KANT'S TRANSCENDENTAL IDEALISM

KANT'S TRANSCENDENTAL IDEALISM
AN INTERPRETATION AND DEFENSE

HENRY E. ALLISON

YALE UNIVERSITY PRESS
NEW HAVEN AND LONDON

Published with assistance from the foundation established in memory of Calvin Chapin of the Class of 1788, Yale College.

Designed by Nancy Ovedovitz and set in Times Roman type by Huron Valley Graphics, Inc. Printed in the United States of America by Edwards Brothers Inc., Ann Arbor, Michigan.

Library of Congress Cataloging in Publication Data

Allison, Henry E.
  Kant's transcendental idealism.

  Bibliography: p.
  Includes index.
  1.Kant, Immanuel, 1724-1804. I. Title.
B2798.A634 1983 193 83–5756
ISBN 0–300–03002–9
    0–300–03629–9 (pbk.)

11 10 9 8 7 6 5 4 3 2

To the memory of Aron Gurwitsch,
with whom I began my study of Kant

Contents

Acknowledgments

The following work is the product of many years of labor, during which time I have become indebted to a large number of individuals and to some institutions. Beginning with the institutions, I would like to express my gratitude to the National Endowment for the Humanities for its award of a fellowship for the year 1980 and to the Academic Senate of the University of California, San Diego, which provided me generous funding over the years for research assistance and for the preparation of the manuscript.

All of my colleagues and many of the students in my Kant seminars have assisted in the progress of my work. I am particularly grateful, however, for the help which I have received from Karl Ameriks, Lewis White Beck, Gerd Buchdahl, and my colleague Robert Pippin. Each of these distinguished scholars has been of enormous assistance to me with his criticisms and suggestions. For all its faults, this book is considerably better than it would have been without their aid. I must also include in this group William McKnight, who served both as editorial assistant and sympathetic critic. Without his timely and substantial assistance, I certainly would not have been able to complete this work while meeting my teaching and administrative duties. In addition, I would like to thank Jeffry King for the preparation of the index.

Outside of the academic community, special thanks are due to two people. One is my wife, Norma, who continues to be an inspiration to me, as well as the one person capable of deciphering my handwriting. In addition to doing all her own work, she typed several versions of the manuscript over the years. The other is Celia Shugart, who has worked with me on the preparation of the manuscript on the computer for the past three years, and who has patiently incorporated all my changes.

I would also like to thank the other members of the philosophy department staff at the University of California, San Diego: Catherine Asmann, June Frowiss, and Gale Vigliotti, each of whom has always been exceedingly cooperative. I am keenly aware of the fact that without the help of all these people, this work would never have seen the light of day.

Finally, it must be noted that chapters 2, 3, 8, and 10 make extensive use of material that appeared in three separate papers in *Dialectica,* and chapter 15 of material that was first published in *Kant-Studien.* My thanks are, therefore, also due to the editors of these journals for their kind permission to reuse this material here.

PART ONE
THE NATURE OF
TRANSCENDENTAL IDEALISM

1

An Introduction to the Problem

The aim of this work is to provide both an interpretation and, where possible, a defense of Kant's transcendental idealism. Since this idealism is inseparable from Kant's views on the nature, conditions, and limits of human knowledge, as well as his critique of other philosophical positions, this project involves a discussion of many of the central topics of the *Critique of Pure Reason*.[1] Some familiar and important topics are omitted, however, both in order to keep the focus as much as possible on Kant's idealism and to allow room for a sufficiently detailed treatment of those topics that are covered. Thus the work also can be characterized as a more or less comprehensive study of Kant's theoretical philosophy, organized around the theme of transcendental idealism. It differs from other treatments of Kant in the recent literature first in its emphasis on the connection between Kant's idealism and his substantive claims, and second in the philosophical weight that it gives both to this idealism and to these claims. Unlike most writers on Kant, I take much of the *Critique* to be not only "interesting" or to "contain more of value than is sometimes supposed," but to be philosophically defensible. At the very least, I believe that with a bit of help from the sympathetic interpreter it can be defended against many of the familiar criticisms that are repeatedly presented as "devastating."

As a first step in this admittedly ambitious project, I shall briefly characterize what I take to be the standard picture of Kant's idealism (which is the source of the familiar criticisms) and attempt to indicate its inadequacy as an account of what Kant actually maintained. I shall then introduce and discuss in a preliminary way the conception of an epistemic condition. My claim is that this conception, although merely implicit in the *Critique,* is the real key to the understanding of transcendental idealism, and with it Kant's philosophical achievement. This will provide the basis for the more extended discussion, in the next two chapters, of transcendental idealism and of the frequently misunderstood argument that Kant advances in support of it in the Antinomy of Pure Reason.

I. THE STANDARD PICTURE AND ITS INADEQUACY

According to the standard picture, Kant's transcendental idealism is a metaphysical theory that affirms the unknowability of the "real"(things in themselves) and relegates knowledge to the purely subjective realm of representations (appearances). It thus combines a phenomenalistic account of what is actually experienced by the mind, and therefore knowable, with the postulation of an additional set of entities which, in terms of the very theory, are unknowable. In spite of the obvious difficulties that it creates, this postulation is deemed necessary to explain how the mind acquires its representations, or at least the materials for them (their form being "imposed" by the mind itself). The basic assumption is simply that the mind can only acquire these materials as a result of being "affected" by things in themselves. Thus, such things must be assumed to exist, even though the theory denies that we have any right to say anything about them (presumably including the claim that they exist).

Although this picture, which can be traced back to Kant's own contemporaries,[2] has been repeatedly criticized, it is still widely accepted, especially in the Anglo-American philosophical world. To a considerable extent this acceptance is due to the influence of P. F. Strawson, who, echoing the standard picture, defines transcendental idealism as the doctrine that "reality is supersensible and that we can have no knowledge of it."[3] Starting with this understanding of Kant's idealism, Strawson sets as his avowed task the separation of what he terms the "analytic argument" of the *Critique* from the transcendental idealism with which he believes Kant unfortunately and unnecessarily entangled it.[4] In the latter respect he has been followed by numerous commentators who have tried to formulate and defend some vaguely Kantian "transcendental arguments" that are uncontaminated by any idealistic premises.[5]

But Strawson not only rejects transcendental idealism as incoherent and attempts, as it were, to save Kant from himself; he also provides an account of what led Kant to this "disastrous" doctrine. As Strawson sees it, transcendental idealism is the direct consequence of Kant's "perversion" of the "scientifically minded philosopher's" contrast between a realm of physical objects composed of primary qualities and a mental realm consisting of the sensible appearances of these objects (including their secondary qualities). This mental realm, like its Kantian counterpart, is thought to be produced by means of an affection of the mind, in this case by physical objects. Kant allegedly perverts this model by assigning the whole spatiotemporal framework (which according to the original model pertains to the "real," that is to say, to physical objects) to the subjective constitution of the human mind. The resulting doctrine is judged to be incoherent because, among other reasons, it is with reference only to a spatiotemporal framework that one can talk intelligibly about "affection."[6]

Although Strawson himself does not put it in quite this way, the usual manner of making essentially the same point is to claim that Kant is an inconsistent Berkeley.[7] The Berkeleian element consists of Kant's subjectivism, namely, the limitation of knowledge to appearances, with these being understood as "mere representations." The alleged inconsistency stems from Kant's combination of his essentially Berkeleian phenomenalistic idealism with his postulation of an inaccessible realm of things in themselves. This conception of what Kant was up to generates, in turn, the standard criticisms, many of which are reflected in Strawson's account. I shall deal with those criticisms that are directed against the Kantian conception of the thing in itself and the associated doctrine of affection in chapter 11. For the present I wish to consider merely those which concern the claim that we know only appearances.

Since it equates 'appearance' with 'mere representation', the standard picture takes Kant's claim that we know only appearances to mean that we know only the contents of our minds, that is, ideas in the Berkeleian sense. This reading of Kant is then sometimes used as the basis for a critique of the doctrine of the ideality of space and time, which Kant presents in the Transcendental Aesthetic. Simply put, the claim is that Kant's subjectivistic starting point forces him to choose between the following equally unpalatable alternatives: either (1) he must maintain that things only *seem to us* to be spatial (or temporal), a doctrine which entails that our consciousness of a world of objects extended and located in space is somehow illusory; or (2) he must claim that appearances, that is to say, representations, really are spatial, a doctrine which is absurd because it requires us to regard mental items as extended and as located in space.

Although this line of criticism has echoes in Strawson,[8] it has been developed most fully by H. A. Prichard, who concentrates much of his attack on the alleged incoherence of Kantian "appearance talk." According to Prichard's highly influential critique, Kant's whole conception of appearance is vitiated by a confusion of the claim that we know only *things as they appear to us* with the quite different claim that we know only a particular class of things, namely, *appearances*. He also suggests that Kant's tendency to slide from one of these claims to the other prevented him from confronting the dilemma posed by the abovementioned alternatives. Thus, on his reconstruction, what Kant really wished to claim is that we know things only as they appear to us; but since this, according to Prichard, entails that these things only seem to us to be spatial (the illusion thesis), in order to defend his cherished empirical realism, Kant is forced to shift to the doctrine that we know appearances and that they really are spatial.[9]

The most basic and prevalent objection stemming from the standard picture is that by limiting knowledge to appearance, that is, to the subjective realm of representations, Kant effectively undermines the possibility of any genuine knowledge at all. In short, far from providing an antidote to Humean skepticism, as was his intent, Kant is seen as a Cartesian skeptic *malgré lui*. Some version of this line of objection is advanced by virtually every proponent of the standard picture, including Strawson.[10] Once again, however, the sharpest formulation is provided by Prichard, whose account can be taken as paradigmatic for the standard picture.[11] Prichard construes Kant's distinction between appearances and things in themselves in terms of the classic example of perceptual illusion: the straight stick that appears bent to an observer when it is immersed in water. Given this analogy, he has little difficulty in reducing to absurdity Kant's doctrine that we know only appearances. His analysis proceeds through various stages, but the main point is simply that this claim is taken to mean that we can know things only as they "are for us" or "seem to us" (in virtue of the distortion imposed by our perceptual forms), not as they "really are." Since to know something, according to Prichard, just means to know it as it really is, it follows that for Kant we cannot really know anything at all. Clearly, such a conclusion amounts to a *reductio* of the Kantian theory.

It seems obvious that, if this is how Kant's transcendental idealism is really to be understood, the Strawsonian project of trying to locate in the *Critique* a philosophical core that can be neatly separated from the idealistic trappings is very attractive. Indeed, it presents itself as the only philosophically fruitful way of dealing with Kant's thought. Nevertheless, in spite of the fact that it does seem to have some textual support, one can raise serious doubts about the adequacy of this interpretation, which is so frequently accepted as a matter of course. The root of the problem is that it tends to neglect altogether, or at the very least to minimize, certain distinctions that are central to Kant's whole transcendental enterprise.

Specifically, it fails to distinguish sharply between the empirical and the transcendental versions of two generally acknowledged and closely related distinctions. These are the distinctions between ideality and reality and between appearances and things in themselves. The issues here are complex, and at this point I can only attempt to provide a rough sketch of what these distinctions involve. I believe, however, that even this rough sketch should suffice to demonstrate the inadequacies of the standard picture as an interpretation of Kant's actual teaching.[12]

'Ideality', in the most general sense in which Kant uses the term, signifies mind dependence or being in the mind (*in uns*); while 'reality' (*Realität*), in the sense in which it is opposed to 'ideality', signifies independence of mind or being external to the mind (*ausser uns*).[13] In both the Transcendental Aesthetic and the Transcendental Dialectic, Kant distinguishes between an empirical and a transcendental sense of 'ideality', and, by implication at least, of 'reality'. Taken in its empirical sense, 'ideality' characterizes the private data of an individual mind. This includes ideas in the Cartesian-Lockean sense or, more generally, any mental content in the ordinary sense of 'mental'. 'Reality', construed in the empirical sense, refers to the intersubjectively accessible, spatiotemporally ordered realm of objects of human experience. At the empirical level, then, the ideality-reality distinction is essentially between the subjective and the objective aspects of human experience. When Kant claims that he is an empirical realist and denies that he is an empirical idealist, he is really affirming that our experience is not limited to the private domain of our own representations, but includes an encounter with "empirically real" spatiotemporal objects.

The transcendental version of the distinction is quite another matter. At the transcendental level, which is the level of philosophical reflection upon experience (transcendental reflection), 'ideality' is used to characterize the universal, necessary, and, therefore, a priori conditions of human knowledge.[14] In the Transcendental Aesthetic, Kant affirms the transcendental ideality of space and time on the grounds that they function as a priori conditions of human sensibility, that is, as subjective conditions in terms of which alone the human mind is capable of receiving the data for thought or experience.[15] He terms these conditions "forms of sensibility." Things in space and time (empirical objects) are ideal in the same sense because they cannot be experienced or described independently of these sensible conditions. Correlatively, something is real in the transcendental sense if and only if it can be characterized and referred to independently of any appeal to these same sensible conditions. In the transcendental sense, then, mind independence or being external to the mind (*ausser uns*) means independence of sensibility and its conditions. A transcendentally real object is thus, by definition, a nonsensible object or noumenon.[16]

The transcendental conception of ideality provides the basis for the transcendental conception of appearance and for the transcendental version of the contrast between appearances and things in themselves. Thus, to speak of appearances in the transcendental sense is simply to speak of spatiotemporal entities (phenomena), that is, of things insofar as they are viewed as subject to the conditions of human sensibility. Correlatively, to speak of things in themselves transcendentally is to speak of things insofar as they are independent of these conditions. In several places Kant insists upon the importance of not confusing this distinction with its empirical counterpart. One of the clearest of these is in "On the Progress of Metaphysics," where, in a discussion of the transcendental ideality of space and time, Kant writes:

> Furthermore, it is to be noted that appearance, taken in the transcendental sense, wherein it is said of things that they are appearances (phenomena), means something completely different than when I say, this thing appears to me in some manner or other, which should designate appearance in the physical sense, and which can be called semblance [*Apparenz*] and illusion [*Schein*]. For although these objects of the senses are mere appearances, since I can only compare them with other sensible objects . . . by the lan-

guage of experience they are nevertheless thought as things in themselves. Thus, if it is said of such a thing that it has the look [*Anschein*] of an arch, in this context the seeming refers to the subjective aspect of the representation of a thing, which can be a cause for it to be falsely taken in a judgment as objective. And, therefore, the proposition that all sensible representations only yield knowledge of appearances is not at all to be equated with the claim that they contain only the illusion [*Schein*] of objects, as the idealist will have it.[17]

The "language of experience," of which Kant speaks here, includes both ordinary and scientific experience. Both involve a distinction between those properties that a given object actually possesses and those it merely seems to possess for a particular observer under certain empirically specifiable conditions. The object as it "really is" (with its actual properties) is the thing in itself in the physical or empirical sense, while the representation of the object possessed by a particular observer under given conditions is what is meant by the appearance or semblance of the object. The main point here is simply that at the empirical level, or in "the language of experience," 'appearances' and 'things in themselves' designate two distinct classes of entity with two distinct modes of being. The members of the former class are "mental" in the ordinary (Cartesian) sense and the members of the latter are "nonmental" or "physical" in the same sense. At the transcendental level, however, things are quite different. There the distinction between appearances and things in themselves refers primarily to two distinct ways in which things (empirical objects) can be "considered": either in relation to the subjective conditions of human sensibility (space and time), and thus as they "appear," or independently of these conditions, and thus as they are "in themselves." Indeed, as Gerold Prauss has pointed out, when Kant is concerned with articulating the transcendental sense of his distinction, he usually does not use such expressions as *Ding an sich, Ding an sich selbst,* or *Sache an sich;* rather, he uses locutions, such as *Ding* or *Sache an sich selbst betrachtet.*[18]

It is certainly possible to detect a dim grasp of the distinction between the transcendental and the empirical conceptions of appearance in Prichard's contrast between things as appearing and appearances. Transcendental-level talk about appearances can be described as talk about things as appearing. Similarly, talk about appearances belongs naturally to the "language of experience." The problem here lies in Prichard's contention that Kant slides from one notion to the other. Given the preceding analysis, this is equivalent to the claim that Kant systematically confuses the transcendental and the empirical versions of his basic distinction. This is itself highly implausible, especially in light of Kant's frequent efforts to distinguish between these two senses of 'appearance'. Even apart from this, however, it can easily be shown that Prichard is guilty of the very confusion of which he accuses Kant. We have seen that part of Prichard's basic objection to what he views as Kant's empirical realism is that it involves the absurd notion that appearances (mental contents) are spatial (extended). Kant is thus judged guilty of spatializing sensations, a charge that with much greater propriety can be directed against Hume. But obviously this "absurdity" arises only if Kant's claim about the spatiality of appearances is taken in the empirical sense. If, as Kant clearly wishes us to do, we construe claims about the spatiality of appearances in the transcendental sense, the absurdity disappears; for then spatiality (together with temporality) can be seen as a defining characteristic of things considered as they appear, not as a property mysteriously attributed to sensations.

The objection to Kant's alleged skepticism can be dealt with in a similar fashion.[19] It is clear from his use of the bent stick analogy that Prichard construes the distinction between appearances and things in themselves in the empirical sense. This, in turn, enables him to take Kant to be claiming that we can know only how things seem (appear) to us, which entails the skeptical conclusion. It is by no means certain, however, that this follows if we construe Kant's claim about the limitation of knowledge to appearances in the transcendental rather than in the empirical sense. Understood in this sense, which is the sense in which Kant intended it, it is an epistemological claim about the dependence of human knowledge on certain a priori conditions which reflect the structure of the human cognitive apparatus. These conditions do not determine how objects "seem" to us or "appear" in the empirical sense; rather, they express the universal and necessary conditions in terms of which alone the human mind is capable of recognizing something as an object at all. Thus the doctrine that we can know things only as they appear, not as they are in themselves, can be regarded as equivalent to the claim that human knowledge is governed by such conditions. If, in fact, there are such conditions, and if they function in the ways in which Kant contends, then it hardly makes sense to accuse him of being a skeptic because he denies the possibility of knowledge of things as they are independently of them, that is, of things as they are in themselves.

To say this is not, of course, to endorse Kant's account. We will not be in a position to evaluate Kant's claims regarding the a priori conditions of human knowledge until we have examined the arguments of the Transcendental Aesthetic and Transcendental Analytic. Nevertheless, it is not necessary to do so in order to realize the inappropriateness of the skepticism objection as formulated by Prichard and other proponents of the standard picture. The problem with this objection is that it fails completely to come to grips with Kant's intent, and thus to see what his transcendental claims actually involve. Instead, these claims are routinely interpreted as empirical or quasi-empirical. Similarly, Kant's talk about the "conditions" of human knowledge is taken in a psychological sense. The inevitable consequence of this is that Kant is seen as a proponent of the very empirical idealism which he took such great pains to repudiate.

II. THE CONCEPT OF AN EPISTEMIC CONDITION

The interpretation of transcendental idealism which I hope to develop in this study will, in contrast to the standard picture, emphasize its connection with Kant's claims regarding the conditions of human knowledge: I shall argue that the claim that human knowledge has such conditions is the distinctive, indeed, the revolutionary thesis of Kant's philosophy, and that transcendental idealism is at bottom nothing more than the logical consequence of its acceptance. So far, however, the crucial notion of 'condition' has remained undefined, even unexamined. Any number of things—for example, the brain, the central nervous system, sense organs, and so forth—could legitimately be described as conditions of human knowledge; yet none of these would have very much to do with Kant's central claim or with transcendental idealism. In an effort to clarify and to pinpoint the relevant sense of the term, I propose to introduce the notion of an *epistemic condition*.[20]

Even though this notion is central to Kant's whole transcendental enterprise, the fact that he never explicitly deals with it makes it difficult, if not impossible, to define in any very precise way. For present purposes, then, it must suffice to characterize an epistemic condition simply as one that is necessary for the representation of an object or an objective state of affairs. As such, it could also be called an "objectivating condition"; for it is in virtue of such conditions that our representations relate to objects or, as Kant likes to put it, possess "objective reality." In this respect epistemic conditions are to be distinguished from what Kant terms "logical conditions of thought," for example, the principle of contradiction. The latter serves as a rule of consistent thinking, but not for the representation of objects. Thus it is not an epistemic condition in the sense in which this notion is taken here. Roughly speaking, the distinction between logical and epistemic conditions reflects Kant's own distinction between general and transcendental logic. In fact, the main business of transcendental logic is to establish a set of epistemic conditions, namely, the pure concepts of the understanding.

In addition to the pure concepts of the understanding, which Kant defines as "concepts of an object in general," space and time (the forms of human sensibility) must also be regarded as epistemic conditions. Although together these two types of condition constitute what Kant himself terms "necessary conditions of the possibility of experience," there are two reasons for believing that the broader notion of an epistemic condition better captures the essential thrust of Kant's thought. The first is simply that Kant is not solely, or even primarily, concerned with experiential knowledge. Epistemic conditions must, therefore, also figure in the Kantian account of nonempirical knowledge, that is, of mathematics and metaphysics. Indeed, as we shall see in chapter 6, the pure concepts in their "logical use" can even be regarded as epistemic conditions of analytic judgments.

The second and main reason for talking about epistemic conditions, rather than about conditions of the possibility of experience, is that this term makes it easier to grasp the difference between this central Kantian conception and other senses of 'condition' with which it is frequently confused. Such confusions are reflected in many of the stock criticisms of Kant, including those discussed in the previous section, as well as in the standard picture as a whole. Moreover, many of Kant's own criticisms of other philosophical positions can be seen to turn on the claim that they involve confusions of what are here called epistemic conditions with conditions of other sorts. One of these is, of course, the confusion of merely logical with epistemic conditions, which figures largely in Kant's polemic with Leibnizian rationalism. This distinction has already been noted and needs no further comment at this point. For the present, it is important to distinguish epistemic conditions from psychological conditions on the one hand and from ontological conditions on the other.

By a psychological condition I mean some mechanism or aspect of the human cognitive apparatus that is appealed to in order to provide a genetic account of a belief or an empirical explanation of why we perceive things in a certain way. This can be understood to include physiological as well as narrowly psychological factors. Custom or habit, as used by Hume in his account of causality, is a prime example of such a psychological condition. As is well known, Kant was insistent in claiming that, although the appeal to such factors may be necessary to explain the origin of our beliefs and perceptions, or even of our knowledge "in the order of time" (*der Zeit nach*), it cannot account for its objective validity. In Kant's terms it can answer the *quaestio facti* but not the *quaestio juris*. The latter is the proper concern of the *Critique,* and this requires an appeal to epistemic conditions.[21] In fact, Kant's basic charge against Hume is that he confuses these questions and thus, implicitly at least, these two kinds of conditions. The clearest example of this is Kant's claim in the *Prolegomena* that, in his analysis of causality, Hume "mistook a subjective necessity (habit) for an objective necessity arising from insight."[22] Ironically enough, this very same line of criticism is frequently raised against the *Critique* by critics who find in it a dangerous subjectivism.

It is equally important to distinguish epistemic from ontological conditions. By the latter I mean conditions of the possibility of the being of things. Since the being of things is here contrasted with their being known, an ontological condition is, by definition, a condition of the possibility of things as they are in themselves (in the transcendental sense).

Newtonian absolute space and time are clear examples of conditions of this sort. Kant describes them as "two eternal and infinite self-subsistent [*für sich bestehende*] non-entities . . . which are there (yet without there being anything real) only in order to contain in themselves all that is real" (A39/B56). In a Second Edition addendum to the Transcendental Aesthetic, Kant indicates the dangerous theological consequences of such a view by pointing out that "as conditions of all existence in general, they must also be conditions of the existence of God" (B71). Even apart from theology, however, Kant believes that this conception of space and time leads to absurdities:

> For if we regard space and time as properties which, if they are to be possible at all, must be found in things in themselves, and if we reflect on the absurdities in which we are then involved, in that two infinite things, which are not substances, nor anything actually inhering in substances, must yet have existence, nay, must be the necessary condition of the existence of all things, and moreover, must continue to exist, even although all existing things be removed,—we cannot blame the good Berkeley for degrading bodies to mere illusion. Nay, even our own existence, in being made thus dependent upon the self-subsistent reality of a non-entity, such as time, would necessarily be changed with it into sheer illusion—an absurdity of which no one has yet been guilty. [B70–71][23]

Kant's point is that, for all its absurdity, Berkeley's idealism, which he interprets as involving the denial of the reality of material objects ("degrading bodies to mere illusion") makes a certain amount of sense when it is viewed as a response to Newton.[24] This is because once the empirical reality of material objects and persons is seen to depend on the absolute (transcendental) reality of space and time, the absurdities connected with the latter make it plausible to deny the former. But this consequence can easily be avoided if, instead of viewing space and time with Newton as conditions of the possibility of things in themselves, we view them as conditions of the possibility of our knowledge or experience of things. In Kantian terms, instead of being "two eternal and infinite, self-subsistent non-entities," they now become two "sources of knowledge" (*Erkenntnisquellen*) (A38/B55). By analyzing the situation in this way, Kant claims to be able not only to distinguish his idealism from that of Berkeley, but also to provide a critical alternative to both the Newtonian and the Leibnizian conceptions of space and time.

Consequently, just as Kant's strategy with Hume is to show that the skeptical consequences of his analysis stem from a confusion of psychological and epistemic conditions, his strategy with Newton is to show that the untenable consequences of the latter's theory of space and time are the results of a confusion of epistemic with ontological conditions. We shall also see that this mode of analysis can be applied to the Kantian critique of many other thinkers. For the present, however, the key point to note is the connection between these two distinctions and the consequent confusions. Although the above account may have suggested otherwise, it is not simply the case that there are some philosophers who just happen to be guilty of one of these confusions and others who just happen to be guilty of the other. The fact of the matter is rather that, from a Kantian standpoint, the two kinds of confusion represent two sides of the same coin, namely, the failure to recognize the role in human knowledge of a set of distinctively epistemic conditons.

Indeed, one can claim that the fundamental issue raised by the *Critique* is whether it is possible to isolate a set of conditions of the possibility of knowledge of things (in the sense already indicated) that can be distinguished from conditions of the possibility of the things themselves. Since the former kind of condition would count as a condition of things as they appear and the latter of things as they are in themselves, an affirmative answer to this question entails the acceptance of the transcendental distinction, and with it of transcendental idealism. If, on the other hand, the question is answered in the negative, as it is by the standard picture, then any purportedly "subjective" conditions are inevitably construed in psychological terms. The subjectivistic, psychologistic, phenomenalistic reading of Kant, which is characteristic of the standard picture, is thus a direct consequence of its negative answer to this question. The real problem with the picture, however, is not that it answers this question in the negative, for Kant's position may very well turn out to be incoherent or otherwise untenable. It is rather that, by presupposing a negative answer, it never really addresses itself to the question at all. An explicit focus on this question should, therefore, at the very least lead to a more accurate interpretation of Kant's intent and of the nature of transcendental idealism. Beyond that, I also hope to be able to indicate that it makes it possible to regard transcendental idealism as a powerful philosophical position rather than as a curious anachronism or a mass of confusions.

Transcendental Realism and
Transcendental Idealism

The function of this chapter is primarily exegetical. Its goal is to develop more fully the interpretation of transcendental idealism sketched in the previous chapter. This time, however, the analysis will proceed in an indirect manner. My strategy is to interpret transcendental idealism by means of the transcendental realism with which Kant on occasion contrasts it. The operative assumption is that transcendental realism and transcendental idealism can be understood as mutually exclusive and exhaustive metaphilosophical alternatives. I thus begin by developing an interpretation of transcendental realism. The essential claims of this interpretation are that all noncritical philosophies can be regarded as realistic in the transcendental sense and that transcendental realism can be characterized in terms of a commitment to a theocentric model or conception of knowledge. I then use these results to construct an interpretation of transcendental idealism, with its contrasting commitment to an anthropocentric model. The main contention is that this approach enables us to see clearly the connection between transcendental idealism and the conception of an epistemic condition, which, in turn, leads to the recognition of the nonphenomenalistic, nonpsychological nature of this idealism.

I. THE NATURE OF TRANSCENDENTAL REALISM

The first difficulty confronting the interpretation for which I wish to argue is that the significance that I attribute to transcendental realism seems to be belied by the paucity of references to it in the text. One would normally expect to find a conception of such alleged importance analyzed in great detail and subjected to a searching criticism. To be sure, Kant does claim that "were we to yield to the illusion of transcendental realism, neither nature nor freedom would be possible" (A543/B571). This certainly suggests that transcendental realism is an illusion of some significance and that it must be a major concern of the *Critique* to eradicate it. Nevertheless, Kant refers explicitly to transcendental realism in only two other places. Both are in the Transcendental Dialectic, and in each case Kant contrasts it with transcendental idealism.

The first is in the First Edition version of the Fourth Paralogism. Kant

14

is there concerned to refute empirical idealism, which he contrasts with his own transcendental version. In this context he writes:

> By *transcendental idealism* I mean the doctrine that appearances are to be regarded as being, one and all, representations only, not things in themselves, and that time and space are therefore only sensible forms of our intuition, not determinations given as existing by themselves, nor conditions of objects viewed as things in themselves. To this idealism there is opposed a *transcendental realism* which regards time and space as something given in themselves, independently of our sensibility. The transcendental realist thus interprets outer appearances (their reality taken as granted) as things-in-themselves, which exist independently of us and of our sensibility, and which are therefore outside us—the phrase 'outside us' being interpreted in conformity with pure concepts of understanding. It is, in fact, this transcendental realist who afterwards plays the part of empirical idealist. After wrongly supposing that objects of the senses, if they are to be external, must have an existence by themselves, and independently of the senses, he finds that, judged from this point of view, all our sensuous representations are inadequate to establish their reality. [A369]

Kant is here arguing that transcendental realism leads to empirical idealism, which is the doctrine that the mind can only have immediate access to its own ideas or representations (the "ideal" in the empirical sense). The point is that because the transcendental realist misconstrues the reality of spatial objects ("objects of the senses") he is forced to deny that the mind has any immediate experience of such objects. Transcendental realism is thus presented as the source of the pseudo-problem of the external world and of the typically Cartesian version of skepticism that is associated with it.

The second passage is from the Antinomy of Pure Reason. Kant there defines transcendental idealism as the doctrine that "all objects of any experience possible to us, are nothing but appearances, that is, mere representations, which, in the manner in which they are represented, as extended beings, or as series of alterations, have no independent existence outside our thoughts." In contrast to this, the transcendental realist is said to regard "these mere modifications of our sensibility as self-subsistent things, that is, treats *mere representations* as things in themselves" (A490–91 / B518–19).

Both of these passages indicate that the defining characteristic of transcendental realism is its confusion of appearances or "mere representations" with things in themselves. The first passage limits this charge to objects of "outer perception" (empirically external, spatial objects), although it does connect it with the conception of time as well as space as "given in themselves, independently of our sensibility." This emphasis on space and outer experience no doubt reflects Kant's concern at that point with empirical idealism and its connection with transcendental realism.

The second passage, which does not reflect this particular concern, goes somewhat further by presenting transcendental realism as the view that considers *all appearances,* those of inner as well as those of outer sense, as if they were things in themselves. I think that this latter passage expresses Kant's considered view on the subject. It is a central tenet of the *Critique* that inner as well as outer sense presents us with objects as they appear, not as they are in themselves. Transcendental realism thus manifests itself as much in a confused view of the former as of the latter.

This of itself should make it clear that the usual interpretation of transcendental realism as equivalent to the scientific realism of the Cartesians and Newtonians (roughly what Berkeley meant by "materialism") is far too narrow.[1] For while Kant only infrequently makes use of the expression 'transcendental realism', he repeatedly accuses philosophers of a variety of stripes of treating appearances as if they were things in themselves or, equivalently, of granting "absolute" or "transcendental" reality to appearances.[2] Indeed, at one place in the *Critique* he terms this confusion the "common prejudice" (A740/B768), while at another he refers to the "common but fallacious presupposition of the absolute reality of appearances" (A536/B564). Moreover, this general claim is found in even stronger form in other texts. Indeed, he goes so far as to assert that prior to the *Critique* the confusion was unavoidable,[3] and even that "until the critical philosophy all philosophies are not distinguished in their essentials."[4]

Such statements support the contention that the transcendental distinction between appearances and things in themselves or, more properly, between things as they appear and the same things as they are in themselves, functions as the great divide in the Kantian conception of the history of philosophy. Only the "critical philosophy" has succeeded in getting this distinction right. Consequently, despite their many interesting differences, all of the others are at bottom nothing more than variant expressions of the same underlying confusion. Thus, if transcendental realism be understood as the point of view which systematically confuses appearances with things in themselves, it can be assigned the same role in Kant's theoretical philosophy that he assigns to heteronomy in his moral philosophy. In other words, it constitutes the common assumption, prejudice, or confusion which is shared by all philosophers who do not achieve the critical standpoint.[5]

A. Some Varieties of Transcendental Realism

The best way to test this contention is to see the extent to which it is applicable to various "noncritical" philosophies. It should be noted, however, that in so doing we will explicitly be viewing these philosophies through Kantian spectacles. The question at issue is not whether the charge that these philosophies confuse appearances with things in themselves, and are thus transcendentally realistic, is "fair" according to some independent standard of evaluation. It is rather whether, given Kant's assumptions, it is possible to view these philosophies in such a manner.

We have already seen that Kant maintains that empirical idealism is a form of transcendental realism, which arises from the recognition of the fact that the human mind has no direct access to the putatively "real" things, that is, to physical objects construed as things in themselves in the transcendental sense. This recognition, in turn, leads to the claim of Descartes and his followers that the only objects of which we are, in fact, immediately aware are ideas in the mind. Such idealism, together with its skeptical consequences, is therefore the result of an implicit commitment to transcendental realism. Kant's First Edition version of the Refutation of Idealism turns on this point. As he succinctly puts the matter:

> If we treat outer objects as things in themselves, it is quite impossible to understand how we could arrive at a knowledge of their reality outside us, since we have to rely merely on the representation which is in us. For we cannot be sentient (of what is) outside ourselves, but only (of what is) in us, and the whole of our self-consciousness therefore yields nothing save merely our own determinations. [A378]

At first glance this seems reminiscent of Berkeley's critique of "materialism," and it has frequently been taken in just this way.[6] On such a reading Kant, like Berkeley, succeeds in avoiding skepticism only by identifying the "real" with the immediate objects of consciousness. But such a reading is a gross oversimplification and fails to capture the real thrust of Kant's position. In order to capture this thrust, it is necessary to focus, as Kant does, on the key term *ausser* or *ausser uns*. The empirical idealist, Kant points out, understands this term in its transcendental sense. In other words, this species of idealist takes the "externality" of the "real" spatiotemporal objects with which science supposedly deals to entail the independence of such objects from the subjective conditions of human knowledge. This would be perfectly acceptable if, in describing these transcendentally external objects, one would refrain from ascribing to them any spatial or temporal predicates. In that case one would be a good transcendental idealist. The problem is that the Cartesian empirical idealist does not do this. Instead, he regards these experientially external objects as belonging to *res extensa*. He therefore conflates the transcendental with the empirical senses of *ausser uns*. It is this conflation or category mistake that generates the skepticism connected with this form of idealism. Kant's refutation consists essentially in pointing this out.

An even more obvious example of a transcendentally realistic mode of thought is provided by the Newtonians or "mathematical students of nature." We have already seen that their absolutistic conception of space and time can be viewed as the consequence of a confusion of epistemic with ontological conditions, and that this is equivalent to the confusion of appearances with things in themselves. It is, however, not only Newton but also his great opponent, Leibniz, who can be characterized as a transcendental realist. In fact, Kant explicitly claims that Leibniz "took the appearances for things in themselves" (A260/B320). I propose to reserve a consideration of this perplexing claim, as well as of the Leibnizian version of transcendental realism, for the next section.[7] For the present, I wish to consider only the most obvious candidates to serve as counterexamples to the thesis of this section. These are provided by phenomenalistic positions such as those of Berkeley and Hume. If these thinkers can be said to have confused appearances with things in themselves, then it can be claimed with some justice that the confusion is virtually universal.

I have already suggested that Berkeley's "dogmatic idealism," which Kant equates with "degrading bodies to mere illusion," can be viewed as a direct offshoot of the Newtonian version of transcendental realism. In that respect it stands to Newtonian absolute space and time as empirical idealism stands to Cartesian *res extensa*. In other words, it is a form of subjectivism or idealism to which one is driven on the basis of certain transcendentally realistic assumptions. But Berkeley's position is more than a mere offshoot of transcendental realism. It is itself realistic in the transcendental sense. Admittedly, Kant never says precisely this with regard to the "good Bishop." He does so, however, with regard to Hume, and his claim is equally applicable to Berkeley. The crucial passage occurs in the *Critique of Practical Reason*, where Kant, summarizing some of the essential tenets of the First Critique, reflects: "I granted that when Hume took the objects of experience as things in themselves (as is almost always done), he was entirely correct in declaring the concept of cause to be deceptive and an illusion."[8]

Since Kant was certainly well aware of the fact that Hume characterized the objects of human experience as "impressions," we are inevitably led to ask why Kant should describe such private, subjective objects as things in themselves. The obvious answer is that Hume treats those impressions as if they were given to the mind as they are in themselves. This can be seen as a consequence of his failure to recognize the existence of a priori forms of sensibility through which these impressions are received (even the private data of inner sense are, for Kant, given to the mind under the form of time and hence count as appearances). Since Hume did not recognize any a priori forms of sensibility, he was not in a position to acknowledge the possibility of any a priori rules of synthesis through which these impressions are brought to the unity of consciousness. In the absence of such rules, there is no reason why, given object (or impression) *A*, something else, object (or impression) *B*, must likewise be given; this, as Kant sees it, is the source of Hume's skeptical doubts concerning causality.[9] But, for the present purpose at least, Berkeleian ideas have precisely the same status as Humean impressions. They too are given to the mind as they are in themselves, a point that is evidenced by Berkeley's denial of the a priori nature of the representation of space. Such ideas, therefore, count as things in themselves in the Kantian sense.

It follows from this that, from a Kantian perspective, both Berkeley and Hume can be judged guilty of confusing appearances with things in themselves. Consequently, both may be termed transcendental realists. The peculiar features of their subjectivism stem from the fact that they regard appearances (in the empirical sense) as if they were things in themselves (in the transcendental sense). In this respect their position can perhaps be contrasted with Cartesian dualism, which regards appearances (in the transcendental sense) as if they were things in themselves (in the same sense). The key point, however, is that Berkeley and Hume share with other transcendental realists a failure to recognize the role in human experience of a set of epistemic conditions.

B. Transcendental Realism and the Theocentric Model of Knowledge

I have suggested that transcendental realism can also be understood in terms of an appeal, either implicit or explicit, to a theocentric model of knowledge. By such a model I understand a program or method of epistemological reflection, according to which human knowledge is analyzed and evaluated in terms of its conformity, or lack thereof, to the standard of cognition theoretically achievable by an "absolute" or "infinite intellect." By the latter I understand one that is not encumbered by the limitations of the human intellect, and which, therefore, knows objects "as they are in themselves." Such an intellect functions in this model essentially as a regulative idea in the Kantian sense. Thus the appeal to it does not commit one either to the existence of such an intellect or to the assumption that knowledge of this type is actually possessed by the human mind. The point is only that a hypothetical "God's-eye view" of things is used as a standard in terms of which the "objectivity" of human knowledge is analyzed.

This model is the common heritage of the Platonic tradition, but it is particularly evident in the great rationalists of the seventeenth century. One thinks in this connection of Malebranche, who claimed that we "see all things in God," and of Spinoza, who maintained that the goal of human cognition is to view things *sub specie aeternitatis*.[10] It is also central to Leibniz; in fact, I intend to show that his appeal to this model is the key to the understanding of the specifically Leibnizian version of transcendental realism. Moreover, the empiricists are also committed to this model, although this fact is somewhat obscured by their essentially psychological orientation. This is readily apparent in Berkeley, who was always something of a Platonist,[11] but it is equally true of Locke and Hume. Since the transcendentally realistic dimension of Hume's thought has already been noted, I shall here limit myself to a brief consideration of Locke. Finally, in an effort to suggest the prevalence of this model and to provide a further basis for understanding the nature of Kant's "Copernican revolution," I shall attempt to show how it underlies Kant's own precritical thought.

Leibniz. Leibniz's appeal to the theocentric model is quite explicit and has often been noted in the literature.[12] Following Augustine and Malebranche, he depicts the divine understanding as the realm of eternal truths, and he claims, in typically picturesque fashion, that it is there that one finds "the pattern of the ideas and truths which are engraved in our souls."[13] This is not to say that the human mind for Leibniz is infinite, or that it is somehow capable of thinking "God's thoughts." On the contrary, he constantly emphasizes the insurmountable limits of human knowledge. He explains these limits in terms of the confusedness of our representations, and this is itself seen as a consequence of our finitude. The point, however, is not that human knowledge is infinite or even adequate; it is rather that it approaches adequacy as it approaches divine knowledge. Thus, despite the infinite difference in degree or scope, there is a commensurability or similarity in kind between human and divine knowledge.[14]

The model is also reflected in Leibniz's key claim that in any true proposition the predicate is contained in the concept of the subject. Leibniz's adherence to this principle leads him to regard demonstration as requiring reduction to identity. He thinks that this is quite possible for arithmetical propositions and possible at least in principle for the axioms of Euclidean geometry. More important, he holds that this principle is not only applicable to necessary truths or "truths of reason," which are true in all possible worlds, but also to contingent truths or "truths of fact," which hold only in the actual world. This, as Leibniz puts it in an early formulation of the principle, is because "it is the nature of an individual substance or complete being to have a concept so complete that it is sufficient to make us understand and deduce from it all the predicates of the subject to which the concept is attached."[15] Since the complete concept of an individual substance involves an infinity of elements, and since a finite mind is not capable of infinite analysis, the human intellect can never arrive at such a conception. Consequently, it cannot demonstrate or deduce truths of fact. Nevertheless, such truths remain deducible in principle, that is, for God, who is capable of an intuitive grasp of the infinite. Expressed in Kantian terms, this means that all propositions are ultimately analytic and that the syntheticity of truths of fact is merely a function of the limits of analysis, not of the nature of the propositions themselves.

These considerations should better enable us to grasp the main outlines of Kant's critique of Leibniz and to understand the claim that Leibniz "took the appearances for things in themselves." Much of Kant's quarrel with Leibniz and his followers focuses on the closely related conceptions of sensibility and appearance. By and large, Kant defines his philosophy vis à vis that of Leibniz in terms of their different understanding of these conceptions. He claims that Leibniz and his followers "falsified" both conceptions, and he sees this as the direct result of their misconstrual of the distinction between the "sensible" and the "intelligible." Instead of viewing the difference between these two aspects of human cognition as "transcendental," that is, as a difference of origin, content, and kind, they regard it as merely "logical," that is, as a difference of degree of clarity and distinctness of the representations.[16] All of this is captured by the claim that Leibniz (here being contrasted with Locke), "*intellectualized appearances*" (A271 / B327). Now, to "intellectualize appearances" is to abstract from their irreducibly sensible (spatiotemporal) character. But since this character is a defining feature of a Kantian appearance, while independence of it is a defining feature of a thing in itself, it can easily be seen that this charge is equivalent to the charge that Leibniz "took the appearances for things in themselves."

Moreover, in his response to Eberhard, Kant makes it clear that the heart of the difficulty with Leibnizianism is that it fails to recognize that human sensibility has its own a priori forms or conditions (space and time), which serve to determine positively the nature and relations of the objects of human experience. That is why Leibnizians tend to regard sensible (perceptual) knowledge of appearances merely as a confused version of the purely intellectual knowledge of these objects obtained by God. Consequently, all of the sensible components of human experience, including spatiotemporal relations, are deemed reducible (for God) to the purely intellectual (logical) determinations which pertain to things in themselves (monads). This reducibility thesis is the logical consequence of Leibniz's appeal to the theocentric model of knowledge and thus of his transcendental realism. It is also the real point behind Kant's contention that Leibniz and his followers "falsified" or "intellectualized" appearances or, equivalently, "took the appearances for things in themselves." Finally, Kant suggests, in the *Critique* and again in his response to Eberhard, that the same failure also serves to explain the distinctive doctrines and confusions of Leibnizian metaphysics.[17] In chapter 5 we shall see how this is reflected in the Leibnizian theory of the ideality of space and in the Kantian critique thereof.

Locke. Locke's use of the theocentric model is not as obvious but is just as real as Leibniz's. Perhaps the best example of this is his much discussed distinction between nominal and real essence. By the nominal essence of a substance, really of a "sort," Locke understands the complex idea of that sort. This idea is formed by the mind on the basis of the experience of a number of instances, and it constitutes the sense of the term denoting that sort. The real essence, by contrast, is the inner nature or the "real constitution" of a thing. Locke uses the example of gold to illustrate this thesis: "The nominal essence of gold," he tells us, "is that complex idea the word gold stands for, let it be, for instance, a body yellow of a certain weight, malleable, fusible and fixed," whereas the real essence is characterized as "the constitution of the insensible parts of that body, on which those qualities and all other properties of gold depend."[18]

Locke's distinction between the two kinds of essence raises a number of issues, but for our purposes the important point is simply that he correlates it with the distinction between divine and human knowledge. A clear illustration of this is his analysis of the "essence" of man. After briefly categorizing those features that are contained in the complex ideas constituting the nominal essence of man, Locke writes:

> The foundation of all those qualities which are the ingredients of our complex idea, is something quite different: and had we such a knowledge of that constitution of man, from which his faculties of moving, sensation, and reasoning, and other powers flow, and on which his so regular shape depends, as it is possible angels have, and it is certain his Maker has, we should have a quite other idea of his essence than what now is contained in our definition of that species, be it what it will: and our idea of any individual man would be as far different from what it is now, as is his who knows all the springs and wheels and other contrivances within the famous clock at Strasburg, from that which a gazing countryman has of it, who barely sees the motion of the hand, and hears the clock strike, and observes only some of the outward appearances.[19]

Knowledge of real essence is here explicitly equated with the knowledge which our "Maker has," that is, divine knowledge. Human knowledge, by contrast, is limited to "some of the outward appearances of things." Clearly then, human knowledge is judged by the ideal standard of divine knowledge and found wanting. Locke's agnosticism is mitigated considerably, however, by his characteristic insistence that our knowledge of nominal essence and the classifications based thereupon are sufficient for our needs. As he so eloquently expresses himself in the introduction to the *Essay*, "The candle that is set up in us shines bright enough for all our purposes."[20] These purposes include, of course, knowledge of God and of our duty; but they also include what Locke calls "the conveniences of life."[21] The point here is that our classification of things into sorts and, more generally, our empirical knowledge, suffices to attain these "conveniences," even though it does not acquaint us with the true nature of things. Locke, therefore, combines his appeal to the theocentric model with an essentially pragmatic account of perceptual knowledge. In this respect his position is not far from that of rationalists such as Descartes and Malebranche.[22]

The primary difference between Locke and the rationalists on this score is that Locke tends to conceive of adequate and, therefore, divine knowledge as basically more of the same; that is to say, he regards divine knowledge as if it were perceptual in nature, albeit involving greatly expanded perceptual powers, such as "microscopical eyes."[23] This contrasts sharply with the usual rationalist version of "adequate" knowledge as infinite reason. Although this may not be the whole story with regard to Locke's theory, it is certainly an important part of it.[24] It also seems to be the part that Kant underscores when, in contrasting Locke with Leibniz, he remarks that Locke "sensualized all concepts of the understanding," and that he viewed sensibility "as an immediate relation to things in themselves" (A271 / B327). Thus, in spite of the fact that their views are diametrically opposed, Kant holds that Leibniz and Locke share a common and erroneous assumption: that "genuine" knowledge, whether it be sensible as with Locke or intellectual as with Leibniz, is of things in themselves.

Kant. Perhaps the most instructive example of an appeal to the theocentric model of knowledge is provided by Kant himself. Indications of this can be discerned in virtually all of his precritical writings, but for illustrative purposes we can limit our consideration to the early metaphysical essay, "A New Exposition of the First Principles of Metaphysical Knowledge" (1755). This essay reflects a stage in his development at which Kant philosophized very much in a Leibnizian mold. Thus, in support of his claim that the principle of identity is the first principle of all truths, the young Kant writes:

> since all our reasoning is resolved into the discovery of an identity of predicate with subject, considered either as it is in itself or in a combination, as is evident from the ultimate rule of truths, hence we see that God does not require the process of reasoning because, since all things are crystal clear to his gaze, one act of re-presentation puts before his intelligence which things are identical and which are not, and he has no need of analysis as the darkened night of our intelligence necessarily has.[25]

Kant here expresses as clearly as one could wish his commitment to the theocentric model of knowledge. Being finite, we are forced to have recourse to analysis in order to grasp the identities which the divine intellect sees immediately. Kant's commitment to this model is revealed not only in this formulation of the ideal of knowledge, but also in some of the central arguments of the work. Two examples will suffice to make this apparent. The first occurs within Kant's argument for the existence of God as the ground of the possibility and hence of the essence of things. In developing this argument Kant appeals to the example of the essence of a triangle:

For the essence of a triangle which consists in the conjuction of its three sides is not in itself necessary. What sane person would contend that it is in itself necessary that the three sides should always be conceived as conjoined? This indeed I concede is necessary to a triangle, that if you think a triangle you must necessarily think its three sides, and that is the same as saying "if anything is, it is". But how it comes about that to the thought of the sides, of the enclosing of space, the other ideas follow, namely that it be in a genus which is thinkable (whence every notion of a thinkable thing comes by combining, limiting, or determining), this could not in any wise be conceived unless in God, the source of all reality, there existed everything that is in a real notion.[26]

The second example occurs in connection with the claim that the principle of the coexistence of substances is to be located in the divine intellect. In support of this contention Kant reflects:

It must be confessed that this relation depends upon a community of cause, namely upon God, as the general principle of existence. And since the mutual reciprocity between these things does not follow from the fact that God has fixed their existence *simpliciter,* unless the same *schema* of the divine intellect which gives them existence has fixed their reciprocities by conceiving their existence as correlated, it is evident that the general intercourse of things is secured by the mere conceiving of the divine idea.[27]

The primary import of both these passages lies in the light which they shed on the elements of continuity and change in Kant's thought. Both the "precritical" and the "critical" Kant were concerned with the determination of the conditions of possibility, although these conditions are explained in quite different ways. In the first passage the question at issue is the nature of the ground or the condition of the possibility of three straight lines being able to enclose a space. The answer of the young Kant is that the possibility of such a figure is grounded in its conceivability by the divine intellect. By contrast, in his account of mathematical possibility in the *Critique,* Kant argues that the impossibility of two straight lines enclosing a space is based upon the conditions of the constructability of figures in space (A221/B268); and these conditions (which define the Euclidean nature of space) are themselves determined by the nature of human sensibility. The second passage is even more striking in this regard, for Kant poses the very same problem that he later deals with in the Analogies, namely, the ground of the unity of experience. In the *Critique* this unity is explained in terms of the "Principles of Pure Understanding." These principles, as we shall see, function as the conditions of the possibility of the consciousness of a unified time order, and they express the necessary conformity of appearances to the schemata of the pure concepts of the understanding. Here, by contrast, the objects (substances) are held to conform necessarily to the schema of the divine intellect. The appeal to the divine intellect in this early essay thus fulfills much the same function as does the appeal to the human intellect in the *Critique*.

II. THE TRANSCENDENTAL NATURE OF KANT'S IDEALISM

I have argued in the preceding section that all noncritical philosophies, including that of the young Kant, can be regarded as transcendentally realistic. These philosophies are united in the "common assumption" or "prejudice" that the objects of knowledge are things in themselves. Since this assumption is shared by philosophers with radically different ontologies and epistemologies, such as Spinoza and Berkeley, it cannot be defined in either ontological or epistemological terms. Instead, it must be characterized as a metaphilosophical or methodological assumption concerning the "standpoint" in terms of which human knowledge is to be analyzed and evaluated. In the endeavor to characterize further this standpoint, I have also suggested that it involves a failure to recognize that human knowledge has its own a priori conditions, which in turn leads to a failure to make the transcendental distinction, and that it is necessarily connected with a theocentric model of knowledge.

The remainder of this chapter explores the implications of this result for the interpretation of transcendental idealism. Clearly, the most basic of these implications is that, like its opposite, transcendental idealism must be characterized primarily as a metaphilosophical or methodological "standpoint," rather than as a straightforwardly metaphysical doctrine about the nature or ontological status of the objects of human cognition. Moreover, just as transcendental realism is defined negatively in terms of its failure to recognize the role of epistemic conditions in human knowledge and its consequent failure to make the transcendental distinction between things as they appear and the same things as they are in themselves, so transcendental idealism is defined positively in terms of its acceptance of this conception and its insistence upon this distinction. To say this is not to deny that transcendental idealism has important metaphysical consequences. It certainly does, and these will be examined in later chapters.[28] The point is that these consequences follow from the acceptance of the transcendental distinction and must, therefore, be understood in connection with it. A further point deserving emphasis here is that it is only if one assumes that human knowledge has a priori conditions of the kind already noted that it becomes possible to "consider" objects in relation to these conditions. In fact, it is only in light of this assumption that the distinction between two ways of "considering" objects can be viewed as anything other than the familiar contrast between "how things seem to me" (given certain psychological and physiological conditions, and so forth) and "how they really are."

Since the basic thrust of the Kantian position is reflected in his own characterization of transcendental idealism as "formal" or "critical," I shall begin with a brief consideration of how this claim is to be understood. The next step is to examine Kant's account of his "Copernican revolution" in philosophy and the sense in which it can be said to involve a shift from a theocentric to an anthropocentric model of knowledge. Finally, in light of all of this, I hope to establish definitively the fundamental difference between transcendental idealism and a phenomenalism or idealism of a Berkeleian type.

A. Transcendental Idealism as Formal Idealism

In response to the pervasive misunderstanding and criticism of his idealism as it was formulated in the First Edition of the *Critique,* Kant notes in the appendix to the *Prolegomena* that he now wishes transcendental idealism to be termed " 'formal' or, better still, 'critical' idealism." In so doing he hoped to distinguish it from both "the dogmatic idealism of Berkeley and the skeptical idealism of Descartes."[29] Moreover, in a note added in the Second Edition to the previously cited definition of transcendental idealism he remarks, "I have also, elsewhere, sometimes entitled it *formal* idealism, to distinguish it from *material* idealism, that is, from the usual type of idealism which doubts or denies the existence of outer things themselves" (B519).

The predominance of the standard picture strongly suggests that Kant would have been well advised to follow more consistently his own terminological recommendation. Kant's idealism is "formal" in the sense that it is a theory about the nature and the scope of the *conditions* under which objects can be experienced or known by the human mind.[30] This is to be contrasted with idealisms of the Cartesian or Berkeleian sort, which are first and foremost theories about the *contents* of consciousness (understood in the empirical sense). Again, this idealism is "critical" because it is grounded in a reflection on the conditions and limits of human knowledge, not on the contents of consciousness or the nature of *an sich* reality.

Unfortunately, much of this is obscured by Kant's tendency to refer to the objects of human experience not only as "appearances" but also as "mere representations." The latter locution in particular, which is extremely frequent in Kant, is mainly responsible for the standard picture. Nevertheless, even here careful attention to the text suffices to raise serious questions about the correctness of this picture. Consider, for example, the characterization of transcendental idealism to which Kant appended the abovementioned note. We saw earlier that Kant there describes transcendental idealism as the doctrine that "everything intuited in space or time, and therefore all objects of any experience possible to us, are nothing but appearances, that is, mere representations, which, in the manner in which they are represented, as extended beings, or as series of alterations, have no independent existence outside our thoughts." The equation of appearances with "mere representations" in the main clause certainly suggests the standard picture. In the subordinate clause, however, Kant effectively undercuts any such reading by indicating that the characterization of appearances as "mere representations" must be understood to refer to "the manner in which they are represented." The claim, therefore, is not that objects have no independent existence (as one might maintain with regard to Berkeleian ideas or the sense data of the phenomenalists); it is rather that such existence cannot be attributed to them "in the manner in which they are represented."

The "manner" in which objects are represented is as spatiotemporal entities. The claim is thus that this description, together with all that it entails, can be applied to objects only in virtue of our manner of representing them, and not to these same objects as they may be in themselves. Kant states that this result is established in the Transcendental Aesthetic, where he argues that space and time are "forms" or "conditions" of human sensibility. We shall consider the specific argument for the transcendental ideality of space and time in chapter 5; for the present, I wish simply to note that behind this argument and, indeed, behind Kant's formal idealism, lies a principle that is implicit in the *Critique* as a whole, but is nowhere made fully explicit: that whatever is necessary for the representation or experience of something as an object, that is, whatever is required for the recognition or picking out of what is "objective" in our experience, must reflect the cognitive structure of the mind (its manner of representing) rather than the nature of the object as it is in itself. To claim otherwise is to assume that the mind can somehow have access to an object (through sensible or intellectual intuition) independently of the very elements that have been stipulated to be the conditions of the possibility of doing this in the first place. This involves an obvious contradiction.[31] The transcendental realist avoids this contradiction only because he rejects the assumption that there are any such conditions. In so doing, however, he begs the very question raised by the *Critique*.

Similar considerations apply to the pure concepts of the understanding, which serve as the intellectual conditions of human knowledge. Although a detailed analysis of Kant's conception of the understanding must await the second part of this study, it should be kept in mind here that all human knowledge is judgmental for Kant (as opposed to being intuitive) and that the pure concepts are claimed to function as the ultimate rules or conditions of judgment. Now, insofar as by 'object' is meant simply the subject of a possible judgment, which is how Kant sometimes construes the term, these concepts are both necessary and sufficient to determine what can "count," that is, be represented as an object. In other words, they define the very meaning of 'object', insofar as by an object is meant merely something conceptually represented. On the other hand, insofar as 'object' is taken to mean an object of possible experience, which, as we shall see, is the "weighty" Kantian sense of the term, these same concepts are necessary but not sufficient conditions for the representations of objects or objective states of affairs.[32] They are still necessary conditions because experience involves judgment; but they are not sufficient conditions because they require supplementation by space and time, the forementioned sensible conditions. The main point, however, is that they possess coequal transcendental status with these sensible conditions. Consequently, the transcendental ideality of the objects of possible experience must be understood to involve their conformity to these concepts as well as to the forms of sensibility. Both count as "forms" of experience, and both, therefore, enter into the characterization of Kant's idealism as "formal." Much of this is usually lost sight of because of Kant's tendency to define transcendental idealism almost exclusively in terms of his theory of sensibility, and, therefore, as a doctrine that receives its primary support and proof from the Transcendental Aesthetic. This same tendency is also exhibited in his frequent characterization of appearances as "modifications" or "determinations" of our "faculty of sensibility" or of the "subjective condition of the senses." Nevertheless, there are passages in which Kant does indicate that the transcendental conception of appearance must be understood in terms of the understanding and its a priori concepts, as well as of sensibility and its a priori forms.[33] Moreover, as we shall see in the next chapter, the so-called "indirect proof" of the Antinomy of Pure Reason rests upon an appeal to a much broader conception of transcendental idealism, one that is ultimately inseparable from the "critical" or "transcendental" method. These passages and the argument in the Antinomy, as well as the Transcendental Aesthetic, must be taken into consideration if one is to understand the "formal" or "critical" thrust of Kant's idealism and its rootedness in the notion of an epistemic condition.

B. Kant's "Copernican Revolution" and the Anthropocentric Model of Knowledge

In a famous passage in the preface to the Second Edition, Kant compares the "changed point of view" (*Umänderung der Denkart*) which he advocates for philosophy with the revolution in astronomy initiated by Copernicus. Not surprisingly, a considerable literature has developed regarding the precise point of the comparison and the appropriateness of the Copernican analogy. The main point at issue is whether Kant has committed what is called the "anthropocentric fallacy" in his reading of Copernicus.[34] Fortunately, we need not concern ourselves with that issue here. The central question is simply how Kant's own philosophical "revolution" is to be understood, and this obviously remains a question even if, as is frequently maintained, the analogy with Copernicus is not particularly apt. Kant describes his revolution in this way:

Hitherto it has been assumed that all our knowledge must conform to objects. But all attempts to extend our knowledge of objects by establishing something in regard to them *a priori,* by means of concepts, have, on this assumption, ended in failure. We must therefore make trial whether we may not have more success in the tasks of metaphysics, if we suppose that objects must conform to our knowledge. [Bxvi]

Given the preceding analysis, it should be clear that Kant is here contrasting the "standpoints" of transcendental realism and transcendental idealism. To begin with, the assumption that "all our knowledge must conform to objects" is readily identifiable as the "common assumption" associated with transcendental realism. Consequently, the "objects" to which our knowledge presumably conforms must be characterized as things in themselves in the transcendental sense. From this point of view, then, we can be said to know objects just to the extent to which our thought conforms to their "real" nature or, equivalently, to God's thought of these same objects. On this model, Kant tells us, we cannot account for the possibility of a priori knowledge of objects, because we cannot explain how the mind could "anticipate" any of the properties of objects so defined, which is required for a priori knowledge. The problem is that this model assumes that all knowledge rests ultimately upon a direct acquaintance with its object, which would, in effect, make all knowledge a posteriori. In the *Prolegomena,* however, Kant goes beyond this to suggest that if the objects of human knowledge are things in themselves, it is not even possible to account for a posteriori knowledge.[35] I think it apparent from what has already been said that this stronger claim represents Kant's considered opinion. In short, his position is that transcendental realism, with its theocentric model, is incapable of explaining knowledge of any sort. That is why a philosophical revolution is necessary.

The contrary "supposition," that "objects must conform to our knowledge" (*die Gegenstände müssen sind nach unseren Erkenntnis richten*), expresses the central tenet of transcendental idealism. It also appeals to an anthropocentric model, the defining characteristic of which is that the cognitive structure of the human mind is viewed as the source of certain conditions which must be met by anything that is to be represented as an object by such a mind. Clearly, this model presupposes that there are such conditions (epistemic conditions); this presupposition, in turn, allows us to attach a meaning to the supposed conformity of objects to our knowledge. To say that objects "conform to our knowledge" is just to say that they conform to the conditions under which we can alone represent them as objects. Moreover, given this presupposition, there is no difficulty in accounting for either a priori or a posteriori knowledge of such objects, for it is an analytic truth that any object represented must conform to the conditions under which it can alone be represented as an object. As already indicated, the key question is whether there are in fact any such conditions and, if so, whether they can be specified.

Since the preface does little more than entertain the possibility that there might be such conditions to which objects must conform, the whole account of the "Copernican hypothesis" must be regarded as a promissory note which will have to be made good in the actual text of the *Critique*.[36] We shall, of course, be concerned with the question of the success of this endeavor throughout the balance of this study. For the present, however, the point to be emphasized is that this "changed point of view" brings with it a radically new conception of an object. An object is now to be understood as whatever conforms to our knowledge, and this, as we have seen, means whatever conforms to the mind's conditions (both sensible and intellectual) for the representation of it as an object. Consequently, an object is by its very nature something represented; and in that sense a reference to mind and its cognitive apparatus is built into the definition of the term. This new conception of an object, which is the correlate of the conception of an epistemic condition, is the major outcome of Kant's so-called Copernican revolution.

Finally, it should be noted that one cannot object to this account of the revolutionary nature of Kant's "supposition" on the grounds that other philosophers before him had developed a conception of the object of human knowledge which involves an essential reference to mind. The fact is readily granted; what is denied is simply its relevance to the present point. Everything depends on how this "essential reference to mind" is understood. For Kant, it must be understood in such a way as to allow one to speak of objects as conforming to our knowledge. But the mind-dependent objects of philosophers such as Berkeley and Hume (ideas and impressions) can no more be said to "conform to our knowledge" than can a humanly inaccessible "object" such as a Lockean real essence.

C. Transcendental Idealism and Phenomenalism

I shall conclude this chapter by returning to the question of the contrast between transcendental idealism and phenomenalism in general and Berkeleian idealism in particular. Jonathan Bennett's fairly standard characterization of the nature of phenomenalism and its distinction from idealism provides a convenient starting point for this discussion. According to Bennett, phenomenalism is essentially a theory about object language statements. It holds that all such statements are translatable into complex statements about sense data (including counterfactual hypotheticals). He further suggests that this is equivalent to the claim that "*objects are logical constructs out of sense data.*" Idealism, by contrast, is characterized as the metaphysical view that "objects are *collections* of sense data." He attributes the latter view to Berkeley.[37]

The first and most basic point to be made here is that phenomenalism, as Bennett describes it, is transcendentally realistic in the same sense and for the same reasons as Berkeleian idealism: in spite of its conception of objects as "logical constructs," it treats (implicitly, of course) the sensible data out of which "objects" are supposedly constructed as things in themselves. Consequently, it is no more suitable for explicating transcendental idealism than is Berkeleian idealism. In short, transcendental idealism is neither a theory about the translatability of object language statements into some more precise or primitive sense datum language nor a theory about the ontological type (material object or collection of sense data) of the objects of human experience. Admittedly, the latter interpretation is suggested by much of Kant's language, in particular by his characterization of objects as "mere representations." Nevertheless, we have seen that this manner of expression, which is primarily responsible for the standard picture, must itself be interpreted in light of the conception of the a priori forms or conditions of human knowledge.

We need not, however, stop with these very general considerations. The whole issue can be clarified further by means of a comparison of Berkeley's analysis of statements about unperceived objects in *The Principles of Human Knowledge* with Kant's treatment of the same topic in the Antinomy of Pure Reason. In the *Principles* Berkeley offers two distinct analyses of propositions of the form: *x* exists, although *x* is not currently being perceived by myself or by another "created spirit." On one of these analyses, *x* can be said to exist, if *x* is being perceived by God.[38] On the other analysis, which is obviously much closer to contemporary phenomenalism, *x* can be said to exist if statements about *x* can be translated into hypotheticals of the form: if one were in position or had the proper instruments, and so forth, one would perceive *x*.[39] Both of these analyses are based upon the correlation between existence and perception which is the hallmark of Berkeley's philosophy.

Kant's account of propositions about unperceived entities and events bears a superficial resemblance to Berkeley's second version, and therefore to phenomenalistic accounts. Thus, he allows that we can perfectly well speak of inhabitants on the moon, even though no one has even seen them, but he goes on to note that

> this, however, only means that in the possible advance of experience we may encounter them. For everything is real [*wirklich*] which stands in connection with a perception in accordance with the laws of empirical advance. They are therefore real if they stand in an empirical connection with my actual consciousness, although they are not for that reason real in themselves, that is, outside this advance of experience.

Moreover, he continues:

> To call an appearance a real thing prior to our perceiving it, either means that in the advance of experience we must meet with such a perception, or it means nothing at all. For if we were speaking of a thing in itself, we would indeed say that it exists in itself apart from relation to our senses and possible

experience. But we are here speaking only of an appearance in space and time, which are not determinations of things in themselves but only of our sensibility. Accordingly, that which is in space and time is an appearance; it is not anything in itself but consists merely of representations, which, if not given in us—that is to say, in perception—are nowhere to be met with. [A493–94 / B522–23]

We can see from this that Kant, like both Berkeley and the contemporary phenomenalist, translates first-order statements about unperceived entities or events into second-order statements about the possible perception thereof. Nevertheless, this superficial resemblance really masks the distinctive feature of the Kantian analysis: the role given to a priori laws or principles. The "laws of empirical advance," or, as he calls them elsewhere, the "laws of the unity of experience" (A494 / B522), are nothing other than the Analogies of Experience. We shall deal in detail with the first two of these Analogies and with Kant's endeavor to justify them in the second part of the study. For the present, the important point is only that, on a transcendentally idealistic analysis, the claim that a certain entity or event is to be met with in the "advance of experience" turns out to be an elliptical way of affirming some lawful connection or "causal route" between the entity or event in question and present experience. It does not, however, in any sense involve the postulation of a hypothetical mental episode in the history of some consciousness (whether human or divine).

The role of intellectual conditions and, more generally, the epistemic or transcendental thrust of Kant's theory, is brought out particularly clearly in the analysis of 'actuality' (*Wirklichkeit*) in the Postulates of Empirical Thought. Kant there defines the actual as "that which is bound up with the material conditions of experience, that is, with sensation" (A218 / B266). Because of the explicit reference to sensation, this definition of actuality certainly seems to invite a phenomenalistic or even an idealistic (in the Berkeleian sense) reading. Kant's discussion of the postulate, however, suggests a somewhat different story. The claim that something is actual, we are told,

does not, indeed, demand immediate *perception* (and, therefore, sensation of which we are conscious) of the object whose existence is to be known. What we do, however, require is the connection of the object with some actual perception, in accordance with the analogies of experience, which define all real connection in an experience in general. [A225 / B272]

At first glance, this might still suggest phenomenalism as Bennett defines it. To be sure, it rules out the extreme idealistic requirement that for an empirical object to be actual (real) it must actually be perceived, but it does seem to require the supposition that the object *could* be perceived, which is just the thesis of phenomenalism (with its appeal to counterfactuals). Nevertheless, this is not quite Kant's position. He does hold that whatever is actual must be an object of possible perception, but this is merely a consequence, not a criterion, of actuality. As the passage above indicates, the criteria of actuality are provided by the Analogies of Experience, that is, by a set of a priori principles or intellectual conditions. The full critical position is that whatever can be connected with some given perception in accordance with these principles, or "laws of the empirical connection of appearances," is to be deemed "actual." The appeal to perception or sensation here functions merely as the point of departure, which gives empirical content to the claim of actuality. The claim itself is not about any "subjective experiences."

Kant's illustration of this principle is also highly instructive. It concerns the hypothetical case of the perception of some magnetically attracted iron filings. Such a perception, he notes, would clearly justify the inference to the existence (*Wirklichkeit*) of some material responsible for this attraction. Moreover, it would do so even though our sensory apparatus is not adequate for the perception of this material. Admittedly, he then suggests that if our sense organs were more powerful or more refined we might be able to perceive it. This once more calls to mind the phenomenalist's characteristic appeal to counterfactuals in order to justify the meaningfulness of existence claims. Kant, however, does not appeal to counterfactuals in this manner. Instead, he remarks that "the grossness of our senses does not in any way decide the form of possible experience in general. Our knowledge of the existence of things reaches, then, only in so far as our perception and its advance according to empirical laws can extend" (A226/B273). The key point here is that the meaningfulness of the reference to this magnetic material is not a function of the possibility of sufficiently improving our sensory apparatus so as to enable us to have experiences that we are not presently able to have. It is rather a function of the connectibility of this material with our present experience in accordance with empirical laws and, ultimately, a priori principles or intellectual conditions.

Finally, the same point can be made with respect to the notion of a possible perception. As is already implicit in his *esse est percipi* principle, and as is perfectly manifest in his account of the *minimum sensibile*, Berkeley's account of possible perception is essentially psychological in nature. To be possible means to be actually perceivable. Consequently, anything too small to be perceived, or below the *minimum sensibile,* can simply be dismissed as impossible.[40] In sharp contrast to this, Kant defines the possibility of perception in terms of the conformity to rules, that is, to a priori principles. Thus he writes:

All that the rule requires is that the advance from appearances be to appearances; for even if these latter yield no actual perceptions (as is the case when for our consciousness they are too weak in degree to become experience), as appearances they nonetheless still belong to possible experience. [A522/B550]

This passage almost seems as if it were written with Berkeley in mind. In any event, it nicely illustrates the radical difference between Kant's transcendental or formal idealism and a phenomenalism or material idealism of the Berkeleian mold. The transcendental concept of appearance is linked here specifically to the notion of a possible experience. The latter notion, however, is defined in terms of conformity to a set of a priori conditions (conditions of the possibility of experience), not in terms of the possibility of a perceptual state. Once again, then, we see that the appeal to such conditions is the defining characteristic of transcendental idealism. We shall see in the next chapter that a similar conception of transcendental idealism emerges from a consideration of the argument of the Antinomy of Pure Reason.

3

The Antinomy of Pure Reason

Although Kant is engaged in a continous battle with the various forms of transcendental realism throughout the *Critique* as a whole, the great pitched battle between transcendental realism and transcendental idealism is contained in the Antinomy of Pure Reason. This is why, in a well-known letter to Christian Garve, Kant remarks that it was the Antinomy of Pure Reason that "first aroused me from my dogmatic slumber and drove me to the critique of reason itself, in order to resolve the ostensible contradiction of reason with itself."[1] It may seem strange to find Kant using virtually the same language to describe the discovery of the Antinomies as he had used to characterize the effect of his famous "recollection of David Hume" some fifteen years earlier.[2] It is particularly strange in light of the fact that Anglo-American students of Kant have come to see the "problem" of the *Critique* almost exclusively in terms of the question of the possibility of synthetic a priori knowledge. Nevertheless, a similar characterization of the Antinomies may be found even in the *Prolegomena,* where the focus is clearly on the problem of the synthetic a priori.[3] More important, such a characterization accurately reflects both the actual development of Kant's thought and the role of the Antinomies within the *Critique of Pure Reason.*

In his analysis of the Antinomies, Kant makes the apparently audacious claim that reason necessarily falls into contradiction with itself in dealing with the traditional cosmological questions. This occurs because reason generates two equally compelling but incompatible answers to each of these questions. He further contends that this contradiction can be removed by the simple expedient of uncovering an incoherent and transcendentally realistic assumption which underlies the cosmological questions themselves. Moreover, since this assumption is unavoidable, given the standpoint of transcendental realism, this also serves as a refutation of such realism. Finally, since transcendental idealism and transcendental realism are mutually exclusive and exhaustive metaphilosophical alternatives, the refutation of the latter provides an indirect proof of the former.

My central concern in this chapter is with this indirect proof of transcendental idealism, rather than with the details of the arguments for the thesis and antithesis of the various Antinomies. Nevertheless, after some preliminary considerations, I shall look closely at the temporal portions of the arguments of the First Antinomy. (The Third Antinomy will be discussed in chapter 15.) These are the most widely criticized of Kant's arguments, and my goal is to show that, although hardly free from difficulty, they are not as hopelessly confused as Kant's critics generally assume. In analyzing the argument for idealism, I shall first consider the official form it takes in the *Critique,* which presupposes the soundness of the proofs of the thesis and antithesis of at least one Antinomy, and then show that the argument can be reformulated so as to avoid this highly questionable premise. The treatment of this topic will be closely related to the account of the connection between transcendental realism and transcendental idealism given in the preceding chapter. In fact, we shall see that if we are to make any sense out of Kant's claim to have provided an indirect proof of transcendental idealism in the Antinomy of Pure Reason, we must understand this idealism in the manner suggested in chapter 2.

I. THE ANTINOMIES: SOME PRELIMINARY CONSIDERATIONS

According to Kant, this great conflict of reason with itself, which, if unresolved, would lead to the "euthanasia of pure reason" (A407/B434), has its roots in reason's demand for an absolute totality of conditions (grounds) for any conditioned. This demand is itself a consequence of the principle that if "*the conditioned is given, the entire sum of conditions, and consequently the absolutely unconditioned* (through which alone the conditioned has been possible) *is also given*" (A409/B436). It will be necessary to return to this principle and its application later when we consider the argument for transcendental idealism. For the present, it is important merely to note its logical status. In Kant's own characterization, the principle affirms the need of reason to aim at "such completeness in the series of premises as will dispense with the need of presupposing other premises" (A416/B444). As such, it reflects the logical requirement of a complete justification or explanation for every assertion. This is equivalent to what Kant sometimes refers to as "the logical principle of sufficient reason," which may be defined as the principle that every true proposition must have a ground or reason.[4]

Problems begin with the application of this principle to the spatiotemporal world. Such an application immediately gives rise to the set of cosmological Ideas. Kant contends that these Ideas arise naturally through the extension, from the elements within the world to the world as a whole, of the demands for serial ordering or synthesis that are thought in the various categories. He therefore describes these Ideas as "simply categories extended to the unconditioned" (A409/B436). The connection between category and Idea makes it possible to construct a table of cosmological Ideas corresponding to the table of the categories. Not every category, however, is capable of such an extension: the category of substance is a clear example of one that is not. The decisive question is whether a given category involves the thought of a synthesis of subordinate elements or conditions. Only if it does is it capable of generating the thought of an unconditioned.

Such a capacity must obviously be granted to the category of quantity. Moreover, this category is intimately involved in the effort to think space and time, which Kant here characterizes as "the two original quanta of all our intuition" (A418/B438). As a consequence of such "quantification," we naturally regard the present moment of time as "conditioned" by past moments in the sense that it is conceived as the result of a completed synthesis of these past moments. As Kant himself admits, the situation with respect to space is not quite so clear. We do not conceive of a given space as conditioned by adjoining spaces in the way in which a moment of time is conditioned by preceding moments; that is, we do not conceive of space in serial terms. Nevertheless, Kant maintains that something analogous is involved in the apprehension or measurement of space; for each part of space is limited by other parts, and in this sense it presupposes these other parts as "the conditions of its limits." Consequently, the apprehension or measurement of a determinate space necessarily involves a synthesis or regress from the conditioned to its condition. On this basis Kant contends, "I can as legitimately enquire regarding the absolute totality of appearance in space as of that in past time" (A413/B440). He also intimates, however, that the real question is whether either enquiry is legitimate.

The other categories that involve the thought of a regress from conditioned to condition, and are thus capable of generating an Idea of the unconditioned, are reality, causality, and necessity. Apart from the case of causality, the connection between category and cosmological Idea seems forced; hence it is tempting to join Kemp Smith in regarding the whole argument as nothing more than another product of Kant's architectonic.[5] Fortunately, very little rides on the question of the exact derivation or the precise number of cosmological Ideas. What is important is Kant's claim that in each case the cosmological Idea generates two equally compelling but contradictory conceptions of the unconditioned. Thus, in reason's endemic need to "think the whole," it seems equally "natural" or "rational" to recognize some first element or limit (an "intellectual beginning") or to reject any such purportedly first element by extending the enquiry into its grounds or conditions ad infinitum.

These broad intellectual options constitute the thesis and antithesis positions respectively of the four Antinomies. The former offer arguments affirming a first beginning of the world in time and a limit in space, a simple element in the matter that occupies space, an uncaused "free" cause outside the series of natural causes that grounds the whole series, and a necessary being that serves as the ground of the contingent beings in the world. The latter maintain that there can be no such beginning, limit, simple, and free cause, or necessary being in the world. It has been argued by Al-Azm that these claims reflect the respective positions of Newton and Leibniz, as presented in the correspondence between Leibniz and Clarke,[6] and this is certainly true of the First Antinomy, with which we shall alone be concerned in this chapter. Kant characterizes the former (Newtonian) position as "dogmatism" and the latter (Leibnizian) position as "empiricism." It seems strange to find Leibniz included amongst the empiricists, but this reflects the actual manner in which he tended to argue against Newton.[7] Moreover, we shall see that this empiricistic position turns out to be as dogmatic as the one to which it is opposed.

Kant contends that the equal success of each side in refuting the other demonstrates the impossibility of a dogmatic solution to the conflict. In other words, we cannot decide for or against either party in any of the questions under dispute by simple inspection of the arguments. This suggests a skeptical impasse, and such a conclusion had already been drawn by Pierre Bayle from a consideration of similar arguments.[8] Kant's own strategy for avoiding this impasse is to adopt what he calls the "skeptical method," which consists essentially of an examination of the presuppositions underlying the dispute. The result of this examination is the realization that both sides share an initially plausible but ultimately incoherent conception of the sensible world as a whole existing in itself. If one assumes this conception, it follows logically that one of the two contradictory claims must be true. But once this assumption is rejected as incoherent the contradiction vanishes and is replaced instead by a "dialectical opposition" between contraries, both of which are false. This reflects Kant's solution to the first two, or "mathematical," Antinomies. The second two, or "dynamical," Antinomies receive a very different treatment. There the thesis claim is referred to the noumenal world and the antithesis claim to the phenomenal world, so that it becomes at least conceivable that both thesis and antithesis are true. They are thus treated as subalternates rather than contraries, although the conflict between them is still regarded as merely dialectical.[9]

As already indicated, this incoherent conception of the sensible world as a whole existing in itself will turn out to be a logical consequence of transcendental realism. The demonstration that transcendental realism gives rise to such a conception, therefore, serves both as a refutation of it and as an indirect proof of transcendental idealism. This demonstration and the implications which Kant claims to derive from it require a detailed examination. But since Kant rests his analysis of the antinomical conflict on the presumed soundness of the arguments for the incompatible positions, it will first be necessary to examine at least some of these arguments. As I have also previously indicated, the analysis will be limited to the First Antinomy, or more specifically, to the temporal portion of the argument.

II. THE FIRST ANTINOMY

The thesis of the First Antinomy states that the world has both a beginning in time and a limit in space. The antithesis denies each of these claims and contends instead that the world is infinite with respect to both time and space. Taking x to refer to the world and F and I to refer to the finitistic and infinitistic positions respectively, the common assumption underlying this dispute can be symbolized as $(\exists x)(Fx \vee Ix)$.[10]

It must be emphasized at the outset that the dispute concerns the nature of the relationship between the *world* and space and time, not, as is sometimes assumed, the nature of space and time themselves.[11] The concept of a world, specifically a spatiotemporal world, is therefore central to the whole analysis. Within the context of the Antinomies, Kant defines 'world' as "the mathematical sum-total [*Ganze*] of all appearances and the totality [*Totalität*] of their synthesis, alike in the great and the small, that is, in the advance alike through composition and through division" (A418/B446). Elsewhere in the *Critique* he defines it as "the object of all possible experience" (A605/B633). Common to both definitions is the emphasis upon totality or wholeness. This reflects Kant's earlier account in the Inaugural Dissertation, where he maintains that the concept of a world in general (whether sensible or intelligible) requires not merely a whole of representation, but the actual representation of a whole.[12] Kant underscores the same point in his *Lectures on Metaphysics*, where he notes that the concept of a world involves not merely the thought of a plurality of discrete items (an aggregate or multiplicity), but also the thought of these items as constituting a whole (*Ganze*).[13] The symbolization offered above attempts to capture the fact that this conception is shared by both sides in Kant's idealized dispute, just as it was in the actual dispute between Newton and Leibniz.

A. The Thesis

Like all the proofs used in the Antinomies, that of the thesis of the First Antinomy is apagogic: it demonstrates that the world must be finite in the relevant respects by showing that it cannot be infinite in these same respects. The temporal portion of the argument turns largely on Kant's analysis of the notion of an infinite series and on the question of the compatibility of this notion with the concept of a world. Its central claim is that the doctrine that the world has no beginning in time (the infinitistic position advocated by Leibniz) logically requires one to hold that at any given moment of time—for example, the present—an eternity has "elapsed" (*abgelaufen*). Since the dispute concerns the sequence of things in time and not time itself, this is taken to mean that at any given moment in time "there has passed away [*verflossen*] in the world an infinite series of successive states of things." Presumably, this entails that an infinite series has been completed. But, the argument continues, "the infinity of a series consists in the fact that it cannot be completed through successive synthesis." In the observation on the thesis, Kant characterizes this as "the true transcendental concept of infinitude" (A432/B460). In light of this concept, the argument concludes: "It thus follows that it is impossible for an infinite world-series to have passed away, and that a beginning of the world is therefore a necessary condition of the world's existence" (A426/B454).

The argument can be broken down into the following six steps:

1. Assume the opposite: the world has no beginning in time.

2. It follows from this that up to any given moment (the present) an eternity has elapsed.

3. This means that an infinite number of successive changes in the states of things (an infinite number of successive events) has actually occurred; that is, an infinite series has been completed.

4. But, according to the "true transcendental concept of infinitude," the infinity of a series consists in the fact that it can never be completed through successive synthesis.

5. The concept of an infinite world-series that has "passed away" (been completed) is, therefore, self-contradictory.

6. Consequently, there must be a beginning of the world in time, that is, a first event.

Some Standard Criticisms. Given its extreme crypticness and apparent appeal to arbitrary assumptions, it is not surprising that this argument has not met with much favor. The most prevalent criticism is that it involves a rather crude form of psychologism (or, alternatively, that it presupposes transcendental idealism). As Kemp Smith succinctly puts it, "From a subjective impossibility of apprehension he infers an objective impossibility of existence."[14]

Much the same point is also made by Russell, who combines it with an appeal to the Cantorian conception of infinite or transfinite number. In light of this conception, he dismisses Kant's characterization of the infinitude of a series as involving "the impossibility of the completion of a successive synthesis." Russell contends, and he has here been followed by many others, that reference to synthesis, which presumably presupposes the mental activity of synthesizing, is completely out of place in a discussion of the concept of infinity. By including it, Kant succeeds only in introducing, in Russell's words, "more or less surreptitiously, that reference to mind by which all Kant's philosophy was infected."[15] But the notion of infinity (like that of all number) refers primarily to a property of classes and is only derivatively applicable to a series. Moreover, Russell points out, "classes which are infinite are given all at once by the defining property of their members, so that there is no question of 'completion' or of 'successive synthesis'."[16] With this analysis, Kant's objections against the supposed infinity of the world are swept aside.

Moreover, almost as an afterthought, Russell introduces a second, independent criticism. According to this new objection, Kant's argument would be hopeless, even if one were to allow him his talk about 'successive synthesis'.

> When Kant says that an infinite series can "never" be completed by successive synthesis, all that he has even conceivably a right to say is that it cannot be completed in a finite time. Thus what he really proves is, at most, that if the world had no beginning, it must have already existed for an infinite time. This, however, is a very poor conclusion, by no means suitable for his purposes.[17]

This line of criticism, which has been reiterated by Strawson,[18] amounts to the charge that Kant is guilty of a *petitio principii*. The reasoning goes roughly as follows: either (1) the world has a first beginning in time, or (2) it has existed for all time. If, as the argument assumes, the synthesis cannot be complete (in a finite time), it follows that the world could not have had a first beginning. The whole purpose of the argument, however, is to show what follows from the denial of the first conclusion. Thus, the proper conclusion is the second. Kant avoids this conclusion by stating that the second is impossible, but in so doing he begs the whole question.

A somewhat similar, although distinct, criticism was first offered by G. E. Moore, whose critique of Kant's argument is part of his attack on idealism in all its forms (between which he does not bother to distinguish very carefully). Moore's position is that if the argument proves anything at all, it proves that time does not exist (which is hardly the conclusion that Kant drew from it). He acknowledges that such a result would follow if Kant could really prove that neither the thesis nor the antithesis were true. Moreover, he accepts the claim of the antithesis that time and space cannot have first moments or parts. He therefore presents the issue in such a way that everything turns on the proof of the thesis. This proof, however, is dismissed summarily on the grounds that it is a "pure fallacy based on an ambiguity in the notion of end."[19]

Moore's contention, which is reiterated by Bennett, is that Kant confused the true proposition that an infinite series does not have two ends—that is, is not bounded at both ends—with the manifestly false claim that it cannot have one end—that is, that it cannot be bounded at all.[20] He cites the series of natural numbers as an example of a series that is bounded at one end (the beginning) and is yet infinite. In light of this, he claims that Kant's mistake was to infer falsely from the fact that the temporal series has one end (the present moment) that it cannot be infinite. The most, however, that can be legitimately inferred from this fact is that, if infinite, the series could not have had a beginning, which is precisely what the infinitistic position asserts. From this he concludes:

> It is, therefore, a pure fallacy to suppose that there cannot have been an infinite series of past hours, simply because that series has an end in one direction and has come to an end now; all that we mean by calling it infinite is that it has no end in the other direction or, in other words, no beginning.[21]

Response to These Criticisms. Keeping Russell's critique in mind, let us begin with a brief look at some of Kant's remarks about the infinite. Now, Kant is at least careful to distinguish his "true transcendental concept of infinitude, according to which the successive synthesis of units required for the measure [*Durchmessung*] of a given quantum can never be completed" (A432/B460), from what he terms "a defective concept of the infinitude of a given magnitude" (A430/B548). This "defective concept" is simply that of a maximum or greatest number. Since there can be no greatest number, this conception enables one to gain an easy but spurious victory over the infinitistic position. Kant's concern is, therefore, to distinguish his argument from one based on that conception.[22] The important point here is that, according to the Kantian definition, the notion of the infinite is not incoherent, and this allows the infinitistic position at least to get off the ground.

Moreover, in a footnote appended to his characterization of the infinite, Kant remarks that such an infinite quantum "contains a quantity [*Menge*] of given units which is greater than any number which is the mathematical concept of the infinite" (A432/B460 n.). Assuming, as I think we must, that by 'number' (*Zahl*) Kant means natural number, the mathematical concept of the infinite can be taken as a schematized version of the transcendental concept, rather than as a distinct concept. It contains a specific reference to number, the schema of quantity (A142/B182), and it expresses in numerical terms what the "transcendental," or "pure," concept expresses in strictly conceptual terms; namely, the thought of the incompletability or inexhaustibility of the enumerative process.[23] According to this conception, then, to say that a set contains infinitely many members is just to say that however many of its members one has picked out or enumerated, there are still more to count.[24] This is compatible with Russell's own characterization of infinite classes as "given all at once by the defining property of their members," and presumably, therefore, with the Cantorian conception of the infinite as well.[25] Thus, whatever fault we may find in Kant's argument, I do not think that we can locate the trouble in his conception of the infinite.

Also crucial for understanding the argument is the distinction drawn in the observation on the thesis of the Second Antinomy between a *compositum* and a *totum* (A438/B467). Elsewhere Kant refers to these as a *totum syntheticum* and a *totum analyticum,* respectively.[26] A totum syntheticum is a whole composed of parts that are given separately (at least in thought). Not only does the concept of such a whole presuppose its distinct, pregiven parts, it also is conceived as the product of the collection (in Kant's term, "synthesis") of these parts. Consequently, the question of whether a particular totum syntheticum is possible is equivalent to the question of whether a complete collection of its parts is conceivable. A totum analyticum, by contrast, is a whole, the parts of which are only possible, or conceivable, with reference to that whole. Space and time, according to Kant, are tota analytica, which, as we shall see, is why they can be characterized as infinite, but the material universe, the world in space and time, is conceived as a totum syntheticum.

Given this characterization of the material universe as a totum syntheticum, it is clear that the alleged contradiction in the infinitistic position must be located in its application of the concept of the infinite, which is itself perfectly legitimate, to the material universe. Since this universe is conceived as a totum syntheticum (it could hardly be regarded as a totum analyticum), the thought of the complete enumeration or "synthesis" of its parts, which is built into this concept, contradicts the thought of inexhaustibility, which is similarly built into the concept of the infinite. Kant himself makes this explicit at the end of the observation on the thesis when he remarks:

> Now since this synthesis must constitute a never to be completed series, I cannot think a totality either prior to the synthesis or by means of the synthesis. For the concept of totality is in this case itself the representation of a completed synthesis of the parts. And since this completion is impossible, so likewise is the concept of it. [A433/B461][27]

The above analysis suggests the nature of the Kantian response to the general charge of subjectivism or psychologism, because it shows that the critique of the infinitistic position turns on a conceptual claim and has nothing to do with the presumed psychological impossibility of grasping or comprehending the infinite.[28] The position can be clarified by noting that the concept of a totum syntheticum is here operationally defined in terms of the intellectual procedure through which it is conceived, much as geometrical figures were thought to be given "real" or "genetic" definitions through the articulation of the rules for their construction. The problem, then, is that the rule or procedure for thinking a totum syntheticum clashes with the rule or procedure for thinking an infinite quantity. The former demands precisely what the latter precludes: namely, completability (at least in principle). In short, we are given two incompatible rules for thinking the same object, which amounts to a genuine contradiction.

Admittedly, this argument does not eliminate all reference to mind or to conceptual abilities, and for this reason alone it would hardly satisfy a philosopher of Russell's persuasion. In addition, it presupposes the Kantian notion of concepts as rules (a topic with which we shall deal in subsequent chapters) and a particular theory of definition.[29] It does not, however, involve either a blatant psychologism or a question begging appeal to the specific doctrines of transcendental idealism.

Similar considerations apply to the Russell-Strawson and Moore-Bennett objections. First, in response to the Russell-Strawson petitio charge, it must be noted that the assumption that the series is infinite does not entail merely that it cannot be completed in a finite time, but rather that it cannot be completed at all. If, however, it cannot be completed at all, then it does not constitute a world (totum syntheticum). We thus have two alternatives: either (1) the series does not constitute a world, or (2) there is a first moment. The correct Kantian option is, of course, the first; but since the argument presupposes that the series does constitute a world, the proper conclusion is the second. Consequently, there is no petitio, although there is the highly questionable premise that the series constitutes a totum syntheticum.

The Moore-Bennett objection, it will be recalled, maintains that the argument commits a "fallacy of ambiguity," confusing an infinite series, which by definition is open at one end, with a series that has no end at either point. Because of this initial confusion, Kant is said to have reasoned falsely that, since the series does have one end (the present moment), it cannot be infinite. Kant, however, does not claim that a series cannot be infinite if it has one end. (As his critique of the "defective concept" of the infinite makes clear, he would have no objection to the infinity of the series of natural numbers.) His point is rather that since, as infinite, the series has only one end, it cannot constitute a totality. In other words, the conception of an infinite series that "cannot be completed by successive synthesis" is rejected on the grounds that it violates the totality condition built into the concept of the world as a totum syntheticum.

Unfortunately, this defense of the thesis argument, which I think is about the best that can be done for it, brings to the fore its real weakness: even if one accepts the analysis of the infinite, the Kantian notion of concepts as rules, and the implicit theory of definition, the argument still turns on the presumed necessity of conceiving of the series of past events or states of the universe as constituting a totum syntheticum. This requirement, however, seems completely arbitrary. Why, after all, can't we simply think of this series as infinite in the sense of being closed at only one end, like the series of natural numbers, without also assuming (per impossibile) that it somehow constitutes a "totality"? As Kant himself acknowledges, there is no difficulty in doing this for the series of future states, which can be conceived as infinite.[30] Why should the situation be any different for the series of past states? Granted, in that case the series would not constitute a totum syntheticum, but why should that rule out the very possibility of such a series?

Although Kant does not neglect this question entirely, his answer is hardly persuasive. Indeed, it seems to reduce to the bald assertion that, because of reason's endemic need to think a totality of conditions (the unconditioned) in its ascent from a given conditioned, "we necessarily think time as having completely elapsed up to the given moment, and as being itself given in this completed form" (A410/B437). There is undoubtedly much to quarrel with here, but the main problem with this claim is simply that Kant himself explicitly rejects it. In Kantian terms, the assumption that the temporal series is "complete" in the sense that it constitutes a totum syntheticum (which is what is really being claimed) is a form of "transcendental illusion." We shall see in the third section of this chapter that Kant regards this illusion as an inevitable consequence of the transcendentally realistic assumption underlying the Antinomy as a whole. This lends some justification to its appearance within the argument (as an implicit premise of the transcendental realist), but it also requires that we abandon the pretense that the argument is "compelling."

Moreover, this is not an isolated difficulty in a particular argument; it is rather a reflection of a fundamental tension running throughout Kant's whole treatment of the antinomical conflict. On the one hand, in order to present this conflict in its strongest light and to underscore the necessity of a solution (if one is to avoid the "euthanasia of pure reason"), he tends to characterize the proofs as "equally clear, evident and irresistible" and even to vouch for their correctness.[31] On the other hand, in order to show that the conflict is "merely dialectical" and to prepare the way for the introduction of transcendental idealism as the key to its resolution, he must insist that these proofs rest upon illicit, transcendentally realistic premises. The conception of the temporal (and spatial) series as complete in the sense that it constitutes a totum syntheticum is just such a premise. We shall see later in this chapter why the transcendental realist is committed to this premise. First, however, we must consider the argument of the antithesis.

B. The Antithesis

Like the thesis, the antithesis deals with the world in space and time, not with space and time themselves. It presupposes the same concept of a world, but asserts that this world can have no beginning in time and no limit in space. Also, in accordance with the logic of the antinomical reasoning, it assumes that a demonstration that the world can have no such beginning or limit, that is, that it is not finite, is logically equivalent to a demonstration that it is actually infinite. As before, we shall concern ourselves mainly with the temporal portion of the argument. In the text this runs as follows:

> For let us assume that it has a beginning. Since the beginning is an existence which is preceded by a time in which the thing is not, there must have been a preceding time in which the world was not, *i.e.,* an empty time. Now no coming to be of a thing is possible in an empty time, because no part of such a time possesses, as compared with any other, a distinguishing condition of existence rather than of non-existence; and this applies whether the thing is supposed to arise of itself or through some other cause. In the world many series of things can, indeed, begin; but the world itself cannot have a beginning, and is therefore infinite in respect of past time. [A427 / B455]

This argument can also be broken down into six steps:

1. Assume the opposite: the world has a beginning in time.

2. The concept of a (temporal) beginning presupposes a preceding time in which the thing that comes into being does not yet exist.

3. It follows from this that if one is to speak of "the world" coming into being, it is necessary to assume the existence of an empty, premundane time.

4. But it is impossible for anything to come into being in empty time because "no point of such a time possesses, as compared with any other, a distinguishing condition of existence rather than nonexistence."

5. We therefore cannot meaningfully speak of the "world itself" as having a beginning in time.

6. Consequently, the world is infinite with respect to past time.

The key steps are 4 and 6. If one assumes that nothing can come into being in empty time, then a fortiori the world cannot have a beginning (in time), for any time prior to the world is by definition "empty." This step involves the verificationist claim that one cannot meaningfully refer to the location or date of an event in an empty time because the moments ("parts") of such a time are indistinguishable from one another. The same point can also be made by noting that there would be no conceivable empirical difference between a universe that came into being at an empty time t_1 and an otherwise identical universe that came into being at empty time t_2. It follows from this that one cannot meaningfully claim that the world came into being at one moment in such a time rather than in another. But if we cannot speak meaningfully of the world as coming into being at one particular moment of time rather than another, then we cannot speak meaningfully of it as coming into being in time at all. Basically the same argument applies, *mutatis mutandis,* to the location of the world in space.

Step 6 involves a jump from the presumed meaninglessness of the claim that the world has a beginning to the assertion that it is infinite. This is, of course, a non sequitur, and Kant clearly recognizes it as such. The point, however, is that the conclusion does follow, given the operative assumption of the whole debate: that the world must be either finite or infinite. With such an assumption one can infer the infinity of the world just as easily from the meaninglessness as from the falsity of the finitistic claim. Since this assumption will be a main focus of the next section, I shall limit the present consideration to the argument for the meaninglessness of the finitistic claim.

There appear to be two major strategies for defending the finitistic position (or something like it) against the verificationist attack contained in step 4. One, suggested by Strawson, involves trying to legitimize the question, Why did the world begin when it did? by construing it as an internal rather than an external question.[32] As an internal question, it concerns the order or arrangement of the elements within the world, as in, Why a before b? As an external question, it involves a reference to some external factor or condition, which might explain why the world began at t_1 rather than t_2. The operative assumption is that its concern with the world as a whole rules out the possibility of treating it as an external question (the notion of totality thus enters the picture once again), but that this does not preclude one from regarding it as a perfectly meaningful internal question. So construed, the question becomes, Why was a given event the first in the series of events constituting the history of the world? This question is meaningful because one can always assume the possibility either of events prior to the designated event or of the actual series of events being ordered in some other way.

The major problem with this move can be easily demonstrated by means of Keith Donnellan's distinction between a "referential" and an "attributive" use of a definite description.[33] If the definite description, 'the first event', is taken referentially as a "rigid designator," then the question, Why did the world begin with *that* event rather than some other? becomes a perfectly meaningful internal question in the manner suggested above. If, however, 'the first event' is taken attributively to denote the earliest event in the series (whatever it may have been), then the only question to be asked is, Why did the first event occur when it did? And this cannot be regarded as an internal question (it involves reference to an external temporal framework). It is clear, however, that only the attributive use of the expression 'the first event' is relevant to the problematic of the First Antinomy; consequently, the reinterpretation of the question as internal does not meet the verificationist challenge posed by the argument of the antithesis.

The second strategy, developed by Bennett, attempts to show that the denial that the world has a beginning does not follow from the stated premises. Bennett admits that, although it is possible to give some sense to the notion of an extramundane space (a claim he uses against the spatial portion of the argument), the same probably cannot be done for a premundane time. Nevertheless, he denies that this justifies the conclusion actually drawn in the argument for the antithesis. As Bennett puts it: "From the impossibility of a premundane time I do not infer the impossibility of a first event. Rather, I infer that if there was a first event, it occurred at the first time."[34] Moreover, he continues, "From the true premise that 'empty time prior to the world' is a 'non-entity', he [Kant] immediately infers not that the first event must have occurred at the first time but rather that there cannot have been a first event."[35]

Given this analysis, Bennett's task is to defend the coherence of the assumption that the first event occurred at the first time. This requires defending the intelligibility not only of the notions of a first time and a first event taken individually, but also of their conjunction. I believe that Bennett succeeds with the first and that one can easily give sense to the second, but that he fails with the third, which is the decisive factor. In other words, while the notions of a first time and a first event are themselves perfectly coherent, the same cannot be said of the notion of a first event at a first time.

In order to conceive of a first time, Bennett suggests that we take as our point of reference any historical event H and assume that n represents the number of years from H back to the first time. The phrase 'n years before H' thus designates the first time.[36] The obvious problem suggested by this analysis concerns the possibility of conceiving of times more than n years before H and, therefore, before the "first time." If n has a finite value (as is required by the argument), then it must be possible to conceive of such times. Bennett's solution is to contend that any phrase of the form 'K years before H,' where $K > n$, "makes sense but does not refer to any time."[37] The point, I take it, is that we can easily imagine times more distant from H than n. Thus, even though 'K years before H' does not in fact refer to a time (since ex hypothesi n is the first time), it conceivably could do so, and this is enough to guarantee the coherence of the notion of a first time. This analysis seems perfectly acceptable.

Although Bennett does not specifically discuss the notion of a first event, it too can be given a coherent meaning. Since by 'event' (Begebenheit, Ereignis) Kant (and presumably Bennett) means roughly a change of state or alteration of a thing in time,[38] the phrase 'the first event' designates the earliest such change to have occurred in the universe. Conceivable events prior to this can be dealt with in the same way that Bennett deals with conceivable times prior to the first time.

As already indicated, however, the difficulty concerns the location of the putative first event at the putative first time. The problem is that, since by 'event' is meant a change in the state of a thing, every event presupposes a prior time in which the thing existed in a different state.

Consequently, the notion of a first event at a first time, that is, an event not preceded by a time in which the world (the "thing" in question here) was in a different state, turns out to be incoherent. But a beginning of the world at the first time would, on Bennett's analysis, be just such an "event." Its possibility can, therefore, be rejected on the same ground.

The obvious retort at this juncture is to grant that a putative beginning of the world is not an 'event' in the abovementioned sense (in Kantian terms it is not an "object of possible experience"), but to insist that this does not rule out its conceivability. This move is perfectly appropriate, and it does allow one to defend the conceivability of a creation or first beginning of the world. The problem is simply that it does not allow one to contend, as Bennett wishes to do, that this first beginning occurred at the first (or any other) time. Although the issues here are complex and cannot be dealt with adequately prior to the treatment of the First and Second Analogies (chapters 9 and 10), the main point is that, quite apart from the question of whether a change is termed an 'event', it is a condition of the possibility of conceiving of the change of a thing in time that we are able to contrast the state of a thing at an earlier with its state at a later time. The upshot of the matter, then, is that one can perhaps hold with Augustine and many others (including Leibniz) that time began with creation, but one cannot meaningfully claim that creation occurred at the first time.[39] It is, however, the latter that must be established in order to refute the argument presently under consideration.

It is important to keep in mind that the strategies discussed so far are both attempts to criticize the argument of the antithesis from within the verificationist framework which it assumes. We have seen that these strategies fail, but to show this is certainly not equivalent to establishing the cogency of the overall argument. In fact, this exercise serves mainly to make it clear that the real crux of the argument is the verificationist assumption to the effect that, if the world had a beginning in time, it must be possible (at least in principle) to specify criteria for determining at what point in time it began. In other words, it presupposes something very much like the Leibnizian principle of the identity of indiscernibles (in the form in which he used it against Newton). Moreover, insofar as this is merely presupposed rather than argued for, the critique of the finitistic position cannot be regarded as any more compelling than Leibniz's critique of Newton. The situation, of course, becomes much worse when we consider the sixth step, which involves the jump from the verificationist rejection of the finitistic position to the posivitive claim for the infinity of the world. Thus we must conclude that, even though the argument for the temporal position of the antithesis can be defended against some of the standard objections, it still falls far short of the claims that Kant makes for it.[40] I also think it fair to say that, for similar reasons, the same can be said about the spatial portion of the argument.

III. THE ANTINOMICAL CONFLICT AND
TRANSCENDENTAL IDEALISM

The remaining issue of this chapter is Kant's use of the antinomical conflict as the basis for an indirect demonstration of transcendental idealism. In considering this issue, I shall first abstract from the fact that the dogmatic proofs of the thesis and antithesis positions (at least in the First Antinomy) do not have the force that Kant claims for them. The goal is to see what follows, if, for the sake of argument, we assume the cogency of these proofs. The next step is to consider what, if anything, can be salvaged of Kant's argument for idealism, if, as seems to be the case, the proofs are not sound. Finally, we shall deal with the question of what the nature of Kant's transcendental idealism must be, assuming that its truth is established by his indirect demonstration.

A. Assuming That the Proofs are Sound

Kant spells out the consequences of his analysis of the antinomical conflict in a single dense passage. After remarking that, in each case, the conflict between thesis and antithesis is "merely dialectical" (since it is due to a "transcendental illusion"), he states:

> From this antinomy we can, however, obtain, not indeed a dogmatic, but a critical and doctrinal advantage. It affords indirect proof of the transcendental ideality of appearances—a proof which ought to convince any who may not be satisfied by the direct proof given in the Transcendental Aesthetic. This proof would consist in the following dilemma. If the world is a whole existing in itself, it is either finite or infinite. But both alternatives are false (as shown in the proofs of the antithesis and thesis respectively). It is therefore also false that the world (the sum of all appearances) is a whole existing in itself. From this it then follows that appearances in general are nothing outside our representations—which is just what is meant by their transcendental ideality. [A506–07 / B534–35]

The logical form of this argument is a *modus tollens* combined with an immediate inference. The denial of the consequent ("the world is either finite or infinite") is used, in turn, to deny the antecedent ("the world is a whole existing in itself"), which is then taken to entail the conclusion: "appearances in general are nothing outside our representations." This latter statement is the thesis of transcendental idealism. Assuming that the proofs of the thesis and the antithesis are sound, the modus tollens is in order. The same, however, cannot be said about the immediate inference. In fact, it seems perfectly possible to accept the conclusion of the modus tollens, that the world (the sum of all appearances) is not a whole existing in itself, and to reject the idealistic result that is presumed to follow immediately from this conclusion.

Part of the problem can be attributed to the way in which this idealistic result is expressed. The claim that "appearances in general are nothing outside our representations" might be taken to be analytic. It can, after all, be derived directly from the definition of 'appearance', without any reference to the preceding argument. This, however, is only a minor defect, which can be avoided simply by reformulating the claim to read "spatiotemporal objects are appearances"; as such, they are also "mere representations, which, in the manner in which they are represented, as extended beings, or as series of alterations, have no independent existence outside our thoughts." But this reformulation also brings to sharper focus the main problem: how can one infer transcendental idealism from the simple denial of the antecedent? The move from the statement "the world (the sum of all appearances) is not a whole existing in itself" to transcendental idealism seems to be another example of the kind of gross non sequitur that critics have frequently claimed to find in Kant.

The difficulty can also be put in another way. The proof for transcendental idealism seems to rest ultimately upon the assumption that it provides the only possible basis for avoiding the antinomical conflict. But this assumption seems manifestly false. The problem with both the thesis and antithesis positions stems from their construing 'world' or 'the sum of all appearances' as a naming expression or definite description. Given this assumption, it makes perfectly good sense to enquire about the magnitude of the referent of 'world' and to presuppose that this magnitude must be either finite or infinite in whatever respects are being considered. This suggests, however, that all that is required to resolve the dispute is to show that 'world' does not refer. Indeed, this is surely the most natural reading of the conclusion of the modus tollens. Since 'world' does not refer to any entity at all, its referent can be neither finite nor infinite. To be sure, it follows from the fact that 'world' does not refer at all that it does not refer to a thing in itself; but it also follows that it does not refer to the appearance of some unknown thing. In any event, it seems both unwarranted and unnecessary to make the further assumption that the spatiotemporal objects which, when taken collectively were mistakenly supposed to provide the referent of 'world', are themselves mere appearances.[41]

It must be admitted that this criticism indicates the inadequacy of the argument for idealism as Kant actually presents it in the *Critique*. The reason for this, however, is that Kant misstates his own real argument. Although Kant presents the move from the denial of the antecedent to the affirmation of transcendental idealism as if it were an immediate inference, the actual argument involves two suppressed premises. The first is that the antecedent is entailed by transcendental realism. The second is that transcendental realism and transcendental idealism are contradictory philosophical standpoints. Thus, to negate the one is to affirm the other. It follows from the first premise that the conclusion of the

modus tollens, which is the negation of the antecedent, entails the negation of transcendental realism; and it follows from the second that this
negation is equivalent to the affirmation of transcendental idealism.
Given these premises, Kant's overall argument is clearly valid. The main
question, therefore, concerns the truth of these additional premises. Since
one of the central concerns of the preceding chapter was to show that
transcendental realism and transcendental idealism together constitute
two mutually exclusive and exhaustive metaphilosophical alternatives, I
shall here take the second premise as given. Unfortunately, the first
premise cannot be treated quite so casually, for it is certainly not immediately evident that there is a relationship of entailment between transcendental realism and the proposition "the world (the sum of all appearances) is a whole existing in itself."

In light of the analysis of transcendental realism sketched in the preceding chapter, let us, then, consider the connection between such realism
and this proposition. We must, however, resist the temptation to assume
that the connection turns simply on a gratuitous addition of 'in itself' to
the description of the world. This move is tempting because the assumption that the world must be either finite or infinite seems to follow directly from the prior assumption that 'world' has a referent without requiring any additional assumption to the effect that this referent "exists in
itself." This temptation is to be resisted because Kant does provide at
least the materials for an argument linking the assumption that we can
refer meaningfully to the world (the sum of all appearances) and the
conception of these appearances, both individually and collectively, as
real in the transcendental sense.

These materials are contained in Kant's analysis of the source of the
antinomical conflict, where he takes up again, from a different perspective, some of the considerations previously introduced in the account of
the derivation of the cosmological Ideas. He begins with the claim that
"the whole antinomy of pure reason rests upon the dialectical argument:
If the conditioned is given, the entire series of all its conditions is likewise
given; objects of the senses are given as conditioned; therefore, etc."
(A497/B525). Kant later adds that the "dialectical" nature of this argument stems from the fact that it commits the fallacy entitled *sophisma
figurae dictionis* (A499–500/B527–28).

The basic idea here is that 'condition' and 'conditioned' can refer either
to propositions or to states of affairs. The major premise of the "dialectical argument" construes these terms in the former sense, and the minor
premise in the latter.[42] Now, Kant maintains that it is "evident beyond all
possiblility of doubt, that if the conditioned is given [*gegeben*], a regress
in the series of all its conditions is set as a task [*aufgegeben*]" (A497–
98/B526). He presents this as an analytic truth, applicable to both senses
of 'condition' and 'conditioned'. He also characterizes it as a "logical

postulate of reason," which suggests that it has the status of an intellectual categorical imperative; namely, always seek conditions. The problem is that, although this imperative is applicable to both senses of 'condition' and 'conditioned', it operates differently in each case. In the case of propositions, it requires that we assume that all of the conditions (premises) are already *gegeben,* that is, thought or presupposed. This, Kant tells us, is "simply the logical requirement that we should have adequate premises for any given conclusion" (A500/B529). In other words, the thought of a conclusion presupposes the thought of the premises from which it is derived. The situation, however, is quite different for states of affairs. Here the regress is always from some actual state of affairs, regarded as conditioned, to another state of affairs, viewed as its condition. Kant terms such a regress or search for conditions "empirical synthesis," and he notes that in this case the conditions are only given in and through the synthesis. This means that states of affairs can only be considered as gegeben insofar as they are in some manner empirically accessible. Consequently, the intellectual categorical imperative has here a merely regulative function: it requires us always to seek further conditions, but it does not entitle us to assume that the totality of these conditions is itself gegeben.

Transcendental realism, however, makes just this illicit assumption, thereby generating the antinomical conflict. Moreover, it does not simply happen to make this assumption, nor is it an assumption that can be attributed only to a certain kind of transcendental realism, namely, an extreme rationalism of a Spinozistic or Leibnizian type, which is frequently accused by Kant and others of confusing the "logical" with the "real," the "conceptual" with the "factual." The point is rather that transcendental realism is compelled by the logic of its position to commit this fallacy, and that this applies to every form of transcendental realism that respects the intellectual categorical imperative. As Kant describes the situation:

> if the conditioned as well as its condition are things in themselves, then upon the former being given, the regress to the latter is not only *set as a task,* but therewith already really *given.* And since this holds of all members of the series, the complete series of the conditions, and therefore the unconditioned, is given therewith, or rather, is presupposed in view of the fact that the conditioned, which is only possible through the complete series, is given. The synthesis of the conditioned with its condition is here a synthesis of the mere understanding, which represents things *as they are,* without considering whether and how we can obtain knowledge of them. [A498/B526–27]

The basic point here is that anyone who regards appearances as if they were things in themselves is thereby committed, in virtue of the intellectual categorical imperative, to presuppose the presence of sufficient conditions for every given conditioned. But since this applies in turn to every specified condition, it requires that the absolute totality of conditions be presupposed as given. This absolute totality is just what is meant by 'the world'. The world is thus presupposed to exist or, equivalently, 'world' is taken to have a referent. The phrase 'in itself' in this context reflects the independence of the world, so conceived, from the conditions of empirical synthesis; for the synthesis that generates this conception of the world is a "synthesis of mere understanding," which is equivalent to what Kant elsewhere calls an "intellectual synthesis."[43] The mark of such a synthesis is that it deals merely with conceptual connections, thereby ignoring all spatiotemporal, or sensible, relations. That is why Kant maintains that it "represents things as they are; without considering whether and how we can obtain knowledge of them." This does not, of course, mean that such a synthesis or conceptual process actually provides knowledge of things as they are in themselves; rather it indicates that it represents, or conceives, things in abstraction from the conditions through which they are alone empirically accessible. To consider things in this way is to consider them "according to their mere concept," and thus as if they were noumena or things in themselves.

There would be nothing wrong with this were it not for the fact that the objects or states of affairs that the transcendental realist regards in this manner are empirical. Consequently, they cannot be meaningfully referred to in abstraction from the conditions under which they are given in the empirical synthesis. For example, the transcendental realist dismisses as irrelevant the successive manner in which the objects or states of affairs are given. As Kant puts it, "There is no reference to a time order in the connection of the conditioned with its condition, they are presupposed as given *together* with it" (A500/B528). Having done this, the transcendental realist is led by means of the intellectual categorical imperative to assume a tenseless logic with respect to objects or states of affairs that are inherently temporal. All of the difficulties follow from this move.

It might seem from the above account that the whole analysis involves a colossal petitio, but such is not really the case. There would be a petitio if this were taken as a direct argument for transcendental idealism. It must be kept in mind, however, that what Kant is doing here is arguing indirectly from his transcendental perspective, showing the consequences of the failure to make the transcendental distinction. In other words, he is arguing that without this distinction, which makes it possible to, as it were, factor in the conditions of human knowledge, it is perfectly "natural," that is, rational, to assume that the totality of conditions for any conditioned is gegeben, even when the conditioned and its conditions are states of affairs.

Admittedly, there is one restriction on the scope of the overall claim linking transcendental realism with the conception of the world as a whole existing in itself. Since the transcendental realist is only led to this conception through the application of the intellectual categorical imperative, any form of transcendental realism that rejects this imperative would thereby presumably avoid any commitment to the conception of the world, and thus to the antinomical conflict. But this is not a major difficulty, since the rejection of this "logical postulate of reason" is tantamount to the rejection of a necessary condition of meaningful discourse. In short, the legitimacy of this principle is simply not an issue between transcendental realism and transcendental idealism.[44]

We conclude, therefore, that both sides in the antinomical dispute, indeed, all forms of transcendental realism that respect the intellectual categorical imperative, are necessarily led to regard the absolute totality of conditions for any given conditioned (state of affairs) as constituting a world existing in itself. Transcendental realism is thus logically committed to the proposition "the world (the sum of all appearances) is a whole existing in itself," which was the point to be established. We have also seen that this result is a direct consequence of the transcendental realist's neglect of, or abstraction from, the conditions under which objects are given to us in experience. This, in turn, leads to the conflation of the merely regulative Idea of totality, which is grounded in the intellectual categorical imperative, with the thought of an actual object (the world). Kant considers this conflation to be a species of "transcendental illusion." Moreover, since apart from the adoption of the transcendental distinction there can be no reason to give epistemic weight to these conditions in dealing with the cosmological questions, there is no ready way for the transcendental realist to avoid this illusion. That is why Kant maintains both that this illusion is "natural," even "inevitable," and yet that it can be overcome by transcendental idealism.

The remaining steps of the argument are easy to supply. Since transcendental realism entails the doctrine that the world (the sum of all appearances) is a whole (totum syntheticum) existing in itself, independently of the conditions of human knowledge, it is committed to the assumption that this world must be either finite or infinite in the relevant respects. But (assuming the soundness of the proofs) the analysis of the antinomical conflict has shown that the world is neither finite nor infinite. Consequently, both the conception of the world as a whole existing in itself and transcendental realism must be rejected. Finally, given the dichotomy between transcendental realism and transcendental idealism, the negation of the former is, at the same time, the affirmation of the latter. This, in essence, is what I take to be the argument for transcendental idealism contained in the Antinomy of Pure Reason. The actual structure of this argument is obscured by Kant's failure to spell out some of its premises. Nevertheless, this argument goes through, if one accepts the account of the relationship between transcendental realism and transcendental idealism given in the last chapter and the soundness of the proofs for the thesis and antithesis positions.

B. Without Assuming That the Proofs are Sound

Although the preceding reconstruction of Kant's argument involves the assumption of the soundness of the proofs for the thesis and antithesis of at least one of the Antinomies, it also suggests a way in which the argument can be reformulated so as to avoid having to make use of that highly dubious premise. This is possible because the truth of transcendental idealism follows directly from the negation of the proposition "the world (the sum of all appearances) is a whole existing in itself." All that is necessary, therefore, is to find independent grounds for this negation. Since this claim is entailed by transcendental realism, and since transcendental realism and transcendental idealism are exclusive disjuncts, this would suffice to demonstrate the truth of transcendental idealism.

In the endeavor to construct such an argument, it is crucial to keep in mind that the conception of the world as a "whole existing in itself" is equivalent to what Kant calls the "cosmological Idea." The particular cosmological Ideas, which appear in the thesis and antithesis of the various Antinomies, are merely expressions or determinations of this Idea. Accordingly, what must be done is to show the incoherence of this Idea, and to do so in a way that does not already presuppose the truth of transcendental idealism.[45]

The incoherence can be seen by considering the difference between the cosmological Idea and the other "Ideas of reason." Kant notes that "the cosmological Ideas alone have the peculiarity that they can presuppose their object, and the empirical synthesis required for its concept, as being given" (A479/B507). This, in effect, means that these Ideas all involve empirical existence claims. Indeed, the theses and antitheses of the first two Antinomies contain just such claims. In this respect the cosmological Idea differs radically from the Idea of God, which is not the concept of an object that is assumed to be "given" in possible experience, that is, located in space and time. The unique feature of the cosmological Idea is also captured by noting that it is really a synthetic proposition. It asserts that there exists a high-order empirical object, the world. As we have already seen, the transcendental realist is led to this assertion through obedience to the intellectual categorical imperative.

The problem here is not simply that no such "object" can be found in experience and, therefore, that 'world' has no referent. This would make the cosmological Idea empty (in the manner of an *ens rationis*), but not incoherent. The incoherence stems from the fact that it both purports to refer and explicitly exempts itself from the conditions under which reference is possible. In this respect, the situation provides a theoretical analogue to the contradiction which, according to Kant, emerges within practical reason whenever, out of self-interest, one exempts oneself from what one otherwise recognizes as a universal law.

The whole matter can be put in a clearer light if we regard Kant's conditions of possible experiences as conditions of empirical reference. Let us note first that the conception of an absolute totality of conditions (states of affairs) that is supposed to constitute the world violates these conditions, whether the totality is finite or infinite. Kant expresses this clearly in the *Prolegomena* when he states, "neither assertion can be contained in experience, because experience either of an infinite space or of an infinite elapsed time, or again, of the boundary of the world by a void space or by an antecedent void time, is impossible; these are mere Ideas."[46] The identical point is made in the passage discussed in the previous section where Kant states that the absolute totality of conditions cannot be contained in the empirical synthesis. Equivalent formulations of this claim would be that the concept of such a totality violates the "conditions of empirical advance" or the "laws of the unity of experience." Common to all these formulations is the thought that, in the endeavor to conceive of such a totality (a totum syntheticum), one is compelled to suspend these "laws" or rules of reference. As already indicated, this is precisely why Kant terms the synthesis, or conceptual process, through which the concept of such an absolute totality is formed a "synthesis of mere understanding."

So far there is no incoherence. There is nothing inherently wrong with a "synthesis of mere understanding," just as there is nothing wrong with the endeavor to think things as they are in themselves. The incoherence emerges, however, as soon as we introduce the second aspect of the situation: the fact that the cosmologist purports to be making an empirical or quasi-empirical claim. He is, after all, referring to the spatiotemporal world, not to some underlying and inaccessible *mundus intelligibilis*. But in the very effort to conceive of, or refer to, such a world, the cosmologist, as we have already seen, suspends the conditions under which such reference is alone possible. Consequently, he produces what must be regarded as a pseudo-empirical concept. According to Kant's own characterization of the situation, the cosmologist falls victim to "that amphiboly which transforms an Idea into a supposed representation of an object that is empirically given and therefore to be known according to the laws of experience" (A484/B512). The transcendentally realistic conception of the world as a whole existing in itself is the product of this amphiboly or, as Kant also terms it, the "transcendental subreption" that consists in the ascription of "objective validity to an Idea that serves merely as a rule" (A509/B537).

The preceding analysis of the incoherence of the cosmological Idea might appear to involve a petitio, since it turns on the validity of the putative "laws of the unity of experience," which are, for Kant, also conditions of the possibility of experience. The Kantian response to this obvious line of objection is to admit that the argument presupposes these laws or conditions, but to deny that this presupposition amounts to a begging of the question with respect to transcendental idealism. This move is possible because the transcendental realism with which Kant is here contending is committed to the same laws (although not, of course, to the idealistic interpretation Kant gives to them). Indeed, it is through these very laws and under the direction of the intellectual categorical imperative that transcendental realism arrives at the specific cosmological Ideas (which are produced by extending the categories to the unconditioned). Kant, therefore, can assume a common ground with transcendental realism when he claims, with regard to empirical objects, "even supposing they were given as things in themselves, without relation to possible experience, it still remains true that they are nothing to me, and therefore are not objects, save insofar as they are contained in the series of the empirical regress" (A496 / B524).

Since being "contained in the series of the empirical regress" is equivalent to being subject to the "laws of the unity of experience," or the Analogies, Kant is in effect maintaining that even transcendental realism acknowledges the validity of these principles within experience. But this means that the issue between transcendental realism and transcendental idealism does not arise at the empirical level. On the contrary, it arises only when transcendental realism endeavors, as it does with the cosmological Ideas, to extend these "laws" beyond the limits of possible experience. Only then, Kant reflects, "does distinction of the mode in which we view the reality of those objects of the senses become of importance, as serving to guard us against a deceptive error which is bound to arise if we misinterpret our empirical concepts"(A407 / B525). The key point here is the last: that under these conditions this "deceptive error" is "bound to arise," given transcendentally realistic assumptions, is the real basis of Kant's indirect argument for transcendental idealism.

Admittedly, such an argument, which presupposes (among other things) the Analogies, is not likely to strike many contemporary philosophers as particularly compelling. I would hope that, to some extent at least, this defect will be remedied by the analysis of the First and Second Analogies in chapters 9 and 10. Even apart from that, however, this argument does at least show how, given certain commonly accepted presuppositions, transcendental realism inevitably falls into contradiction with itself when, under the direction of the intellectual categorical imperative, it endeavors to "think the whole." Moreover, this argument shows this without either appealing to the proofs of the thesis and antithesis of the various Antinomies or presupposing the truth of transcendental idealism. If one also accepts the account of the relationship between transcendental realism and transcendental idealism contained in the last chapter, this can be seen as the basis for a powerful argument for transcendental idealism.

C. Transcendental Idealism

We are now prepared to deal with the final question of this part of the study: What must be the nature of transcendental idealism, assuming that this idealism is established by the preceding line of argument? The answer, in brief, is that the idealism that follows from the negation of the proposition "the world (the sum of all appearances) is a whole existing in itself" is identical to the idealism described in the last chapter. Certainly, despite a good deal of misleading language on Kant's part, it cannot be regarded as "phenomenalistic" in any of the ordinarily accepted meanings of the term.[47] There are two very simple and compelling reasons for this. The first is that Kant himself tells us that the argument is, among other things, intended to refute rather than to establish a "dogmatic idealism." The second is that, as Kant's critics continually point out, the argument itself does not entail any "phenomenalistic" conclusions.

Kant declares his intention in the First Edition version of the Refutation of Idealism, the Fourth Paralogism. After attacking Descartes's "empirical idealism," which he contrasts with his own transcendental variety, Kant makes passing reference to the "dogmatic idealist," whom he characterizes as one who denies, rather than merely doubts, the existence of matter. He further suggests that such an idealist "must base his view on supposed contradictions in the possibility of there being such a thing as matter at all." Finally, he notes that this position has not yet been dealt with, but will be in "the following section on dialectical inferences" (A377). This "following section" is the Antinomy of Pure Reason. Thus Kant explicitly claims to have refuted this form of idealism in the very section of the *Critique* where his critics see an argument intended to establish it.

There is also a historical point that should be noted in this context. Normally, when Kant speaks of dogmatic idealism he is referring to the views of Berkeley. The passage presently under discussion, however, suggests that it is not Berkeley, but rather his lesser-known countryman and contemporary Arthur Collier, whom Kant has in mind. In the second half of his main work, *Clavis Universalis,* which was probably known to Kant,[48] Collier advances the thesis that the very concept of an "external," or mind-independent, world is self-contradictory. Moreover, he does so on the grounds that such a world can be shown to be both finite and infinite. Something that must be both finite and infinite, he argues, is really neither, and a thing that is neither finite nor infinite is nothing at all.[49] Superficially, at least, this certainly suggests Kant's own argument.[50] It is, therefore, not surprising to find scholars who view Collier's argument as an anticipation of, if not an actual influence on, Kant's.[51] Once again, however, the problem with this interpretation is that it completely neglects the fact that Kant claims to have refuted an idealism of this type in the Antinomy of Pure Reason.[52]

With regard to the second point, the outcome of Kant's argument is more properly described as methodological or epistemological than as ontological. If it establishes anything at all, it is the necessity for making the transcendental distinction between things as they appear and the same things as they are in themselves. It does this indirectly by showing that if we fail to make this distinction, that is, if we completely ignore the epistemic function of the subjective conditions of human knowledge by regarding them as psychological conditions, or if we consider them as conditions of things in themselves by regarding them as ontological conditions, then we inevitably fall into contradiction. To be sure, this does not occur in the case of our ordinary empirical or scientific judgments. We have just seen that the transcendental distinction is not relevant at that level. It does occur, however, and the distinction does become relevant when, under the impetus of the intellectual categorical imperative, we endeavor to "think the whole."

The "critical" outcome of Kant's argument can also be seen by noting the connection between the endeavor to "think the whole" and the theocentric model of knowledge.[53] It should be obvious that the two go together. To attempt to "think the whole" is simply to attempt to gain a "God's-eye view" of things, to consider them *sub specie aeternitatis;* and this, we have seen, leads inevitably to the adoption of a tenseless logic, which completely abstracts from the successive manner in which objects are given to us in experience. A contradiction then arises because the objects which are being thought in this atemporal manner exist in time; their temporality is constitutive of their very "objectivity." Seen from this perspective, the lesson to be learned is the necessity of shifting from the theocentric to the anthropocentric model of knowledge, of making the "Copernican revolution" or the "transcendental turn." Kant himself says as much in his own account of the "revolution" in the *Critique.* He does so again in one of his many important letters to Marcus Herz, where, discussing Solomon Maimon (who himself criticized Kant for rejecting the theocentric model), Kant reflects:

> The antinomies of pure reason could provide a good test stone for that, which might convince him that one cannot assume human reason to be of one kind with the divine reason, distinct from it only by limitation, that is, in degree—that human reason, unlike the divine reason, must be regarded as a faculty only of *thinking,* not of *intuiting;* that it is thoroughly dependent on an entirely different faculty (or receptivity) for its intuitions, or better, for the material out of which it fashions knowledge; and that, since intuition gives us mere appearances whereas the fact itself is a mere concept of reason, the antinomies (which arise entirely because of the confusion of the two) can

never be resolved except by deducing the possibility of synthetic a priori propositions according to my principles.[54]

These considerations make it possible to deal in summary fashion with a prevalent criticism of Kant's procedure that has been given its sharpest expression by Strawson.[55] Strawson assumes that what Kant intended to establish by means of his resolution of the Antinomies was a phenomenalistic, essentially Berkeleian, form of idealism. Having started with this assumption, he draws the obvious conclusion that the argument fails. He suggests that, instead of establishing a genuine form of idealism, the argument has at most established a version of verificationism. He then infers from this that, for some unexplained reason, Kant saw fit to combine this more or less acceptable verificationism with the excess baggage of a phenomenalistic metaphysics.

The falsity of this assumption about Kant's intent has already been shown, but a word about Kant's "verificationism" may be in order. Certainly one cannot deny that Kant frequently argues in a verificationist fashion. It is, after all, a central tenet of the *Critique* that a concept must have a sensible referent if it is to have objective reality, that is, empirical significance. It is just this tenet that Strawson calls "the principle of significance" and Bennett calls "concept empiricism." Moreover, as Kant says explicitly with regard to the cosmological Idea, "possible experience is that which can alone give reality to our concepts; in its absence a concept is a mere Idea, without truth, that is, without relation to an object" (A489/B519). One cannot, however, stop here. The real question concerns the precise nature of the verificationism, that is, of the appeal to possible experience that is at work in the *Critique*. As we saw in the preceding chapter, the Kantian appeal to possible experience is not to a hypothetical perceptual episode in the history of some sentient organism or even to a set of empirical laws. It is rather to a set of formal, a priori conditions. When, as in the Antinomies, Kant rejects concepts or principles on basically verificationist grounds, he typically does so by showing that they are the result of either a neglect or a misunderstanding of these conditions.

Once again, then, the point is that the appeal to the formal, a priori conditions of human experience and their characterization as "epistemic" are the defining features of Kant's idealism. The position is idealistic because, as we have seen, it grants to these conditions the function of defining the meaning of 'object' or, equivalently, of determining what can count as "objective" for the human mind. The world considered as a "whole existing in itself" (the object for transcendental realism) is rejected as an object by Kant precisely because it violates these conditions. This essentially verificationist argument is, therefore, at the same time an argument for transcendental idealism, properly construed.

PART TWO
HUMAN KNOWLEDGE AND ITS CONDITIONS

4
Discursivity and Judgment

In the first part of this study I argued that Kant's idealism can be defined in terms of its commitment to a set of epistemic conditions—conditions that determine what can count as an object for the human mind. Since, on this interpretation, the success of Kant's whole transcendental approach depends on the cogency of his claims about these conditions, we must now consider the specific conditions designated by Kant and the arguments which he provides in support of his claims for them. But since the epistemic conditions to which Kant appeals are conditions of discursive knowledge, and since Kant claims that discursive knowledge is not the only conceivable kind of knowledge (although it is the only kind possible for man), it is necessary to begin with an examination of Kant's account of the discursive nature of human cognition and the theory of judgment that underlies it. This is the task of the first two sections of the present chapter. The final two sections attempt to clarify the connection between Kant's theory of judgment and both his distinction between analytic and synthetic judgments and his conception of synthetic a priori judgments. The chapter as a whole serves as a prolegomenon to the analysis of the sensible and intellectual conditions of human knowledge that follows in the next two chapters.

I. DISCURSIVE KNOWLEDGE AND ITS ELEMENTS: CONCEPTS AND INTUITIONS

Kant on occasion contrasts the discursive or conceptual knowledge of which human beings are capable with the problematic conception of an intuitive intellect.[1] Such an intellect is thought to grasp its object immediately, without the need for any conceptualization and without being affected by the object. For the latter reason it must also be characterized as archetypal or creative rather than echtypal: its act of intuition literally produces its object. This is, of course, precisely the kind of cognition generally thought to pertain to God. Since classical empiricism appeals to a model of cognition that is both nonconceptual and receptive (the immediate apprehension of simple ideas or sensible impressions), it seems strange that Kant connects a nonconceptual, intuitive mode of cognition specifically with a creative, divine mind. This can be understood, however, as a direct consequence of his rejection of the empiricists' assumption that there can be a purely receptive apprehension of an object, without any conceptualization. Given this, it follows that any intuition which is deemed adequate to provide knowledge of an object, that is, to present a determinate object to the mind, must also be regarded as non-sensible or archetypal. Although Kant regards the conception of such an intellect as problematic, he nonetheless uses its bare conceivability heuristically in order to underscore his central claim that human cognition is not the only (logically) possible kind of cognition. This, in turn, enables him to drive a "critical" wedge between the conditions of human or discursive knowledge and conditions of things in themselves.[2]

Our immediate concern, however, is with discursive knowledge and its elements: concepts and sensible intuitions. In his *Lectures on Logic* Kant defines a concept as "a general representation or a representation of what is common to several objects."[3] It follows from this definition that it is a mere tautology to speak of general or common concepts, as if concepts could be divided into general, particular, and singular: "Not the concepts themselves, but merely their use can be so divided."[4] In the parallel definition in the *Critique,* Kant remarks that a concept, again in contrast to an intuition, refers to its object "mediately by means of a feature [*eines Merkmals*] which several things may have in common" (A320/B377). In other words, because of its generality, a concept can refer to an object only by means of features which are also predicable of other objects falling under the same concept.

In the *Critique* Kant remarks that a concept "is always, as regards its form, something universal which serves as a rule" (A106). This means that a concept functions as an organizing principle for consciousness, as a means for holding a series of representations together in an "analytic unity." For example, to form the concept of body is to think together the features of extension, impenetrability, figure, and so forth—the components of the concept. To apply this concept is to conceive of some actual or possible object or objects under the general description provided by these features. This is equivalent to forming a judgment about the object or objects. Thus Kant claims that "the only use which the understanding can make of these concepts is to judge by means of them" (A68/B93), and he characterizes concepts as "predicates of possible judgments" (A69/B94).

Kant also distinguishes between pure (a priori) and empirical concepts and between the matter, or content, and form of a concept; but only the latter distinction is directly relevant to our present concerns. By the *content* of an empirical concept, Kant means the sensible features that are thought in it as its marks. These are derived from experience and correspond to the sensible properties of things. By the *form* of a concept, Kant means its universality or generality, which is the same for all concepts. Kant's point is that simply having a set of sensible impressions that are associated with one another is not the same as having a concept. A concept requires the thought of the applicability of this set of sensible impressions to a plurality of possible objects. With this thought, these impressions become transformed into "marks," that is, partial conceptions. This thought, however, is not itself derived from experience; rather, it is produced by a series of "logical acts" of the understanding that Kant terms "comparison," "reflection," and "abstraction." Taken together, these acts consist in the combining together of the common, sensible features shared by diverse particulars into the abovementioned "analytic unity," while disregarding or abstracting from the differences.[5] Kant sometimes characterizes this whole process as "reflection" (*Reflexion, Überlegung*),[6] and the concepts produced thereby "reflected [*reflectirt*] representations."[7]

Kant defines an intuition as a "singular representation" (*repraesentatio singularis*),[8] and he contends that it "refers immediately to its object" (*bezieht sich unmittelbar auf den Gegenstand*) (A320/B377). Recognizing that the definition of 'intuition' as "singular representation" does not involve any reference to sensibility, Hintikka has argued that only the singularity criterion is essential and the immediacy criterion is a mere corollary.[9] This ignores, however, the presentational function of intuition, for it is precisely in virtue of its "immediacy," that is, its direct, nonconceptual mode of representing, that an intuition can present a particular object to the mind and, therefore, serve as a "repraesentatio singularis." Moreover, this is true of both species of intuition, the problematic intellectual variety as well as the sensible intuition operative in human or, more generally, finite cognition.

Nevertheless, a tension, if not outright contradiction, has often been noted between the official definition of 'intuition' as a "singular representation" and the account of sensible intuition.[10] The problem is that, according to Kant's theory of sensibility, sensible intuition provides the mind with only the raw data for conceptualization, not with the determinate knowledge of objects. Such knowledge requires not only that the data be given in intuition, but also that it be taken under some general description or "recognized in a concept." Only then can we speak of the "representation of an object." Kant gives clear expression to this central tenet of his epistemology in the famous formula, "Intuitions and concepts constitute, therefore, the elements of all our knowledge, so that neither concepts without an intuition in some way corresponding to them, nor intuitions without concepts, can yield knowledge" (A50/B74).[11]

The key to the resolution of this tension is well expressed by W. H. Walsh, who remarks that a Kantian sensible intuition is only "proleptically" the awareness of a particular.[12] The point here is simply that, although intuitions do not in fact represent or refer to objects apart from being "brought under concepts" in a judgment, they *can* be brought under concepts, and when they are they *do* represent particular objects.[13] In this respect they differ from purely subjective or aesthetic "representations," such as feelings, which can have no representative function. Thus, as we shall see in more detail in subsequent chapters, it is really necessary to draw a distinction between determinate or conceptualized and indeterminate or unconceptualized intuitions. Moreover, this distinction applies to both pure and empirical intuitions.

Unfortunately, this does not exhaust the complexity or, perhaps better, the ambiguity inherent in the Kantian conception of intuition. In fact, it applies to only one of three distinguishable senses in which Kant uses the term: the sense in which it refers to a particular kind of representation (repraesentatio singularis) or mental content. In addition to this more or less official sense of 'intuition', Kant also uses the term on occasion to refer both to the object represented by such a content, the *intuited,* which is always an appearance, and to the act of directly representing an individual, the *intuiting.* In short, it is necessary to distinguish between a mental content, an object, and an act sense of 'intuition'.[14] While it is generally clear from the context when the term is being used in the third sense, it is frequently difficult to determine whether it is being used in the first or second sense or, indeed, whether or not Kant himself conflates the two senses. In what follows, we shall see that at times a good deal rides on these questions, including the proper way to understand the role of intuition in synthetic judgments. But before we are in a position to deal with this issue, we must consider Kant's general theory of judgment.

II. KANT'S THEORY OF JUDGMENT

As already indicated, discursive knowledge is judgmental. It is in and through judgments that we apply concepts to given data, while concepts themselves are characterized as "predicates of possible judgments." Kant makes all of this quite explicit when he states that "we can reduce all acts of the understanding to judgments, and the *understanding* may therefore be represented as a *faculty of judgment*" [*ein Vermögen zur urtheilen*] (A69/B94). One of the main problems, however, confronting any interpretation of Kant's theory of judgment is that he defines 'judgment', meaning both the act (judging) and the product (the judgment), in a wide variety of ways, especially in the various extant versions of his lectures on logic. In the standard "Jäsche Logik," for example, he states simply that "a judgment is the representation of the unity of the consciousness of several representations or the representation of their relation so far as they make up one concept."[15] In the "Wiener Logik," by contrast, he writes:

Judgment in general is the representation of the unity in a relation of many cognitions [*Erkenntnisse*]. A judgment is the representation of the mode in which the concepts generally belong objectively to a consciousness. If one thinks two representations as bound together as cognitions and as thereby constituting a single cognition [*Eine Erkenntniss*], then that is a judgment. Every judgment therefore involves a certain relation of different representations insofar as they pertain to a cognition.[16]

The basic difference between these accounts is that whereas the first seems to equate making a judgment with forming a complex concept, the second takes every judgment to involve the cognition of an object and, therefore, to possess "objective validity." Moreover, precisely the same contrast is to be found in the two accounts of judgment contained in the *Critique of Pure Reason*. The first, corresponding to the Jäsche version, is located in the Logical Employment of the Understanding section, which provides an introduction to the Metaphysical Deduction. The second, reflecting the conception of the Wiener version, is located in §19 of the Second Edition version of the Transcendental Deduction. Because of this contrast, it is sometimes claimed that these texts embody two distinct, even incompatible, theories of judgment.[17] I believe, however, that they deal with different aspects of a single, coherent theory that became fully explicit only in the Second Edition of the *Critique*. In order to make this clear, I shall briefly consider each in turn. This should also put us in a position to consider the nature and significance of Kant's distinction between analytic and synthetic judgments.

A. Concepts and Judgment: The Initial Account

Kant's major concern in the first of these two accounts is to make explicit the identification of discursive knowledge with judgment. Every judgment, for Kant, involves an act of conceptualization, and vice versa.[18] Since Kant's conception of concepts commits him to the doctrine that "no concept is ever related to an object immediately, but to some other representation of it, be that other representation an intuition or a concept," he proceeds to define judgment as "the mediate knowledge of an object, that is, the representation of a representation of it" (A68/B93). Immediately after this definition, Kant provides a capsule account of his theory of judgment. Because of its brevity and importance, I shall quote it in full.

In every judgment there is a concept which holds of many representations, and among them of a given representation that is immediately related to an object. Thus in the judgment, 'all bodies are divisible', the concept of the divisible applies to various other concepts, but is here applied in particular to the concept of body, and this concept again to certain intuitions [or appearances][19] that present themselves to us. These objects, therefore, are mediately represented through the concept of divisibility. Accordingly, all judgments are functions of unity among our representations; instead of an immediate representation, a *higher* representation, which comprises the immediate representation and various others, is used in knowing the object, and thereby much possible knowledge is collected into one. [A68–69 / B93–94]

We see from Kant's example that the judgment involves two concepts, 'body' and 'divisibility', which are related both to each other and to the object judged about, that is, to the complete set of x's thought under the general description contained in the concept 'body'. Of these, the subject concept, 'body', stands in the more direct, though still not immediate, relation to the object. It does not relate to the object *simpliciter* (no concept can do that), but rather to an immediate representation of it. Such an immediate representation is, by definition, an intuition; so the subject concept in Kant's illustration refers directly to the intuition, and only mediately to the object. Roughly put, the intuition provides the sensible content for the judgment, while the concept provides the rule in accordance with which the content is determined. It is precisely by determining this content that the concept is brought into relation with the object. That is why Kant characterizes the relation between concept and object as mediate.

The judgment then asserts that the object so determined (the subject of the judgment) is also thought through the predicate 'divisibility'. This is a second determination or conceptualization of the object, one that is mediated by the first. It is this second determination to which Kant refers when he claims that in a judgment "much knowledge is collected into one." Presumably, the collection or unification effected by this particular judgment is of the x's thought through the concept 'body' with the other x's that may be thought through the concept 'divisibility', such as lines and planes. Kant's claim that "all judgments are functions of unity among our representations" is intended to underscore the point that every judgment involves a unification or "collection" of representations under a concept, that is, an act of conceptualization. The term 'function' here must obviously be taken in the Aristotelian sense as equivalent to 'task' or 'work'. Kant is thus saying that the essential task of every act of judgment is to produce a unity of representations under a concept.[20]

More detailed accounts of this same conception of judgment are to be found in many of Kant's *Reflexionen*. These accounts are generally intended as introductions to the distinction between analytic and synthetic judgments, but the treatment of the generic features of judgment can be considered independently of that issue. One of the most important of these Reflexionen is referred to by Paton in connection with his discussion of Kant's theory of judgment.[21] I here cite only that portion of Kant's text that is directly relevant to our present concern:

Every object is known only through predicates which we think or assert of it. Before this, any representations that may be found in us are to be regarded only as material for cognition, not as themselves cognitions. An object, therefore, is only a something in general which we think to ourselves through certain predicates which constitute its concept. Every judgment, therefore, contains two predicates which we compare with one another. One of these, which constitutes the given knowledge of the object, is called the logical subject; the other, which is compared with it, is called the predicate. When I say 'a body is divisible' this means that something *x,* which I know through the predicates that together constitute a concept of body, I also think through the predicate of divisibility.[22]

The first two sentences of this passage reiterate the previously made point about unconceptualized representations. Of more immediate significance, however, is the fact that Kant infers from this that every judgment must have two predicates. Certainly this claim cannot simply be accepted as it stands, because it applies only to categorical judgments; hypothetical and disjunctive judgments can have many more than two predicates. Nevertheless, since Kant regards these latter forms of judgment as logical compounds of categorical judgments, this is a mere detail that can safely be ignored. The crucial point here is that when Kant characterizes concepts as "predicates of possible judgments" he is not limiting their function to that of logical or grammatical predicates. If he were, he could not claim that judgments have more than one predicate. His major contention is that predicates, or concepts, function to determine the very content to be judged about. They do this by providing a general description under which this content can be thought. Insofar as a concept fulfills this function it is regarded as a "real" rather than a merely "logical" predicate. Such a predicate is also called a "determination" (*Bestimmung*).[23]

In the judgment under consideration, the logical subject, 'body', functions as a real predicate. In Kant's own terms, it "constitutes the given knowledge of the object," which means that it provides the initial description under which the subject *x* is to be taken in the judgment. Correlatively, since the judgment is analytic, the predicate 'divisibility' is only a logical predicate; that is to say, it does not add any further determinations to the subject beyond those already established by the characterization of it as a body. Leaving aside for the present, however, the whole question of analyticity, we see that the judgment "compares" these predicates with one another and asserts that they pertain to an identical *x*. It thus asserts that the same (or some, or every) *x* that is thought through the predicate 'body' is also thought through the predicate 'divisibility'. This is the basic Kantian schema for judgments of the categorical form, whether analytic or synthetic. Since, as previously noted, the other relational forms are logical compounds of categorical judgments, it can be taken as the Kantian schema for judgment in general. From it we can see how deeply Kant's analysis of judgment is rooted in his conception of the discursive nature of human thought.

B. Judgment and Objectivity: The Second Account

The objectivity of judgment is the focal point of the brief discussion of judgment in the Second Edition version of the Transcendental Deduction. Kant is here concerned with the explication of the distinction, first made in §18, between an "objective unity" of self-consciousness, which presumably involves the categories, and a "subjective unity," which is a product of the reproductive capacity of the imagination. He begins by criticizing logicians who define a judgment as the "representation of a relation between two concepts." Although he notes in passing that the definition is inadequate because it applies only to categorical judgments, Kant's real complaint is that it does not specify in what this relation consists. In an effort to answer this question Kant writes:

> I find that a judgment is nothing but the manner in which given modes of knowledge are brought to the objective unity of apperception. This is what is intended by the copula 'is'. It is employed to distinguish the objective unity of given representations from the subjective. [B141–42]

The distinguishing characteristic of the relation of representations in a judgment is thus seen to lie in its objectivity. It is an "objective unity," and, as such, it is correlated with the objective unity of apperception. In view of Kant's definition of the objective or transcendental unity of apperception, this must be taken to mean that every judgment involves "that unity through which all the manifold given in an intuition is united in a concept of the object" (B139). Kant's doctrine of apperception will be discussed in some detail in chapter 7, but for the purposes of this preliminary sketch he can be understood to be claiming that every judgment involves a synthesis or unification of representations in consciousness, whereby the representations are conceptualized so as to be referred or related to an object.[24] So far this tells us nothing that could not be gleaned from the previous analysis. But Kant proceeds to remark that a judgment can be described as "a relation [of representations] which is *objectively valid,* and so can be adequately distinguished from a relation of the same representations that would have only subjective validity, as when they are connected according to laws of association" (B142). The claim that every judgment involves the reference of representations to an object is thus taken to be equivalent to the claim that every judgment is objectively valid. Objective validity is, therefore, a definitional feature of judgment for Kant, not merely a value that can be assigned to some judgments. It serves to distinguish the unification of representations in a judgment from their unification in an associative act of imagination.

If this claim is to make any sense, it is obvious that objective validity cannot be equated with truth (otherwise, Kant would be committed to the absurdity that every judgment is true). Thus, it seems reasonable to follow Prauss on this point, who suggests that that 'objective validity' for Kant means simply the capacity to be true or false.[25] On this interpretation Kant's claim that every judgment is objectively valid is really equivalent to the claim that every judgment has a truth value. This is certainly true of all genuinely empirical judgments, although it raises certain problems about metaphysical judgments that need not concern us here.[26] It is not, however, true of a merely imaginative or associative unification of representations, such as my association of heat with the thought of the sun, or of the mere entertaining of a concept, such as the thought of a black man. Both of these are simply events in my mental history. As such, they can be neither true nor false, which is not to say that one cannot form true or false judgments about them. The full significance of this distinction between a judgmental and an imaginative or associative unification of representations will emerge in chapter 7; for the present our concern must be with the distinction between analytic and synthetic judgments.

III. THE ANALYTIC-SYNTHETIC DISTINCTION

Although it is clear from the *Reflexionen* and his response to Eberhard that Kant's distinction between analytic and synthetic judgments is deeply rooted in his theory of judgment and, therefore, in his conception of the discursive nature of human cognition, none of this is readily apparent from his official presentation of the distinction in the introduction to the *Critique of Pure Reason*. Moreover, this is one of the main reasons why the distinction has been so frequently misunderstood and subjected to so much misguided criticism.

The introduction contains two different, but purportedly equivalent, versions of this distinction. According to the first version, analytic judgments are those in which "the predicate B belongs to the subject A, as something which is (covertly) contained in this concept A." Equivalently, they are described as those in which the connection of the predicate with the subject is "thought through identity." Synthetic judgments, by contrast, are those in which "B lies outside the concept A, although it does stand in connection with it." The connection between subject and predicate in such judgments is thus said to be "thought without identity" (A6–7/B10–11). According to the second version, the distinction is between merely explicative (analytic) and ampliative (synthetic) judgments. The former, Kant maintains, add "nothing through the predicate to the concept of the subject, merely breaking it up into those constituent concepts that have all along been thought in it, although confusedly." The latter, on the other hand, "add to the concept of the subject a predicate which has not been in any wise thought in it, and which no analysis could possibly extract from it" (A7/B11). Only much later in the *Critique* does Kant make explicit what is implicit in his entire discussion; namely, that the law of contradiction is the principle of all analytic judgments.[27] In the *Prolegomena* Kant follows the second version, but adds that the distinction concerns the content of judgments (what they assert) rather than their origin or logical form. Moreover, he states explicitly that analytic judgments depend wholly on the law of contradiction, and that this is a basic point of contrast with synthetic judgments.[28]

The first version, which is the one usually cited, is particularly subject to misinterpretation and vulnerable to criticism, because it suggests that the distinction is a logical one and that it concerns the relationship between the subject and predicate concepts in a judgment (whether or not one is included in the other). Indeed, this seems to support Eberhard's contention, summarily dismissed by Kant, that the analytic-synthetic distinction is equivalent to the distinction between identical and nonidentical judgments.[29] It also gives rise to the obvious and frequently stated objection that the distinction applies only to judgments of the categorical form, and thus, that it can hardly be the universal distinction that Kant claims it to be. The major problem, however, is that this version provides no hint as to how syntheticity is to be understood (except as the negation of analyticity), or why Kant should insist in the *Prolegomena* that the distinction concerns the content rather than the logical form of judgments.

Beyond this, there are the familiar difficulties concerning how one determines whether one concept is "contained" in another. As Lewis White Beck has pointed out, Kant seems to recognize two distinct criteria for deciding such questions. He calls one "phenomenological" and the other "logical."[30] According to the former, the question whether one concept is "contained" in another is resolved by introspection: we reflect on what is "actually thought" in a given concept. According to the latter, the question is resolved by considering whether the contradictory of the original judgment is self-contradictory. If it is, then the original judgment is analytic and its truth can be determined in accordance with the principle of noncontradiction.

An obvious problem here is that these two criteria do not always produce the same result; it seems possible that a judgment could be analytic under one criterion and synthetic under the other. At best the first version does nothing to dispel such a possibility. Moreover, the phenomenological criterion itself seems to be a singularly unreliable guide, because it leaves it unexplained how in any given instance one can determine whether the failure to find one concept contained in another is due to the actual syntheticity of the judgment or to the limited insight of the person making the judgment. In short, it leaves open the possibility that any and every apparently synthetic judgment is covertly analytic. Unfortunately, the logical criterion fares no better. The problem with it is that except for manifest tautologies ($a = a$), it cannot be applied without appealing to "phenomenological" considerations, that is, to meanings. How, after all, can one determine whether the contradictory of a given judgment is self-contradictory without appealing to the meanings of the terms and, therefore, without determining whether the one concept is "contained" in the other?[31]

Although it hardly suffices to resolve all of the difficulties just mentioned, the second version is greatly superior to the first because in it the notion of a synthetic judgment, the real focus of Kant's concern, "wears the trousers." We learn that a synthetic judgment is one through which we extend rather than merely clarify our knowledge. This suggests that the two species of judgment differ in their epistemic functions; it also suggests why Kant insists in the *Prolegomena* that the distinction concerns the content of the judgments. What is more, it serves to put to rest the objection that the distinction is only relevant to judgments of the subject-predicate form. It does not, however, tell us in what sense and by what means we extend our knowledge through synthetic judgments, and it retains much of the psychological or subjectivistic flavor that is suggested by the appeal to the phenomenological criterion in the case of the first.[32]

These difficulties are alleviated somewhat by the brief account in the *Lectures on Logic,* where Kant presents the analytic-synthetic distinction in terms of the contrast between a "formal" and a "material" extension of knowledge.[33] Analytic judgments, he tells us, extend our knowledge in the former and synthetic judgments in the latter sense.[34]

Analytic judgments provide a formal extension of knowledge by clarifying or explicating what is merely implicit in a concept. This involves the uncovering of implications of which one may not previously have been aware, but which are derivable by strictly logical means from a given concept. Once again, Kant takes 'all bodies are extended' as his example of an analytic judgment, and he renders it schematically as "To every x to which appertains the concept of body $(a + b)$ appertains also extension (b)."[35] This is the basic formula for an analytic judgment. It shows that in such a judgment the predicate (b) is related to the object x (the subject of the judgment) by virtue of the fact that it is already contained (as a mark) in the concept of the subject. Analytic judgments are, therefore, "about" an object: they have a logical subject and, as Kant's example shows, they can also have a real subject. Nevertheless, since the truth or falsity of the judgment can be determined merely by analyzing the concept of the subject, the reference to the object x is otiose.[36] That is why it is perfectly possible to form analytic judgments about nonexistent, even impossible objects, and why all analytic judgments are known a priori.

In his response to Eberhard, Kant supplements this by introducing what amounts to a distinction between immediately and mediately analytic judgments.[37] 'All bodies are extended' is immediately analytic because 'extension' (together with 'figure', 'impenetrability', and so forth) is a mark of the concept *body.* In the scholastic terminology interjected in the debate by Eberhard, these marks are parts of the "logical essence" of the concept. 'All bodies are divisible' is mediately analytic because 'divisibility' is not itself part of the concept (logical essence) of body, but rather of one of its constituent concepts (*extension*). In other words, it is a mark of a mark. This implies that the judgment rests on an inference, and in that sense does extend our knowledge. But this does not amount to a difference in kind; for in each case the predicate is derived from the concept of the subject by a process of analysis, and thus on the basis of the principle of contradiction. In each case, then, the extension is merely formal.

This makes it clear that Kant's conception of analyticity is of a piece with his basic thesis regarding the discursive nature of human thought: it rests upon his notion of a concept as a set of marks (themselves concepts), which are thought together in an "analytic unity," and which can serve as a ground for the recognition of objects. These marks collectively constitute the intension of a concept. One concept is "contained in" another if and only if it is itself either a mark of the concept or a mark of one of its marks. Unlike most contemporary conceptions of analyticity, Kant's is thoroughly intensional. As Beck quite correctly points out, it rests upon the doctrine of the fixity of a concept, that is, on the thesis that the marks of a concept can be sufficiently determined (even without an explicit definition) for the purpose of analysis.[38] The notorious difficulties that arise concerning analytic judgments involving empirical concepts such as *water,* which we need not consider here, all stem from the difficulty of sufficiently determining such concepts.[39]

A synthetic judgment, by contrast, extends our knowledge in a "material" sense. The example of a synthetic judgment given in the *Lectures on Logic* is 'all bodies have attraction', which Kant renders schematically as "For every x to which appertains the concept of body $(a + b)$ appertains also attraction (c)."[40] Like its analytic counterpart, this judgment asserts a connection between the predicate (c) and the subject (x), which is thought through the concept $(a + b)$. In other words, it asserts that every x, known under the general description contained in the concept $a + b$ also possesses the additional property c. But unlike its analytic counterpart, it asserts this independently of any connection between the predicate and the concept of the subject. To be sure, in the judgment the predicate (c) is connected with the subject concept $(a + b)$; but the connection is grounded in, and mediated by, the reference of both to the identical object (x), which serves as the subject of the judgment. It, therefore, extends our knowledge of x (in this case, of all x's) by providing a determination or property of x that is not already contained in the concept $(a + b)$. This is what is meant by a "material extension."

Kant explicates this further by suggesting that the synthetic judgment contains a "determination," whereas the analytic judgment contains only a "logical predicate."[41] Since Kant maintains both that existential judgments are synthetic and that 'existence' is not a real predicate, this account of synthetic judgments obviously cannot be accepted as it stands. In other words, it cannot be maintained that the possession of a logical predicate that is also a real predicate is criterial for the syntheticity of a judgment. An existential judgment is synthetic, not because its logical predicate 'existence' is a real predicate or determination, but rather because its logical subject is one, and the judgment simply asserts the existence of an object corresponding to this subject.

It might also seem that in analytic judgments such as 'all bodies are divisible', the logical predicate, 'divisibility', is likewise a real predicate. After all, it is a property of every x that answers to the general description thought in the concept *body*. Indeed, this is just what the judgment asserts. Nevertheless, the point is that in the analytic judgment the predicate is related to the subject (x) simply in virtue of the fact that it is already contained (either immediately or mediately) in the concept of this subject. Thus the "reality" of the predicate does not come into consideration in the judgment. In synthetic judgments, however, the reference to the subject and, therefore, the reality of the predicate are just the points at issue. That is why the question of how such judgments are possible a priori is so perplexing.

In any case, a synthetic judgment (of theoretical reason)[42] can materially extend our knowledge only if the concepts in it are related to intuition. The reason for this is to be found in the very nature of discursive thought. As we have already seen, concepts can never relate immediately to objects, but only to other representations (either concepts or intuitions). Consequently, no judgment can ever relate a concept directly to an object, but only to some given representation of that object. That is why discursive knowledge is mediate. But, if the concept is held to be a real predicate or determination, then it must be related to some representation that itself stands in an immediate relation to the object, that is, to an intuition. In fact, it is only if the subject and predicate concepts in a synthetic judgment are both related to the intuition of the object that the connection of these concepts thought in the judgment can be grounded or objectively valid. Although all of this is obscured by the way in which Kant formulates the analytic-synthetic distinction in the *Critique,* he does clarify matters considerably in his response to Eberhard and in the related correspondence with Reinhold. Thus, in a letter to Reinhold, Kant remarks concerning Eberhard's claim that he (Kant) failed to provide a principle of synthetic judgment:

> But this principle is completely unambiguously presented in the whole *Critique,* from the chapter on the schematism on, though not in a specific formula. It is: *All synthetic judgments of theoretical knowledge are only possible through the relation of a given concept to an intuition.*[43]

It only remains to consider whether this principle enables us to understand the possibility of judgments that are both synthetic and a priori.

IV. THE PROBLEM OF THE SYNTHETIC A PRIORI

Kant held that the question of the possibility of synthetic a priori judgments emerges as the central problem of metaphysics as soon as the distinction between analytic and synthetic judgments is properly drawn. He thus points to the failure of past philosophers to recognize this problem as evidence of their failure to make the distinction. No such claim, however, is made for the distinction between a priori and a posteriori knowledge. In fact, in his response to Eberhard he notes that it is a distinction "long known and named in logic."[44] Kant is certainly correct on this score, although a contemporary philosopher would view the distinction as epistemological rather than logical. To ask whether a given judgment or proposition is a priori or a posteriori is to ask how it is known or, in Kantian terms, how it is grounded or legitimated. The key issue is the role of experience in this grounding. A priori judgments are grounded independently of experience, while a posteriori judgments are grounded by means of an appeal to experience. Following Leibniz, Kant regards necessity and universality as the criteria for the a priori. His fundamental assumption is that the truth value of judgments which lay claim to universality and necessity cannot be grounded empirically.

Analytic judgments obviously fit into this category. Their truth value is determined by means of an analysis of the constituent marks of a given concept. This is true even when the concept is empirical. The real question is whether it is likewise possible for synthetic judgments to have nonempirical grounds. Since they are synthetic, they cannot have a purely conceptual or logical grounding; since they are known a priori, they cannot be grounded in experience. The problem of the synthetic a priori is, therefore, that of explaining how a nonempirical, yet extraconceptual and extralogical grounding of a judgment is possible. An equivalent way of formulating the problem is to ask how it is possible to extend one's knowledge (in the material sense) beyond a given concept, independently of any experience of the object thought through that concept.[45]

Kant's clearest answer to this general question is contained in a passage, not published in Kant's lifetime, in "On the Progress of Metaphysics."

> Knowledge is a judgment from which a concept arises that has objective validity, i.e., to which a corresponding object in experience can be given. All experience, however, consists of the intuition of an object, i.e., an immediate and singular representation, through which the object is given to knowledge, and of a concept, i.e., a mediate representation through a mark which is common to several objects, through which it is thought. One of these two modes of representation alone cannot constitute knowledge, and if there is to be synthetic knowledge *a priori*, there must also be *a priori* intuitions as well as concepts.[46]

The key point here is the claim that synthetic a priori judgments require a priori or pure intuitions as well as concepts. Kant emphasizes the same point in "On a Discovery" and the related correspondence with Reinhold, where he is particularly concerned to distinguish his position from that of Leibnizian rationalism.[47]

The need for a priori or pure concepts in synthetic a priori judgments is easily shown. Suppose that the predicate in a synthetic judgment is an empirical concept. In that case, its connection with an object (its objective reality) would have to be established by empirical means. But this connection is precisely what is asserted in a synthetic judgment, so the resulting judgment must be empirical (and thus known a posteriori). As obvious as this conclusion is, however, it is partly obscured by two features of Kant's position: one is that analytic judgments, which are always a priori, can be made on the basis of empirical concepts; the other is that Kant sometimes speaks of "impure" a priori judgments, which involve empirical concepts as well.[48] With regard to analytic judgments, we need only note once again that they abstract from the whole question of objective reference and thus from the objective reality of the concept. The appeal to experience is therefore otiose, even when the concept itself is empirical. With regard to "impure" a priori judgments, it is sufficient to point out that they always involve pure concepts as predicates. In Kant's own example of such a judgment, 'every alteration has a cause', the emphasis is placed upon the fact that 'alteration' is an empirical concept. Nevertheless, causality is a pure concept; and that is precisely why the connection asserted in the judgment between this concept and every instance of an alteration cannot be established by an appeal to experience.

The role of pure intuition in synthetic a priori judgments, which is the point on which Kant particularly insists in all of his anti-Leibnizian moments, is considerably more complex. It involves three questions, each of which must be considered separately. The first is why synthetic a priori judgments require intuitions at all. The second is why they require pure rather than merely empirical intuitions. The third is whether such judgments can be said to relate pure concepts to pure intuitions or, equivalently, whether they require that pure intuitions be "subsumed" under pure concepts.

First, a synthetic a priori judgment requires intuition for the same reason that any synthetic judgment does: the mutual reference to intuition of the concepts connected in a judgment is what alone makes possible the material extension of our knowledge. Indeed, it is precisely because of the impossibility of providing an intuition answering to the concepts that Kant holds the judgments of transcendent metaphysics to be ungrounded. From the standpoint of theoretical knowledge at least, the limits of our sensibility (the source of all of our intuitions) are at the same time the limits of our world.

But why can't we make do with empirical intuition? Why is it necessary to introduce the hybrid notion of a pure, yet sensible, intuition, which Eberhard and so many others dismiss as a contradiction in terms? Although the notion of a pure intuition is a murky one, perhaps the murkiest in the entire *Critique,* the reason for its introduction is clear: the insufficiency of empirical intuition to ground synthetic a priori judgment. The problem with an empirical intuition is its particularity. A determinate, or conceptualized, empirical intuition is the representation, under a certain description, of a particular spatiotemporal object; for example, this desk in front of me. As particular, the representation is incapable of expressing the universality and necessity that is thought in a pure concept and asserted in a synthetic a priori judgment. To cite a single and obvious mathematical example: as synthetic, the judgment that the sum of the three interior angles of a triangle is equal to two right angles must somehow be grounded in the intuition of a triangle; but as a priori, it cannot be grounded in the intuition (image) of any particular triangle. Its possibility thus rests upon there being some nonempirical or pure intuition of a triangle, that is, a singular representation that nonetheless can "attain that universality of the concept which renders it valid of all triangles, whether right angled or obtuse angled or acute angled" (A140/B180).[49]

Finally, we come to the question of whether pure intuitions, construed as representations, function as ingredients in synthetic a priori judgments in the same way that empirical intuitions function in synthetic a posteriori judgments. At this stage of the analysis, before we have fully investigated Kant's conception of pure intuition, we can only argue in general terms that the very same considerations advanced in support of the contention that synthetic judgments in general require the relation of concepts to intuitions (or, equivalently, the "subsumption" of the latter under the former) must also apply here with respect to pure intuition. How, after all, can a pure intuition provide the ground of the connection of concepts asserted in such a judgment unless it provides a representation of the real subject of which the concepts are predicated? Again, how can a pure concept apply universally and necessarily to a sphere of objects, for example, alterations—and it must do so, if the judgment is to be both synthetic and a priori—unless it is related in the judgment to the universal and necessary conditions, that is, the "form," of our intuition of these objects? But these universal and necessary conditions of intuition are, as we shall soon see, themselves pure intuitions. Consequently, if synthetic a priori judgments are to be possible, pure concepts as predicates must be related in these judgments to pure intuitions as the representations of their subjects. The questions of how a pure intuition is possible and what it can contain, or represent, are among the main concerns of the next chapter. In chapter 8 we shall further see that the transcendental schemata must also be regarded as pure intuitions.

5

The Sensible Conditions of Human Knowledge

After providing definitions of some key terms and briefly linking space with outer sense and time with inner sense, Kant turns abruptly at the beginning of the Transcendental Aesthetic to the question of the ontological status of space and time. Three possibilities are introduced, and although Kant does not say so explicitly, it is obvious that the list is intended to be exhaustive. The first is the absolutistic theory, advocated by Newton, according to which space and time are "real existences." The second is the relational view, advocated by Leibniz, according to which they are determinations or relations of things "such as would belong to things even if they were not intuited." The third is the "critical" view, according to which "they belong only to the form of intuition, and therefore to the subjective constitution of our mind, apart from which they could not be ascribed to anything whatsoever" (A23 / B37–38).

The central concern of the Transcendental Aesthetic is to demonstrate the truth of the last alternative. Kant takes this to be equivalent to a direct proof of transcendental idealism. The argument moves from an analysis of the representations of space and time, which purports to show that these representations are both a priori and intuitive, to the ontological claim about space and time themselves. Unfortunately, this argument is seldom taken very seriously. In fact, it is widely assumed that Kant's real argument for the ideality of space turns on his conception of Euclidean geometry as a synthetic a priori science of space.[1] Since this conception is almost universally rejected, there is little sympathy (at least among contemporary philosophers) for the central claims of the Transcendental Aesthetic. In opposition to this dominant interpretation, I hope to show in this chapter that Kant's argument from the representation of space is still worthy of serious consideration, especially when it is considered in light of the alternative possibilities available to him (basically, the Leibnizian and Newtonian theories and variants thereof). I also contend that both the argument from geometry and the argument from the "paradox" of incongruent counterparts, which is sometimes advanced as an independent proof of the ideality thesis, derive whatever force they possess from the primary argument from the representation of space. Consequently, the rejection (or at least radical modification) of Kant's views on geometry, which seems to be required by the development of non-Euclidean geometries, does not entail the rejection of the doctrine of the ideality of space.

I. THE REPRESENTATIONS OF SPACE AND TIME

Kant's analysis of the nature and origin of the representations of space and time is contained in the Metaphysical Exposition of these "concepts." This exposition has two goals. The first is to show that the representations of space and time are a priori; the second is to show that they are intuitions. Since the analysis of space and time parallel one another for the most part, I shall concentrate on the former, referring to the latter only in those instances where Kant's analysis differs significantly. Specific problems concerning the representation of time will be dealt with in subsequent chapters.

A. The Apriority Thesis

The argument for the a priori nature of the representation of space is contained in two brief paragraphs which have become the topic of endless controversy. For convenience sake, I quote them both in full:

> Space is not an empirical concept which has been derived from outer experiences. For in order that certain sensations be referred to something outside me (that is, to something in another region of space from that in which I find myself), and similarly in order that I may be able to represent them as outside and alongside one another, and accordingly as not only different but as in different places, the representation of space must be presupposed. The representation of space cannot, therefore, be empirically obtained from the relations of outer appearance. On the contrary, this outer experience is itself possible at all only through that representation.

> Space is a necessary *a priori* representation, which underlies all outer intuitions. We can never represent to ourselves the absence of space, though we can quite well think it as empty of objects. It must therefore be regarded as the condition of the possibility of appearances, and not as a determination dependent upon them. It is an *a priori* representation, which necessarily underlies outer appearances. [A23–24 / B38–39]

The interpretive problem begins with the question of the relationship between the two arguments. Are they two independent proofs of the apriority thesis or one argument with two steps? Not surprisingly, the main commentators are divided on this issue. Vaihinger maintains that Kant presents one theorem with two proofs, the first direct and the second indirect.[2] By contrast, both Kemp Smith and Paton, influenced by what they take to be the inadequacy of the first argument, tend to see them as two steps in a single proof.[3] The position which I propose to defend is that they constitute two distinct proofs, each of which suffices to establish the apriority of the representation of space, but that the second calls attention to a crucial feature of this representation that is not suggested by the first.

The First Apriority Argument. This argument involves two distinct claims, both of which are presuppositional in nature.[4] The first claim is that the representation of space must be presupposed if I am to refer my sensations to something "outside me" (*ausser mir*). The second is that this representation must be presupposed if I am to represent objects as outside or external to one another. Since 'ausser' is normally a spatial term, the claim that space must be presupposed in order to refer my representations (sensations) to something ausser mir might appear to be a mere tautology. A similar objection can be raised against the second claim, as well as against the contention that space is the form of outer sense.

This way of construing the argument is, however, misleading. The crucial point is that by 'outer sense' is meant a sense through which one can become perceptually aware of objects as distinct from the self and its states. Similarly, by 'inner sense' is meant a sense through which one can become perceptually aware of the self and its states. It follows from this that 'ausser' here does not already involve a reference to space. Consequently, Kant's claim that the representation of space functions as the condition by means of which we can become aware of things as ausser uns is no more tautological than the corresponding claim about time. On the contrary, its significance stems precisely from the fact that no logical necessity is involved. Thus, it is at least conceivable that other "sensible beings" might possess this awareness under other conditions. Correlatively, it is equally conceivable that other "sensible beings" might be aware of themselves and their mental states through a vehicle other than the representation of time. The gist of the first claim is, therefore, that the representation of space is the condition or presupposition of human awareness, but not of any conceivable awareness of objects as distinct from the self and its states.

The second claim can be dealt with in a similar fashion. Once again, the claim that space must be presupposed in order to represent objects as "outside [*ausser*] and next to one another, as not only different [*bloss verschieden*], but as in different places," initially appears to be tautological. This, however, is not the case if we take 'bloss verschieden' to refer to qualitative diversity, and thus to suggest a contrast between qualitative and numerical diversity.[5] Given this reading, Kant can be taken to be arguing that in order to be aware of things as numerically distinct from one another, it is necessary to be aware, not only of their qualitative differences, but also of the fact that they are located in different places. In other words, the representation of place, and therefore of space, functions within human experience as a necessary condition of the possibility of distinguishing objects from one another. Moreover, as in the previous case, it is not a logically necessary condition. There is no contradiction in the thought that there might be some other, nonspatial mode of awareness of numerical diversity; we simply do not know what such a mode of awareness would be like.

Here, as well as in many other places in the Transcendental Aesthetic, Kant is directly challenging the Leibnizian theory of space, particularly as it is articulated in the correspondence with Clarke. After contending against the Newtonian theory that space is simply the order of coexisting phenomena, Leibniz turns in the fifth letter to the question of why we nevertheless conceive of space as something more than and independent of this order. Reduced to its essentials, his answer is that this concept of space is a sort of imaginative gloss, the result of our inability to perceive distinctly minute differences between situations. This inability, he argues, leads in turn to a confounding of resemblance or agreement with actual numerical identity.[6]

In opposition to this view, Kant is here arguing that the something extra, which according to Leibniz is superimposed by the mind upon the order of coexisting phenomena, is a necessary condition for the awareness of the order in the first place. Moreover, although this argument was undoubtedly developed by Kant with Leibniz in mind, it is equally applicable to the standard empiricistic analyses of the origin of the idea of space or extension, for example, Locke's. The main point is simply that the features of experience to which one appeals in the endeavor to account for the origin of this idea already presuppose it. The same holds, *mutatis mutandis,* for time.

These considerations put us in a position to deal with two basic objections that have frequently been raised against Kant's argument. The first of these can be traced back to Maass, and it reflects his endeavor to defend the Leibnizian position against Kant's attack. According to Maass, it is possible to accept Kant's premises and yet deny his conclusion. A representation A, he reasons, may underlie or be presupposed by another representation B, and thus not be derivable from it. But it does not follow from this that A is a priori. An equally plausible alternative is that those representations are correlative and that they mutually condition one another. Assuming this possibility, which Maass claims Kant completely ignores, the concept A could be obtained only by abstraction from the complete concept AB. A would therefore be an empirical concept.[7] This is obviously intended by Maass not to be a mere possibility, but to reflect the essence of the Leibnizian position. Thus A refers to the order or situation of things, and B to the things themselves. The point, then, is that while we cannot represent the things (B) without also representing their order or situation (A), we only arrive at the concept of the latter by an act of abstraction from the complete concept (AB). In this sense it is empirical.

Much the same line of objection is also raised by Paton. Although he neither suggests that space might be an empirical concept, nor asserts that

Kant completely neglected the possibility that the representations of space and of the things therein might somehow mutually condition each other, he does contend that this latter possibility is only removed by the second-space argument. Consequently, the first argument is viewed as of itself insufficient to establish the apriority of the representation of space.[8] It is on this basis that Paton claims that the two arguments must be taken to constitute two steps in a single proof rather than two distinct proofs.

But this objection misses the force of Kant's argument. The argument does not merely contend that we cannot have the representation of things as distinct from ourselves and from each other without also having the representation of space. This would be the case even if space were nothing but the order of coexisting phenomena, which was just Maass's point. What the argument claims is rather that the representation of space functions within human experience as a means or vehicle for the representation of objects as distinct from the self and from each other. Moreover, we cannot, as Maass suggests, argue in the other direction: we cannot maintain that the awareness of things as distinct from ourselves and from each other is similarly a condition of the possibility of the representation of space. Again, this would hold only if space were nothing more than the order of these things.[9] The argument for the apriority of the representation of space is thus at the same time an argument against any purely relational theory of the nature of space. The parallel argument concerning time functions in precisely the same way.[10] In both cases the key lies in the epistemic function claimed for the representation.

Whereas the first objection maintains that Kant's argument does not prove enough, the second holds that it proves too much. According to this objection, if the argument proves anything at all, it proves that even our empirical concepts must be a priori in precisely the same sense as space is a priori. The operative assumption here is that Kant's argument moves directly from the claim that the representation of space is necessary in order to recognize spatial relations and determinations to the conclusion that it is a priori. It is then suggested that an analogous claim can be made about any empirical concept. Dryer, who himself rejects this objection, describes the problem:

> In order to recognize objects as red, one must already have the concept of redness. But this does not establish that the concept of red is not an empirical concept. In order to observe things about us, we must represent them in space. How then can this show that the concept of space is not likewise empirical?[11]

Dryer's formulation of the objection already serves to indicate the disanalogy between the two cases. In spite of the opaqueness of Kant's own formulation, it is clear that he is not arguing that the representation of space must be presupposed in order to recognize things as spatial. Such an argument would make the claim tautological. As we have already seen, he is arguing instead that the representation of space is necessary in order to be aware of things as distinct from ourselves and from each other (in Dryer's terms, as "about us"). Since a reference to space is not already built into these distinctions, as a reference to red is built into the thought of red things, the two cases are not analogous. Moreover, as Dryer suggests, the ability to make these distinctions is itself a necessary condition of the possibility of experience.[12] Therefore, unlike the ability to distinguish between red and blue things, it cannot be acquired through experience. The argument shows, however, that this ability presupposes (although not logically) the representation of space. Consequently, Kant's argument can be said to show that the representation of space is a priori by showing that it functions as an epistemic condition. This fact is completely neglected by both of the abovementioned objections.

The Second Apriority Argument. This argument asserts that "space is a necessary *a priori* representation, which underlies all outer intuitions." Although this seems to be stronger than the claim made at the beginning of the previous argument, it is really an equivalent claim formulated in a positive way. The proofs, however, are quite different. The premise of this argument is contained in the second sentence: "We can never represent to ourselves the absence of space [*Man kann sich niemals eine Vorstellung davon machen dass kein Raum sei*], though we can quite well think it is empty of objects." This suggests the following argument, which is presumably what Kant had in mind: if x can be (or be represented) without A, B, C and their mutual relations, but A, B, C cannot be (or be represented) without x, then x must be viewed as a condition of the possibility of A, B, C and their mutual relations. Applying this to space, Kant concludes, "It must therefore be regarded as the condition of the possibility of appearances, and not as a determination dependent upon them."

Because of its reference to the impossibility of representing the absence of space, this argument is frequently dismissed on the grounds that it involves a psychological claim (and a questionable one at that). Thus, Kemp Smith, who interprets it in this way, notes that "the criterion is not the impossibility of thinking otherwise, but our own incapacity to represent this specific element as absent."[13] By contrast, other commentators suggest that Kant is here asserting something much closer to a logical than to a psychological impossibility. On this interpretation Kant is making a claim about the inconceivability of the nonexistence of space that is analogous to Spinoza's claim about the inconceivability of the nonexistence of substance.[14]

The latter reading is clearly unacceptable. Kant nowhere affirms that space (or time) is logically necessary. On the contrary, we have already seen that it is not logically necessary for space to be the form of outer or time of inner sense. This enables us to recognize the (logical) possibility of other forms of sensible representation, and to recognize such a possibility is already in a sense to "represent to ourselves the absence of space." More important, Kant's doctrine that we can think, although not know, things as they are in themselves requires him to allow for this possibility. For how can we think about things as they are in themselves unless we can "represent to ourselves the absence of space"?

Nevertheless, simply because Kant is not talking about a logical impossibility, it does not follow, as Kemp Smith assumes, that he is doing psychology. There is a third alternative; namely, that Kant is concerned with the determination of epistemic conditions. Moreover, that this is in fact Kant's concern emerges quite clearly in the parallel argument regarding time. Kant there writes: "We cannot, in respect of appearances in general, remove [*aufheben*] time itself, though we can quite well think time as void of appearances." He further remarks that "In it [time] alone is actuality of appearances possible at all." Finally, in a parenthetical phrase added in the Second Edition, time is characterized as "the universal condition of their [appearances'] possibility" (B46). The significance of this lies in the fact that the scope of the claim regarding "removing time," which is presumably the temporal analogue to representing the absence of space, is strictly limited to appearances. In addition, we are told that the reason we cannot remove time from appearances is that time is a condition of their very possibility, that is, their representation. This is an epistemic and not a psychological claim.

Since only outer appearances are in space, whereas all appearances are in time, the scope of the corresponding space argument must be limited to outer appearances. Nevertheless, given this limitation, it seems reasonable to assume that Kant is trying to make the same point about the representation of space that he makes about time. So construed, the claim is that we cannot represent to ourselves outer appearances without representing them as in space.[15] Indeed, we saw in the analysis of the first argument that it is precisely by representing appearances as spatial that we represent them as "outer," that is, as distinct from states of our consciousness. Kant's point, therefore, is not that it is either psychologically or logically impossible to remove (in thought) space or time. It is rather that it is impossible to do so and still have any sensible content to intuit. Kant perhaps put the matter best in the observation on the antithesis of the First Antinomy, where, in commenting on the Leibnizian project of reconciling the finitude of the world with the rejection of a void, extra-mundane space, he remarks, "If that void, and consequently space in general as *a priori* condition of the possibility of appearances, be set aside, the entire sensible world vanishes" (A433 / B461).

It does not, however, follow from the fact that we cannot think of appearances without also thinking of them as in space and time, that these representations are a priori. Here is where Maass's point, mistakenly presented as a criticism of the first argument, becomes relevant. The problem can also be expressed by noting that this claim, taken by itself, is perfectly compatible with the Leibnizian doctrine that space and time are merely orders or systems of relations. Every monad, after all, contains in its complete concept something that corresponds to every other monad in the universe. At the phenomenal level this is reflected in the order or situation of things vis à vis one another. One cannot, in thought, negate this order without also negating the very being of the things ordered. Nevertheless, this hardly establishes that this order is a priori, that is, logically prior to and independent of the thought of the things ordered.

The conclusion to be drawn from this is simply that the second part of the claim is equally necessary for the establishment of the apriority thesis. In other words, it is necessary to show both that we cannot remove space and time from the thought of appearances and that we can represent to ourselves space and time independently of these appearances. Together they prove that the representations of space and time are conditions of appearances and thus a priori. By the same token, they also prove that space and time themselves cannot be construed in the purely relational sense advocated by Leibniz. The key point here is that Leibniz can accept the first but not the second of these claims. To be sure, we have already seen that there is a sense in which he grants that we have an idea of space as something existing independently of things and their relations. The whole thrust of his analysis, however, is to show that the idea contains nothing more than the order of things, confusedly represented as existing independently of them. Consequently, space, so conceived, is for Leibniz a "mere ideal thing," an *ens imaginarium*. That is precisely why Kant contends that for Leibniz the representations of space and time are "merely creatures of the imagination, whose source must really be sought in experience" (A40/B57).

By contrast, Kant insists that the representations of space and time have a content that is logically independent of, and thus irreducible to, the representations of the things in them. This is the meaning of the claim that we can think space and time as empty of objects. It does not follow from this that we can experience or perceive empty space or time. Kant denies this repeatedly. Moreover, even if this were possible, it is hard to see what bearing it would have on the apriority issue. It does follow, however, that space and time remain accessible to thought when we abstract from the entire empirical content of our experience, that is, from everything that can be attributed to sensation. Kant states this cryptically in the *Prolegomena* with regard to both space and time when he notes: "If we omit from the empirical intuition of bodies and their alterations (motion) everything empirical, that is, belonging to sensation, space and time still remain."[16] In the *Critique* he expresses himself more expansively with respect to space:

> Thus, if I take away from the representation of a body that which the understanding thinks in regard to it, substance, force, divisibility, etc., and likewise what belongs to sensation, impenetrability, hardness, colour, etc., something still remains over from this empirical intuition, namely, extension and figure. These belong to pure intuition, which, even without any actual object of the senses or of sensation, exists in the mind *a priori* as a mere form of sensibility. [A21 / B35].

We see from this that the extension and figure of body is the primary content of the representation of space. Since this content remains when one abstracts from the other properties and relations thought in connection with the representation of a body, whereas these do not remain when one abstracts from it, it cannot be viewed as derived from these other properties and relations. In a word, it is a priori. Kant is not making the claim, ridiculed by Berkeley, that we can somehow sense or imagine figure without color or, more generally, primary without secondary qualities. His point is rather that in our experience of body we necessarily regard the spatial properties as primary, because it is in virtue of these properties that we deem it a representation of a body in the first place. This certainly cuts against Berkeley, although Kant's main target is obviously Leibniz. In fact, with this argument, Kant can be said to have turned the Leibnizian position on its head. Recall that for Leibniz we can perfectly well have an order or situation of things without space, that is, without the superimposed complex of reified places, but we cannot have place or space without the things and their order and situation. Everything in the representation of space is, therefore, reducible (in principle) to the representation of this order or situation. For Kant, however, it is only in terms of the prior and independent representation of space that we can represent to ourselves this order or situation of things. It is, therefore, not space, but the things in space that are eliminable, not, to be sure, in experience, but in thought. The same applies, *mutatis mutandis,* to time.

Like the first argument, this argument establishes the a priori status of the representations of space and time by indicating their unique, foundational role in human experience. This does not, however, make the second argument superfluous. In addition to putting the contrast between the Kantian and the Leibnizian positions in a clearer light, it also calls attention to a feature of these representations that is both central to Kant's position and completely neglected by the first argument: the fact that they have a content of their own, which remains when abstraction is made from everything empirical. By bringing this out Kant not only underscores their a priori status, but also prepares the way for the claim that they are pure intuitions.[17] It is to this claim that we now turn.

B. The Intuition Thesis

Once again Kant offers two distinct arguments in support of a single thesis. This time, however, the situation is complicated by the fact that he substitutes a completely different version of the second argument in the Second Edition. For convenience sake, I here cite both versions of this second argument, although I shall concentrate on the second in my analysis.

> Space is not a discursive or, as we say, general concept of relations of things in general, but a pure intuition. For, in the first place, we can represent to ourselves only one space; and if we speak of diverse spaces, we mean thereby only parts of one and the same unique space. Secondly, these parts cannot precede the one all-embracing space, as being, as it were, constituents out of which it can be composed; on the contrary, they can be thought only as *in* it. Space is essentially one; the manifold in it, and therefore the general concept of spaces, depends solely on (the introduction of) limitations. Hence it follows that an *a priori,* and not an empirical, intuition underlies all concepts of space. [A25 / B39]
>
> Space is represented as an infinite given magnitude. A general concept of space, which is found alike in a foot and in an ell, cannot determine anything in regard to magnitude. If there were no limitlessness in the progression of intuition, no concept of relations could yield a principle of their infinitude. [A25]
>
> Space is represented as an infinite *given* magnitude. Now every concept must be thought as a representation which is contained in an infinite number of different possible representations (as their common character), and which therefore contains these *under* itself; but no concept, as such, can be thought as containing an infinite number of representations *within* itself. It is in this latter way, however, that space is thought; for all the parts of space coexist *ad infinitum.* Consequently, the original representation of space is an *a priori* intuition, not a concept. [B39–40]

The First Intuition Argument. This argument assumes the exhaustive nature of the concept—intuition distinction. Given this assumption, it attempts to show, by means of an analysis of the nature of the representation of space, that this representation cannot be a concept and must, therefore, be an intuition. Since Kant has already shown that the representation is "pure," or a priori, he now concludes that it is a pure intuition. The total proof involves two distinct steps. In the first Kant contrasts the relation between space and particular spaces with the relation between a concept and its extension.[18] In the second he contrasts it with the relation between a concept and its intension. As we shall see, both steps are necessary in order to produce the desired conclusion.

The first step turns on the singleness of space. The basic claim is that "we can represent to ourselves only one space." If the argument is to work, it must be assumed that this is not a contingent matter, as if the class of spaces just happened to have only one member. But neither can it be a logically necessary truth, like the truth that we can conceive of only one "most perfect being" or only one substance, in Spinoza's sense. In support of this claim, however, Kant offers only the observation that we are somehow constrained to think of particular spaces as parts of a single space. Although Kant asserts in the corresponding time argument that "the representation which can only be given through a single object is an intuition" (A32 / B47), it should be clear that this still does not prove that the representation of space (or time) is an intuition. Consider the concept of the world as analyzed in the discussion of the Antinomies. Since it is the concept of a complete collection or totality, we can conceive of only one (actual) world.[19] Nevertheless, we would hardly infer from this that the representation is an intuition. On the contrary, it is a cosmological Idea. In order to prove that the representation of space is an intuition, Kant must show how it differs from the concept of a complete collection or totality.

It is difficult to determine whether Kant actually had this problem in mind; nevertheless, it is effectively resolved in the second part of the argument. As indicated, Kant here contrasts the relationship between space and its parts (particular spaces) with the relationship between a concept and its intension. The main point is that the marks or partial concepts out of which a general concept is composed (its *Bestandteile*) are all logically prior to the whole. A general concept is thus a collection of marks. A similar claim can be made about a concept of a collection or a totality such as the world. Here too, although in a different sense, the parts are prior to the whole. This, however, is not the case with space and its parts. Rather than being pregiven elements out of which the mind forms the idea of a single space, the parts of space are only given in and through this single space which they presuppose. Space, in other words, is not only presented as single (*einzig*), but as a unity (*einig*). Consequently, it cannot be conceived as a collection or aggregate. To return to the language used in the discussion in the First Antinomy, it is a totum analyticum and not a totum syntheticum or, more simply, a Totum and not a Compositum. Precisely the same holds for time.

In the remainder of the paragraph Kant acknowledges that we can form general concepts of space, but insists that these are only the results of the limitation of the one, all-inclusive space. He further claims that this proves that the underlying intuition is a priori. Kant seems to have in mind a two-step procedure. First, through the introduction of limitations, which is itself a conceptual activity, we produce the idea of determinate spaces (figures and magnitudes); then, on the basis of these determinations, we form by abstraction general concepts of spaces. Although Kant does not explain the matter, it is precisely the precedence of the intuition over all spatial concepts that provides the basis for the assertion of the apriority claim. Thus, even in the Transcendental Aesthetic, which is explicitly devoted to a consideration of the sensible conditions of human knowledge, Kant does not deny the role of conceptualization in the representation of space. The main point, however, is that the possibility of such conceptualization rests upon some given content, that is, an intuition. In Kant's own terms, space is *intuitus, quem sequitur conceptus.*[20] This is the position that Kant consistently maintains.

The Second Intuition Argument. This argument is both more complex and more problematic than the preceding one. It assumes that space is represented as an infinite given magnitude and concludes from this that the representation must be an intuition. A brief glance at the First Edition version of the argument makes it clear why Kant completely recast it in the Second Edition. Its nerve is the claim that a general concept of space, which is formed by abstraction from particular spatial measurements, "could not determine anything with regard to magnitude." This is obviously true but nonetheless completely irrelevant. First, it does not have anything in particular to do with the infinity of space. Precisely the same point could be made if space were represented as a finite given magnitude. Second, even if we accept the infinity premise, this does not require us to assume that the representation is an intuition. All that this premise does is rule out the possibility that the representation could be acquired by abstraction, in the manner of an empirical concept. Certainly, it leaves open the possibility, already alluded to in connection with the preceding argument, that the representation of space is analogous to the representation of an infinite collection, for example, the world. Since we do not infer that the representation of the world is an intuition from the fact that the world is conceived as infinite (at least by the proponents of the infinitistic position), why should we do so in the case of space?

The Second Edition version can be read as an endeavor to meet these difficulties by showing the different senses in which concepts and intuitions involve infinity. In so doing Kant also sheds additional light on the differences between the logical form or structure of concepts and intuitions.[21] A concept has a complex logical form, involving both an extension and an intension. Viewed extensionally, every concept has various other concepts contained *under* it. These concepts are arranged hierarchically in terms of generality, and they stand in the relationship of genus to species. Lower concepts, that is, species, are introduced by adding differentia. Thus, by adding differentia, the genus "physical body" can be divided into the species "inanimate" and "animate," and the latter into the species "animal" and "vegetable." Viewed intensionally, every concept contains other concepts *within* it as its component parts. But here the ordering is just the reverse of the extensional ordering, because the lower or more specific concepts, which are obtained by adding differentia, contain the higher or more general concepts within themselves. There is thus an inverse correlation between the extension and the intension of a concept: the smaller the extension, that is, the more limited the sphere of objects to which it applies, the richer the intension, and vice versa.

As the first intuition argument makes clear, this contrasts markedly with the structure of an intuition. Since it is the representation of an individual, all the parts of an intuition are contained in and presuppose the whole. Similarly, intuitions are not divided by adding differentia but by introducing limitations or boundaries.[22] This gives to an intuition a structure analogous to that of a totum analyticum, which is what the first argument implies. The second argument really does nothing more than build on this by showing how the difference in structure is reflected in the different ways in which concepts and intuitions involve infinity. A concept involves infinity with respect to its extension: it can have an infinite or, better, an indefinite number of concepts falling under it. In fact, since Kant denies that there can be an *infima* species, he is committed to the view that the search for subordinate concepts can be pursued ad infinitum.[23] A concept, however, cannot involve infinity with respect to its intension, because such an infinite concept, for example, the Leibnizian complete concept of an individual substance, could not be grasped by the human mind. An intuition, by contrast, can have an infinite number of parts within it. Moreover, Kant points out, this is precisely the way in which space is thought, "for all the parts of space coexist *ad infinitum.*" From this he concludes that "the original representation of space is an *a priori* intuition, not a concept."

One fundamental question raised by this analysis concerns the sense of infinity that is to be assigned to space. The claim that the parts of space "coexist *ad infinitum*" certainly suggests that the infinity of space consists in the innumerability of its parts. It would also seem, however, that the very same considerations that Kant advances against the doctrine of the infinity of the world in space and time in the thesis of the First Antinomy apply equally to the infinity of space and time themselves so conceived.[24] Consequently, either the Aesthetic stands in blatant contradiction to the Dialectic, or Kant had some other sense of 'infinity' in mind.

Fortunately, there is considerable evidence to suggest that the latter is the case. First, we note that in the First Edition version of the argument Kant makes it clear that the infinity of space has to do with the "limitlessness in the progression of intuition." The point here is that however large a region of space one takes, it is always represented as bounded by more of the same. Presumably, the same principle holds in the case of division, and this serves to explain the infinite divisibility of space. This is also consistent with Kant's claim that a point is a limit and not a part of space. Second, in the parallel time argument, contained in both editions, Kant asserts that "the infinitude of time signifies nothing more than that every determinate magnitude of time is possible only through limitations of one single time that underlies it. The original representation, *time,* must therefore be given as unlimited" (A32/B47–48). Since there is nothing to indicate that Kant construed the infinity of space any differently from that of time, it seems reasonable to assume that the same sense of infinity as limitlessness also applies to space. On this interpretation the argument differs somewhat from the First Edition version, but it is not incompatible with it. Whereas the First Edition emphasizes that every single given region or extent of space, no matter how large, is encompassed by a surrounding homogeneous space, the Second Edition emphasizes the fact that any given number of distinct regions, no matter how many, are encompassed by a single homogeneous space. Both, however, lead to the same result; namely, the limitlessness of this single, all-encompassing space.[25]

C. The Givenness of Space (Form of Intuition and Formal Intuition)

Although the preceding analysis of the infinity of space resolves the apparent conflict between the Transcendental Aesthetic and the Transcendental Dialectic, it also seems to raise the spectre of another and potentially more serious conflict between the Transcendental Aesthetic and the Transcendental Analytic. The heart of the problem lies in the "givenness" upon which Kant insists in the proposition "Space is represented as an infinite *given* magnitude." First, it is difficult to see how Kant can claim that space and time are given as infinite, since the recognition of their infinity would seem to require conceptual determination. For similar reasons, this claim in the Aesthetic is frequently taken to contradict the doctrine of the Axioms of Intuition that space can only be represented by means of a successive synthesis.[26] Second, the claim that space and time are given at all (quite apart from their infinity) seems to conflict with the claim at the end of the Analytic that "pure space and time are indeed something, as forms of intuition, but are not themselves objects which are intuited" (A291/B347). If they are not given as objects of intuition, in what sense can they be said to be given at all? As we shall see, this question is crucial for the understanding of Kant's overall argument for the transcendental ideality of space and time.

In order to understand this difficult notion of the "givenness" of space in Kant, it will be helpful to return to the formula *intuitus, quem sequitur conceptus.* As already indicated, this formula expresses the thought that the conceptualization of space, such as occurs in geometry, presupposes a preconceptual framework (in Kant's terms a "pure manifold"), which both guides and limits this conceptual activity. Since this framework guides and constrains our conceptual activity (not only in geometry but also in "outer experience"), it can be said to confront thought "from without" as a brute, irreducible datum. Consequently, it is necessary with respect to human cognition (and thus a priori) without being logically necessary.[27] As is so frequently the case, the basic idea was clearly articulated by Schulze, who wrote:

> If I should draw a line from one point to another, I must already have a space in which I can draw it. And if I am to be able to continue drawing it as long as I wish, without end, then this space must already be given to me as an unlimited one [*als ein uneingeschrankter*], that is, as an infinite one. Correlatively, I cannot successively generate any cylinder or body except in space, that is to say, I can only do so because this space is already given, together with its quality which allows me to suppose that points are everywhere, and which enables me to generate, without end, the three dimensions of extension.[28]

In the recent literature a similar thesis is maintained by Arthur Melnick. Concerned with the apparent contradiction between Kant's infinity claim and the main doctrines of the Analytic, Melnick writes:

> We do not perceive spatial regions (extents of objects in space) that are limitless or without bounds. Rather, we perceive space under the pre-conception (or, better, under the "*pre-intuition*") that the bounded spatial extents we do perceive are parts of a limitless or unbounded space.[29]

The expression "pre-intuition" is particularly appropriate here, because it captures perfectly Kant's point that every determinate space is represented as a part or determination of the one unbounded space. This one unbounded space can be said to be "preintuited," in the sense that it is given together with every determinate intuition as its original ground or condition. It is not, however, itself actually intuited as an object. Moreover, we can see from this that the claim that "space is represented as an infinite *given* magnitude" must be taken as a claim about the "form," or essential structure, of every determinate representation of space, not as a claim about a unique representation of this infinite space itself.

The same considerations also suffice to resolve the apparent contradiction between the Aesthetic and the Axioms of Intuition. The main point is that Kant is concerned in the latter place with the representation of determinate spaces and with the connection between such representation and the intuition of objects in them. The claim is that this representation presupposes a successive synthesis of homogeneous parts, and thus that every determinate space must be conceived of as the product of such a successive synthesis. This is equivalent to the claim that it must be conceived of as an extensive magnitude. Clearly, this is a claim about the conceptual conditions (rules) under which it is possible to represent a determinate portion of space. Equally clearly, however, such a successive synthesis presupposes the givenness of the homogeneous portions of space and, therefore, the givenness of the single, all-inclusive space of which they are parts. In fact, it can only be thought of as the successive determination of this space.[30]

Perhaps the most illuminating Kantian text on this issue is a frequently discussed footnote in the Second Edition of the Transcendental Deduction, where Kant deals explicitly with the problem of the connection between the "original," "given," and "unlimited" space and time and determinate representations of space and time. Although this note is attached to the discussion of the synthesis of apprehension, that is, the empirical synthesis which Kant contends is involved in sense perception, it is intended to explicate the claim made in the text that space and time are not only a priori forms of intuition but also themselves a priori intuitions with a manifold, or content, of their own. In an effort to explain this and the unity of space and time, Kant remarks:

> Space, represented as *object* (as we are required to do in geometry), contains more than mere form of intuition; it also contains *combination* of the manifold, given according to the form of sensibility, in an *intuitive* representation, so that the *form of intuition* gives only a manifold, the *formal intuition* gives the unity of representation. In the Aesthetic I have treated this unity as belonging merely to sensibility, simply in order to emphasize that it precedes any concept, although, as a matter of fact, it presupposes a synthesis which does not belong to the senses but through which all concepts of space and time first become possible. For since by its means (in that the understanding determines the sensibility) space and time are first *given* as intuitions, the unity of this *a priori* intuition belongs to space and time, and not to the concept of the understanding. (Cf. §24.) [B160–61]

We shall return to this note in chapter 7 in connection with the analysis of the Transcendental Deduction. For the present, our concern is merely with the contrast drawn between a 'form of intuition' and a 'formal intuition', both of which come under the generic label 'pure intuition'. This contrast reflects, at the level of pure intuition, the general distinction made in the preceding chapter between an indeterminate (unconceptualized) and a determinate (conceptualized) intuition. Kant's failure to introduce this distinction in the Transcendental Aesthetic, where he is concerned to demonstrate that the representations of space and time are pure intuitions, is the source of a good deal of the confusion and obscurity of his analysis.[31] This note, however, clearly indicates that Kant thought it important to interpret the argument of the Aesthetic in light of this distinction.

Actually, the situation is even more complex than the above account indicates. The problem is that if we apply the analysis of 'intuition' sketched in the last chapter to the case of 'pure intuition', we are forced to distinguish three senses of the term. Not only must we contrast a 'form of intuition' (indeterminate pure intuition) with a 'formal intuition' (determinate pure intuition), but we must distinguish two senses of the former term. This can be taken to mean either the form or manner (*Art*) of *intuiting,* which can be characterized as an innate capacity or disposition to intuit things in a certain way, such as spatially and temporally,[32] or the form, the essential structure, of that which is *intuited.*[33]

At first glance it might seem that the notion of a form of intuiting has no place in the present context; for it does appear absurd to suggest that a mere capacity to intuit things could itself contain a manifold. This, in turn, leads directly to Kemp Smith's view that Kant himself was fundamentally confused about the matter and tried to combine two irreconcilable views of space.[34] To a considerable extent, however, the confusion is due to Kemp Smith's rendering of *gibt* as "contains." A better translation is "gives" or, as he elsewhere translates it, "supplies."[35] Such a rendering makes it clear that Kant is not saying or implying that a mere capacity to intuit somehow itself contains a manifold, but rather that it is the ultimate source or ground of the manifold contained in the actual intuition. Presumably, by 'the manifold' here is to be understood the spaces that are given in and through the original representation of space. Kant usually characterizes it as the "pure manifold" in order to indicate its apriority and independence of sensation.

The notion of a form of the intuited, distinct from both a form of intuiting and a formal intuition, is needed in order to characterize the given, infinite, single, and all-inclusive space which contains within it the manifold of spaces. Clearly, this space, which is the main focus of Kant's analysis in the Transcendental Aesthetic, can be described neither as a mere capacity to intuit nor, since it is not itself represented as an object, as a formal intuition.[36] As the preceding analysis indicates, it must be construed as the "preintuited" framework or structure that conditions and is presupposed by the actual representation of regions or configurations of space.[37] This is what Gerd Buchdahl refers to as "indeterminate space" or "spatiality."[38] We shall see later in this chapter that it is space so construed that Kant claims to be transcendentally ideal, and that the argument for this ideality turns on the contention that such a form can be understood only as the product of a subjective manner of intuiting.

Finally, by 'formal intuition' is meant a determinate intuitive representation of certain "formal," or universal and necessary, features of objects qua intuited. The crucial point here is that, as determinate, a formal intuition is a hybrid, requiring both the form of intuition and a concept by means of which this form is determined in a certain way. A spatial formal intuition, with which the geometer is concerned, is the intuitive representation of the form or essential properties of the figure corresponding to a given geometrical concept. Such representations are the products of mathematical construction, which is itself ultimately governed by the given nature of space as the form of the intuited. In other words, this given nature, rather than merely the laws of logic, determines what is geometrically possible, that is, constructible. This, of course, is precisely why Kant contends that geometry is synthetic, though the nonempirical nature of the representation ("preintuition") of this form is the basis of his explanation of why geometry is an a priori science.

III. GEOMETRY AND INCONGRUENCE

We must now consider the relevance of the preceding claims about geometry to the overall argument for the transcendental ideality of space. As was noted at the beginning of this chapter, the so-called argument from geometry is frequently taken to be the main, indeed, the sole support for the ideality thesis. More recently, a similar claim has been made for Kant's analysis of incongruent counterparts, a topic that is not even discussed in the *Critique*. My concern in this section is to show that neither of these claims can stand up under scrutiny.[39] Fortunately, since nothing in my argument turns on the merits or defects of either Kant's views on geometry or his analysis of incongruent counterparts, it is possible to make the discussion relatively brief.

A. Geometry

The connection between geometry, construed as a body of synthetic a priori propositions, and the transcendental ideality of space is indicated in the Transcendental Exposition, and it serves as the focal point in the analysis in the *Prolegomena*. Since in the latter work Kant makes use of an explicitly analytic or regressive method, the move from the alleged "fact" of geometry to the transcendental ideality of space as its necessary condition cannot be taken as a proof of this ideality. The key text must, therefore, be the Transcendental Exposition, which is only characterized as such in the Second Edition. Kant tells us that the purpose of such an exposition is to show how a concept (representation) can function as a principle through which one can explain a body of synthetic a priori knowledge. This requires showing, first, that the knowledge in question "does really flow from the given concept," and second, "that this knowledge is possible only on the assumption of a given mode of explaining the concept" (B40). In other words, a transcendental exposition is designed to show that a given body of synthetic a priori knowledge (P) is only possible if there is a representation (Q) with certain specified properties. Q is thus a necessary condition for P, or equivalently, $P \rightarrow Q$.

This is precisely the connection which Kant proceeds to establish between geometry and the representation of space as analyzed in the Metaphysical Exposition. It is simply assumed here that "geometry is a science which determines the properties of space synthetically and yet *a priori*." The question is "What, then, must be our representation of space, in order that such knowledge of it may be possible?" (B40). It should be noted that the question concerns our *representation* of space, not space itself. Not surprisingly, Kant maintains that this representation must be both an intuition (because the knowledge is synthetic) and a priori (because the knowledge is a priori). The science of geometry is thus linked with the preceding analysis of the representation of space, without a word being said about the ideality of space itself. Then suddenly, however, Kant asserts:

> How, then, can there exist in the mind an outer intuition which precedes the objects themselves, and in which the concept of these objects can be determined *a priori?* Manifestly, not otherwise than in so far as the intuition has its seat in the subject only, as the formal character of the subject, in virtue of which, in being affected by objects, it obtains *immediate representation, that is, intuition,* of them; and only in so far, therefore, as it is merely the form of outer *sense* in general. [B41]

Here Kant does seem to affirm that space is transcendentally ideal, or at least that it is the form of outer sense. The argument, such as it is, consists of two steps. The first and previously noted step is the assertion that the a priori and intuitive character of the representation of space is a necessary condition of the possibility of geometry. The second is the claim that this a priori and intuitive character entails that space itself must be a form of outer sense or of sensibility. A similar logical structure is to be found in other texts where Kant argues from the synthetic and a priori nature of geometry to the transcendental ideality of space. In each case the move is mediated by an appeal to the a priori and intuitive character of the representation of space.[40]

Two important results follow from this. First, the transcendental ideality of space, like the a priori and intuitive character of the representation, is only a necessary and not also a sufficient condition of geometry, construed as a synthetic a priori science of space. Consequently, the denial of the latter does not entail the denial of the former. Second, the argument from geometry only moves to ideality by way of an appeal to the a priori and intuitive character of the representation of space. Consequently, if this can be established independently, then the ideality argument can proceed without any appeal to geometry. But the whole point of the Metaphysical Exposition is to show that the representation of space has just this character. It follows, therefore, that the argument for ideality can bypass completely the Transcendental Exposition or any considerations about the nature of geometry. In fact, the most that any such considerations can provide is independent support for the contention that the representation of space is a priori and intuitive. Even given this, however, it is still necessary to prove that space itself is transcendentally ideal.

B. Incongruent Counterparts

Kant means by such counterparts, objects that are completely similar to one another with respect to their intrinsic properties, but which cannot be contained within the same spatial parameters. These include both geo-metrical objects, such as spherical triangles, and physical objects, such as left and right hands. In the *Prolegomena* (§13), and again in the *Metaphysical Foundations of Natural Science,* he appeals to the "paradox" of such counterparts in support of the transcendental ideality of space.[41] Nowhere, to my knowledge, does he even suggest that there might be a comparable argument concerning time. Nevertheless, the existence of incongruent counterparts is even less capable of providing an independent proof of the ideality of space than is the argument from geometry. Indeed, scholars have often noted that at different times Kant drew different conclusions from the same phenomenon. Thus, when he first appeals to incongruent counterparts in his 1768 essay "Concerning the Ultimate Foundation of the Differentiation of Regions in Space," it is to show, presumably in support of the Newtonian position, that space is a fundamental datum of human experience, prior to and independent of things and their relations.[42] But just two years later, in the Inaugural Dissertation, he appeals to counterparts to support the claim that our knowledge of space rests on intuition, and is thus not purely conceptual.[43] Finally, in the last two texts mentioned above, he appeals to it in support of the ideality thesis. This apparently constant shift of opinion has led Bennett, for one, to assume that "Kant could not decide which if any of his doctrines about space can draw strength from the special facts about the right/left distinction."[44]

Tempting as it is, this extreme view must be rejected. There is a consistent development in Kant's use of incongruent counterparts, and this development reflects his growing awareness of the connection between Leibniz's relational theory of space and the theory of sensibility as confused perception.[45] Thus, while the appeal to incongruent counterparts is always used to refute the Leibnizian theory of space, in the Inaugural Dissertation and other later writings it is also used to show that the representation of space is intuitive rather than conceptual. But, as with the argument from geometry, the move from this to transcendental ideality still has to be made, and the phenomenon or "paradox" of incongruent counterparts does not of itself enable us to make this move. In fact, if, as seems reasonable, one acknowledges that the existence of such counterparts does not even prove that the representation of space is a priori,[46] then it is even less powerful than the argument from geometry (assuming the truth of Kant's characterization of geometry).

In order to see this more clearly, let us consider briefly the argument in its most fully developed form, which is contained in the *Prolegomena*. Kant there suggests that incongruent counterparts present a "paradox" that can be resolved only by transcendental idealism. The alleged "paradox" is that there are objects (Kant again refers to both geometrical and physical objects) which are qualitatively identical (that is, they have "complete internal agreement") and yet cannot be substituted for one another because they differ in external relations. This would indeed be a paradox for the Leibnizians, as it constitutes a counterexample to the principle of the identity of indiscernibles. It also shows that the incongruence of these counterparts can only be understood in terms of their orientation in a three-dimensional global space that is independent of these objects and their relations. This, we have seen, was Kant's original use of the argument in 1768. Moreover, given the concept-intuition distinction, it also shows that the representation of this global space in relation to which the objects are oriented is an intuition. Again, Kant had already drawn this conclusion in 1770. One would, therefore, expect Kant simply to reiterate the same points; but instead he writes:

> What is the solution? These objects are not representations of things as they are in themselves and as some mere understanding would know them, but sensuous intuitions, that is, appearances whose possibility rests upon the relation of certain things unknown in themselves to something else, namely, to our sensibility. Space is the form of the external intuition of this sensibility, and the internal determination of every space is possible only by the determination of its external relation to the whole of space, of which it is a part (in other words, by its relation to the outer sense). That is to say, the part is possible only through the whole, which is never the case with things in themselves, as objects of the mere understanding, but which may well be the case with mere appearances.[47]

To be sure, the points alluded to above are contained in this "solution." What is noteworthy, however, is how much more is also contained in it. Not only does Kant here affirm that space is the form of external intuition, but also that the objects experienced therein are appearances. Kant clearly assigns much more work to this argument than it can possibly perform. Most, if not all, of the ontological mileage comes from the equation of things as they are in themselves with things as some "mere understanding might conceive them." Since a "mere understanding" is by definition incapable of intuition, and since the argument does show that the distinction between incongruent counterparts requires an appeal to intuition, it does follow that the objects are not such as a "mere understanding might conceive them." But this really only proves that we cannot regard these objects as Leibnizian monads, and thus that we cannot construe our perception of them as an obscure conception. It is still quite a jump from this to the positive conclusion that these objects are appearances in the transcendental sense, or that the space in which they are intuited is a form of outer sense. This move might be legitimate, if there were no other alternatives. In the present case, however, there is a very obvious alternative; namely, the Newtonian theory. Not only is this theory compatible with the phenomenon of incongruent counterparts, but Kant's earliest appeal to this phenomenon was to provide support for such a theory. Consequently, incongruent counterparts can hardly provide the basis for an independent proof of the transcendental ideality of space and of the objects experienced therein.

IV. THE IDEALITY ARGUMENT

All of this suggests that Kant's real argument for the transcendental ideality of space is contained in the Conclusions from the Above Concepts, which follows immediately upon the Metaphysical and Transcendental Expositions. It is here that we find the move, such as it is, from the nature of the representation of space to the ontological status of space itself. Here Kant first draws two explicit conclusions regarding the content of this representation and then proceeds to claim that space is empirically real and transcendentally ideal. The remainder of the section is devoted to an explanation of the notion of transcendental ideality. The treatment of time has a similar logical structure. Kant does add that time, as the form of inner sense, is a formal, a priori condition of *all* appearances, since all appearances, as modifications of the mind, belong to inner sense. This will turn out to be of great significance for the argument of the Transcendental Analytic, but it is not directly relevant to our present concern. Accordingly, I shall once again concentrate on the spatial portion of Kant's analysis.

A. Kant's Conclusions

The first of these "conclusions," like the first argument for the apriority of the representation of space, is expressed in negative terms. Kant asserts: "Space does not represent any property of things in themselves, nor does it represent them in their relation to one another." Aside from the preface, this is the first reference to 'things in themselves' in the *Critique,* and the uninstructed reader is not in a position to know how to interpret it. Kant, however, does help matters somewhat when he indicates that this claim must be taken to mean that "space does not represent any determination that attaches [*haftete*] to the objects themselves, and which remains even when abstraction has been made from all the subjective conditions of intuition." This clearly indicates that 'things in themselves' is to be taken in the transcendental sense. The claim is thus that the representation of space (the a priori intuition) does not contain any properties (including relational properties) that can be predicated of things when they are considered apart from their relation to the subjective conditions of intuition. In support of this sweeping claim, Kant remarks only that "no determination, whether absolute or relative, can be intuited prior to the existence of the things to which they belong, and none, therefore, can be intuited a priori." (A26/B42). This claim itself does not receive any justification.

The second "conclusion," like the second apriority argument, is expressed in positive terms. Kant now claims that "space is nothing but [*nichts anders als*] the form of all appearances of outer sense." Although there is a brief reference to the distinction between the matter and form of appearance at the beginning of the Transcendental Aesthetic, the reader is once again not really prepared for Kant's claim. Evidently realizing this, Kant endeavors to clarify matters by remarking that "it [space] is the subjective condition of sensibility, under which alone outer intuition is possible for us" (A26 / B42). In the German text this is an explanatory clause, the function of which is to indicate what is meant by calling space the "form of all appearances of outer sense." Unfortunately, Kemp Smith confounds matters for the English reader by translating this clause as a separate sentence, thereby suggesting that Kant is making a new claim rather than explicating the previous one. Keeping this in mind, we can see that Kant's claim here is that the *content* of the representation of space, that is, what is actually represented (or, better, presented) therein, is only a subjective condition of human sensibility. The remainder of the paragraph is dedicated entirely to an account of the favorable consequences of the view for the understanding of the possibility of a priori knowledge.

Finally, on the basis of these claims about the representation of space, Kant asserts:

> It is, therefore, solely from the human standpoint that we can speak of space, of extended things, etc. If we depart from the subjective condition under which alone we can have outer intuition, namely, liability to be affected by objects, the representation of space stands for nothing whatsoever. This predicate can be ascribed to things only in so far as they appear to us, that is, only to objects of sensibility. [A26–27 / B42–43]

It is here and in the remainder of this paragraph that Kant affirms the transcendental ideality of space, as well as the compatibility of this ideality with its empirical reality. As already indicated, this is a claim about the nature of space itself, which is presumably based upon the preceding analysis of the representation. In essence, the transcendental ideality thesis is that spatial predicates are limited to "objects of sensibility," that is, appearances, or, equivalently, that these predicates are not applicable to things "when they are considered in themselves through reason, that is, without regard to the constitution of our sensibility" (A28 / B44). Correlatively, the empirical reality thesis is that these predicates are applicable to outer appearances, which is equivalent to the assertion of the "objective reality of space in respect of whatever can be presented to us outwardly as object" (A28 / B44).

The empirical reality of space can easily be seen to follow from the preceding analysis of the function within experience of the representation. As a condition of human experience, the representation is obviously applicable to objects qua experienced or, more generally, to things considered as objects of possible experience. The problem is to see how the transcendental ideality of space follows from this same analysis. Undoubtedly, it is the difficulty in finding any such argument that has led so many interpreters to assume that Kant's "real" argument is based on the synthetic a priori character of geometry. Moreover, many interpreters, who do find an argument here that is independent of an appeal to geometry, see it as resting on nothing more than the general connection between apriority and subjectivity, which is itself regarded as a basic presupposition of Kant's thought.[48] Such a line of argument, however, suffers from two fatal defects. First, it renders the whole discussion of the intuitive nature of the representation of space completely idle in the ideality argument. Second, it is incapable of explaining how the subjective origin of the representation of space can justify the claim of the transcendental ideality of space itself, that is, the nonapplicability of spatial predicates to things as they are in themselves. What is needed, then, is an argument that appeals to the intuitive as well as the a priori nature of the representation of space, and that is capable of generating this ontological result.

B. In Search of an Argument

The formulation in the *Prolegomena* contains important clues for the reconstruction of Kant's argument. After noting that the possibility of mathematics rests upon a priori intuition, Kant raises the question of the possibility of intuiting something a priori. It is significant that this problem does not arise for concepts, at least not in the same way. Kant writes: "Concepts indeed are such that we can easily form some of the *a priori*, namely, such as contain nothing but the thought of an object in general; and we need not find ourselves in an immediate relation to the object."[49] Kant's point here is that since concepts never relate immediately to objects, they can be formed independently of any experience of them. In fact, it is possible to form concepts for which no corresponding object can be given, and thus to think (although not know) things as they are in themselves. An intuition, however, since it relates immediately to its object, does not so much represent as actually present the object to the mind. It is the apparent incompatibility of this immediacy or presentational requirement with its presumed apriority that renders the notion of an a priori intuition problematic. This seems to require that an object somehow be given to the mind before it is actually experienced, which is a contradiction in terms. There is thus a need to explain how an intuition can "take place [*stattfinden*] a priori," or, as he also puts it, "how an intuition of the object can precede the object itself."[50]

This initial formulation, in particular, is highly misleading, although it is also fairly typical of Kant. He frequently speaks of intuitions or syntheses that "take place *a priori*," suggesting thereby some mysterious transcendental activity. The real problem, however, concerns the possibility, not of an activity (intuiting a priori), but of a representational content. Simply put, the problem is this: How is an intuition possible, the content of which is nonempirical, that is, not derived from an affection by an object? Kant notes that this would be impossible if the intuition represented (that is, presented) things as they are in themselves. This is merely a reiteration of the first conclusion of the *Critique*. He here goes further, however, and suggests that even an empirical intuition would be impossible on this assumption. He writes: "It is indeed even incomprehensible how the intuition of a present thing [*einer gegenwärtigen Sache*] should make me know this thing as it is in itself, as its properties cannot migrate into [*hinüber wandern*] my faculty of representation."[51] Kant's manner of expression is once again somewhat fanciful, and it seems to involve an allusion to the scholastic theory of perception (the doctrine of intentional species). Nevertheless, the point he is making here is the same point that he made in the First Edition of the *Critique* regarding the relation between transcendental realism and empirical idealism: the impossibility of explaining intuition (perception) in terms of a direct contact between the mind and the independently real (as was attempted by the scholastic theory) leads inevitably to the positing of representative entities (ideas) as the immediate objects of awareness.

Kant's present concern, however, is with a priori, not empirical, intuition; the problem is to explain how such an intuition can be possible, that is, to show what it must actually contain or present to the mind. Since the possibility that it contains or presents to the mind any properties or relations of things as they are in themselves has already been ruled out, he concludes:

> Therefore in one way only can my intuition anticipate the actuality of the object, and be a cognition *a priori,* namely: if my intuition contains nothing but the form of sensibility, antedating in my mind all the actual impressions through which I am affected by objects.[52]

This corresponds to the second conclusion in the *Critique*. It asserts that an a priori intuition is possible, if and only if it contains or presents to the mind a form of its own sensibility. This claim is perfectly general; it does not involve a specific reference to either space or time, the putative forms of human sensibility. Nevertheless, it does help to clarify the implicit argument of the *Critique,* an argument that is obscured by the order in which Kant presents his conclusions. This implicit argument consists of two steps. The first shows that an a priori intuition is possible *if* it contains or presents to the mind a form of sensibility. The second shows that such an intuition is possible *only if* it does this. Since the Metaphysical Expositions have already shown that the representations of space and time are a priori intuitions, it follows from the present argument that space and time themselves, the contents of these representations, are forms of sensibility.

The "If" Portion of the Argument. This first part of the argument makes a minimal claim and is relatively unproblematic. All that it really maintains is that, in general, an a priori intuition is possible if it contains or presents to the mind its own form of sensibility. The major issues here are the meaning of 'form of sensibility' and whether such a form is the sort of thing that can be intuited. Unfortunately, Kant's own definitions at the beginning of the Transcendental Aesthetic, where one would expect to find answers to these questions, are not very helpful. As Paton points out, Kant tends to treat 'form of appearance', 'form of intuition', 'form of sensibility', and even 'pure intuition' as if they were virtually equivalent expressions.[53] This, in turn, seems to make the contention that a pure intuition is, or has as its content, a form of sensibility almost a matter of definition. Moreover, since it is precisely the claim that space and time themselves (the contents of a pure intuition) are forms of sensibility that entails their subjectivity, this tends to reduce the whole ideality argument to a matter of definition.

In order to see that this is not really the case, it is necessary to consider some of these definitions. We begin with the expression 'form of appearances', which is in many ways the most basic. 'Appearances' must be taken here in an ontologically neutral sense, that is, as not already implying any subjectivity or ideality. Instead, it refers merely to the objects that are actually given in experience, in contrast to objects that are merely conceived. Correlatively, 'form' must be taken to mean condition, while 'matter' means that which is conditioned or determined by the form.[54] Thus, in the Second Edition, Kant defines the form of appearance as "that which so determines the manifold of appearance that it allows of being ordered in certain relations" (B34). Otherwise expressed, a form of appearance is a feature of the appearance in virtue of which its elements are viewed as ordered or related to one another in experience. The first apriority argument maintains that the representation of space functions as a form in this sense.

We have already discussed the expression 'form of intuition' and its inherent ambiguity. We saw that the expression can designate either the formal features or structure of the objects intuited or the mode or manner (*Art*) of intuiting. In the former sense it is equivalent to 'form of appearances', and, therefore, is ontologically neutral. In the latter sense, however, it involves an explicit reference to mind. It is a characteristic of mind and, more particularly, of its receptive capacity, not of things as they may be apart from their relation to mind.

Like 'form of intuition', 'form of sensibility' can be taken in two senses. Unlike those of the former expression, however, both of these senses involve a reference to mind, and thus carry with them mentalistic implications. More precisely, 'form of sensibility' can designate either a form of *sensibly intuiting,* which Kant sometimes also terms a 'form of receptivity', or a form of *objects qua sensibly intuited.* I shall henceforth refer to these as "form of sensibility$_1$," and "form of sensibility$_2$," respectively. The main point here is that, in claiming that a form of appearances or of intuited objects is a form of sensibility$_2$, one is also claiming that it is a form which pertains to these objects in virtue of the subjective constitution of the mind, that is, in virtue of its form of sensibility$_1$. This is just what the Conclusions from the Above Concepts is supposed to establish.

Given these preliminaries, we are now in a position to formulate the "if" portion of the argument more precisely. It maintains that if the content of a given intuition is a form or formal feature of objects of intuition (the *intuited*) that pertains to these objects only in virtue of the constitution of the mind (its form of *intuiting*), then that intuition must be a priori. This is because, first, the content of such an intuition would be universal and necessary (at least for all subjects equipped with the same form of intuiting), and second, its source would not lie in the objects themselves, nor in any sensible data (sensations) produced by the affection of the mind by these objects. For the second reason it would also be "pure," that is, independent of sensation. This claim is, of course, completely general, applying to pure intuition in general, without any specific reference to Kant's analysis of the representation of space. Nevertheless, it does, I think, establish the minimal result that we can account for the possibility of an a priori intuition of space, if we assume that it is (or contains) a form of sensibility$_2$.

The "Only If" Portion of the Argument. Given the minimal nature of the result established in the "if" portion of the argument, it is apparent that most of the work must be assigned to the "only if" portion. As this characterization indicates, this is an argument by elimination; and, once again, the two alternatives to the Kantian view are the Leibnizian and Newtonian positions. This, of course, immediately suggests the possibility of other radically different alternatives, which are completely neglected by the Kantian formulation. I believe that this problem can be dealt with adequately by construing these alternatives broadly to encompass all relational and absolutistic (in the sense of nonrelational) concepts of space respectively. Even granting this, however, we are still left with the question of whether the Newtonian conception of space (broadly construed) is in fact ruled out by the argument of the Metaphysical Exposition. Clearly, if this argument establishes anything at all, it is the inadequacy of the Leibnizian (relational) conception; but its relevance to the Newtonian conception is another matter. Paton, for one, suggests that this argument is pefectly compatible with the Newtonian conception and that Kant's real critique of this conception rests on other, strictly metaphysical grounds, such as the inconceivability of space and time as "real things." Thus Paton indicates the limitations of Kant's argument in the Metaphysical Expositions with a query:

> Granting that by means of our pure intuitions of space and time we can know *a priori* the conditions, or forms, of all appearances, why should not space and time be real things which are at the same time conditions, or forms, of things, not only as they appear to us, but as they are in themselves?[55]

As formulated, this question is ambiguous. In fact, it encompasses two questions: (1) Why can't space and time be conditions or forms of *both* appearances *and* things as they are in themselves (assuming the transcendental distinction between things as they appear and the same things as they are in themselves)? and (2) Why can't space and time be "real things" (in the transcendental sense) and conditions or forms of the experience of "real things" *rather than* of "mere appearances"? Both questions are perfectly appropriate, but only the second, which reflects the Newtonian position, need concern us here, because only it challenges directly the contention that space is a form of human sensibility. The first, which is the topic of the next section, assumes that space (the content of the a priori intuition) is such a form and asks why this precludes the possibility that things in themselves are also spatial or in space.

Admittedly, the arguments discussed so far (for the apriority and intuitive nature of the representation of space) are mainly of an anti-Leibnizian nature. Nevertheless, it must be realized that to limit them in this way is to abandon any hope of finding a "direct proof" of transcendental idealism in the Transcendental Aesthetic. This, as we have seen, requires demonstrating that it is *only if* we take space and time to be forms of human sensibility that we can account for the salient features of our representations of space and time; namely, that they are a priori intuitions. But, if the accounts in the Metaphysical Expositions are, indeed, compatible with the Newtonian view (broadly construed), then Kant's Conclusions simply do not follow from his premises, no matter how cogent these premises themselves may be.

In spite of Paton's doubts, it is at least clear that Kant himself took the account of the representation of space as a pure intuition to rule out the Newtonian as well as the Leibnizian view. Thus in his first Conclusion in the *Critique,* he contends specifically that "space does not represent any property of things in themselves," which amounts to an explicit rejection of the Newtonian position as he construes it. Again, in the previously discussed passage from the *Prolegomena,* Kant denies the possibility of an a priori intuition of something existing in itself. Although Newton is not mentioned here by name, the clear implication is that his theory cannot account for the presumed "fact" that our representation of space is both intuitive and a priori. Finally, in "On the Progress of Metaphysics," Kant repeats the argument from the conditions of the possibility of an a priori intuition and contends that such an intuition would not be possible if it concerns the form of an object as it is in itself.[56]

It is, however, one thing to show that Kant held such a view and quite another to show that he was entitled to do so. Moreover, here we must deal with the fact that much of the Metaphysical Exposition does seem to be perfectly compatible with the Newtonian theory. For example, both the conception of space as a "condition" of objects and the claim that we can conceive of space as empty of objects but cannot "think away" space appear to be points which the Newtonian could readily acknowledge. Clearly, both are compatible with the assumption that space is a "real thing" and a condition of things in themselves (an ontological condition). It should also not be forgotten at this point that in 1768 Kant appealed to the phenomenon of incongruent counterparts in support of the Newtonian theory, though he later used the same phenomenon to show that the representation of space is an a priori intuition. This certainly suggests that the epistemological status that Kant assigns to the representation of space is compatible with the ontological status that Newton assigns to space itself.

As a first step in the resolution of this difficulty, which threatens to undermine the overall argument of the Transcendental Aesthetic, it is important to remember that the real issue raised by the Metaphysical Exposition concerns the function of space as a form or condition of human experience. Given this reminder, we can distinguish between two questions: (1) Does a particular theory of space hold that space functions in this way? and (2) Is this theory capable of accounting for the possibility of space functioning in this way? These are, as it were, two tests for any theory of space suggested by the argument of the Metaphysical Exposition. Now, although nowhere to my knowledge does Kant make this explicit, I take his position to be that the Leibnizian theory fails both tests, while the Newtonian theory fails only the second. If correct, this explains why Kant can derive anti-Newtonian conclusions from the Metaphysical Exposition, in spite of the facts that the bulk of the argument is directed against the Leibnizian theory and that portions of it (taken out of context) seem to be perfectly compatible with the Newtonian theory.[57]

The question, then, is why the Newtonian theory is incapable of accounting for the possibility that space (or, better, the representation of space) functions as a form or condition of human experience. In terms of the language introduced in this study, this is equivalent to the question, Why is regarding space as an ontological condition incompatible with also regarding it as an epistemic condition? Once again, we must appeal to an argument by elimination. Since the Kantian claim that space is a form of sensibility is ruled out *ex hypothesi*, two obvious alternatives remain: (1) We have an innate idea of space, and between this idea and space itself there exists a kind of "preestablished harmony"; and (2) Our idea of space is derived from the experience of these "real things" and represents a property and condition of them.

Admittedly, Kant does not take the first alternative very seriously (and for good reason), but he does not neglect it completely. In fact, in the Second Edition of the Transcendental Deduction he explicitly considers such a possibility in the case of the categories, characterizing the position as "a kind of preformation system of pure reason." Apart from its completely ad hoc nature and its reliance upon dogmatic metaphysical assumptions concerning, for example, the goodness of God, the basic problem with this hypothesis is that it fails to account for the necessity that is to be explained.[58] I think it obvious that precisely the same considerations apply in the case of space.

The second alternative, which Kant does take seriously, does not fare much better. The problem here is that, by assuming that the representation of space is somehow derived from our experience of things as they are in themselves, this formulation denies the possibility that space can function as a condition of the possibility of the experience of such things. As was already suggested in chapter 2, there is a contradiction involved in the assumption that the representation of something that is supposed to function as a condition of the possibility of the experience of objects can have its source in the experience of these objects. This is contradictory because it entails that experience be possible apart from something that is stipulated to be a condition of its possibility.

It might seem that there is another, far more reasonable, alternative: that we have a direct acquaintance with space itself, and that this enables it to serve as a "condition" of experience in the sense that it provides a fixed framework with respect to which we can orient ourselves and distinguish between the real and apparent (relative and absolute) motion of bodies. We have already seen, however, that Kant explicitly denies that space (and the same holds for time)[59] is ever given to us as such an object. The Newtonian theory likewise denies this, although it does insist upon assigning to absolute space the abovementioned epistemic function. The problem, however, is that in order to give such a function to space (conceived as something real in the transcendental sense) this theory is forced to regard space as a kind of quasi object after all. This is the point of Kant's previously cited claim that "the mathematical students of nature," that is, the Newtonians, "have to admit two eternal and infinite self-subsistent [für sich bestehende] non-entities [Undinge] (space and time), which are there (yet without there being anything real) only in order to contain in themselves all that is real" (A39/B56). The metaphysical absurdities involved in the conception of absolute space and time are the direct consequences of this "admission," which the Newtonians cannot avoid because of their transcendentally realistic assumptions.[60]

It is noteworthy that this anti-Newtonian argument, like the anti-Leibnizian arguments discussed previously, involves neither an appeal to a psychological, genetic conception of the a priori nor any assumption about the synthetic a priori character of geometry. On the contrary, it turns entirely on the epistemic function within human experience of the representation of space, a function that is supposedly established in the Metaphysical Exposition. Since it is really this function that Kant has in mind when he claims that the representation of space is a priori intuition, this suggests that Kant's question, How is an intuition possible a priori? ought to be replaced by the question, How can the representation of space (or time) play the foundational role in human experience that is claimed for it in the Metaphysical Exposition? Not only is this actually the question that Kant is asking, but, when the issue is posed in this way, the argument from the nature of the representation of space becomes much more plausible than it first appears. Clearly, the representation can function in this way if space (the content of the representation) is a form of human sensibility; and having ruled out the Leibnizian and Newtonian alternatives (broadly construed) it is difficult to see on what other basis this could be understood. In the last analysis then, everything turns on Kant's claim that the representation of space functions as a form or condition of human experience.

C. Space and Things in Themselves
(The Problem of the Neglected Alternative)

Although Kant himself infers the transcendental ideality of space directly from his conclusion that space is a form of human sensibility, it is frequently maintained that this conclusion, even if it be granted, does not suffice to prove that space is transcendentally ideal, that is, that it does not pertain to things as they are in themselves. After all, might it not be the case both that space is such a form and that things as they are in themselves are spatial or in space? Indeed, how can Kant deny such a possibility without contradicting his cherished critical principle that things as they are in themselves are unknowable? Surely to know that things, so considered, are not spatial (or temporal) is to know a good deal about them. These seem like perfectly good questions to raise at this point in the argument, and the belief that Kant has no ready answer to them underlies the famous neglected alternative objection, which, in its various forms, can be traced back to Kant's contemporaries. Fortunately, there is no need here to survey these forms or the history of the controversy surrounding them,[61] for the gist of the objection is succinctly expressed by Kemp Smith.

> Kant recognizes only two alternatives, either space as objective is known *a posteriori,* or being an *a priori* representation it is subjective in origin. There exists a third alternative, namely that although our representation of space is

subjective in origin, space is itself an inherent property of things in themselves.[62]

One of the standard strategies for dealing with this objection is to admit that the alternative is left open or neglected by the Transcendental Aesthetic, but to claim that it is removed by the resolution of the Antinomies.[63] Such a move is certainly compatible with the interpretation of the Antinomies offered here, and it is attractive as a last resort. Nevertheless, it is worthwhile considering whether the argument of the Transcendental Aesthetic itself can be saved. This would require showing that Kant's conclusion regarding the inapplicability of spatial and/or temporal predicates to things as they are in themselves does not involve a neglect of the alleged third alternative.

An interesting attempt in this direction was undertaken by Karl Reinhold.[64] Rather than discussing space and time specifically, Reinhold argues directly from the notion of a form of representation. His key claim is that the form of a representation is precisely what distinguishes it from everything else, that is, what makes it into a representation. He concludes from this that, unless one assumes that by 'a thing as it is in itself' is meant simply a representation, which the proponents of the neglected alternative objection would hardly be willing to acknowledge, one must deny that a form of representation can pertain to a thing as it is in itself. Admittedly, this argument as it stands will not do. As Reinhold's contemporaries already recognized, and as Vaihinger reiterates, it involves a petitio principii.[65] The presumably neglected alternative is not that a form of representation (sensibility) is also a form of things as they are in themselves (as if the two forms could be numerically identical), but rather that there is something in the things as they are in themselves corresponding to this form of representation. Whether this correspondence is understood in terms of qualitative identity or similarity is here irrelevant.

Although technically correct, this criticism nevertheless ignores an essential aspect of Reinhold's analysis: the suggestion, never really developed by Reinhold, that Kant's argument moves from the notion of a form of sensibility to transcendental ideality, and not simply, as critics tend to assume, from the apriority of a representation to its subjectivity. When properly developed, this suggestion puts Kant's argument in a completely different light and makes it clear that he did not neglect the third alternative.

Since Reinhold's chosen expression, 'form of representation', has precisely the same logic as Kant's 'form of sensibility', the significance of his suggestion can be gleaned from our previous consideration of the latter expression. Thus, a 'form of representation' can designate either a form (mode or manner) of representing or a form of what is represented. The second sense of the term is obviously the one that is at issue in the present argument. The key point, however, is that such a form, like Kant's form of sensibility$_2$, pertains only to what is represented in virtue of a specific mode or manner of representing. A reference to mind and its capacities is, therefore, built into the very notion of such a form, just as a reference to a sensibly affected or receptive mind is built into the Kantian conception. It follows from this that if space is such a form, then neither it nor any properties thereof can be meaningfully predicated of objects, when these objects are considered in abstraction from their representation by a mind endowed with that manner of representing. It is conceded, however, by the proponents of the neglected alternative objection that space is such a form. Consequently, it likewise follows from the above that spatial predicates cannot be applied to things as they are in themselves.

Still, it might be objected at this point that this does not suffice to eliminate the neglected alternative. One might argue that this alternative assumes a space pertaining to things as they are in themselves that is qualitatively identical or similar to the space that is represented in virtue of our peculiar mode or manner of representing. The preceding line of argument, however, has succeeded only in showing that one cannot speak of a numerical identity between space characterized as a form of sensibility$_2$ and space viewed as pertaining to things as they are in themselves.[66] Indeed, this was precisely the problem with Reinhold's original argument; hence, the above "improvement" has not really changed matters at all.

Against this it must be maintained first that the preceding analysis does demonstrate the meaninglessness of talking about a qualitative identity. It does so because it shows that the presumed identity would be between a property that only pertains to things in virtue of their being represented in a particular way and one that pertains to things as they are independently of being represented at all. Mind dependence is thus a defining characteristic of the former, and mind independence of the latter. Speaking of a qualitative identity here is like speaking of such an identity between a sensation and something that is exactly like a sensation, except for the fact that it cannot be sensed. Moreover, essentially the same considerations apply if one speaks of a similarity or analogy rather than a qualitative identity between the space of sensibility and the presumed space of things in themselves. Once again, one would be speaking of a similarity or analogy between something that involves an essential reference to mind and something that, *ex hypothesi,* is totally independent of mind. If such a notion escapes the charge of being self-contradictory, it is only at the cost of its utter vacuity.

In order to clarify this point, let us consider briefly the notorious colored spectacle analogy, which is frequently used to interpret Kant's claim that space is a form of human sensibility, and which itself strongly suggests the neglected alternative objection. According to this all too common interpretation, Kant's claim that space and time are forms of human sensibility is taken to mean that the mind somehow imposes a spatiotemporal form on experience in much the same manner as colored spectacles impose their own color on whatever is perceived through them (with the major difference being that the forms of sensibility cannot be removed). Given such an interpretation of Kant's claim, the neglected alternative objection makes perfect sense. Körner explains:

> It is always logically possible that what we perceive under the form of space and time is so ordered independently of our perception. It is quite possible that what a person sees through his irremovable spectacles as, let us say, pink, is also pink in fact, and would be seen so even if *per impossibile* the spectacles were removed.[67]

The problem with this argument is simply that it works for colored spectacles but not for the Kantian forms of sensibility. Leaving aside any consideration of the subjectivity of colors, which is certainly not relevant to the analogy, the main point is that color is a property that can perfectly well belong either to the glasses or the objects perceived through them. By contrast, a Kantian form of sensibility is, as we have seen, a form that only pertains to objects in virtue of our peculiar mode or manner of representing them. One can, of course, still quarrel with the claim that space and time are such forms, although I have tried to show that arguments in support of this claim are much stronger than is generally assumed. What one cannot do, however, is claim that it is possible both for space to be such a form and for things as they are in themselves to be spatial. Thus, given his conclusion that space is a form of human sensibility, Kant is entitled to infer that it is transcendentally ideal.

We thus conclude that it is possible to construct an argument for the transcendental ideality of space and time on the basis of materials provided in the Transcendental Aesthetic. Moreover, this argument is independent of any assumptions about the nature of mathematics. It rests rather upon the results of Kant's analysis of the representations of space and time in the Metaphysical Expositions, and it consists of two parts. The first part, which itself involves two steps, demonstrates that the content of these representations must be forms of human sensibility, that is, products of our peculiar mode or manner of representing. The second part spells out the ontological implications of this result. It shows that, as products of our peculiar mode or manner of representing the data given to the mind in intuition, neither spatial nor temporal properties can be meaningfully assigned to things as they are in themselves. This, as we have seen, is equivalent to demonstrating that space and time are transcendentally ideal. The ideality thesis is therefore really a consequence of Kant's claim that space and time are epistemic conditions.

6

The Intellectual Conditions of Human Knowledge

By the "intellectual conditions of human knowledge" I mean the pure concepts of the understanding. Following Aristotle, Kant also terms these concepts 'categories'. The demonstration of the objective reality of these categories is the explicit task of the Transcendental Deduction. Before this can be undertaken, however, it is first necessary to show that there are such concepts and to identify them. This is the function of the section of the *Critique* called the Clue to the Discovery of all Pure Concepts of the Understanding. In the Second Edition of the *Critique* Kant entitles this section the Metaphysical Deduction, and he claims that in it "the *a priori* origin of the categories has been proved through their complete agreement with the general logical functions of thought" (B159).

This description of the matter, however, is somewhat misleading. It suggests that the Metaphysical Deduction presupposes that there are certain concepts that possess categorial status, and that its task is merely to show that these concepts are of a priori rather than empirical origin. In other words, it suggests a parallel with the Metaphysical Expositions of space and time in the Transcendental Aesthetic, which take these "concepts" as the initial data to be analyzed and argue that they must be both a priori and intuitive. In reality, however, the data of the Metaphysical Deduction are not concepts but the forms of judgment derived from general logic. The forms are claimed to provide the "clue to the discovery of the pure concepts of the understanding." The actual argument thus moves to these concepts rather than from them. Its explicit concern is to catalogue them on a systematic basis by deriving them from a single principle; namely, the nature of judgment. Kant contends that this derivation makes it possible not only to guarantee the completeness of the catalogue, but also to explain "why just these concepts, and no others, have their seat in the pure understanding" (A81/B107). By so doing, Kant also claims to have made a major advance upon Aristotle.

But even this does not give us a fully accurate picture of what the Metaphysical Deduction is about, for it implies that Kant is concerned merely with the subsidiary question of how to guarantee the completeness of a list of pure concepts, and that he thus ignores the more fundamental question of whether there can be any such concepts at all. Admittedly, Kant does not raise the latter question in an explicit fashion, as he frequently does with respect to the complementary notion of pure intuition. Nevertheless, I do not think that Kant completely neglects it. In fact, I contend that the real, albeit mainly implicit, starting point of the Metaphysical Deduction is the thesis that a set of pure concepts must be presupposed as necessary conditions of judgment. As such, these concepts can be regarded as the intellectual conditions of human knowledge. After sketching this thesis in the first part of the chapter, I turn in the second to a consideration of the explicit argument of the Metaphysical Deduction.

I. PURE CONCEPTS OF THE UNDERSTANDING

In the case of concepts, unlike that of intuitions, 'pure' cannot be equated with 'a priori'. This is because it follows from Kant's theory of sensibility that there are a priori concepts that express formal conditions of intuition. These are the very concepts with which the mathematician is concerned and which he constructs in pure intuition. Kant, on occasion, terms these "pure sensible concepts," where 'pure' does mean 'a priori'.[1] Strictly speaking, however, the expression 'pure concept' for Kant is a shortened version of 'pure concept of the understanding'. Pure concepts can, therefore, be characterized as concepts that have their origin ("seat") in the nature of human understanding or, equivalently, as those that express a fundamental law or function of the understanding.

It follows from Kant's theory of judgment that there must be some concepts that are pure in this sense. Two essential features of this theory are here relevant. The first is the role assigned to judgment as the fundamental act of thought. So construed, the function of judgment is not limited to the combination of given representations (concepts and other judgments); it is also required to provide determinate representations in the first place. Consequently, even empirical concepts, which for the empiricist are derived directly from experience by abstraction, are viewed by Kant as products of a judgmental activity (synthesis). The second relevant feature is the role of concepts in judgment. As we have seen, every act of judgment is also an act of conceptualization and vice versa. The unification of representations in a judgment, which provides a determinate content for thought, occurs by bringing these representations under a concept. Every judgment thus necessarily makes use of some pregiven concept (or concepts). Of course, it does not follow from the fact that every judgment presupposes some concept or other that there are some concepts that are presupposed by every judgment. It might be the case that a concept applied (and thus presupposed) in a judgment is itself the product of an antecedent judgment. For example, the judgment "Socrates is a man" obviously presupposes the concept *man,* which it predicates of the individual Socrates. This concept, however, is itself the product of a prior judgment in which the real definition of 'man' is determined.[2] Nevertheless, it is clear that this process cannot be continued indefinitely. For one thing, we soon arrive at certain very general concepts, such as entity, property, individual, class, and totality, that cannot themselves be regarded as products of prior judgments; for another, these very general concepts can be shown to be necessarily involved in all judgments as conditions of the very possibility of the activity. Although we become explicitly aware of such concepts only by a reflection on the nature of judgment, we become aware of them *as presuppositions* of this activity. Such concepts are the pure concepts of the understanding; they are second-order concepts or rules for the generation of rules.[3] Given Kant's theory of judgment, there must be some such second-order concepts if there are to be any concepts at all.

This general line of argument, which I take to be implicit in the Metaphysical Deduction, not only proves that there must be some pure concepts, but also indicates where we should go to look for them; namely, the nature of judgment. Kant's own procedure involves an appeal to the notorious table of the forms of judgment, which he claims to have borrowed from general logic. Some of the issues regarding the adequacy and the origin of the table will be discussed in the next section. For the present, our concern is solely with the idea of a possible correlation or agreement between a judgmental form and a pure concept.

The first task obviously is to determine what Kant means by 'forms of judgment'. This can easily be accomplished if we keep in mind that Kant characterizes judgments as "functions of unity among our representations." The forms of judgment are thus the various ways in which the unity is possible, irrespective of the nature of the content that is unified. In other words, they are the modes through which the general function of judgment (unification of representations) can be exercised. For example, this function can be exercised through affirmation or negation,[4] with respect to an individual, a whole class, or some members of the class. In addition, the items unified can be related in a categorical, hypothetical, or disjunctive manner. Finally, the unification can be taken problematically, assertorically, or apodictically. Kant also terms these individual forms "logical functions" or "moments of thought."[5] If we follow Kant in grouping them under the headings "Quantity," "Quality," "Relation," and "Modality," then we can say that each of these headings contains a set of logical functions and that at least one from each set must be exercised in every judgment.[6]

By specifying these logical functions, we arrive at a set of concepts that relate directly to the activity of judgment. It would also seem, however, that they are purely syntactical or formal. In Melnick's terms, they are "concepts of judgment forms rather than concepts of the objects judged about."[7] Moreover, if such concepts are regarded as rules, then they are more properly described as rules for the classification of judgments than as rules for judging itself. In short, they do not seem to be the pure concepts that we are seeking. As we have already seen, these must be rules that are presupposed by, and necessarily involved in, the activity of judging. More important, since Kant himself describes these concepts as "concepts of object in general," it is clear that they cannot be merely syntactical rules.

In order to see how this table of logical functions might be capable of yielding a set of pure concepts, it is necessary to recall some of the specifics of the Kantian theory of judgment. Once again, the crucial point is the connection between judgment and conceptualization. Since every judgment is at the same time an act of conceptualization, it seems plausible to assume that each of the various forms or functions of judgment involves its own peculiar mode of conceptualizing given representations. In other words, to judge under a specific form is to conceptualize given representations in a determinate manner. Consequently, the ability to conceptualize in that way or, equivalently, the possession of the appropriate concept, is a necessary condition of the possibility of judging under a certain form.[8]

Another important aspect of Kant's theory of judgment is the claim that every judgment involves the relation of given representations to an object, that is, the thought of the objective validity of the synthesis. It follows from this that the concept that is presupposed is one through which this objective validity is thought. In Kantian terms, it is a "concept of an object in general." Such a concept is a rule under which an object must be thought, if it is to be determined by means of a judgment of a certain form. A rule of this sort is a pure concept of the understanding or a category.

The point can be clarified by considering the pure concepts of substance and causality (ground and consequent) and their connections with the categorical and hypothetical forms of judgment; but first a reminder and a warning are in order. The reminder concerns the intimate connections among Kant's transcendental idealism, his analysis of judgment, and his view of concepts as rules. We have already seen in Part 1 of this study that the sense of 'object' for Kant is always to be explicated in terms of the conditions of the representation of an object, and that this involves an essential reference to judgment (and, therefore, to mind). An object in the broadest sense is the correlate of a judgmental act. The pure concepts are the categorial rules through which objects of any ontological type must be conceptualized by a discursive intelligence. They are, in short, rules for the "pure thought of an object." Experience itself for Kant consists of judgment (not the mere reception of sensible data). An object of possible experience is thus the correlate of a certain kind of judgment (a "judgment of experience"). Such judgments make use of the pure concepts, but they also presuppose the sensible conditions (schemata) under which objects corresponding to these concepts can be given in experience.

The warning is closely related to the above reminder. It is simply that we are presently concerned only with the pure and not with the so-called "schematized" categories. In other words, our immediate concern is with the pure concepts themselves in their capacity as judgmental rules, not with the sensible conditions under which these concepts can be applied concretely to objects of possible experience. Although it is a central thesis of the Transcendental Analytic that it is only by means of their connection with these sensible conditions (schemata) that the categories can yield knowledge of "real" objects (objects of possible experience) in synthetic judgments, Kant is also committed to the doctrine that they have a purely intellectual function as conditions of judgment.[9] Indeed, it is in virtue of this function that they are called "pure concepts of the understanding."

Let us now turn to the pure concept of substance and its presumed connection with the categorical function of judgment. Paton underscores this condition by describing it as "the *concept* of the synthesis of subject and predicate."[10] Kant himself, however, defines it in two ways, both of which, like all the definitions of pure concepts, must be considered merely nominal.[11] On the one hand, it is defined as the relation of subsistence and inherence;[12] on the other, as the concept of something that can be conceived only as subject, and never as predicate of something else.[13] The first can be regarded as the official definition, since it is found in the table of categories, but the second corresponds much more closely to the way in which Kant actually construes the concepts. Accordingly, I shall here adopt the second definition. The problem, then, is to determine the connection between the categorical form or function of judgment and the concept of something that must be conceived in this manner.

Some hint of the connection can be derived from what has just been said. In illustrating the general point about the connection between a particular judgment form and a pure concept, I suggested that the exercise of the categorical function requires the concept of a subject to which properties can be attached and, therefore, the capacity to distinguish between a subject and its properties. Correlatively, the object of a categorical judgment is always conceived as a subject or bearer of properties. For example, in the categorical judgment 'Socrates is mortal', I conceive of the subject (Socrates) as the owner of a property (mortality). Moreover, in so doing I necessarily distinguish between the subject and its property. Unless I could do this, I could not form the judgment.

So far there is little with which to quarrel. The whole difficulty with the analysis stems from the fact that the concept of a subject or bearer of properties does not seem to be equivalent to the pure concept of substance as it has been characterized above. The latter is not merely the concept of something that *can* serve as the bearer of properties, but rather of something that *must* always be conceived in that capacity, that is, something that must always be taken substantively. It is, however, by no means obvious that this concept is required in order to judge categorically. After all, we can make perfectly good categorical judgments about properties and abstract objects, as well as about persons or things (normal substance candidates). To cite Jonathan Bennett's example, we can say 'His amiability cloys'.[14] In making this judgment, we are certainly not assuming that 'amiability' refers to some (real) subject that can never be predicated of anything else. To claim otherwise is to hold that we cannot coherently use this term to refer to a property, which is absurd.

The response to this common line of objection requires a distinction between the manner in which a subject is thought within a given judgment and the manner in which something is thought as an object "in itself," independently of any particular judgment. The pure concept of substance is a rule for the conceptualization of the content of a categorical judgment. It expresses the necessity of conceiving the subject of such a judgment (the object judged about) as a bearer of properties (predicates) and, therefore, as not itself a property of something else. This amounts to the claim that, in order to judge categorically, it is necessary to consider the subject as if it were a substance, not, to be sure, in the full-blown ontological sense, but in the sense that within the judgment it must be taken substantively. The rule "never a predicate of anything else" thus applies within a given judgment. The ontological concept of substance arises from the endeavor to think of some entity that must be conceived in this way in every judgmental context. In short, the ontological concept can be regarded as the product of a hypostatization of the judgmental concept. The fact that the unschematized and hypostatized ontological concept does not have any application to an object has no bearing on the essential function within judgment of the pure concept.

Good evidence for this interpretation is provided by the First Edition version of the First Paralogism. Kant's target here is the rational psychologist who argues for the substantiality of the soul as a thinking being. The argument under attack is a syllogism, the major premise of which is the nominal definition of substance: "That, the representation of which is the *absolute subject* of our judgments and cannot therefore be employed as determination of another thing, is *substance"* (A348). The minor premise, which need not concern us here, states that the I, as object of thought, must always conceive itself in this way. From this the rational psychologist concludes that the I, as thinking being or soul, is a substance. In commenting on this reasoning, Kant remarks, "I can say of any and every thing that it is substance, in the sense that I distinguish it from mere predicates and determinations of things" (A393). His point, of course, is that anything can be made to serve as the logical subject of a judgment and thus can be conceived substantivally; but this hardly justifies the assumption that this subject is a substance in the ontological sense. Presumably, the mistake of the rational psychologist, with which we shall deal in chapter 13, stems from the fact that he does not recognize this. For present purposes, however, the key point is that this analysis implies that we necessarily regard the logical subject of a judgment as if it were a substance, in the sense that we "distinguish it from mere predicates and determinations of things." Unless this were the case, it is hard to see how either the ontological concept of substance or this particular fallacy of the rational psychologist could ever arise.

The question of the relationship between the hypothetical form of judgment and the pure concept of causality (the relation of ground and consequent) can be dealt with more succinctly. It is first necessary to note, however, that this form cannot be construed in truth-functional terms as the material conditional.[15] To judge hypothetically, in the sense in which such judgment is relevant to Kant's argument, is to assert a connection between two states of affairs, such that the assumption of the existence of one of them justifies the inference to the existence of the other. Each of these states of affairs, taken individually, is viewed as merely problematic; the judgment asserts only the connection between the two of them. Kant expresses this by remarking that "it is only the logical sequence which is thought in the judgment" (A73 / B98). It can be seen from this that the exercise of the hypothetical function presupposes a rule for the determination of the thought of the sequence of states of affairs. Just as it is necessary in the case of the categorical judgment to determine which element in the manifold is to be thought of as the subject and which as its predicate, so it is necessary in the case of the hypothetical judgment to determine which of the states of affairs thought problematically in the judgment is to provide the basis ("inference ticket," in Ryle's sense) for the thought of the other.[16] The claim is that the concept of the relation of ground and consequent is the required rule.[17] The justification of this claim is that this concept is simply the thought of such a determinate relation of states of affairs. Consequently, to assert such a determinate relation, that is, to exercise the hypothetical function, is to relate the problematic states of affairs in accordance with this rule.

The issue can be clarified by a look at Kant's own example of a hypothetical judgment: "If there is perfect justice, the obstinately wicked will be punished" (A73 / B98). This was chosen by Kant as an example of a judgment of a hypothetical form, not as an illustration of the connection between judgments of this form and the relation of ground and consequent. Nevertheless, it will serve to illustrate the function in judgment of the pure concept. First, this judgment expresses the logical connection between the thoughts of two states of affairs, neither of which is deemed in the judgment to be actual. As such, it fits the previous characterization of the hypothetical form. Second, these two problematically conceived states of affairs are thought of as connected in such a way that the assumption of the actuality of the first provides a ground ("inference ticket") for the assumption of the actuality of the second. In short, the relation of ground and consequent links the problematic thought of a state of affairs in which there is perfect justice with the equally problematic thought of a state of affairs in which the obstinately wicked are punished.

This judgment, however, does not involve the assertion of a causal connection between the two states of affairs. The reason we assume that the obstinately wicked will be punished in a world in which there is perfect justice is not that we presuppose any causal mechanism capable of accomplishing this task, but simply that punishment for the obstinately wicked constitutes part of the concept or description of a world in which there is perfect justice (at least it constitutes part of Kant's concept of such a world). Nevertheless, the analyticity of the judgment has no bearing on the fact that the elements are thought together in terms of the relation of ground and consequent.

The moral to be drawn from this is that the claim that judgments of the hypotheticai form presuppose, or essentially involve, the concept of the relation of ground and consequent is not to be confused with the claim that they presuppose, or essentially involve, the concept of causality.[18] Like all of the pure concepts, the relation of ground and consequent is a rule for the conceptualization of the manifold of intuition in general, when the corresponding function of judgment is applied to this manifold. In other words, this concept is a rule for the unification of thoughts in a judgment of the hypothetical form, insofar as that judgment is to relate to an object, that is, insofar as it is to be a judgment at all. By contrast, the relation of cause and effect is a relation of events in human experience. Such a relation involves a reference to time, and thus to the schema of the concept of causality (rule-governed succession). No such reference is involved in the logical relation of ground and consequent.

Finally, the fact that Kant uses analytic judgments as examples is itself of significance and should not pass without notice, for it shows that the pure concepts of the understanding are viewed by Kant as conditions of analytic as well as of synthetic judgments. Indeed, the whole argument of the Metaphysical Deduction rests on this assumption, just as it rests on the correlative assumption that the logical functions, which Kant lists in his table, are the forms of all judgments.[19] We cannot view these concepts with Kemp Smith as conditions of "synthetic" or "creative," in contrast with "analytic" or "discursive," thought.[20] They are rather conditions of all human thought, for all such thought is judgmental, and they are the conditions of judgment.

II. THE METAPHYSICAL DEDUCTION "PROPER"

Given this account of Kant's implicit argument for the set of a priori or pure concepts that function as intellectual conditions of judgment, we are now in a position to examine his explicit argument. This argument, which constitutes the "official" Metaphysical Deduction, is intended to establish the agreement between the table of the logical functions of judgment (§9) and that of the pure concepts of the understanding (§10). It is imbedded in a comparison of the respective concerns of general and transcendental logic. The focal point of this comparison, which is cryptic in the extreme, is a brief characterization of the transcendental functions of the imagination and the understanding. The former is said to synthesize our representations, and the latter to "bring this synthesis to concepts" (A78/B103). This is the first discussion in the *Critique* of the transcendental functions of these faculties. It contains, however, little more than a series of bald assertions, and much of it is only intelligible in light of the subsequent treatment of this topic in the Transcendental Deduction. Accordingly, I propose to ignore these considerations for the present and to concentrate instead on the nerve of the argument which connects the pure concepts with the logical functions. This nerve is contained in the following paragraph:

> The same function which gives unity to the various representations *in a judgment* also gives unity to the mere synthesis of various representations *in an intuition;* and this unity, in its most general expression, we entitle the pure concept of the understanding. The same understanding, through the same operations by which in concepts, by means of analytical unity, it produced the logical form of a judgment, also introduces a transcendental content into its representations, by means of the synthetic unity of the manifold in intuition in general. On this account we call these representations pure concepts of the understanding, which apply *a priori* to objects—a conclusion which general logic cannot establish. [A79/B104–05][21]

Although the contrary is commonly assumed to be the case, the central claim of this paragraph is the identity of the understanding and its activity (function) as considered in general and in transcendental logic. In short, these two disciplines are concerned with one understanding, possessing a single characteristic activity, which they analyze at different levels. This activity consists in the unification or synthesis of representations, and this unification occurs in certain determinate ways which can be called 'forms' or 'functions' of unity. In fact, it is precisely because general and transcendental logic deal with the same activity at different levels that Kant thinks it possible to move from the determination of the forms or functions of the former to those of the latter.[22]

Unfortunately, much of this is obscured by the manner in which Kant formulates his own position. His juxtaposition of analytic and synthetic unity, viewed in light of the earlier contrast between analysis and synthesis, has given rise to the widely held view that Kant is here speaking of two distinct but somehow analogous or parallel activities. On this interpretation, which is fully developed by Kemp Smith, the activity studied in general logic is that of analysis, and this activity is manifested specifically in analytic judgments. In contrast, the concern of transcendental logic is with synthesis, particularly when this activity is manifested in synthetic a priori judgments. In support of this it is also pointed out that synthesis is here attributed to the imagination rather than to the understanding. Consequently, instead of a single activity (synthesis) of a single faculty (the understanding), we actually find two distinct activities (analysis and synthesis) assigned to two distinct faculties (understanding and imagination).[23]

One trouble with this doctrine is that it fails totally to explain how one could "deduce" the pure concepts of the understanding from the table of logical functions. The recognition of this has led some interpreters to what can be termed the "presupposition thesis." This thesis is usually presented as the doctrine to which Kant should have adhered, rather than as an interpretation of the actual teaching of the *Critique*. According to this thesis, there is no analogy or parallel between the logical activity of analysis and the transcendental activity of synthesis. On the contrary, their radical heterogeneity is insisted upon, and the claim is made that analysis must somehow presuppose synthesis. In support of this claim it is noted that Kant does, in fact, state that analysis presupposes synthesis.[24] Unlike the doctrine of parallel activities, the presupposition thesis does not reduce Kant's whole position to absurdity. Nevertheless, it shares with that interpretation an inability to explain how one can move from a determination of the functions of judgment to the specific categories. The vague suggestion that one is a presupposition of the other is certainly no help in this regard.

Neither of these interpretations, however, is really warranted by the text. The first sentence speaks unambiguously of the "same function" producing unity in both judgment and intuition, and the second sentence refers to the "same understanding" as well as to the "same operations" thereof. The identity of the understanding in its logical and its transcendental employment is, therefore, the basis for Kant's whole analysis. Since it has not yet been officially established that the understanding has a transcendental employment, this claim seems arbitrary in the extreme. Nevertheless, the difficulty can easily be avoided by reformulating the claim in the hypothetical mode: if the understanding has a real or transcendental employment (as is claimed in the Transcendental Deduction), then it must be the case that this employment involves the same unifying functions and activities as are found in its logical employment. This result follows logically from Kant's earlier claim that "we can reduce all acts of the understanding to judgments, and the *understanding* may therefore be represented as a *faculty of judgment*" (A69 / B94).

The starting point of the "deduction" must, therefore, be the determination of the forms of judgment, a task which Kant assigns to general logic. As already indicated, these forms must be taken to be the forms of all judgments (synthetic as well as analytic), just as the pure concepts of the understanding must be regarded as rules of conceptualization that are involved in all judgments (analytic as well as synthetic). It is, therefore, crucial not to confuse an analytic unity with an analytic judgment or to assume that one intellectual activity (analysis) is being contrasted with another (synthesis). The point is rather that both analytic and synthetic judgments involve the unification of representations in one consciousness, and that the logical functions of judgment are the forms or modes of this unification. Kant puts the matter quite precisely in "On the Progress of Metaphysics" when he writes: "The understanding shows its capacity merely in judgments, which are nothing other than the unity of consciousness in the relation of concepts in general, it being undetermined whether that unity is analytic or synthetic."[25]

In light of these general considerations, which reflect points discussed in the first section of this chapter, we can now proceed to a more detailed analysis of the text. The first point to note here is that the expression 'analytic unity' refers to the concepts that are united in judgments. Nowhere does Kant maintain that judgments themselves are analytic unities.[26] As we have already seen, concepts are analytic unities because they unite in a single representation a series of marks that pertain to a diversity of objects. In fact, it is precisely because concepts are analytic unities that they can be combined with one another in judgments whereby "much possible knowledge is collected into one." Once again, this holds true whether the judgment is analytic or synthetic. Second, by the 'logical form of a judgment', Kant means a judgment of a given logical form. Consequently, Kant's cryptic claim that the understanding "produces the logical form of a judgment," "in concepts" and "by means of analytic unity," must be taken to mean that the understanding produces a judgment of a specific logical form by combining its concepts (analytic unities) in a determinate manner. Insofar as the understanding produces judgments, or judges, it also produces the forms of judgment.[27] The table of logical functions of judgment is supposed to contain a complete specification of these forms.

Kant further contends that the "same understanding" also "introduces a transcendental content into its representations by means of the synthetic unity of the manifold in intuition in general." The expression 'transcendental content' is obscure and is subject to a variety of interpretations. Nevertheless, I believe that the most reasonable reading is to take it as referring to the just-mentioned synthetic unity of the manifold.[28] Moreover, I say this despite the fact that the text states that the transcendental content is introduced *by means of* the synthetic unity, not that it *is* this unity. Strictly speaking, a transcendental content must be an extralogical objective content, that is, one that involves relation to an object or objective reality. Thus, to introduce a transcendental content into representations is merely to relate them to an object. The key point, however, which Kant only develops in the Transcendental Deduction, is that the synthetic unity of the manifold is the form of the thought of an object in general. Consequently, insofar as the understanding produces such a synthetic unity, it also introduces a transcendental content into its representations, that is, its judgments. As we have already seen, the determination of this synthetic unity is inseparable from the act of judgment itself, although it is an aspect of this act that does not fall within the purview of general logic. This enables Kant to talk about the "same operations" or, more generally, to present a picture of the understanding as engaged in one fundamental activity (judging) which can be analyzed at two levels. Finally, the reference to "intuition in general," which is also found in the Second Edition version of the Transcendental Deduction, is intended to indicate that this general transcendental or objectifying function of the understanding is independent of the particular nature of the manifold of intuition.

If we assume that the understanding has such a transcendental or objectifying function, and that it exercises it through the same operations by means of which it judges, then it follows that the logical functions of judgment, which are the forms in accordance with which the understanding unites its concepts in judgment, will also be the forms in accordance with which it unites the manifold of intuition in order to determine an object for judgment. We are thus led to the conclusion that the pure concepts of the understanding, which introduce the requisite transcendental content, are nothing other than the logical functions of judgment, viewed in connection with the manifold of intuition. In addition to being implicit in Kant's analysis, this interpretation of the relation between the logical functions and the pure concepts makes it easy to explain what neither the parallel activity nor the presupposition thesis could account for; namely, the possibility of actually deriving the table of categories from the table of logical functions. Since they are the same forms of unification, considered from different points of view or at different levels, there is no difficulty at all in moving from one to the other.

Although such an interpretation is clearly implicit in Kant's analysis, the fact remains that he does not explicitly state the matter in quite this way in the Clue to the Discovery of all Pure Concepts of the Understanding or, indeed, anywhere in the First Edition of the *Critique*.[29] Fortunately, however, he does make precisely this claim in at least four different texts. Listed in order of composition, the first of these is the *Prolegomena,* where Kant says of the pure concepts of the understanding that "they are themselves [*an sich selbst*] nothing but logical functions, and as such do not produce the least concept of an object, but require sensuous intuition as a basis."[30] The second is in the famous footnote in the preface to the *Metaphysical Foundations of Natural Science,* where Kant asserts that the categories "are nothing but mere forms of judgment insofar as these forms are applied to intuitions (which with us are always sensible only), and that by such application our intuitions first of all obtain objects and become cognitions."[31] The third is in the Transcendental Deduction in the Second Edition of the *Critique,* where he writes: "Now the *categories* are just these functions of judgment, insofar as they are employed in the determination of the manifold of a given intuition" (B143). Finally, in "On the Progress of Metaphysics," after asserting that the pure concepts of the understanding function to determine the manifold of pure intuition, and are thus fundamental concepts of combination (synthesis), he remarks that these concepts are "just the same logical functions, but only insofar as they represent *a priori* the synthetic unity of the apperception of a manifold given in intuition in general."[32]

I have already argued that such a correlation can reasonably be claimed in the cases of the categorical function with the pure concept of substance and of the hypothetical function with the pure concept of causality (the relation of ground and consequent). I also believe, although I do not intend to argue for it here, that similar claims can be made for the correlation of most of the other logical functions with the corresponding pure concepts. The major exception would seem to be the correlation between the disjunctive function and the pure concept of community.[33] Indeed, Kant himself admits that the correlation in this case is far from obvious, and in the Second Edition he even adds an explicit defense of it.[34] Unfortunately, this defense must be deemed a failure. It consists essentially in, first, noting that in a disjunctive judgment the elements (problematic judgments) that are combined are viewed as conjointly constituting a whole (in the sense that they exhaust the possibilities), and second, affirming an analogy between this and the thought of a collection of things as constituting a whole.[35] The analogy breaks down because, in the case of a disjunctive judgment, which Kant understands only in the sense of an exclusive disjunction, the assertion of one element entails the negation of the others, while in the case of the pure concept, which involves the thought of reciprocal connection, the assertion of one element entails the assertion of the others. The only positive result that emerges from this rather contrived analysis is that both the disjunctive form and the pure concept involve the thought of a coordination of elements, which is contrasted with the thought of subordination that is involved in the hypothetical form and the pure concept of causality. This provides sufficient justification for distinguishing the pure concept of community from that of causality, but not for deriving it from the disjunctive form of judgment.

Another major difficulty with Kant's argument concerns his notorious claim regarding the completeness and systematic nature of his list of categories. We have already seen that Kant viewed his great advance upon Aristotle to consist in the fact that he had succeeded in deriving the categories from a single principle; namely, the nature of judgment. Such a derivation presumably gives the list a systematic basis and guarantees its completeness. The operative assumption is that "the functions of the understanding can . . . be discovered if we can give an exhaustive statement of the functions of unity in judgment" (A69 / B94). The functions of unity in judgment are the forms of judgment, and the functions of the understanding are the categories. If one accepts the preceding analysis and ignores the lack of fit between the disjunctive form and the pure concept of community, this claim should not cause any difficulty. Given the established connection between the logical functions and the pure concepts, a complete list of the former would *ipso facto* yield a complete list of the latter. The obvious problem concerns the completeness of the former list. Kant insists upon its completeness, but he does not offer any argument in support of this claim. In addition, it seems highly likely that the list of logical functions is not itself based solely on considerations pertaining to general or formal logic, but actually presupposes the list of categories which is supposed to be derived from it.[36]

Moreover, Kant himself does not seem to have been completely of one mind on the question of the possibility of providing a derivation or deduction of the logical functions. He usually emphasizes the unity of reason and the understanding, and with it the possibility of having insight into their operations.[37] At other times, Kant seems to limit or deny the possibility of such insight. In this context both the categories and the logical functions are regarded as brute, inexplicable givens, much as the forms of sensibility are regarded in the Transcendental Aesthetic. Kant expresses this point of view most sharply in a passage in the Second Edition of the Transcendental Deduction:

> This peculiarity of our understanding, that it can produce *a priori* unity of apperception solely by means of the categories, and only by such and so many, is as little capable of further explanation as why we have just these and no other functions of judgment, or why space and time are the only forms of our possible intuition. [B145–46][38]

If we regard this as Kant's considered opinion on the matter, as I believe we must, then the whole project of providing a derivation of the logical functions of judgment from a single principle, for example, the unity of consciousness, must be abandoned as misguided. This applies not only to the demand for such a derivation by Kant's idealistic successors, but also to the attempt by Klaus Reich actually to provide Kant with one.[39] In that case, however, it is difficult to see what sense can be given to Kant's claim to have demonstrated the completeness of the list of categories or to have shown "why just these concepts, and no others, have their seat in the pure understanding."[40] Nevertheless, Kant's failure to deliver on his more extravagant promises should not be allowed to obscure the positive achievement of his analysis of judgment. This achievement lies in having shown that the activity of judgment presupposes a set of a priori concepts which, because of their essential role in judgment, deserve categorial status.

It is also crucial, however, to be clear as to just what this achievement really amounts to. Given the overall goal of the Transcendental Analytic, it must be regarded as a necessary, albeit relatively modest, first step. The most that it shows is that the exercise of certain judgmental functions requires certain concepts. I have argued that this be taken as a perfectly general thesis that cuts across the distinction between analytic and synthetic judgments. Moreover, it must be kept in mind that the concepts referred to here are "pure" in the sense that they are derived from the very nature of the understanding and have no reference to the spatiotemporal manifold of human experience. Thus, as already indicated, the claims that the categorical judgment involves the pure concept of substance and that the hypothetical judgment involves the pure concept of causality (ground and consequent) are not to be taken to imply that judgments of these forms necessarily involve a reference to enduring physical objects or to causal connections. Finally, and most important, this analysis does not carry with it any implications regarding the objective or empirical reality of these concepts. The basic point is simply that we cannot move directly from the premise that a given concept functions as a condition of judgments of a certain logical form to the conclusion that this concept has any applicability to the data of human experience. This is to be contrasted with the situation in the Transcendental Aesthetic, where Kant did move directly, and nonproblematically, from the assertion of the function of space and time as sensible conditions of human knowledge to the assertion of their empirical reality. That is precisely why a Transcendental Deduction is necessary.

PART THREE
CATEGORIES, SCHEMATA, AND EXPERIENCE

7
Objective Validity and Objective Reality: The Transcendental Deduction of the Categories

In the preface to the First Edition of the *Critique* Kant readily acknowledges that the set of investigations contained in the Transcendental Deduction cost him more labor than any other.[1] He then proceeds to add to his labors, as well as to those of his commentators, by entirely recasting the argument in the Second Edition. Partly as a labor-saving device and partly for more philosophical reasons, I propose to focus my attention in this chapter on the Second Edition version. The First Edition Deduction will not be ignored completely, but will be used mainly to illuminate this later version of the argument. My main philosophical reason for concentrating on the Second Edition Deduction is that the argument is structured in such a way as to make it evident that the central problem is the demonstration of a connection between the intellectual and sensible conditions of human knowledge. Although I believe that this is also the central problem of the First Edition Deduction (indeed, of Kant's theoretical philosophy as a whole), this is largely obscured by the way in which he presents his argument there. Thus, by concentrating on the Second Edition we can consider the central problem in its clearest form.

A basic exegetical difficulty that is unique to the Second Edition Deduction stems from the division of the argument into two parts, each of which presumably establishes the necessity of the categories. The first part (§§15–21) asserts their necessity with respect to objects of sensible intuition in general. The claim is that any sensible content, whatever its inherent nature, must be subject to the categories if it is to be brought to the unity of consciousness, that is, if it is to be thought or conceptualized. Establishing this result is equivalent to demonstrating that the categories are the necessary rules for any discursive intelligence.[2] The second part (§§24–26) argues for the necessity of the categories with respect to human sensibility and its data. This portion of the argument thus presupposes the results of the Transcendental Aesthetic.

The problem is how one is to understand the connection between these two parts and their corresponding arguments. Are they intended as two distinct yet complementary proofs of the categories, or are they rather two steps in a single proof? Kant's statement at the end of the first part that "a beginning is made of a *deduction* of the pure concepts of the understanding" (B144) certainly suggests the latter alternative. This, however, immediately gives rise to the question, Why, if the argument of the first part is sound, is the second part necessary? If the data of *all* sensible intuition are necessarily subject to the categories, then a fortiori the data of human sensible intuition are also. It therefore seems that the only task left for the second part of the argument would be a trivial linear inference from genus (intuition in general) to species (human intuition).[3] But instead of such an inference, Kant introduces an elaborate account of the imagination and its various synthetic activities.

Most commentators who have dealt with this issue at all have attempted to interpret the division in terms of a model borrowed from the First Edition Deduction. The obvious candidates here are the distinctions between an "objective" and "subjective" deduction and between the proofs "from above" and "from below."[4] In an essay which deals with this very problem, Dieter Henrich has shown conclusively that neither of these models is applicable to the structure of the argument of the Transcendental Deduction in the Second Edition. In addition, he has formulated a criterion for the success of any interpretation of this version of the Deduction.

> The interpretation must show that, contrary to the initial impression that the two conclusions merely define the same proposition, . . . sections 20 and 26 offer two arguments with significantly different results, and that these together yield a single proof of the transcendental deduction. We shall call this task the problem of the two-steps-in-one-proof.[5]

Although I cannot fully accept Henrich's own reconstruction of the argument,[6] I believe that he has provided an important criterion for a successful interpretation: the two parts of the argument must be treated as two steps in a single proof. Taking this as a given, I shall attempt to show that the two parts of the Deduction contain two different claims about the categories and operate with two different conceptions of an object. The essence of my interpretation can be expressed in the formula that the first part of the Deduction is concerned with the objective validity (*objective Gültigkeit*) of the categories and the second part with their objective reality (*objective Realität*).

The distinction between objective validity and objective reality is not easy to draw with precision, and it is not clear that Kant himself consistently adheres to it. Nevertheless, he does distinguish between them, and it is necessary to keep this distinction in mind if one is to understand the argument of the Transcendental Deduction.[7] The notion of objective validity has already been considered in connection with the analysis of judgment. The key point is that the objective validity of a judgment is defined as its capacity to be either true or false (in contrast simply to its truth). Using the legalistic metaphor suggested by the notion of validity (*Gültigkeit*), we can also say that a judgment is objectively valid if the synthesis of representations which it contains is "grounded" or "legitimate." The objective validity of the categories is to be explained in terms of their role in judgment. Thus to say that the categories are objectively valid is to claim that they make possible, "ground," or "legitimate" an objectively valid synthesis of representations, that is, a judgment. But since it is only in and through judgments that we represent objects, the objective validity of the categories can also be said to consist in the fact that they are necessary conditions for the representation of objects.[8]

By contrast, the notion of objective reality has an ontological sense. To claim that a concept has objective reality is to claim that it refers or is applicable to an actual object. Thus a fictional concept, such as 'unicorn,' would not have objective reality, although it could very well function as a predicate in an objectively valid judgment, such as 'unicorns do not exist.' In the case of the categories, which alone concern us here, the claim of objective reality is equivalent to the claim that they have a reference or applicability to whatever objects are given to us in intuition (objects of possible experience).[9] That is why the demonstration of the objective reality (but not the objective validity) of the categories requires the establishment of their connection with the forms or conditions of human sensibility. We shall see that this connection is made in the second part of the Deduction by means of the conception of the transcendental synthesis of the imagination.

As already indicated, in the Transcendental Deduction, objective validity and objective reality are connected with different conceptions of an object. Since it is linked to judgment, objective validity goes together with a judgmental or logical conception of an object (an object in *sensu logico*).[10] This is an extremely broad sense of 'object', which encompasses anything that can serve as the subject in a judgment. The term that Kant generally uses (at least in the Deduction) for an object in this sense is *Objekt*. Correlatively, the notion of objective reality is connected with a "real" sense of object, that is, with an object in the sense of an actual entity or state of affairs (an object of possible experience). Kant's term for an object in this sense is *Gegenstand*. Invoking another formula that figures prominently in the argument of this chapter, we can say that the first part of the Deduction endeavors to establish the necessity of the categories with respect to objects in the sense of Objekt, and the second part endeavors to establish their necessity with respect to objects in the sense of Gegenstand.[11]

The claim that Kant operates with two (or more) senses of 'object' is virtually a commonplace in the literature. The point is usually made with reference to Kant's remark in the First Edition that "all representations have, as representations, their object, and can themselves in turn become objects of other representations" (A108).[12] This suggests a distinction, such as the one developed by Prauss, between "objective objects" (spatiotemporal entities and states of affairs) and "subjective objects" (representations and representative states).[13] Such a distinction is perfectly legitimate and even necessary. It corresponds to Kant's own distinction between objects of outer and inner sense. However, as a distinction between two species of Gegenstand, it does not correspond to the Objekt-Gegenstand distinction.[14] Much closer to the point is Strawson's well-known contrast between a very general conception of an object, which encompasses whatever can count as a particular instance of a general concept, and a "weighty" sense, which applies only to what can be said to exist independently of the occurrence of representative states.[15] In addition, however, to the fact that Strawson seems to equate his object in the "weighty" sense with the Kantian object of outer sense (and, therefore, with one kind of Gegenstand),[16] he also contends that the whole concern of the Deduction must be with objects in this sense. The present interpretation, by contrast, attempts to show that the judgmental or logical conception of an object (Objekt) has an essential role to play in Kant's argument.

This chapter as a whole is divided into three main sections. The first is devoted to an analysis of the first half of the Deduction. I there maintain that Kant can be said to have succeeded in establishing the necessity of the categories with respect to objects in the judgmental sense. The second is concerned with an analysis of the important contrast between the objective and the subjective unities of consciousness. I argue that a legitimate sense can be given to this distinction, one that is compatible with Kant's account of objectivity and that differs markedly from the distinction between judgments of perception and judgments of experience contained in the *Prolegomena*. I also acknowledge, however, that Kant himself did not always understand the distinction in this "legitimate" sense, and thus that there is a fundamental incoherence in his account. The third deals with the argument of the second half of the Deduction. I argue that this portion of the proof of the categories is at best only partially successful. The problem is that Kant's endeavor to connect the categories with human experience seems to have been motivated by two distinct concerns. One is to show that they necessarily apply to the sensible data of human intuition, which is enough to establish their objective reality. The other is to show that they somehow make experience possible, with experience understood as empirical knowledge of objects and an objective order distinct from perceptions and their subjective order. I argue that even under the most charitable interpretation, the Transcendental Deduction cannot be taken to have accomplished the latter task.

I. APPERCEPTION, SYNTHESIS, AND OBJECTIVITY

A. The Transcendental Unity of Apperception

Although it is preceded in the text by a general account of synthesis or combination, considered as an activity of the understanding (§15), the real starting point of the Transcendental Deduction is the principle of the transcendental unity of apperception. Kant's best-known formulation of this principle is to be found at the beginning of §16:

> It must be possible for the 'I think' to accompany all my representations; for otherwise something would be represented in me which could not be thought at all, and that is equivalent to saying that the representation would be impossible, or at least would be nothing to me. That representation which can be given prior to all thought is entitled intuition. All the manifold of intuition has, therefore, a necessary relation to the 'I think' in the same subject in which this manifold is found. [B131–32]

Kant presents this as a single principle and regards it, at least in the Second Edition, as analytic.[17] In reality, however, the apperception principle involves several distinct claims, not all of which are obviously analytic. The first, most basic, and obviously analytic claim is contained in the first sentence of the passage cited above: "It must be possible for the 'I think' to accompany all my representations." This applies to each of my representations taken individually; it asserts that in order for any of these to be anything to me, that is, to represent anything for me, it must be possible for me to be aware of it as mine. This is equivalent to the possibility of reflectively attaching the 'I think' to it. Any representation for which this is not possible is *ipso facto* not a representation for me.

Two points must be noted here. First, this principle affirms only the necessity of the possibility of attaching the 'I think', not the necessity of actually doing so. In other words, it does not affirm that I must actually perform a reflective act in order to represent (think) anything. Second, it only affirms the necessity of this possibility if the representation is to function *as a* representation, that is, to represent some object. It therefore neither affirms nor implies that this is necessary in order for the representation to be "mine" in any sense. Although Kant does not develop this theme in the *Critique,* we shall see shortly that he is perfectly willing to allow for unconscious representations which are capable of influencing our feelings and desires. Here, however, he is concerned only with the epistemological or thinking subject. Consequently, the claim that a representation is "nothing to me" means simply that I cannot represent to myself anything by it, not that it is nonexistent.[18]

By itself this does not take us very far. If the Deduction is to get off the ground, Kant must link this principle with the representation of a manifold of intuition, more precisely, with the representation of it *as a* manifold. The first step is to note that any representation of a manifold *as a manifold* is a single complex thought. In Kant's terms, it involves a "synthetic unity of representations." I regard this claim also as obviously analytic: it serves merely to clarify the formal nature of the thought of a manifold, regardless of its particular content. Consequently, it should not be confused with the claim that such a representation requires an act of synthesis.

The next step is to show that a single complex thought requires a single thinking subject. The point here is essentially the one that was noted by William James: a set of distinct thoughts of the elements of a whole can never be equivalent to the thought of the whole itself.[19] Thus, while each of the representations that collectively constitute the single complex thought could conceivably be distributed amongst a multiplicity of thinking subjects, the single complex thought itself could not be so dispersed. I take this claim to be likewise analytic. Support for this interpretation is provided in a passage in the Second Edition version of the Second Paralogism.

> That the 'I' of apperception, and therefore the 'I' in every act of thought, is one [*ein Singular*], and cannot be resolved into a plurality of subjects, and consequently signifies a logically simple subject, is something already contained in the very concept of thought, and is therefore an analytic proposition. [B407][20]

By the "concept of thought" Kant means the idea of a multiplicity of representations grasped as a unity (a single complex thought). Certainly this is an accurate characterization of discursive thought, which is the only kind of thought under consideration in the Deduction. It is this grasping of a multiplicity as a unity that requires, logically, a "logically simple subject": without such a subject we would have merely the multiplicity of elements and not the conception of their unity. But without the conception of their unity, that is, without the thought of the whole, we would not have the thought in question. In a word, the denial of the "logically simple subject" entails a denial of the identity conditions of the thought.

It only remains to connect this last result to the initial claim regarding the necessity of the possibility of reflectively attaching the 'I think' to all of my representations. This is not difficult to do; and it yields the principle of the necessary identity of apperception, which plays a central role in the overall argument of the Deduction. The point is simply this: since a single complex thought logically requires a single thinking subject, it follows (1) that it must be a numerically identical 'I think' that can be reflectively attached to each of the component representations taken individually, and (2) it must (necessarily) be possible for this thinking subject to be aware of the numerical identity of the 'I think'. The latter is a necessary condition of the possibility of a number of discrete representations being united in the thought of a single subject as its representations, and, a fortiori, of its constituting a single complex thought. In other words, if representations *A, B,* and *C* are to be thought together in a single consciousness, which is necessary if they are to constitute a single complex thought, then the I that thinks *A* must be identical to the I that thinks *B,* and so forth. In addition, if the subject is to be conscious of these representations as collectively constituting a unity, then it must also be possible for it to become conscious of its own identity as subject with respect to the thought of each of these representations. This is still analytic. As Kant puts the matter,

> it says no more than that all *my* representations in any given intuition must be subject to that condition under which alone I can ascribe them to the identical self as *my* representations, and so can comprehend them as synthetically combined in one apperception through the general expression, '*I think*'. [B138]

Finally, this analysis of Kant's apperception principle helps us to understand the connection between the unity of consciousness and the numerical identity of the 'I think', which is a central theme of Henrich's recent monograph on the Transcendental Deduction.[21] Henrich notes that, in his various formulations of the apperception principle, Kant sometimes refers to the unity of consciousness and sometimes to its numerical identity. He also points out that Kant himself distinguishes between these two conceptions, and he maintains that only the latter conception, construed as "moderate" rather than "strict" identity, ultimately provides the basis for a successful proof of the categories.[22] I do not intend to engage here in an extended polemic with Henrich. It does, however, seem worthwhile to consider the connection between the conceptions of unity and identity as they function in the above reconstruction of Kant's argument. According to this reconstruction, each of them has a role to play, albeit at different stages of the argument.

Recall that the unity or singularity of consciousness (the single thinking subject) is first introduced as the necessary correlate of a single complex thought. In other words, the unity of consciousness is correlated with the consciousness of unity (it takes one to know one). The notion of the identity of the 'I think' is then invoked in order to provide a condition that must be met by any consciousness that is unified in the appropriate manner. As already indicated, the claim is that if consciousness is to be unified in such a way as to allow for the possibility of a single complex thought, then it must (necessarily) be possible for the subject of that thought to be conscious of its numerical identity with respect to the representation of each of the elements that enters into that thought.

The point at issue can be clarified by a brief consideration of a passage from the First Edition which contains a perplexing ambiguity.

> We are conscious *a priori* of the complete identity of the self in respect of all representations which can ever belong to our knowledge, as being a necessary condition of the possibility of all representations. For in me they can represent something only in so far as they belong with all others to one consciousness, and therefore must be at least capable of being so connected. [A116]

The ambiguity concerns just what it is that we are supposed to be conscious of a priori. Indeed, there would seem to be a prior question concerning what it can mean to be "conscious *a priori*" at all. I believe, however, that this must be taken merely as Kant's rather clumsy way of referring to the awareness of something as necessarily the case. The problem, then, is to determine what it is that we are aware of in this manner. There seem to be two possibilities. The first, suggested by the initial reference to consciousness, is that we are aware of our numerical identity. So construed, the argument posits a kind of Cartesian consciousness of our numerical identity as a necessary condition of knowledge. Such a consciousness is precisely what Henrich regards as the fundamental premise of the Transcendental Deduction.[23] The second possible reading, which I regard as the more plausible one, is suggested by the word 'as.' According to this reading, what we are aware of is not numerical identity; it is rather the "fact" that this identity must be presupposed as a necessary condition of knowledge. This implies, at most, the possibility of such a consciousness, certainly not its actuality or necessity. The awkwardness of the syntax of this passage almost suggests that Kant was torn between these two views at the time of its composition. The important point, however, is that only the second reading is compatible with the Second Edition, where Kant emphasizes the analyticity of the apperception principle in all its forms. Given this reading, what this principle really asserts is the "necessity of a possibility,"[24] the possibility of becoming reflectively aware of an identical 'I think' with respect to each of my representations.

B. The Necessity of Synthesis

Perhaps the most perplexing aspect of Kant's position in the first part of the Second Edition Deduction is that, in spite of his insistence on the analyticity of the principle of the necessary unity or identity of apperception, he also maintains that this principle is not sterile. In fact, he contends that we can derive from it the necessity of a synthesis of the given manifold. Thus, after his initial presentation of the principle, Kant asserts its direct consequence:

> This thoroughgoing identity of the apperception of a manifold which is given in intuition contains a synthesis of representations, and is possible only through the consciousness of this synthesis. For the empirical consciousness, which accompanies- different representations, is in itself diverse and without relation to the identity of the subject. That relation comes about, not simply

through my accompanying each representation with consciousness, but only in so far as I *conjoin* one representation with another, and am conscious of the synthesis of them. Only in so far, therefore, as I can unite a manifold of given representations in *one consciousness,* is it possible for me to represent to myself the *identity of the consciousness in [that is, throughout] these representations.* In other words, the *analytic* unity of apperception is possible only under the presupposition of a certain *synthetic* unity. [B133]

This passage contains two distinct claims, which come together in the conclusion that the analytic unity of apperception presupposes "a certain synthetic unity." The first is that the consciousness of the identity of the 'I think' "contains" a synthesis; the second is that it is possible only through a consciousness of this synthesis. Both are essential to Kant's overall argument, and I intend to discuss each in turn. Before doing so, however, it is necessary to backtrack a bit in order to consider Kant's initial account of synthesis in §15. The manifold, Kant there notes, can be given in a purely sensible intuition, and the form of this intuition can be regarded as nothing more than the mode in which the subject is affected:

But the combination [*conjunctio*] of a manifold in general can never come to us through the senses, and cannot, therefore, be already contained in the pure form of sensible intuition. For it is an act of spontaneity of the faculty of representation; and since this faculty, to distinguish it from sensibility, must be entitled understanding, all combination—be we conscious of it or not, be it a combination of the manifold of intuition, empirical or non-empirical, or of various concepts—is an act of the understanding. To this act the general title 'synthesis' may be assigned, as indicating that we cannot represent to ourselves anything as combined in the object which we have not ourselves previously combined, and that of all representations *combination* is the only one which cannot be given through objects. Being an act of the self-activity of the subject, it cannot be executed save by the subject itself. [B129–30]

This claim is frequently criticized on the grounds that it rests upon some dubious assumptions about what is actually given to the mind: an essentially Humean doctrine of psychological atomism or a "data sensualism."[25] Such criticism, however, is misguided because it neglects the fact that in the Second Edition Kant explicitly abstracts from any consideration of the manner in which the manifold is given. The only assumption is that we are dealing with a mind for which the manifold must be given, that is, with a discursive rather than an intuitive intellect. As Kant makes clear in the passage cited above, the problem is to explain how such a mind can *represent to itself* its data as combined, that is, as constituting a synthetic unity. This problem is generated by the preceding analysis of apperception, not by any assumptions about the manner in which the data are given to the mind. Thus, even if we assume that the data is somehow given to the mind in an organized or unified fashion, the mind must still represent to itself or think, that is, conceptualize, this "given" unity.[26]

Kant puts the point succinctly in a letter to Beck when he writes: "We must *synthesize* if we are to represent anything as *synthesized* (even space and time)."[27] An act of spontaneity (synthesis) must, therefore, be presupposed as a necessary condition of the possibility of the representation of any synthetic unity. This is Kant's essential claim in §15, and it follows logically from the concept of a discursive understanding.

Given these preliminaries, we are now in a position to examine Kant's two claims about the transcendental unity or identity of apperception: that it contains a synthesis, and that it is only possible through a consciousness of this synthesis. An important point to keep in mind here is that apperception involves the actual consciousness of an identical 'I think'. This thought or consciousness is itself an act of spontaneity, not a datum of inner sense, for it involves the unification in a single "universal self-consciousness" of distinct representations, each of which is accompanied by a distinct "empirical consciousness" or act of awareness.[28] That is why Kant claims that this thought "contains" a synthesis. The point is simply that to think this thought (that of the identity of the 'I think') is to unify the distinct representations in a single consciousness.

The situation can be clarified by a consideration of the simplest possible case: where a subject has two representations, A and B, each of which is accompanied by a distinct awareness or "empirical consciousness." In other words, there is an 'I think' A and an 'I think' B pertaining to a single subject. Clearly, in order for the subject of both these thoughts to become reflectively aware of its identity, it must combine A and B in a single consciousness. Only by so combining A and B can it possibly become aware of the identity of the I that thinks A with the I that thinks B. It cannot, therefore, apperceive its own identity as a thinking subject without *in the same act* also unifying these representations. Consequently, this act does necessarily "contain" a synthesis. Obviously, the converse does not hold; not every act of unification of representations in a single consciousness produces an actual consciousness of the identity of the 'I think'. This, however, is irrelevant. As we have already seen, all that the apperception principle requires is that this unification allow for the possibility of such self-consciousness. Kant terms this self-consciousness "universal," which is here equivalent to transcendental, because it constitutes the "logical form of all knowledge."[29] We shall see why shortly.

The claim that apperception is possible only through a consciousness of the synthesis means that the awareness of the identity of the 'I think' involves an awareness of the synthesis or combination that it "contains." This claim is more complex than the preceding one because of the ambiguity that attaches to the terms 'synthesis' or 'combination'. These can refer either to the act itself or to the product of the act. Moreover, it would appear that the claim must be taken in both senses. Understood as a claim about synthesis in the sense of a product, it is unproblematic.

Indeed, this result follows directly from the preceding analysis. The awareness of the identity of the I that thinks *A* with the I that thinks *B* obviously requires an awareness of both *A* and *B*. This is because the I of the 'I think' has no determinate content, and thus cannot be characterized apart from its representations. Consequently, unless I can become aware of both representations together, I cannot become aware of the identity of the I that thinks the one with the I that thinks the other. As Kant puts it, "I should have as many and as diverse a self as I have representations of which I am conscious to myself" (B134). But not only is such an awareness possible only by means of the combination of these representations in one consciousness, it is itself an awareness of the result of their combination. In this sense, then, apperception clearly involves the consciousness of a synthesis or combination of representations.

The claim would seem to be considerably more problematic if consciousness of synthesis is taken to mean an awareness of the activity itself. This is partly because it appears to be an empirical question whether we are ever aware of any such activity through introspection, and partly because it is generally assumed that, as conditions of experience, transcendental activities cannot in principle become objects of awareness. Nevertheless, I believe that here too a case can be made. The crucial point is that apperception involves not only the identification of the I that thinks *A* with the I that thinks *B*, but also, and primarily, the I that thinks each with the I that thinks both together in a single consciousness. Such an identification is necessary if the subject is to be aware of both *A* and *B* as its representations. The subject, however, cannot make this identification unless it is aware of its act of combining both of these representations in a single consciousness. In other words, my consciousness (apperception) that both *A* and *B* are my representations is inseparable from my consciousness of the act of thinking them together in a single consciousness. But this act is just what Kant means by synthesis. In this sense too, then, apperception can be said to be impossible apart from the consciousness of synthesis.

Finally, we must consider the significance of the fact that Kant regards this complex claim concerning the connection between apperception and synthesis as equivalent to the thesis that "the *analytic* unity of apperception is possible only under the presupposition of a certain *synthetic* unity." Here, and in the important footnote attached to this claim, Kant begins to forge the link between apperception and the understanding, a link that is obviously crucial for the whole argument of the Deduction. We have already seen that Kant regards all general concepts as analytic unities, and that this must be taken to mean that they contain within a single representation the thought of what is common to a multiplicity of distinct representations (a set of common marks). We have also seen that Kant regards such concepts as produced by a series of "logical acts," termed "comparison," "reflection," and "abstraction." Our present concern centers on the connection between these claims and the doctrine of apperception. Two points here are highly relevant. First, this identical 'I think', that is, "the bare representation I," which "must be capable of accompanying all other representations, and which in all consciousness is one and the same" (B132), can be regarded as the form or prototype of the analytic unity that pertains to all general concepts. In fact, it is simply this analytic unity considered in abstraction from all content. Consequently, the consciousness of the 'I think' is itself the thought of what is common to all concepts. Second, the act of becoming aware of this identical 'I think' is the form of the act of reflection, by means of which the mind grasps the identity in difference in the formation of general concepts. Once again, it is nothing more than the "logical act," considered in abstraction from all content. The consciousness of this act, that is, the consciousness of synthesis, is, therefore, the consciousness of the form of thinking.[30]

The main conclusion to be drawn from all of this is that the doctrine of apperception, at least in the Second Edition Deduction, is most properly viewed as a formal model or schema for the analysis of the understanding and its "logical" activities. Correlatively, the theory of synthesis implied by this doctrine is to be taken as an analytical account of the mode of operation of the model. As such, it is neither a bit of introspective psychology nor an idealistic ontological thesis concerning the manner in which the mind "creates" the phenomenal world by imposing its forms upon the given sensible data. This modeling function provides the basis for the transcendental status assigned to the principle of apperception and for the claim that all of our representations must conform to its conditions, if they are not to be epistemically null. Moreover, I believe that such a conception of apperception represents the view which Kant himself tries to express at the end of the abovementioned footnote when, after his account of analytic and synthetic unity, he concludes:

> The synthetic unity of apperception is therefore that highest point, to which we must ascribe all employment of the understanding, even the whole of logic, and conformally therewith, transcendental philosophy. Indeed, this capacity [*Vermögen*] is the understanding itself. [B134 n.]

C. Apperception and Objects

The essential move in the first part of the Deduction is the attempt to establish a reciprocal connection between the transcendental unity of apperception and the representation of objects. I shall call this the "reciprocity thesis." It is the specific concern of §17. Given this thesis, Kant can introduce his conception of judgment as "nothing but the manner in which given modes of knowledge are brought to the objective unity of apperception" (§19). This, in turn, provides the basis for the explicit connection between apperception and the categories, defined as the logical functions of judgment "insofar as they are employed in determination of the manifold of a given intuition" (§20). Unfortunately, the argument for this crucial thesis is compressed into a single dense paragraph. Since this paragraph requires a careful analysis, I shall cite it in full:

> *Understanding* is, to use general terms, *the faculty of knowledge*. This knowledge consists in the determinate relation of given representations to an object; and an *object* is that in the concept of which the manifold of a given intuition is *united*. Now all unification of representations demands unity of consciousness in the synthesis of them. Consequently it is the unity of consciousness that alone constitutes the relation of representations to an object, and therefore their objective validity and the fact that they are modes of knowledge; and upon it therefore rests the very possibility of the understanding. [B137]

Kant is here making explicit the connection between apperception and the understanding to which he had alluded in the passage cited above. We are told that the characteristic activity of the understanding is to relate given representations (intuitions) to an object. This immediately gives rise to the question of what is meant by an object (Objekt), and we see that it is defined simply as "that in the concept of which the manifold of a given intuition is *united*." This definition reflects Kant's "Copernican revolution": first-order talk about objects is replaced by second-order talk about the conception of an object, and the conditions of its conception (epistemic conditions). The meaning of 'object' is thus to be determined by an analysis of these conditions. The root claim (merely implicit in this passage) is that the act of conceiving, knowing, understanding, or judging about an object $= x$ (all of these here being regarded as equivalent) consists in the unification of the manifold of the intuition of x by means of a concept. This can be taken as a schematic account of the form of the thought of an "object in general," that is, of any object, regardless of its determinate nature. For our immediate purposes, however, the most noteworthy feature of this definition is its breadth. It follows from it that whatever can be represented by means of the unification of a manifold of intuition under a concept counts as an object. It also follows that a concept through which such unification is achieved counts as a "concept of an object" and is thus objectively valid. The latter point is, of course, central to Kant's endeavor to establish the objective validity of the categories.

This conception of an object also provides the key to the understanding of Kant's attempt to link the unity of consciousness with the representation of objects. The crucial claim is that "it is the unity of consciousness that alone constitutes [*ausmacht*] the relation of representations to an object, and therefore their objective validity." Since Kant presents this claim as a direct consequence of the principle that "all unification of representations demands unity of consciousness in the synthesis of them," it might seem that he is guilty of a gross non sequitur. The problem is that this principle is only strong enough to license the conclusion that the unity of consciousness is a *necessary* condition for the representation of an object; it is not strong enough to prove that this unity is also a *sufficient* condition. In other words, we can infer from the apperception principle that there can be no representation of objects apart from the unity of consciousness, because without such a unity there can be no representation of anything at all. It would seem, however, that we cannot similarly infer that whenever there is a unity of consciousness there is a representation of an object. Yet this is precisely what Kant appears to be claiming. Indeed, it is what he must claim, if he is to establish a necessary connection between the categories and the unity of consciousness.[31]

There is, however, no problem here at all if 'object' is taken in the broad sense indicated in §17. Since it follows from the apperception principle that the unity of consciousness is impossible apart from a synthetic unity of representations, and since this synthetic unity can only be achieved by uniting these representations under a concept, and since (by definition) any such synthetic unity counts as an object, it also follows that the representation of an object is a necessary condition for the unity of consciousness. But this is equivalent to saying that the unity of consciousness is a sufficient condition for the representation of an object, which is just what the reciprocity thesis asserts.

I have stated previously that this broad conception of an object at work in the first part of the Deduction can be characterized as judgmental or logical. It follows from Kant's analysis of judgment that every judgment has such an object, but it does not follow that this object actually exists, or even that it is possible in other than a purely logical sense. Evidence of Kant's continued concern with this conception of an object is provided in a number of Reflexionen, which stem from different periods of his philosophical career. The most revealing of these is a late Reflexion (dated 1797), which is discussed by Henrich. The portion of the text which I cite consists of a number of attempts to articulate this judgmental conception of an object:

> What is an object? That which is represented through a totality of several predicates which pertain to it. The plate is round, warm, tin, etc. 'Warm', 'round', 'tin', etc. are not objects, but the warmth, the tin etc. are.
>
> An object is that in the representation of which other representations can be thought as synthetically connected.
>
> Every judgment has a subject and predicate. The subject of the judgment, insofar as it contains different possible predicates, is the object.
>
> 'Warm', 'rectangular', 'deep' etc. are predicates. The warmth, the rectangle, the depth etc. are objects. The same applies to rational and reason. The determinable in a judgment, the logical subject, is at the same time the real object.

The subject of a judgment, in the representation of which is combined the ground of the synthetic unity of a manifold of predicates, is an object.[32]

This Reflexion provides a clear indication of just how broadly Kant construes the judgmental conception of an object. It includes not only physical objects, such as plates, but also properties of these objects, even abstract objects, such as reason. The only two restrictions on what can count as an object in this sense seem to be that it must be referred to by the subject term of a judgment, that is, it must function as a logical subject, and that its conception must involve the synthetic unity of representations. These restrictions are not really independent of one another. As Henrich notes in his analysis of this text, the point which Kant is trying to articulate here is just the connection between the representation of an object through a judgment and a synthetic unity of representations. The basic claim is that the object or logical subject of a judgment must be such a synthetic unity. Henrich suggests that this claim may be derived from the analysis of judgment, independently of any appeal to the apperception principle.[33] In reality, however, it is already implicit in §17 of the Deduction, where it is a consequence of the apperception principle.

The moral to be drawn from this is that one must keep in mind that by 'object', Kant does not mean in §17 what he means in the supposedly parallel passage in the First Edition, where he introduces the conception of the transcendental object.[34] Linguistic evidence of this difference is provided by the fact that Kant uses the term 'Gegenstand' in the relevant passages in the First Edition, whereas, with one exception, he uses 'Objekt' in the first part of the Deduction in the Second Edition. The important point, however, is that this terminological difference reflects a difference in the questions being addressed in the two texts. In the First Edition, the analysis of 'object' is introduced within the context of a reflection on the subjective nature of appearances. Kant there suggests that since appearances are "nothing but sensible representations, which, as such, and in themselves, must not be taken as objects capable of existing outside our power of representation," the question naturally arises: "What, then, is to be understood when we speak of an object [Gegenstand] corresponding to, and consequently also distinct from, our knowledge?" (A104). The concern, therefore, is with the conditions of the representation of an object in the "weighty" sense, which is schematically characterized as "something in general = x" (A104) and later as the "transcendental object = x" (A109). Kant attempts to link this conception of an object directly to the "formal unity of consciousness" (the unity of apperception) and through this to the categories. The logical or judgmental conception of an object does not even enter the picture.

By contrast, in §17 there is no mention of this problem and, therefore, no appeal to the "weighty" sense of object. The claim is simply that the unity of apperception is an "objective unity" and "objectively valid," because it is the ultimate ground or condition of the representation of an object in the judgmental sense. As Kant aptly puts it:

> The synthetic unity of consciousness is, therefore, an objective condition of all knowledge. It is not merely a condition that I myself require in knowing an object, but is a condition under which every intuition must stand in order *to become an object for me*. For otherwise, in the absence of this synthesis, the manifold would *not* be united in one consciousness. [B138]

The remainder of the argument merely unfolds the implications of this analytic principle. We see first that synthetic unity is a condition of the understanding (analytic unity), and consequently of the representation of an Objekt. The act of understanding is then identified with judgment. It follows from this that the manifold must conform to the logical functions of judgment if it is to be brought to the objective unity of consciousness, or conceptualized. If we accept the results of the Metaphysical Deduction, it also follows that this manifold is necessarily subject to the categories.

It is obvious, however, that this line of argument cannot take us very far. Precisely because it proceeds analytically from the principle of apperception, which is itself analytic, and operates with a judgmental or logical conception of an object, it cannot establish any connection between the unity of apperception and objects in the "weighty" sense. Still less can it establish any connection between the unity of apperception and the experience of a law-governed world of such objects. In fact, it does not involve any mention of experience and the conditions of its possibility. This may seem disappointing, but it should not come as any great surprise. After all, Kant himself remarks at the end of this portion of the argument that only "a beginning is made of a *deduction* of the pure concepts of understanding."

II. THE PROBLEM OF SUBJECTIVE UNITY

Before turning to the analysis of the second part of the Deduction, it is necessary to consider the distinction between an objective and a subjective unity of consciousness, which is drawn in §18 and again alluded to in §19. The question is what sense can be given to this notion of a subjective unity and to the claim that it has subjective validity? This is a problem that first arises in connection with the distinction drawn in the *Prolegomena* between judgments of perception, which are only subjectively valid, and judgments of experience, which have objective validity. The distinction in the *Critique* between subjective and objective unity may be seen as a corrective to the earlier distinction between two kinds of judgment. The necessity for such a corrective stems from the theory of judgment made explicit in the Second Edition, according to which objective validity is an inherent trait of all judgments. After a brief consideration of the *Prolegom-*

ena account and its inadequacies, I shall suggest that one can find in the discussion in the Second Edition of the *Critique* a way of drawing the objective-subjective distinction that is compatible with this theory of judgment. I take this to be the view to which Kant *should have* adhered. I shall also show, however, that there are passages that can be interpreted only as remnants of the inadequate doctrine of the *Prolegomena*. We are thus led to the conclusion that the text contains two incompatible accounts of nonobjective consciousness. This is the source of its great obscurity.

A. Judgments of Perception and Judgments of Experience

Kant intends this as a distinction between two species of empirical judgment. In his presentation of this distinction he remarks:

> Empirical judgments, so far as they have objective validity, are *judgments of experience*, but those which are only subjectively valid I name mere *judgments of perception*. The latter require no pure concept of the understanding, but only the logical connection of perception in a thinking subject. But the former always require, besides the representation of the sensuous intuition, special *concepts originally begotten in the understanding*, which make possible the objective validity of the judgment of experience.[35]

The striking feature of this passage is that judgments of perception are presented as lacking two properties which, in the Second Edition of the *Critique*, Kant holds to be essential to all judgments. Instead of maintaining, as he does in the *Critique*, that all judgments involve an objectively valid, categorially determined unification of representations in a single consciousness, he here suggests that there are two kinds of empirical judgment, only one of which (judgments of experience) fit this general description. The other (judgments of perception) are merely subjectively valid and occur without the use of any categories. Kant later suggests that they involve a connection of perceptions "in a consciousness of my particular state." This is contrasted with the connection in "consciousness in general" that occurs in an objectively valid judgment of experience.[36] An equivalent characterization of this merely subjective mode of unification is that the representations are "referred to a consciousness in one subject only" (again in contrast to consciousness in general).[37]

Moreover, the problem is compounded by the fact that Kant distinguishes between two classes of judgments of perception; namely, those that can and those that cannot become judgments of experience by the application of a pure concept. Examples of those that cannot include 'The room is warm', 'Sugar is sweet', and 'Wormwood is bitter'.[38] Kant's point here is that such judgments are inherently subjective because they refer to feeling states or sensations that can never be attributed to the object. An example of those that can is 'When the sun shines on the stone it grows warm'. He contends that with the addition of the pure concept of causality this becomes converted into the objectively valid judgment of experience: 'The sun warms the stone'.[39]

This lumping together under the same label of first-person reports about feeling states and claims about sequences of perceptions that relate to the "objective world" is initially somewhat puzzling. Kant's point, however, can be understood if we keep Hume in mind. The crucial contrast for Hume is between constant conjunction and genuinely causal, or necessary, connection. Kant obviously construes the claim that when the sun shines on the stone it grows warm as equivalent to the statement that whenever I have seen the sun shining on the stone, I have also observed that it grows warm. In other words, he takes it as a first-person report or statement about "subjective experiences." As such, it is quite distinct from the "objective" causal claim that the sun warms the stone. The latter says nothing about my perceptions; it is rather a claim about a causal connection that holds independently of how I or any other particular subject happen to perceive things.

The distinction between judgments of perception and judgments of experience can be schematically formulated as the contrast between judgments of the form 'It seems to me that p', and those of the form 'It is the case that p'. The function of the categories is to convert claims of the former sort into the latter. They can do this because they are rules for the universally valid and necessary synthesis of representations. To think of my representations as unified in accordance with such a rule is to think of them as unified (and thus to unify them) in a way that is independent of my perceptual state or any other subjective factors. The thought of the objective validity of such a unification is therefore equivalent to the thought of its universality and necessity. Kant makes this explicit when he claims that "objective validity and necessary universality (for everyone) are equivalent terms."[40] By arguing in this way he suggests a connection between objective validity and intersubjective agreement that seems to be lacking in the more Cartesian focus of the *Critique*. This suggestion is, of course, strengthened by the previously noted conception of consciousness in general, which is the *Prolegomena*'s counterpart to the objective or transcendental unity of apperception.

Although I do not believe that there is any real difference between the *Prolegomena* and the *Critique* on this point, I do not intend to deal with this issue here.[41] My present concern is rather with the notion of a judgment of perception and its two anomalous features: its merely subjective validity and its lack of a pure concept. Since Kant's doctrine is that pure concepts are the grounds of the objective validity of our judgments, these two features are really equivalent. Nevertheless, for the purpose of analysis it is helpful to distinguish between them and to discuss each separately. This will also make it easier to contrast the doctrine of the *Prolegomena* with that of the Second Edition of the *Critique*.

The first point to note is that the notion of subjective validity is itself an ambiguous one in Kant. In the Canon of Pure Reason, Kant equates the subjective validity of a judgment with "the holding of a thing to be true" (*Das Fürwahrhalten*) (A822/B850). This means that a judgment is subjectively valid if it is held to be true, that is, if it is believed, by a subject. A judgment that is believed without justifying grounds, that is, grounds which would warrant universal acceptance, is said to possess merely "private validity" (*Privatgültigkeit*). This conception of subjective validity is also present in the *Prolegomena,* at least implicitly, for 'It seems to me that *p*' can be regarded as equivalent to 'I believe that *p*'. Nevertheless, the way in which Kant characterizes judgments of perception in the *Prolegomena* suggests that he construes their subjective validity to consist essentially in the fact that they are *about* the subject and its cognitive and/or affective states. Thus, in one sense of the term a judgment can be said to be merely subjectively valid if it holds only *for* the subject, while in the other sense it is subjectively valid if it is true merely *of* the subject.

The claim that judgments of perception have merely subjective validity is vitiated by Kant's failure to distinguish clearly between these two senses of the term. This can easily be seen from the examples of judgments of perception cited earlier. These judgments all can be taken as first-person reports about how things seem to me, that is, as *es scheint* judgments.[42] Such judgments are certainly subjectively valid in the sense that they refer only to the subject and its states, not to "objective objects." But it hardly follows from this that they are true only for the subject and are thus only subjectively valid in the other sense (which is alone incompatible with objective validity). In fact, such judgments are objectively valid in precisely the same sense and for the same reasons as judgments of experience: they are grounded and can be known to be true or false.[43] It is true that the table on which I am writing seems to me to be brown, that sugar tastes sweet to me, and so forth. Moreover, the truth value remains even if the scope of the judgment is limited to a particular episode in my mental history: for example, 'The sugar tasted sweet to Allison at 1:33 P.M. on July 29, 1980'. Finally, even though such judgments are about me, I am neither the only person able to formulate them nor the only person for whom they can be true. That sugar tasted sweet to me at a particular time is simply a fact about the world.[44]

Given the doctrine of the *Critique,* the denial of any role for the categories in judgments of perception is equally problematic. It would seem obvious that at least the categories of quantity and quality are relevant to such judgments.[45] More important, it follows from the previous analysis that every judgment has an Objekt and must, therefore, employ the categories. This is also implicit in the characterization of the categories as logical functions of judgment applied to the manifold of a given intuition. Since judgments of perception, like judgments of experience, involve the unification of a manifold of intuition in one consciousness, they must make use of the categories. To be sure, Kant claims in the *Prolegomena* that such unification requires merely the "logical connection of perceptions in a thinking subject."[46] It is difficult to see, however, what such a "logical connection" could conceivably involve, if not a connection according to these concepts.

It might be objected at this point that the preceding analysis has misconstrued the Kantian notion of a judgment of perception. What has here been regarded as such a judgment is really a second-order, reflective judgment *about* my perceptual and/or affective state. It is, in short, what Kant will later call a "judgment of inner sense." Judgments of this latter type, so the objection goes, certainly lay claim to objective validity and involve the categories. They are not, however, the judgments of perception with which Kant is concerned in the *Prolegomena*. By such a judgment, Kant means perceptual awareness itself, not a reflective judgment about this awareness. To return once more to Kant's examples, my perceptual consciousness of the bitterness of wormwood and the sweetness of sugar (the "seemings" themselves) are the actual judgments of perception. They are regarded as judgments because they are modes of consciousness with their own peculiar "subjective objects" (appearances). Nevertheless, as judgments about such "subjective objects" they are radically distinct from judgments of experience.[47]

Some such distinction is certainly in order. It is, after all, one thing to perceive sugar as sweet or, to use Lewis White Beck's example, to dream about a three-headed monster, and quite another to judge reflectively about my taste or my dream state.[48] The acceptance of this distinction, however, does not help us to resolve the difficulties raised by Kant's account of such judgments in the *Prolegomena*, because even in the case of a dream, where my "object" is illusory, I must make use of the categories. Moreover, a dream object is located in the spatiotemporal framework of a dream world and stands in connection with other objects in the same dream world. Thus, insofar as dreaming involves the consciousness or awareness of such imaginary objects, it must likewise involve the categories.[49] As Beck suggests, this is perhaps why Kant characterizes representations which do not conform to the conditions of the unity of apperception, and which are therefore without categorial determination, as "less even than a dream."[50]

B. The Subjective Unity of Consciousness: Not Less, but Other Than a Dream

It is no doubt largely because of these considerations that the distinction between a judgment of perception and a judgment of experience is replaced in the Second Edition of the *Critique* by the distinction between a subjective and an objective unity of consciousness. As we have already seen, however, the conception of judgment which lies behind this shift appears to make the whole notion of a subjective unity of consciousness problematic. The difficulty is not that judgments of perception or, more generally, "subjective judgments" are ruled out by this conception; it is rather that this conception commits Kant to the doctrine that such judgments, like "objective judgments," involve an objective unity of consciousness and, therefore, categorial determination. Moreover, although Kant does not deal with the issue at any length in the *Critique,* it is perfectly clear from his comments in other places that he was well aware of this fact. Two passages, which have been much discussed in the literature, are especially worthy of note in this regard. The first is from a letter written to Marcus Herz:

> All sense data [*data der Sinne*] for a possible cognition would never, without those conditions, represent objects. They would not even reach that unity of consciousness that is necessary for knowledge of myself (as object of inner sense). I would not even be able to know that I have sense data; consequently for me, as a knowing being, they would be absolutely nothing. They could still (I imagine myself to be an animal) carry on their play in an orderly fashion, as representations connected according to empirical laws of association, and thus even have an influence on my feeling and desire, without my being aware of them (assuming that I am even conscious of each individual representation, but not of their relation to the unity of representation of their object, by means of the synthetic unity of their apperception). This might be so without my knowing the slightest thing thereby, not even what my own condition is.[51]

The second passage is from a Reflexion.

> Consciousness can accompany all representations, and *thus also those of imagination,* which, and the play of which, is itself an object [*Objekt*] of inner sense, and of which it must be possible to become conscious of as such an object.[52]

In the first of these passages Kant is explaining to Herz his criticisms of Maimon's views and affirming, in opposition to Maimon, the necessity of the categories for all conscious representation. Thus the emphasis on the claim that a unity of consciousness, and with it the categories (as its "conditions"), is required even for a consciousness of our mental states. Apart from this unity and its conditions there can be a play of representations which affects our feelings and desires (Kant should have added our behavior); but since nothing is represented through such a play, it would be nothing to us as "knowing beings." In the second (a Reflexion dealing with problematic idealism) he is discussing the function of the imagination in dreams and fever, that is, in cases where there is obviously no object corresponding to the representations (*Sinnenanschauungen*).[53] Kant's point here is that even this purely subjective play of representations can be brought to consciousness and represented as an object. The clear implication is that such representation is objectively valid and categorially determined. Since both passages affirm the position to which Kant is committed by his analysis of judgment, they underscore the question with which we began: What can possibly be meant by a subjective unity of consciousness, if it is not a unity through which we represent to ourselves our own subjective states or condition?

There is in fact only one thing that could count as a subjective unity in the Kantian sense: a unity or connection of representations through which nothing is represented, not even our subjective states. First, as a unity of consciousness, its elements must be representations and they must stand in some order or connection with one another (otherwise there would be no unity at all). Second, and most important, no object (Objekt) can be represented by means of this order or connection, and this must include a subjective object. For this reason it appears that the term 'subjective' is somewhat of a misnomer, and that 'nonobjective' or 'nonrepresentational' would be more appropriate. Such a unity not only need not, but cannot, accord with the conditions of the unity of apperception (the categories). In other words, it is not a unity by means of which a subject can become conscious of the identity of the 'I think'. This is because such a unity is not itself a product of thought, that is, of the spontaneity of the subject (synthesis). Consequently, it must have determining causes (as a psychological phenomenon), but it cannot have validating grounds or reasons.

The orderly play of representations "connected according to empirical laws of association," to which Kant refers in his letter to Herz, provides a good example of such a subjective unity. Kant evidently has in mind the phenomenon of the association of ideas as it is characterized by Hume and by many other eighteenth-century thinkers. Since this association, or the disposition to associate, is the product of past conditioning (what Hume calls custom or habit), it cannot be attributed to the spontaneity of thought. Kant himself assigns it to the reproductive imagination, or, better, to the imagination in its reproductive and empirically conditioned capacity. Once again, however, the main point is that nothing can be represented by means of such an association. Let us consider a simple case expressed in Humean terms: whenever I receive an impression of smoke I immediately form the idea of fire, and vice versa. It should be clear that my imaginative association of these representations is not equivalent to my representation or thought of the connection of the phenomena corresponding to these representations. Not only can I associate the representations without thinking of any objective connection, but insofar as I merely associate them in this way, I cannot think or represent to myself the connection of the phenomena. It should be equally clear that this imaginative association of representations is not equivalent to the representation of my subjective state. To be sure, it is quite possible for me to represent to myself my own subjective state or disposition to associate. Nevertheless, my empirical knowledge of the fact that I associate or tend to associate these representations does not itself occur by means of their association. On the contrary, it requires a reflective act of thought which must be in accord with the conditions of the objective unity of self-consciousness (the categories). In other words, if I had merely the disposition to associate and not also the capacity to think, I could not even become aware of the fact that I associate. This is the fundamental claim that Kant is making to Herz.

The conception of subjective unity outlined in the preceding paragraphs is, I contend, the one to which Kant is committed in virtue of his theory of judgment. I further believe that this conception is implicit in the letter to Herz and, indeed, in the Reflexion. The main question, however, is whether this same conception can also be found in the Second Edition of the *Critique*. This can only be resolved by considering the few cryptic references to subjective unity contained in §18 and §19. We shall see that the evidence is at best ambiguous.

One of the factors that indicates that Kant has this conception in mind in the *Critique* is that he refers to the subjective unity as a unity of *consciousness* and to the objective unity as a unity of *self-consciousness*. An objective unity can be termed a unity of self-consciousness because it is possible through it to become aware of an identical 'I think'. Since this is not possible in the case of a subjective unity, the latter is appropriately characterized as a unity of consciousness rather than of self-consciousness. Once again, we should not be misled by the fact that it is possible to become conscious of such a subjective unity as a "subjective object." The Kantian conception of self-consciousness, at least as it is presented in the doctrine of apperception, concerns the thought of the 'I' as subject of thought, not the empirical knowledge through inner sense of the 'me'.[54] The apperception of an identical 'I think' must be possible in connection with the reflective and objectively valid representation of the subjective unity in a judgment of inner sense, but it is not possible through the subjective unity itself. In other words, a subjective unity of consciousness is not a unity *of* self-consciousness, although it can (as objectified) become a unity *for* self-conscious thought.

In the same vein, it should be noted that Kant initially describes the subjective unity of consciousness as a "*determination of inner sense—*through which the manifold of intuition for such (objective) combination is empirically given" (B139). This suggests the order in which representations occur in inner sense (what Kant usually calls the "order of apprehension.") Such an order is subjective in two ways. First, as a "determination of inner sense," it is subjective in the sense of being mental. Second, and most important, it is subjective in the sense of being nonobjective or nonrepresentational. Just as we do not represent to ourselves an objective connection between smoke and fire by the simple assertion or juxtaposition of their representations in consciousness, so too we do not represent to ourselves an objective order or sequence of phenomena simply by means of the successive reception of the sensible data (intuitions) in inner sense.

Finally, we must note that in his account of subjective unity Kant refers to an order of association as well as to the order of occurrence in inner sense. In fact, he even seems to treat these orders as equivalent. Thus, in illustration of what he means by a subjective unity, Kant reflects, "To one man, for instance, a certain word suggests one thing, to another some other thing; the unity of consciousness in that which is empirical, is not as regards what is given necessarily and universally valid" (B140).[55] Clearly, Kant should have distinguished between an order of the occurrence of representations in inner sense and an order of the association of representations in the imagination. The former depends solely on physical or physiological factors and pertains merely to sensibility. The latter involves psychological factors, such as Hume's custom or habit, and requires a certain imaginative capacity. In spite of these differences, however, the fact remains that both orders or unities are subjective in the sense we have been discussing.

So far then, what Kant says about the subjective unity of consciousness in the *Critique* accords with what one would expect him to say. Unfortunately, this is not true of everything that Kant has to say about this unity. A case in point is his brief discussion of the empirical unity of apperception. In a passage that occurs immediately before the one just cited, Kant remarks that, in contrast to the transcendental or "original" unity of apperception, which is objectively valid, "the empirical unity of apperception, upon which we are not here dwelling, and which besides is merely derived from the former under given conditions *in concreto,* has only subjective validity" (B140). The context indicates that Kant is here treating the empirical unity of apperception as equivalent to the subjective unity of consciousness. The problem is that Kant also seems to regard empirical apperception as equivalent to empirical self-consciousness, that is, as the mode of consciousness through which we represent ourselves to ourselves as objects in inner sense.[56] Consequently, the subjective unity of consciousness is here being identified with the consciousness or representation of one's subjective states rather than with the subjective states themselves. That is why it is said to be subjectively valid. As we have seen repeatedly, however, Kant's theory of judgment commits him to regard such representations as objectively valid judgments of inner sense. The reference to empirical apperception with its subjective validity must, therefore, be seen as a reversion to the standpoint of the *Prolegomena.*

The same can be said about Kant's claim that this empirical unity is derived from the transcendental unity "under given conditions *in concreto.*" There would seem to be only two possible ways in which this incredibly obscure statement can be interpreted, and each of them involves serious difficulties. According to one of these interpretations, Kant's point is that although the content of empirical apperception is determined by empirical factors (the "given"), its form as a mode of consciousness is subject to the transcendental conditions of unity. I regard this as the most plausible reading of Kant's claim because it does justice to the fact that empirical apperception is a form of consciousness through which something is represented; namely, a subjective state. The problem with the claim on this interpretation is that the assignment of subjective validity to this form of consciousness contradicts the principle that it is subject to the transcendental conditions of unity. It should be noted here that this occurs in the very section in which Kant first claims that the transcendental unity of apperception is an objective unity.[57]

According to the second possible interpretation, the claim is simply that the order in which perceptions occur in inner sense is determined by causal laws and is in that sense subject to the transcendental conditions of experience.[58] If this is what Kant actually meant to say, then things are even more confused. First, although it is true that for Kant the order in which perceptions occur in inner sense is causally determined, it makes no sense to say this order is subjectively valid. The notion of validity is applicable only to the representation of this order, not to the order itself. Second, as already noted, Kant should have said that the representation of this order is objectively, not subjectively, valid. Third, quite apart from the dubiousness of the notion of subjective validity, Kant would never assert that the representation or thought of this causally determined order is itself causally determined. On either interpretation, then, it seems that this claim involves a fundamental incoherence. It also seems that this incoherence, and with it the possibility of two such diverse interpretations, is due to the fact that Kant here conflates the empirical unity of apperception with the subjective unity of consciousness.

Finally, we can detect a similar confusion in §19 in connection with the account of judgment. Immediately after defining judgment in terms of the objective unity of apperception, Kant proceeds to contrast an objectively valid relation of representations in judgment with "a relation of the same representations that would have only subjective validity—as when they are connected according to laws of *association*" (B142). This juxtaposition of judgment and association, together with the suggestion that they would involve the same representations, albeit connected in different ways, calls to mind the contrast between objective and subjective unity. At the same time, however, Kant also attributes subjective validity to this associative or subjective unity. Moreover, to make matters worse, in explaining what he means by this he writes:

In the latter case, all that I could say would be, 'If I support a body, I feel an impression of weight'; I could not say, 'It, the body, is heavy'. Thus to say 'The body is heavy' is not merely to state that the two representations have always been conjoined in my perception, however often that perception be repeated; what we are asserting is that they are combined *in the object,* no matter what the state of the subject may be. [B142]

Kant here conflates the contrast between the objective unity of self-consciousness that occurs in judgment and the subjective unity of consciousness produced by association with the quite different contrast between judgments which refer to objects in the "weighty" sense (judgments of experience) and those which refer to the state of the subject (judgments of perception). Incredibly enough, he does this in the very paragraph in the *Critique* in which he attempts to articulate his conception of judgment. Given this conception, and the contrast between an objective and a subjective unity that goes with it, Kant should have distinguished here between the mere association of the impression of weight with the impression of body (a subjective unity) and the thought "If I support a body, I feel an impression of weight." He should also have noted that this thought is as much a judgment possessing objective validity as its counterpart, "The body is heavy." Both involve the relation of representations to an object. The difference between them is not relevant to the conception of judgment which Kant is here trying to explicate.[59]

III. IMAGINATION, APPREHENSION, PERCEPTION, AND EXPERIENCE

Kant provides two distinct characterizations of the task of the second part of the Deduction. In one (§21) he describes it as showing "from the mode in which the empirical intuition is given in sensibility, that its unity is none other than that which the category . . . prescribes to the manifold of a given intuition in general" (B145). In the other (§26) he depicts the task as explaining "the possibility of knowing *a priori* by means of the category whatever objects may present themselves to our senses, not indeed in respect to the form of their intuition, but in respect of the law of their combination, and so, as it were, of prescribing laws to nature, and even of making nature possible" (B159). The passages agree in contending that the task of the second part of the Deduction involves demonstrating a relationship between the categories and the specifically human mode of sensibility from which abstraction was made in the first part. The first passage defines the problem in terms of demonstrating a connection between the categories and empirical intuition, through which alone we can have access to an actual empirical object (Gegenstand). The second passage obviously goes considerably beyond this, indicating that what must really be done is to show that the categories function to make nature possible. Since by 'nature' is here meant the totality of appearances or objects of possible experience (*natura materialiter spectata*), this is really equivalent to demonstrating that they make experience possible.[60]

Kant should have distinguished between these goals, but the main point is that neither of them was achieved by the first part of the Deduction. As we have seen, this portion of the Deduction establishes the necessity of the categories for representing an object in the judgmental or logical sense. Clearly, it does not follow from this alone that the categories have any application to the actual content of human experience. Still less does it follow that the categories somehow make experience possible, especially if by 'experience' is meant empirical knowledge of objects in the "weighty" sense.

Kant expresses this very point at the beginning of §24, when he remarks parenthetically that, considered simply in connection with the intellectual synthesis (the act of judgment), the categories are "mere forms of thought, through which alone no determinate object [*Gegenstand*] is known" (B150). Later, in a passage contained in both editions, he refers to the employment of the categories with respect to an object of intuition in general (an object, the mode of intuition of which is not specified) as "transcendental." This is to be contrasted with their empirical employment, and this suggests that the first part of the Deduction is concerned with establishing the former and the second with establishing the latter. Kant goes on to note, however, that the transcendental employment of a category is not a real employment, by which he means that it does not provide knowledge of any actual object.[61] Consequently, the first part of the Deduction does not of itself demonstrate that we can gain knowledge through these pure concepts. This requires showing that they have an empirical employment, which involves demonstrating their connection with the mode in which objects are actually given in human experience. As I have already indicated, this is equivalent to demonstrating their objective reality.

The argument consists of two steps, which are separated by a significant discussion of inner sense and apperception that will be considered in Part 4. First, Kant links the unity of apperception, and with it the categories, to time (§24). This linkage turns on the connection of both with the transcendental synthesis of the imagination, which is the synthesis through which space and time are unified and determined. He then relates the categories to the actual data of human sensibility (§26). The focal point of this second step is the analysis of the synthesis of apprehension, which is the synthesis constitutive of empirical intuition. Only by showing that this synthesis is likewise governed by the categories can Kant connect them with the actual content of empirical intuition, and thus establish their objective reality.

A. The Transcendental Synthesis of the Imagination

Kant begins the argument of the second part of the Deduction by introducing the distinction between an intellectual and a figurative synthesis (*synthesis intellectualis* and *synthesis speciosa*). The former notion does not require any additional elaboration. It is the activity of judgment through which a given manifold of representations is brought to the objective unity of apperception. Broadly construed, the notion of a figurative synthesis encompasses any imaginative synthesis, including the formation of an image. Here, however, Kant is concerned only with the a priori or transcendental dimension of this synthesis. If the argument is to work, Kant must show, first, that this synthesis is responsible for the unification and determination of time, and second, that it, like the intellectual synthesis, is governed by the categories. Although it can hardly be said that Kant himself actually establishes either of these claims, I believe that he at least supplies the necessary materials for the construction of the relevant arguments.

Among the most important of these materials is the characterization of the imagination as "the faculty of representing in intuition an object that is not itself present" (B151). The significance of this characterization stems from the fact that it makes clear why the imagination is required for the representation of time and space as they are described in the Transcendental Aesthetic. Let us first consider the case of time, which is crucial for the remainder of the argument of the Transcendental Analytic. The Transcendental Aesthetic showed that each extent of time is represented as a determinate portion of a single all-inclusive time, which is itself characterized as an infinite given magnitude. It follows from this that the actual awareness of a given portion of time, for example, the present time during which I am struggling to explicate Kant's doctrine of transcendental synthesis, involves the awareness of it as a portion of this single time. As we have already seen in the case of space, however, this whole is not itself actually given in intuition as an object. In the case of time, we could say that it is given only one moment at a time. Nevertheless, in order to represent the particular portion of time, and myself as engaged in that activity during that time, I must be able to represent past and future time. In other words, I must be able to represent times that are not "present," and ultimately the single time of which all determinate times are parts. This is what the imagination enables me to do. Similar considerations apply to space. In order to represent a determinate portion of space, such as a line, I must represent it as a determination of a single, all-inclusive space which is itself not given as such. This likewise requires an imaginative capacity, and this capacity is presupposed by the thought of the infinite extendability of a straight line.

This argument, which Kant does not develop, must be distinguished from the related argument that he does present in the First Edition in connection with the account of the synthesis of reproduction (one aspect of the three-fold synthesis). Reproduction is there regarded as a fundamental activity of the imagination. Without it, Kant contends, "not even the purest and most elementary representations of space and time could arise" (A102). Kant illustrates the claim with regard to both space and time. The attempt to draw a line in thought or to think the time from one noon to the next obviously requires the successive apprehension of the component parts of the line or of the time. "But," Kant reflects, "if I were always to drop out of thought the preceding representations (the first parts of the line, the antecedent parts of the time period . . .), and did not reproduce them while advancing to those that follow, a complete representation would never be obtained." This, Kant concludes, warrants the inclusion of reproduction "among the transcendental acts of the mind" (A102). The argument sketched above differs from this account in that it does not limit the transcendental activity of the imagination to reproduction; rather, it gives equal weight to the capacity to project the future, that is, to represent the not yet given. Both are necessary for the representation of time and space as described in the Transcendental Aesthetic, and the characterization of the imagination given in the Second Edition Deduction allows for both.

Finally, since the determinate representation of time is a product of the transcendental synthesis of the imagination, it follows that this synthesis is a sufficient as well as a necessary condition of such a representation (assuming, of course, that time, as form of intuition, is "given"). Thus, there is a reciprocity between the transcendental synthesis of the imagination and its "transcendental product" (the determinate representation of time) which parallels the reciprocity established in the first part of the Deduction between the intellectual synthesis or judgment and its "logical product" (the object in the sense of *Objekt*).

The second and perhaps most problematic aspect of Kant's doctrine is the claim that the imaginative synthesis is governed by the categories. Why, after all, should the imaginative activity have anything to do with the logical functions of judgment? I take this to be the most fundamental question raised by Kant's analysis. Only by establishing such a connection can Kant demonstrate the connection between the categories and human sensibility that is needed for the explanation of the possibility of synthetic a priori judgments. The issue is thus central to the whole program of the *Critique*. Unfortunately, Kant seems to beg rather than to answer this question. Instead of providing an argument, he simply claims dogmatically that the imaginative synthesis is an expression of the spontaniety of thought, that it determines inner sense a priori in respect of its form, and that this determination is in accord with the unity of apperception.[62]

The latter point is obviously crucial. If the determination or unification of time is necessarily in accord with the unity of apperception, then, given the argument of the first part of the Deduction, it follows that it is also necessarily in accord with the categories. It is important to realize, however, that we cannot proceed analytically from the unity of apperception to the unity of time (or space). In a word, the unity of consciousness does not entail the unity of time (or space). There is no logical contradiction in the thought of a number of times (or spaces) that are not parts of a single time (or space). Consequently, there is no purely conceptual constraint on the possibility of uniting under a concept in a judgment the representations of objects located in different time-frames. The moral to be drawn from this is that, because of its a priori forms, the introduction of human sensibility into the argument of the Deduction brings with it an element that cannot be accounted for in terms of the purely conceptual requirements of the unity of apperception. That is precisely why the argument cannot proceed analytically from the genus (manifold of sensibility in general) to the species (manifold of human sensibility). It is also why the conclusions of the Deduction are synthetic and a priori in spite of the analytic nature of the apperception principle itself.

Fortunately, although we cannot argue directly from the unity of apperception to the unity of time (which would make the former a sufficient condition of the latter), we can make the reverse move from the *representation* of the unity of time to the unity of apperception, and by this means we can connect the transcendental synthesis of the imagination with apperception and the categories. In order to do this, we need only combine the results of the first half of the Deduction with the doctrine that the unification or determination of time is produced by the transcendental synthesis of the imagination. The point here is simply that, given the argument of the first part of the Deduction, it follows that the product of the transcendental synthesis of the imagination must accord with the conditions of the unity of apperception. Otherwise it could not be represented as a unity (a single all-inclusive time). But the categories have been shown in the first part of the Deduction to be conditions of the unity of apperception. Consequently, the transcendental synthesis of the imagination, which produces this unity by determining time, must conform to the categories.

Moreover, given the nature of time as a form of human sensibility, it also follows that the unity of the consciousness of a temporal manifold is impossible apart from the combination of the elements of the manifold in a single time. The argument here is simple and direct: if the elements of the manifold cannot be represented together, except insofar as they stand in a determinate relation to one another in a single time, then a fortiori they cannot be thought together in a single consciousness, unless they are so related. This makes the unity of time into a necessary condition of the possibility of human experience. We shall see that the argument of the

Analogies of Experience turns on this principle. For the present, however, the important point to note is that this is a condition imposed on thought (apperception) from "without." It expresses a requirement of human sensibility, not of understanding. Nevertheless, it serves to limit or "restrict" the understanding.

I would hope that this brief analysis suffices to indicate the precise role played by the doctrine of the transcendental synthesis of the imagination in the Second Edition Deduction. Kant links the categories to the forms of human sensibility by connecting them both to this synthesis. We must, therefore, reject the suggestion of Heidegger that Kant somehow "recoiled" from the transcendental imagination in the Second Edition.[63] In fact, if anything, the revision of the argument in the Second Edition brings into sharper focus the function of the imagination and its transcendental synthesis in the overall proof-structure.

Unfortunately, the essential function of the transcendental synthesis of the imagination in the argument is somewhat obscured by Kant's apparent denial of any ultimate distinction between the imagination and the understanding. Thus, in sharp contrast to the formulations of the First Edition, Kant characterizes the transcendental synthesis of the imagination as an "action [*Wirkung*] of the understanding on the sensibility" (B152). In addition, he claims that it is the understanding "under the title of a *transcendental synthesis of imagination*" that determines inner sense (B153). Finally, he maintains that "it is one and the same spontaneity, which in the one case, under the title of imagination, and in the other case, under the title of understanding, brings combination into the manifold of intuition" (B161 n.). Not only do such formulations conflict with the First Edition, where the imagination is treated as a fundamental function of the "soul,"[64] but they also conflict with the Metaphysical Deduction, where the act of synthesis is explicitly assigned to the imagination rather than to the understanding.

Much of this is perfectly understandable in light of Kant's concern to avoid the criticisms that were raised against the First Edition version of the Deduction because of its apparently psychological and phenomenalistic thrust. In addition, this apparent identification of the imagination with the understanding serves to underscore the main point of the argument: that the transcendental synthesis of the imagination is in accordance with the conditions of the unity of apperception and, therefore, with the categories. Nevertheless, we have also seen that it is equally important for the argument of the Deduction that the extraconceptual, figurative nature of the transcendental synthesis be recognized. This is necessary if the categories are to be brought into connection with the forms of human sensibility, and through these forms to the actual content of human experience (empirical intuition). The real question at issue is not to which psychological faculty the figurative synthesis is to be assigned; it is rather whether the determination of time requires a synthesis that is governed by the categories, but yet differs from the purely intellectual synthesis that occurs in judgment in that it is also conditioned by the form of inner sense. I have tried to show here that, in spite of Kant's tendency to minimize the role of the imagination in the Second Edition, the argument requires such a synthesis.

B. The Synthesis of Apprehension

The demonstration of the objective reality of the categories requires more than simply establishing their connection with the forms of human sensibility; it is also necessary to establish their relationship to empirical intuition.[65] Kant attempts to achieve this goal by linking the categories to the synthesis of apprehension. In the Second Edition he defines this synthesis as "that combination of the manifold in an empirical intuition, whereby perception, that is, empirical consciousness of the manifold [*derselben*] (as appearance) is possible" (B160).[66] This corresponds to what is referred to in the First Edition as the "empirical synthesis of apprehension."[67] The key point, which is evident from the definition, is that this synthesis is concerned with the sensible content or matter (in contrast to the form) of appearances. Although Kant attempts to argue at some length in the First Edition that sense perception as such requires a synthesis, he here simply assumes this to be the case. The concern of the argument is to show that this empirical synthesis, like the transcendental synthesis of the imagination, is governed by the categories.

The argument consists of five steps that are compressed into another of Kant's typically dense paragraphs (B160–61). For convenience' sake, I shall cite each step in turn and then comment briefly upon it. An attempt at an overall assessment is reserved for the next section.

[Step 1.] In the representations of space and time we have *a priori forms* of outer and inner sensible intuition; and to these the synthesis of apprehension of the manifold of appearance must always conform because in no other way can the synthesis take place at all.

As already noted, Kant here simply assumes the actuality of a synthesis of apprehension. Taking this for granted, he reminds us that this synthesis must conform to space and time, which have been shown to be the a priori forms of human intuition. The point of this reminder is that whatever turns out to be a necessary condition for the representation of space and time will also be a necessary condition for the apprehension or perception of anything that is intuited in space and time. The same principle also underlies the arguments of the Axioms of Intuition and the Anticipations of Perception.

[Step 2.] But space and time are represented *a priori* not merely as *forms* of sensible intuition, but as themselves *intuitions* which contain a manifold of their own, and therefore are represented with the determination of the *unity* of this manifold (*vide* the Transcendental Aesthetic).

This is the passage to which Kant attaches the important and previously discussed footnote in which he distinguishes between a form of intuition and a formal intuition. The main function of the note is to explicate the point made in the text that space and time are not only forms of intuition but themselves intuitions with a manifold (content) of their own. As such, they can only be represented insofar as their manifold is unified. This much follows from the first part of the Deduction. Although Kant does not refer explicitly to it in either the text or the note, it is clear that the transcendental synthesis of the imagination is assumed to be the vehicle for this unification, and thus for a determinate representation of space or time (formal intuition). Moreover, the imaginative, extraconceptual nature of the synthesis is evident from Kant's remark in the final sentence of the note that "the unity of the *a priori* intuition belongs to space and time, and not to the concept of the understanding" (B161 n.). In light of what was said in the last section, this cryptic remark can be taken to express the view that the intuited unity of space and time is distinct from the conceptual unity that is imposed upon representations in a judgment. In the case of a judgment the unity belongs to the pure concept of the understanding, whereas in the case of the intuition it belongs to the intuited content.[68] The unity of consciousness in the representation of space and time is thus itself conditioned by the intuited content. Once again, that is why the synthesis involved in this representation must be viewed as an act of the imagination rather than of the understanding.

[Step 3.] Thus *unity of the synthesis* of the manifold, without or within us, and consequently also a *combination* to which everything that is to be represented as determined in space or in time must conform is given *a priori* as the condition of the synthesis of all *apprehension*—not indeed in, but with these intuitions.

Kant here states that the conditions of the unity of the representations of space or time are also conditions of the apprehension of anything in space or time. Consequently, anything that is apprehended in a determinate position in space or time must conform to the conditions of the representation of their unity. This makes explicit the point that is already implicit in step 1. Since the unification of the representation of space or time is achieved through the transcendental synthesis of the imagination, it also serves to connect the synthesis of apprehension to this transcendental synthesis. Kant makes the same point in the First Edition by claiming that the empirical synthesis of apprehension presupposes a pure synthesis.[69] The claim that this synthetic unity is given "not indeed in, but with these intuitions" reflects Kant's basic principle that the representation of unity presupposes a synthetic activity, and is not simply passively received through sensibility.

> [Step 4.] This synthetic unity can be no other than the unity of the combination of the manifold of a given *intuition in general* in an original consciousness, in accordance with the categories, insofar as the combination is applied to our *sensible intuition*.

This is the key step, for it is here that Kant actually links the synthesis of apprehension with the categories. There is, however, obviously no argument offered in support of this step. Instead, Kant dogmatically asserts that the unity required for apprehension is an application to human sensibility of the unity of the manifold of an intuition in general that is required for apperception. This licenses the claim that the former, like the latter, is governed by the categories. Although Kant does not bother to provide us with the argument, we can see that this result does follow from the assumption that the transcendental synthesis of the imagination is governed by the categories taken in connection with step 3. At least it follows if, as seems reasonable, we construe step 3 to assert that the synthesis of apprehension is subject to the conditions of the transcendental synthesis of the imagination. Virtually the whole weight of the "argument" thus falls on the claim, itself unsupported by Kant, that the transcendental synthesis of the imagination is governed by the categories. As I attempted to show in the last section, this does not follow analytically from the apperception principle itself, but it does follow from this principle taken in conjunction with the synthetic propositions that time is the form of inner sense and that imaginative synthesis is necessary for the representation of time.

> [Step 5.] All synthesis, therefore, even that which renders perception possible, is subject to the categories; and since experience is knowledge by means of connected perceptions, the categories are conditions of the possibility of experience, and are therefore valid *a priori* for all objects of experience.

This is Kant's general conclusion to the preceding argument. If we assume that there are only three kinds of synthesis (intellectual synthesis, figurative synthesis, and apprehension), then the first part of this conclusion clearly follows. Indeed, the Transcendental Deduction as a whole has been concerned to show that each of these syntheses in turn is governed by the categories. The second part, however, which involves a contrast between perception and experience, defined as "knowledge by means of connected perceptions," interjects for the first time a whole new theme into the Deduction. The contrast naturally calls to mind the distinction drawn in the *Prolegomena* between judgments of perception and judgments of experience; but the crucial difference is that Kant here contends that both perceptions and experience are governed by the categories. More important, it also calls to mind the two distinct formulations of the task of the second part of the Deduction which were cited at the beginning of this section of the chapter. Recall that according to one formulation the task is to establish a connection between the categories and empirical intuition, while according to the other it is to show that the categories function to make experience possible. Since the connection of the categories with perception, and thus with empirical intuition, follows from their role as conditions of the synthesis of apprehension, it is at least plausible to claim that the argument has established the first of these goals. The remaining question is whether it can also be said to have established the second. In order to deal with this question, it is necessary to consider the distinction between perception and experience and to analyze the function of the categories with respect to each of them.

C. Perception and Experience

We have already seen that Kant defines perception in the Second Edition Deduction as the empirical consciousness of an intuition as appearance. The claim is that this consciousness presupposes a synthesis of apprehension. This accords with Kant's other characterizations of perception in both editions of the *Critique*. Despite differences in details or in emphasis, they all agree in defining 'perception' as a mode of empirical consciousness which involves sensation and which has as its object an appearance.[70] The term is also used to refer to the objects of such consciousness, that is, appearances. Kant is notoriously slippery on this point, but the notion of 'appearance', when it is treated as equivalent to 'perception' or as the object of a perception, must be distinguished from the transcendental conception of the thing as it appears. Appearances in the sense presently under consideration are modifications of inner sense; they are "in us" in the empirical sense, and this holds true even though the actual content of the appearance (the sensible data) derives from outer sense. We can, therefore, say that perception is a mode of consciousness that has as its objects modifications of inner sense. The order of perception, or equivalently, of apprehension, is the order in which perceptions or appearances occur in empirical consciousness. It follows from the preceding argument that the consciousness of this order, and therefore perception itself, is subject to the categories. This is because the argument shows, or at least purports to show, that the synthesis of apprehension, whereby perceptual consciousness is determined, is subject to the conditions of the transcendental synthesis of the imagination, and this synthesis itself is governed by the categories.

The main difficulty with Kant's argument concerns the move from perception to experience. 'Experience' is here defined as "knowledge by means of connected perceptions," which corresponds to Kant's usual characterization of it as empirical knowledge of objects through perception.[71]

What Kant wishes to show is not simply that the categories apply to whatever is experienced (this much follows from the definition of experience together with the results of the preceding argument), but also (and primarily) that the categories make experience possible. In other words, what must be demonstrated is that by serving as rules for the unification of perceptions (themselves "subjective objects") the categories make possible the knowledge of an objective order of things and events ("objective experience") distinct from the subjective order of perceptions. This is precisely what Kant endeavors to show in the Analogies of Experience with respect to the relational categories (really their schemata) and an objective, temporal order of events. The problem with the argument of the Transcendental Deduction is that no such result follows from the role of the categories in the synthesis of apprehension. The most that follows from this role is that the categories are necessary for the connection of perceptions in "empirical consciousness"; it does not follow from it that they also function to relate these perceptions to an objective order and thus produce experience.[72] Indeed, it does not follow from the argument of the Transcendental Deduction alone that experience in the Kantian sense is even possible.

The problem can be clarified by a brief consideration of the two specific examples which Kant provides as illustrations of his general thesis. The first involves the category of quantity and its role in the apprehension of a spatial object (a house). Kant's choice of a "weighty" object such as a house may be misleading, especially in light of his subsequent treatment of the same example in the Second Analogy, but it is clear from the context and from his choice of terms that he is talking about the formation of a perception or image of a house in "empirical consciousness," not about the actual experience of the object. Because of the nature of human sensibility, the parts of such an "object" are apprehended as external to one another in space. Kant's point is thus that the apprehension presupposes a synthesis of the various spaces in which its constituent parts are apprehended.

> When . . . by apprehension of the manifold of a house I make the empirical intuition of it into a perception, the *necessary unity* of space and of outer sensible intuition in general lies at the basis of my apprehension, and I draw as it were the outline of the house in conformity with this synthetic unity of the manifold in space. [B161]

The point here is that the formation of the image of a spatial object is subject to the conditions of the representation of space. The connection between this necessary synthetic unity and the category of quantity stems from the homogeneity of the parts of space. Since the pure concept of quantity is just the concept of the "synthesis of the homogeneous in an intuition in general" (B162), Kant concludes that the apprehension or perception of a house must be governed by that category. This is an anticipation of the argument of the Axioms of Intuition, where Kant endeavors to prove that "all appearances are, in their intuition, extensive magnitudes" (A160). This principle applies to all objects, but it does so as a condition of their apprehension in empirical consciousness, not as a condition of the actual experience of such objects as distinct from our representation of them.

Kant's second example is designed to illustrate the role of the concept of causality in the perception of an event, such as the freezing of water. Kant begins by noting that the perception of such an event involves the successive apprehension of two states of the water: fluidity and solidity. The problem is to explain how such apprehension is possible. To this end Kant writes:

> But in the time with which I underlie all appearances as inner intuition I necessarily represent to myself the synthetic unity of the manifold, without which the relation could not be given in an intuition as being determined in respect of the time sequence. [B162–63]

The sentence is almost unintelligible, but the basic point seems to be that the apprehension of a determinate sequence in time presupposes the representation of the synthetic unity of time, and thus a synthesis. In other words, Kant appears to be suggesting a parallel with the previous example of the parts of a house. Just as that apprehension presupposes a synthesis which determines the pure manifold of outer sense (space) so too this apprehension presupposes a synthesis which determines the pure manifold of inner sense (time). Only as the result of such a determination of time, which is presumably accomplished by the transcendental synthesis of the imagination, is it possible to apprehend a sequence of perceptions in time. The claim, which Kant does not even attempt to justify, is that the ground of this determination or synthetic unity is the category of causality. Given this, he concludes:

> Thus my apprehension of such an event, and therefore the event itself, considered as a possible perception, is subject to the concept of the *relation* of *effects* and *causes,* and so in all other cases. [B163]

Since Kant's account of causality will be discussed at some length in chapter 10, it would be redundant to deal with that matter here. Our present concern is rather with the more immediate question of just what this example is intended to illustrate. Given the contrast between perception and experience and the fact that the previous example illustrates the role of the concept of quantity in apprehension or perception, one would naturally assume that it is intended to illustrate the function of the category of causality as a condition of the experience of an objective order of events distinct from the subjective order in which perceptions appear in empirical consciousness. This is further indicated by the fact that this example seems to anticipate the argument of the Second Analogy (where Kant does make such a claim), just as the first anticipates the argument of the Axioms of Intuition. None of this emerges, however, from the actual argument which Kant provides. If this argument establishes anything at all, it is only that the category of causality is necessary for the apprehension of a sequence of perceptions in inner sense. Thus, rather than the expected contrast of experience with perception, what we actually find in the second example is a parallel account of the role of a category in connection with the synthesis of apprehension or perception. They differ only in that the first example is concerned with the connection between apprehension, the category, and the synthesis of the manifold of outer sense, while the second is concerned with the connection between apprehension, the category, and the synthesis of the manifold of inner sense. In the second example Kant does, of course, refer to the perception of an event, and therefore to an instance of objective succession (a change of state of an enduring physical object). The problem is that not only does Kant fail to distinguish between the subjective order of apprehension and the objective order of the event, but he actually identifies them.[73]

It might be objected that I have placed too much weight on what is in fact a mere illustration or addendum rather than an integral part of Kant's argument. Such an objection, however, ignores the fact that the treatment of the category of causality in the second example is the logical extension of the argument of the second part of the Transcendental Deduction. It thus serves perfectly to illustrate the inadequacy of this argument to achieve the result which Kant desires. We have seen that Kant's overall strategy is to argue first that the transcendental synthesis of the imagination is necessary for the representation of space and time and that this synthesis must accord with the categories. He then claims that the synthesis of apprehension, whereby perception is produced, must likewise conform to the same categories, because it must conform to the conditions of the transcendental synthesis. I have tried to argue that a strong case can be made for the claim that this strategy does succeed in establishing a connection between the categories and empirical intuition, and that this is sufficient for a demonstration of their objective reality. Under no circumstances, however, can it also be claimed that it succeeds in showing that the categories make experience possible.

D. Some Conclusions

The first and most obvious conclusion to be drawn from the preceding analysis is that the argument of the Transcendental Deduction is at best only partially successful. It can also be seen that the problem does not really lie where it is generally thought to lie, in the doctrine of apperception and the analytic accounts of synthesis and objectivity. It lies rather in the second and synthetic portion of the argument, where Kant endeavors to connect the categories with experience by first linking them with the synthesis of apprehension. Even if we accept all of Kant's premises, including his doctrine of transcendental synthesis, his conclusion that the categories make experience possible and prescribe a priori laws to nature does not follow.

One should not infer from this, however, that the difficulty is due merely to the proof-strategy that Kant adopts in the Second Edition, and that this provides justification for preferring the First Edition version. Although in the First Edition Kant does attempt to link the categories directly to the experience of objects in the "weighty" sense, and even contends that such experience is itself a necessary condition for apperception, it can easily be shown that this version is subject to similar difficulties.[74]

Moreover, we cannot avoid the conclusion that the argument is only partially successful by suggesting, as Prauss does, that the function of the categories as conditions of "objective objects," and thus of experience, is already established in the first part of the Deduction, and that the second part is concerned merely with establishing their connection with "subjective objects."[75] In the key footnote from the preface to the *Metaphysical Foundations of Natural Science,* Kant does assert that he now sees that the solution to the problem of determining "how experience is possible by means of these categories, and only by means of them," can be derived "almost by a single conclusion from the precisely determined definition of a judgment in general (an act by which representations first become cognitions of an object)."[76] Depending upon the weight that one attaches to "almost," one could conceivably claim that Kant is here, in effect, suggesting that the desired result follows logically from the argument of the first part of the Deduction. Nevertheless, quite apart from the question of what Kant himself may have thought about the matter (either in 1785, when this was published, or in 1787, when the Second Edition of the *Critique* appeared), the fact remains that the argument of the first part of the Deduction establishes no such result. It merely demonstrates the objective validity of the categories with respect to objects in the judgmental or logical sense.

But if the first part of the Transcendental Deduction is analytic and the second part fails to demonstrate that the categories make experience possible, then much, if not all, of its philosophical significance would seem to be denied. This is especially true for the contemporary analytic reading of the Deduction. At least since Strawson, philosophers within this tradition have tended to regard the Deduction as an attempt, albeit a seriously muddled one, at a self-contained transcendental argument. The purported goal of Kant's argument, on this interpretation, is to refute the skeptic (whether Cartesian or Humean is rarely made clear)[77] by showing that we have genuine experience of "weighty" objects that are distinct from our perceptions of them.

There is, however, no need to conclude, as Bennett contemptuously does, that the Transcendental Deduction is a "botch."[78] First, in spite of the analytic nature of its basic claims, the first part of the argument provides a good "beginning," because it establishes a necessary connection between the unity of consciousness and the representation of an object in the judgmental or logical sense (the reciprocity thesis). This lays the foundation for the remainder of the argument, since it makes possible the subsequent connection between the unity of consciousness and the categories as concepts of an object in general.

Second, even though it is not completely successful, the second part of the Deduction can hardly be deemed a total failure. In fact, I have tried to argue that a strong case can be made for the claim that it does establish the objective reality of the categories and thereby achieves one of the goals which Kant set for it. Its failure to achieve the second and more ambitious goal is, therefore, not grounds for its outright rejection. Finally, even if it does not provide a self-contained transcendental argument, capable of silencing the skeptic by demonstrating synthetic a priori claims about human experience and the objects thereof, it may very well still turn out to provide an essential step in such an argument. In that case, the problem would not lie so much in the argument of the Deduction itself as in Kant's tendency to assign to it a task that should properly have been assigned to the Transcendental Analytic as a whole. We shall explore that possibility at length in the next three chapters, which deal with the Schematism and the first two Analogies of Experience.

8

The Transcendental Schematism

The Schematism of the Pure Concepts of the Understanding is the place in the *Critique* where Kant deals explicitly with the products of the transcendental synthesis of the imagination, which unites the pure concepts with pure intuition (the intellectual with the sensible conditions of human knowledge). Taking this as a clue, my main goals in the present chapter are to explain just what is meant by a "transcendental schema" and to delineate the function of Kant's theory of a transcendental schematism in the overall argument of the Transcendental Analytic. In so doing, I also hope to cast some additional light on Kant's claim in his letter to Reinhold (discussed in chapter 4) that the Schematism chapter contains the first statement in the *Critique* of the principle of synthetic judgments.

> *All synthetic judgments of theoretical knowledge are only possible through the relation of a given concept to an intuition.* If the synthetic judgment is experiential, the underlying intuition must be empirical; if it is a judgment *a priori,* the intuition must be pure.[1]

The chapter is divided into four parts. The first deals with Kant's own account of the function of the Schematism and with the question of why he describes the problem of schematizing the pure concepts in terms of subsumption. The second examines the chief ways in which Kant characterizes the transcendental schemata, both in the Schematism chapter and elsewhere; it contends that the schemata are to be regarded as determinate, or conceptualized, pure intuitions. The third considers the issue of the nature and justification of the claim that a particular schema belongs to a given category, for example, "the permanence of the real in time" to substance; it contends that such claims constitute a special class of synthetic a priori judgments ("schema judgments"). It also attempts to show how such judgments might be justified, a project which Kant himself completely neglects, but which turns out to be crucial for the overall argument of the Transcendental Analytic. The fourth discusses the connection between the schemata and the Principles; it argues that the interpretation of the schemata as determinate pure intuitions provides the key to the understanding of the synthetic a priori nature of the Principles.

173

I. SCHEMATISM AND SUBSUMPTION

The official task assigned to the Schematism is to explain how the categories, which have their seat in the nature of the human understanding, can apply to what is sensibly given to the mind, that is, to appearances. The task thus reflects Kant's insistence on the distinction between sensibility and understanding as two sources of knowledge. In the brief section called Transcendental Judgment in General, which serves as an introduction to the Analytic of Principles, the second book of the Transcendental Analytic, Kant states that the Schematism accomplishes this task by providing the "sensible conditions under which alone pure concepts of the understanding can be employed" (A136/B175). By "sensible conditions" for the employment of a concept, Kant means the specific features or properties of what is sensibly given which reflect or correspond to what is thought in the concept. These could also be called the "empirical meaning conditions" of the concept. The basic idea here is that apart from such conditions (the schemata) the pure concepts of the understanding have a "logical use" (as logical functions of judgment), but not a "real use," that is, an application to "real" objects.

To specify these conditions is also to specify just what is being claimed about the phenomenal world (the sum of all appearances), when it is claimed that particular categories apply to it. Thus the determination of these conditions is an integral part of what Kant terms "metaphysics in its first part" (Bxviii) and Paton a "metaphysic of experience";[2] namely, a body of synthetic a priori propositions (Principles of Pure Understanding), in which categorial claims are made about the phenomenal world. In fact, given this understanding of metaphysics, one can even subscribe to Heidegger's dictum that "the doctrine of the schematism of the pure concepts of the understanding is the decisive stage in the laying of the foundations of *metaphysica generalis*."[3]

In spite of this, however, it is sometimes argued that the account of the Schematism is superfluous because the desired results, if they are established at all, must already have been established in the Transcendental Deduction. This was originally maintained by Prichard, for whom it applies to the whole of the second book of the Transcendental Analytic, not just the Schematism chapter.

> We naturally feel a preliminary difficulty with respect to the existence of this second part of the *Analytic* at all. It seems clear that if the first part is successful, the second must be unnecessary. For if Kant is in a position to lay down that the categories must apply to objects, no special conditions of their application need be subsequently determined. If, for instance, it can be laid down that the category of quantity must apply to objects, it is implied either that there are no special conditions of its application, or that they have already been discovered and shown to exist. Again, to assert the applicability of the categories is really to assert the existence of principles, and in fact of

just those principles which it is the aim of the *System of Principles* to prove. Thus to assert the applicability of the categories of quantity and of cause and effect is to assert respectively the principles that all objects of perception are extensive quantities, and that all changes take place according to the law of cause and effect.[4]

More recently, a similar objection, albeit with specific reference to the Schematism, has been raised by J. G. Warnock, who maintains that the presence of this chapter in the *Critique* is due entirely to Kant's illicit separation of the possession of a concept from the ability to use it. According to Warnock, the goal of the Transcendental Deduction is to prove that we possess a certain set of concepts (the categories); and if this goal were achieved, there would be no remaining questions about the applicability of these concepts and, therefore, no problem requiring a theory of schematism for its solution.[5]

Neither form of this objection can stand up under any scrutiny, but a brief consideration of both forms should help to clarify further the function of Kant's theory of a transcendental schematism. The main point here is the completely general nature of the outcome of the Transcendental Deduction.[6] As we saw in the last chapter, the most that can be claimed for the Transcendental Deduction is that it establishes the objective reality of the categories; namely, the fact that they have a sensible reference or application to the data of human sensibility. This is accomplished in the second part of the Deduction by connecting the categories first with the forms of sensibility (particularly time) through the transcendental synthesis of the imagination, and then with the empirical content of sensibility through the synthesis of apprehension. If sound, this argument shows that the categories stand in a necessary connection with time, and, therefore, with objects qua temporal. By itself, however, this result hardly enables us to arrive at any specific metaphysical propositions. To cite Prichard's own example: it simply is not true that "to assert the applicability of the categories of quantity and cause and effect is to assert the principle that all objects of perception are extensive quantities, and that all changes take place according to the law of cause and effect." To know that the concept of quantity is applicable to the objects of human experience is not yet to know either that it applies universally or that the objects to which it applies are extensive quantities. The latter conclusion, in particular, requires the additional knowledge of how this concept is expressed in sensible terms, that is, how it is schematized. Again, to know that the category of causality is applicable to objects of human experience is not to know either that it relates specifically to alterations of the state of substances or that it relates to all such alterations.[7]

Similar considerations apply to the objection in its Warnockian form. The purpose of the Transcendental Deduction is not, as Warnock suggests, to prove that we possess a certain set of concepts. On the contrary, it assumes on the basis of the Metaphysical Deduction that we do possess the pure concepts and that they have at least a "logical use" (as logical functions of judgment). The question with which it deals is whether they also have an extralogical or "real use," that is, an application to objects of possible experience.[8] Once again, the argument, if sound, proves that they do have such a use, but it does not show how and under what specific conditions the particular concepts are to be employed. For example, it does not tell us what property or relation of appearances in time is to be taken as the sensible expression or analogue of the logical relation of ground and consequent. This is the task which the Schematism must perform for each of the categories. As Kant puts the matter in an important Reflexion, "The Schematism shows the conditions under which an appearance is determined in respect to a logical function and, therefore, stands under a category."[9]

Another difficulty which critics have found in Kant's account is that he casts the whole problem of finding sensible conditions which license the application of specific categories to appearances in terms of subsumption. This occurs twice, and 'subsumption' seems to be used in a different sense in each case.[10] The first is in the introduction to the Transcendental Doctrine of Judgment, where Kant defines judgment as "the faculty of subsuming under rules, that is, of distinguishing whether something does or does not stand under a given rule (*casus datae legis*)" (A132/B177). Here the rules are the pure concepts, and the schemata function as the means for determining whether a given appearance stands under one or another of these rules. The second and really notorious passage occurs at the opening of the Schematism chapter itself. Kant begins by noting that all cases of subsumption of an object under a concept require some homogeneity between the two. This is presumably illustrated by the relation between the geometrical concept of a circle and the empirical concept of a plate (not, as one would expect, the plate itself). Here the homogeneity is said to consist in the fact that what is intuited in the former (the geometrical concept) is thought in the latter.[11] Then, by way of contrast to this relatively unproblematic situation, comes the decisive passage:

> But pure concepts of understanding being quite heterogeneous from empirical intuitions, and indeed from all sensible intuitions, can never be met with in any intuition. For no one will say that a category, such as that of causality, can be intuited through sense and is itself contained in appearance. How, then, is the *subsumption* of intuitions under pure concepts, the *application* of a category to appearances, possible? A transcendental doctrine of judgment is necessary just because of this natural and important question. [A136–37/B176–77]

Unfortunately, most of Kant's commentators have found this question, at least in the way in which he here formulates it, to be neither natural nor important. According to the standard objection, 'subsumption' is here used in the sense in which it is found in the traditional theory of judgment, that is, to designate the relation between a class concept and the particulars falling under it. To judge on this theory is just to subsume particulars under such a concept. Evidence for this interpretation is presumably supplied by Kant's example of the subsumption relation between the geometrical concept of the circle and the empirical concept of a plate. Given this reading, it is then easy to argue not only that this notion of subsumption is hopelessly inadequate to capture the nature of judgment, but also that such a formulation mistakes the relation which, according to Kant's own doctrine, holds between the categories and the sensibly given. As Kemp Smith puts it, this relation is properly one of form and matter, structure and content, not universal and particular.[12]

Admittedly, the opening paragraphs of the Schematism chapter cannot be characterized as a model of philosophical lucidity. Still, it would be surprising if Kant were in fact as confused as his commentators assume him to be. First of all, one can question whether Kant really intended his example of the relation between the geometrical concept of a circle and the empirical concept of a plate to be taken as an instance of the subsumption of a particular under a class concept. This suggests that the concept of a plate (or rather the plate itself) can be taken as a member of the class of circles, which can hardly be what Kant meant. As Paton has indicated, it seems rather that the key to Kant's intent lies in the initially puzzling reference to "the roundness which is intuited in the former" (the pure geometrical concept of a circle).[13] Assuming this, we can then read Kant to be maintaining that it is the possibility of exhibiting the geometrical concept in pure intuition (constructing a circle) that explains the homogeneity between it and objects, such as plates, that are given in empirical intuition, as well as the empirical concepts that are formed by abstraction from the content of such intuition ("thought in the latter"). The homogeneity, in short, is between pure and empirical intuition, not between a class concept and a member of that class. Moreover, only such a reading enables us to make any sense of the contrast which Kant wishes to draw between the geometrical concept and the pure concepts of the understanding, which "can never be met with in any intuition."

Such an interpretation of the circle-plate relation also relieves us of the need to interpret the still problematic relation between the pure concepts and appearances in terms of the notion of subsumption as it is operative in the traditional theory of judgment. In fact, as the text already indicates, Kant is using 'subsumption' as a synonym for 'application'.[14] Thus, rather than making 'subsumption' into the "trouser word," which would force us to conclude that Kant has mistakenly construed the problem of the application of the categories in terms of the judgmental notion of subsumption, it seems to be both reasonable and in accordance with the text to read 'subsumption' here as simply meaning 'application'.

If we were to stop here, however, we would not so much have interpreted 'subsumption' as interpreted it away. Certainly, an adequate exegesis must show that the term is not completely idle. Fortunately, this is quite easy to do. The key point is that it is the syllogistic, not the judgmental, conception of subsumption that is at work here, and which is supposed to provide an analogy for understanding the problem of the application of the pure concepts of the understanding to appearances.[15] Kant sketches his views on this topic in the *Critique* and in a parallel passage in the *Lectures on Logic* (§58). As he puts it in the *Critique,* inferring or "judging mediately" takes place "by the subsumption of the condition of a possible judgment under the condition of a given judgment." The "given judgment" is the universal rule which functions as the major premise ("everything composite is alterable"). The minor premise is characterized as "the subsumption of the condition of another possible judgment under the condition of the rule" ("bodies are composite"). The conclusion is the "mediate judgment," which results from the application of the rule to the subsumed case ("bodies are alterable") (A330–31 / B386–87). The crucial term here is 'condition'. Recall that in the minor premise, it is the "condition of another possible judgment" (bodies) that is subsumed under "the condition of the rule" (not the rule itself). In addition, Kant tells us that this rule "states something universal, subject to a certain condition." In the categorical syllogism in the text, the condition of the rule is the quality of being composite. The minor premise then asserts that this condition is met in the case of bodies. This licenses the conclusion that all bodies are alterable. The condition of the rule is thus the middle term in the syllogism, the "third thing," which connects the universal rule with the particulars to which it is applied in the conclusion.

Kant hardly wished to construe the application of the categories to appearances as a bit of syllogistic reasoning. Nevertheless, the analogy with such reasoning does serve to underscore the particular problem of understanding how such application is possible. As already noted, the problem is the heterogeneity of the two elements to be brought into connection. This heterogeneity is due to the fact that the pure concepts of the understanding, in contrast even to "pure sensible," or mathematical, concepts, are derived from the very nature of the understanding. As such, they have no direct relation to intuition. Yet, as the Transcendental Deduction demonstrates, they do relate to intuition and, therefore, to appearances. Given all of this, it is easy to see that the whole purpose of the analogy is to suggest that, just as in the case of syllogistic reasoning, the connection between the rule expressed in the major premise and the instance to which it is applied in the conclusion is only established by means of the subsumption of the instance under the *condition* of the rule; so in the present case, where the pure concepts of the understanding are the universal rules, there is a need for some analogue of the condition of the rule, or the middle term of the syllogism, under which appearances can be "subsumed." This analogue will, of course, turn out to be the transcendental schema, the infamous "third thing," which makes possible the mediation between category and appearance.

Finally, this analogy enables us to see the importance, if not the naturalness, of the question which Kant raises. Since concepts for Kant are "predicates of possible judgments" (A69/B94), and since judgments which apply concepts to appearance are synthetic, while those which apply a priori concepts are likewise a priori, it follows that the question with which Kant is concerned at the beginning of the Schematism chapter is really the question of how synthetic judgments are possible a priori.[16] When he first posed this question in general terms in the introduction to the *Critique*, without any specific reference to the pure concepts of the understanding, Kant alluded mysteriously to an "unknown = x" (B13), which is needed to ground the connection between the concepts that is asserted in the judgment. When he returns to it in the Transcendental Analytic, this "unknown = x" is more precisely characterized as a transcendental schema. No doubt this is part of what Kant had in mind when he wrote the letter to Reinhold cited at the beginning of this chapter.

II. THE NATURE OF THE TRANSCENDENTAL SCHEMATISM

What, then, is a transcendental schema, if it is to be capable of playing this significant role? This would seem a straightforward question, for which there must be a direct, unambiguous answer. When we turn to the text, however, we find a bewildering variety of answers, not all of which are obviously compatible with one another. Limiting ourselves to the Schematism chapter, and even there ignoring minor variations, not to mention the important accounts of the schemata of mathematical and empirical concepts, we find the notion of a transcendental schema characterized in the following ways:

1. As a "third thing" or "mediating representation," which is "homogeneous on the one hand with the category, and on the other hand with the appearance, and which thus makes the application of the former to the latter possible." Kant also claims that such a representation must be "pure" (nonempirical), and that "while it must in one respect be *intellectual*, it must in another be *sensible*" (A138/B177).

2. As a "transcendental determination of time," which, as suggested in the first characterization, is homogeneous with both category and appearance, and which therefore "mediates the subsumption of the appearances under the category" (A139/B178).

3. As the "formal and pure condition of sensibility to which the concept of understanding is restricted" (A140/B179).

4. As the "representation of a universal procedure of imagination in providing an image for a concept" (A140/B179–80). This is intended as a general characterization of a schema. It leads directly to the brief account of the schemata of mathematical and empirical concepts as rules for the construction of images.

5. As "simply the pure synthesis, determined by a rule of that unity, in accordance with concepts, to which the category gives expression." This formulation underscores the point that, unlike those of other concepts, the schemata of the pure concepts of the understanding cannot be construed as rules for the construction of images. In this context, it is further described as a "transcendental product of imagination, a product which concerns the determination of inner sense in general according to conditions of its form (time) in respect of all representations, so far as these representations are to be connected *a priori* in one concept in conformity with the unity of apperception" (A142/B181).

6. As "the true and sole conditions under which these concepts obtain relation to objects and so possess *significance*" (A146/B185).

7. As "nothing but *a priori* determinations of time in accordance with rules" (A145/B184).

8. As "only the phenomenon, or sensible concept, of an object in agreement with the category" (A146/B186).

In the face of this plethora of formulations, the thesis for which I wish to argue is that a transcendental schema is to be construed as a pure intuition, and that this is compatible with all of these formulations, with the possible exception of the fourth. Although none of these formulations explicitly identifies a transcendental schema with a pure intuition, such an identification is obviously compatible with the third and the sixth. More germane, however, is the fact that Kant does characterize a transcendental schema explicitly as a pure intuition in both the *Critique of Practical Reason* and the *Critique of Judgment*. In the former work he writes, in connection with the discussion of the *Typic of Pure Practical Judgment:*

> The judgment of pure practical reason, therefore, is subject to the same difficulties as that of the pure theoretical, though the latter had a means of escape. It could escape because in its theoretical use everything depended upon intuitions to which pure concepts of the understanding could be applied, and such intuitions (though only of objects of the senses), as *a priori* and hence concerning the connection of the manifold in intuitions, could be given *a priori* in conformity to the concepts of the understanding, i.e., as schemata.[17]

In the *Critique of Judgment* he notes:

> Intuitions are always required to verify [*darzuthun*] the reality of our concepts. If the concepts are empirical the intuitions are called examples: if they

are pure concepts of the understanding the intuitions go by the name of schemata.[18]

The claim that transcendental schemata are to be construed as pure intuitions is not new. Moltke S. Gram has insisted upon it in his own account of the Transcendental Analytic. Gram, however, grants to this interpretation a somewhat subterranean status, since he connects it with what he calls Kant's "hidden" or "implicit" theory of syntheticity. According to this theory, synthetic judgments predicate concepts of intuitions, and synthetic a priori judgments predicate pure concepts of pure intuitions. Transcendental schemata, construed as pure intuitions, are on this view the referents of the schematized and not the pure concepts.[19] Nevertheless, Gram explicitly denies that this interpretation of a transcendental schema is compatible with all of Kant's accounts. In particular, he denies its compatibility with the "third-thing" account. The heart of the problem, according to Gram, lies in what he takes to be the incoherence of the notion of a "third thing," which is both universal and particular, intellectual and sensible. Since these constitute two sets of contradictory properties, nothing can possess both members of either set. Moreover, even if something could, it would not be pure intuition, which is by definition entirely sensible and particular.[20]

It can easily be seen, however, that this objection is misguided. In fact, it is the direct result of Gram's failure to distinguish between the two senses of 'pure intuition' discussed in chapter 5.[21] These two senses, it will be recalled, correspond to Kant's own distinction between space as a mere *form of intuition* or sensibility and an actual representation of space (as in geometry), which is a *formal intuition*.[22] Of these two, it is obviously only the first that can be said to be purely, or completely, sensible. Consequently, Gram's whole objection to the "third-thing" formulation is a product of his erroneous assumption that the notion of a pure intuition can be understood only in the first sense.

Nor can this second (determinate) sense of pure intuition be taken as an afterthought to which Kant merely alludes in an obscure footnote in the Second Edition. On the contrary, it is a central thesis of the Transcendental Deduction, even in the First Edition, that it is only insofar as the "pure manifold" of intuition (indeterminate pure intuition) is synthesized in accordance with the categories that it can be brought to the unity of consciousness and thus yield an actual content for cognition. As Kant clearly states, apart from such a synthesis, "not even the purest and most elementary representations of space and time, could arise" (A102). Surely, such representations count as pure intuitions in the Kantian sense, and so we are led inevitably to conclude that the conception of a determinate pure intuition is as central to Kant's thought as the doctrine of the transcendental synthesis of the imagination, from which it is in fact inseparable. Moreover, as we have also seen, it is just such a (determinate) pure intuition to which the mathematician appeals when he exhibits or constructs his concepts.[23] The pure (formal) intuition that is produced by such an activity is both sensible and intellectual (it is a *sensible* presentation of a *concept*), and it is also both universal and particular. Indeed, Kant himself claims as much in his account of geometrical construction.

> To *construct* a concept means to exhibit *a priori* the intuition which corresponds to the concept. For the construction of a concept we therefore need a *non-empirical* intuition. The latter must, as intuition, be a *single* object, and yet none the less, as the construction of a concept (a universal representation), it must in its representation express universal validity for all possible intuitions which fall under the same concept. [A713/B741]

If, therefore, we take the notion of pure intuition in the second, determinate sense, there is no longer any difficulty in reconciling the claim that a transcendental schema is a pure intuition with the initial characterization of it as a "third thing." We must now consider whether it is compatible with the second and decisive characterization of such a schema as a "transcendental determination of time." Since most of the other characterizations are clearly equivalent to or derivative from this one, showing the compatibility in this case should suffice to justify the interpretation.

Some apparent plausibility is certainly derived from the fact that time, for Kant, is a pure intuition. Thus far, however, the plausibility is merely apparent, for from the fact that time is a pure intuition it by no means follows that a transcendental determination of time is one also. Moreover, the text is not of very much direct help in this matter. Rather than providing us with an account of just what he means by a "transcendental determination of time," Kant simply affirms its homogeneity with the category "which constitutes its unity, in that it is universal and rests upon an *a priori* rule," and with appearance, "in that time is contained in every empirical representation of the manifold" (A138–39/B177–78). Nevertheless, by paying attention to some of the hints contained here, it should be possible to arrive at some understanding of this difficult notion.

Let us begin with a consideration of what, in general, it means for Kant to "determine an intuition" (keeping in mind that time is an intuition). Such locution is not very frequent in the text, but where we do find it, it clearly means to synthesize, conceptualize, or subsume the given intuition under a concept (all of these here being used synonymously) in such a way that the intuition is related to, or represents, an object.[24] Moreover, only by this means can a concept itself come into relation to an object and thereby gain objective reality. 'Transcendental' is here equivalent to 'a priori', or universal and necessary; hence the equivalence of the second and seventh formulations. Thus a transcendental determination of an intuition would simply be one that is governed by an a priori concept, which is precisely what Kant indicates in the passage cited above. Putting this together and applying it to time, we arrive at the result that a transcendental determination of time must be a conceptualization of time in accordance with an a priori concept, which refers time to an object or objectifies it, while also providing objective reality for the concept involved. To objectify time means to represent a temporal order as an intersubjectively valid order of events or states of affairs in the phenomenal world, in contrast to a merely subjective or "subjectively valid" order of representations in an individual consciousness. Presumably, this is effected by the transcendental synthesis of the imagination. A transcendental determination of time can, therefore, also be characterized as a product of this synthesis or, as Kant puts it in the fifth formulation, a "transcendental product of imagination."[25]

These considerations all seem to lead to the conclusion that transcendental determinations of time, as products of the transcendental synthesis of the imagination, are universal and necessary (a priori) characteristics of objective time or an objective temporal order. This would explain their homogeneity with appearance, since all appearances are contained in such an order, and with the pure concepts, since these concepts provide the rules whereby this order is determined. The situation, however, is considerably complicated by the fact that time (as well as space) is not itself an object and cannot be perceived. Consequently, a transcendental determination of time must be regarded as a universal and necessary characteristic of things in time (phenomena), in virtue of which time can be represented in a determinate manner (objective time relations can be expressed), rather than as a characteristic of time per se. [26] To cite a single example, the schema of the concept of substance is said by Kant to be the "permanence of the real in time" (A143/B183). Kant will argue in the First Analogy that it is only by reference to something permanent that change, and with it the passage of time, can be intuited. Our concern here is not with the cogency of this argument, but simply with the claim itself; namely, that it is only by reference to the permanent that the passage of time can be determined and, therefore, that the presence of something permanent is a necessary feature of any world that can be experienced as temporal. Given this, together with the above considerations, it follows that permanence, although a property of things in time rather than of time itself, can nonetheless be regarded as a transcendental determination of time.

But does not this account of a transcendental determination of time completely undermine the claim that a transcendental schema is a pure intuition? How can such a necessary characteristic of things in time, or even the representation of such a characteristic, be termed a pure intuition? To continue with our example: permanence is a concept which refers to any number of possible objects; and the same can be said, *mutatis mutandis,* of any of the schemata. This is undoubtedly why transcendental schemata are frequently construed as concepts and equated with the schematized categories. Moreover, such an interpretation is not only suggested by the above account, but also seems to be confirmed by Kant's own characterization of the schema in the eighth formulation as "only the phenomenon, or sensible concept, of an object in agreement with the category."

Since a transcendental schema has already been defined as a *determinate* pure intuition, and since this has been seen to mean one that is conceptualized, it should come as no great surprise to find a conceptual component in its characterization. Here the emphasis must fall on the fact that it is a *sensible* concept. Although Kant, of course, begins with the radical separation of sensibility and understanding, intuition and concept, the very heart of his account of knowledge consists in the claim that any cognition of an object involves both elements. With regard to permanence, as well as all of the transcendental schemata, the intuitive element must be located in the irreducibly sensible component of the representation. To think of something permanent is just to think of it as lasting through time. The concept thus "rests upon" or presupposes the intuition of time, which it determines. In this respect it is analogous to a mathematical concept, such as that of a triangle, which has an essential reference to the pure intuition of space, wherein it is exhibited or constructed.

It might here be objected that the comparison ignores the crucial difference between mathematical concepts and pure concepts of the understanding: the former can be constructed, that is, presented in pure (formal) intuition, and the latter cannot. Indeed, it was this very heterogeneity between pure concept and intuition that generated the problem of the Schematism in the first place. Thus the basic justification for characterizing the realized (constructed) mathematical concept as a pure (formal) intuition seems to be totally lacking in the case of the schemata of the pure concepts of the understanding.

In order to deal with this objection, it is necessary to consider the account of pure intuition which Kant provides in the Transcendental Aesthetic. As we have seen, this conception is consistently correlated with the notion of form. The differences between the various characterizations turn on the different ways in which this latter notion is construed. Thus, in the preliminary definitions, "pure intuition" is initially equated with "form of sensibility" (A20/B34–35). But since the defining characteristic of empirical intuition is the presence of sensation, a form of sensibility is likewise termed a "form of empirical intuition." Correlatively, since "appearance" is defined as the "undetermined object of an empirical intuition," a pure intuition can also be designated as a "form of appearance."

We have already considered many of these locutions and their relations to one another in chapter 5, where we saw that 'form' is equivalent to 'condition', with the latter term understood in an epistemic sense. Thus, in the Metaphysical Exposition of space, Kant argues that the representation of space functions as a "condition" of outer experience on the grounds that it is only by reference to this representation that objects can be experienced as external to the mind and to each other. Correlatively, in the conclusions drawn from this Exposition, Kant asserts that space is "nothing but the form of all appearances of outer sense," precisely because he claims to have shown already that it is the "subjective condition of sensibility under which alone outer intuition is possible for us" (A26/B42). Kant here assumes a correlation between 'condition of intuition,' or sensibility, 'form of intuition', and 'pure intuition'. Given this correlation, it would seem plausible to maintain that transcendental schemata are pure intuitions if they can be shown to function as "forms" or "conditions" of sensible intuition.

Kant certainly seems to affirm such a function for transcendental schemata when he characterizes them as 'formal conditions of sensibility' (A140/B179). Indeed, this is strikingly reminiscent of the above mentioned characterization of space as a 'subjective condition of sensibility'. Even apart from this, however, it should by now be clear that this is precisely the function that is assigned to transcendental determinations of time. As conditions of empirical time determination, they are certainly conditions in a different sense than are space and time themselves. The latter are general forms or conditions of sensibility, that is, conditions under and with reference to which the data of empirical intuition are given to the mind, while transcendental determinations of time are specific temporal conditions of actual empirical intuitions. Nevertheless, they are still conditions of empirical intuition and, therefore, pure intuitions in the Kantian sense.

III. THE CATEGORIES AND THEIR SCHEMATA:
THE PROBLEM OF SCHEMA JUDGMENTS

In addition to explicating the function of transcendental schemata and characterizing them in general terms, Kant also provides us with a catalogue of the particular schemata that are connected with the various categories (or at least with eight of them).[27] This catalogue contains a set of claims which I shall here call "schema judgments." By a "schema judgment," I mean simply a judgment that asserts that a certain schema pertains to, or is the sensible expression of, a certain category. An example of such a judgment is the claim "The schema of substance is permanence of the real in time" (A143/B183). Given the nature and function of transcendental schemata, it seems clear that such judgments can be construed as semantic claims. In C. I. Lewis's terminology, as adopted by Lewis White Beck, they provide the categories with a "sense meaning," whereas apart from their schemata they merely have a "linguistic meaning."[28] For much the same reason, these schemata have also been characterized as "semantic rules."[29] In the Schematism chapter Kant himself says emphatically that "the schemata of the pure concepts of understanding are thus the true and sole conditions under which these concepts obtain relation to objects and so possess significance [*Bedeutung*]" (A146/B185). Elsewhere he modifies this claim somewhat by noting that, apart from their schemata, the pure concepts do have a logical significance, and even a "transcendental meaning," but no reference to an object that can be given in possible experience, and thus no "real" significance.[30] As previously noted, I take the latter claim to be the doctrine to which Kant is committed by his theory of pure concepts.

A. The Problem Defined

Our present concern, however, is not with the pure concepts considered apart from their schemata; it is rather with the basis of their connection with these schemata. In particular, it is with the nature and justification of the schema judgments which assert this connection. A fruitful way of coming to grips with the problem raised by judgments of this type is to ask how they are to be classified within the Kantian framework. The fact that Kant does little more than list the schemata pertaining to the particular categories might suggest that the schema judgments are either analytic or merely stipulative claims. A similar interpretation is also indicated by the semantic nature of these claims. Nevertheless, the heterogeneity of the intellectual and the sensible, taken together with the status of the transcendental schemata as pure intuitions or conditions of sensibility, rules out the possibility that the claims are analytic, while the possibility that they are stipulative, which would make the connection arbitrary, is incompatible with Kant's claim that these schemata are the *sole* conditions under which the categories gain significance. Equally clearly, a schema judgment cannot be synthetic a posteriori. This would imply that the connection between category and schema is based on experience; but this is incompatible with the a priori status of both, as well as with Kant's claim that it is only in virtue of these schemata that the categories can relate to experience in the first place. We are left, therefore, with the alternative that a schema judgment is both synthetic and a priori.

But we need not content ourselves with an argument by elimination. We can also see positively that schema judgments must be classified as synthetic a priori. First, although they cannot be equated with real definitions of the categories,[31] schema judgments certainly function analogously to such definitions; and, as we have already seen, such definitions are always synthetic judgments. Moreover, as Lewis White Beck has pointed out, in providing a concept with a schema, which I take to be equivalent to making a schema judgment concerning that concept, "It is not the *concept* of an intuitive condition which might be added to the concept or included in its definition . . . it is the *condition of sensibility itself.*"[32] We have seen that such a "condition of sensibility" is a pure intuition. Beck does not say quite this, but he does note that the condition is "a transcendental addendum, a real predicate, a synthetic predicate, a *Bestimmung,* an element in the *ratio essendi* as well as the *ratio cognoscendi.*"[33] Given the previous account of judgment, there can be no doubt that any judgment that does this is synthetic in Kant's sense; and if the predicate is an a priori representation (as is the case in a schema judgment), then the judgment is also a priori.

The synthetic a priori character of schema judgments indicates that they, like all such judgments, require a "deduction" or justification. Moreover, although Kant never explicitly addresses himself to this problem, there are at least two passages which suggest that he was aware of it. The first is from the general introduction to the Analytic of Principles. In commenting on the "peculiarity" of transcendental philosophy, he there notes that "besides the rule (or rather the universal condition of rules), which is given in the pure concept of understanding, it can also specify *a priori* the instance to which the rule is to be applied." In light of this, he further reflects: "It [transcendental philosophy] must formulate by means of universal but sufficient marks the conditions under which objects can be given in harmony with these concepts" (A136/B175). The second passage is from the Schematism chapter itself. Here Kant notes curtly that "pure *a priori* concepts, in addition to the function of understanding expressed in the category, must contain *a priori* certain formal conditions of sensibility, namely those of inner sense" (A140/B179). We have already seen, with regard to this passage, that these "formal conditions of sensibility" are transcendental schemata.

Unfortunately, neither of these passages helps very much in the resolution of the problem. Both presuppose the general result of the Transcendental Deduction, namely, that the pure concepts stand in relation to time by means of their connection with the transcendental synthesis of the imagination. Given this result, Kant seems to be claiming that it must be possible to specify the schema corresponding to the category or, equivalently, that the category somehow "contains" its schema (the formal condition of sensibility). But he does not offer a trace of justification for this claim, and he provides no account of how one can ever establish the connection between a given category and its schema. We thus find ourselves led to the paradoxical result that the whole problem of the synthetic a priori breaks out *within* the doctrine of the Schematism, even though this doctrine is intended as an essential step in the resolution of this problem.

An initially plausible way of dealing with this problem is through the familiar distinction between pure and schematized categories. Thus one might argue that, since the pure concepts stand in no connection with time, no schemata can be supplied for them; but that, since the schematized categories already stand in connection with time (as rules for the transcendental synthesis of the imagination), the connection between *these* categories and their schemata can be determined analytically. For instance, if, with Paton, we define the pure category of substance as "the concept of the synthesis of subject and predicate" and the schematized category as "the concept of the synthesis of the permanent and the changing in time,"[34] then, while it would be impossible to provide a schema for the former, it would be a trivial matter to do so for the latter.[35]

But this surely will not do. Even assuming the distinction between pure and schematized categories, which Kant himself never explicitly draws,[36] the obvious difficulty with this move is that it only pushes the problem back one step, to the connection between the pure and the schematized categories. Thus, to continue with Paton's distinction between the pure and the schematized categories of substance, we are led to ask about the connection between the concept of the synthesis of subject and predicate (which concerns the relation between representations in a judgment) and the concept of the synthesis of the permanent and the changing in time (which concerns the relation between entities). It is easy to show that this connection must be both synthetic and a priori, and so we come back to our original question.[37]

We must, therefore, find the "ground" of the synthetic a priori judgment connecting category and schema. In order to achieve this goal, we must go beyond what Kant explicitly tell us, but it may still be possible to do so on the basis of materials which the Transcendental Analytic provides. Two points are of particular relevance: (1) that the categories, as rules for the transcendental synthesis of the imagination, serve to determine time (the form of inner sense); and (2) that the schema is in each case the product of such determination.[38] Assuming these premises, I believe that it is possible to construct a plausible case for the connections between at least some of the categories and their designated schemata. I regard the case for the connection between the category of community and its schema as hopeless, for many of the same reasons advanced in chapter 6 regarding the connection between this category and the disjunctive form of judgment. Moreover, an adequate treatment of the connections between the categories of quantity and quality and their schemata would involve lengthy considerations that are not directly relevant to the main line of argument in this study. Consequently, I intend to limit my analysis to the modal categories, where the schema judgments have to be interpreted in light of the corresponding Principles (the Postulates of Empirical Thought), and to the categories of substance and causality, where the discussion of the schema judgments serves as a prelude to the central themes of the next two chapters.

B. The Modal Categories and Their Schemata

The modal categories and their respective schemata are possibility ("the agreement of the synthesis of different representations with the conditions of time in general"), actuality ("existence in some determinate time"), and necessity ("existence of an object at all times"). In his recapitulation of these schemata Kant adds by way of a general comment, "The schema of modality and of its categories is time itself as the correlate of the determination whether and how an object belongs to time" (A145 / B185). Both the general comment and the specific schemata suggest strongly that what Kant is providing here is a set of translations of logical into real modalities. In other words, he is specifying the conditions under which we can designate an empirical object or state of affairs as possible, actual, or necessary. Such translations (and the same can be said for all the schemata), provide rules for thinking about appearances in categorial terms. They tell us how, and in what specific terms, categorial thinking must proceed. Moreover, since categorial thinking is the condition of all thinking, they are at the same time the conditions of all thought about appearances. They can, therefore, be regarded as rules for the application to appearances of rules, and this constitutes the moment of truth in the prevalent "rule theory" of the schematism.[39] The key point, however, is that they can function as rules in this sense only, if it is assumed that they express the result of the translation of the logical functions thought in the categories into temporal terms. For example, only if I already know or assume that the temporal and hence experiential translation of 'actuality' must be "existence at a determinate time" can I use this as a basis for deciding whether something is actual. In each case it is the initial claim that is crucial and that requires justification. Thus, rather than simply describing transcendental schemata as rules, it is more accurate to characterize them as "transcendental products" that can serve or function as rules.[40]

The case of possibility is the most clear cut, although even it is not without its difficulties. Kant understands logical possibility in the traditional manner as lack of contradiction. Even an *ens rationis* is possible in this sense, but not everything that is logically possible is also really possible. 'Real possibility' is defined in terms of the agreement of the thought of an object (the "synthesis") with the "conditions of time in general." Simply put, to be really possible means to be possible in or over a period of time. Kant's own example of real possibility is the case of opposites, both of which cannot pertain to the same thing at the same time, but which can belong to it at different times. This shows that a temporal indexing is necessary in order to determine real possibility. An example of something that is really, although not logically, impossible is a first (or last) event, which was discussed in connection with the argument of the

First Antinomy. This example makes it clear that in order to determine what is really possible we need to refer to the "laws of the unity of experience," that is, the Analogies, as well as directly to time, because these "laws" specify the conditions under which something can be experienced in time. Nevertheless, the fact remains that time provides the field or framework within which, and in terms of which, real possibility is determined.

At this point the question naturally arises: What has happened to space? This question occurs with respect to all of the schemata, but it is especially germane here because, in the Postulates of Empirical Thought, Kant defines the possible as "that which agrees with the formal conditions of experience, that is, with the conditions of intuition and of concepts" (A218/B265). The necessity of an agreement with conceptual conditions has already been noted in the discussion of the notion of a first (or last) event. We have also seen that this is perfectly compatible with the characterization of real possiblity in terms of time. Nevertheless, space is also a form of intuition and would, therefore, seem to have a foundational role with respect to possibility. In fact, Kant notes in the Postulates that constructibility in space is the condition of the objective reality of a geometrical concept, and thus of the real possibility of the object of that concept.[41] This certainly seems to lend support to the frequently voiced objection that Kant unjustifiably ignored space in his designation of the schemata.

I shall first consider the problem in connection with possibility and will then turn to the general issue that Kant's apparent neglect of space raises for the interpretation and evaluation of his whole theory of schematism. First, it must be acknowledged that Kant's characterization of geometrical possibility in spatial terms is not reflected in the schema of possibility, even though it is in the Postulate. There is, however, some justification for this, if we consider that in the Schematism chapter Kant is concerned not with the role of pure concepts in mathematics, but rather with the conditions of their applicability to appearances. Time is characterized in the Transcendental Aesthetic as the "formal *a priori* condition of all appearances whatsoever" (A34/B50), in contrast to space, which is the a priori condition of outer appearances only. The preeminence given to time stems from its being the form of inner sense; and all appearances, as "modifications of inner sense," are in time, whereas only outer appearances are in space. But if not all appearances are in space, then conformity to the conditions of space, or spatiality, can hardly be the criterion of real possibility for objects as appearances. It may be a sufficient condition, but it is certainly not a necessary condition, for such possibility. Thus Kant seems to be fully justified in defining the schema of possibility in exclusively temporal terms.

The general objection is more complex and requires a two-part response. First, as in the case of possibility, it is necessary to distinguish between the sphere of objects to which the categories apply and the necessary conditions in virtue of which they apply. Kant clearly holds that they apply to spatial as well as to temporal objects; but for the reasons cited above, he also maintains that they apply to the former in virtue of their temporality. The transcendental synthesis of the imagination is, after all, concerned with the determination of the manifold of inner sense, and thus with the manifold qua temporal. Second, being a transcendental determination of time is not incompatible with being in space, or of having an essential reference to space. As we have already seen, transcendental determinations of time are properties not of time itself, but of things in time, by means of which we can represent the temporal relations of phenomena. Thus permanence, for Kant, is only a property of things in space, but it nonetheless functions as a transcendental determination of time. Nor can we say, as is sometimes done, that Kant moves away from this position in the Second Edition, with its increased emphasis on space.[42] Admittedly, Kant does there assert that in order to establish the objective reality of the categories we need not merely intuition but outer intuition (B291). Nevertheless, as we have just seen in the case of permanence, the fact that we need outer intuition or, equivalently, the fact that the permanent can be found only in space, does not affect the status of the schema as a transcendental determination of time. Kant's position on this score is certainly not stated as clearly as one might wish, but it is defensible. Moreover, it is essentially unchanged in the Second Edition.

In light of these considerations, we should be in a position to deal with the connections between the remaining modal categories and their schemata in a fairly succinct fashion. The connection between actuality and its schema (existence at a determinate time) seems obvious. The point is simply that for anything to be regarded as actual in the "real," or empirical, sense, it must be assignable a determinate location in time. The reasons why space is not included here are precisely the same as they are in the case of possibility. If there is any problem here at all, it is with the pure concept of actuality, not with its schema. In contrast to 'possibility' and 'necessity', 'actuality' does not seem to have a pure or logical sense. It is, therefore, not clear just what it is that is being translated into temporal terms through schematization. Kant, however, does make use of the notion of "logical actuality" *(logische Wirklichkeit)* in order to express the groundedness or "transcendental truth" of a judgment (A75/B101). Since the pure concept is connected with the assertoric form of judgment, it can perhaps be characterized as the concept of assertion. In the introduction to the *Lectures on Logic,* Kant connects this notion with the principle of sufficient reason.[43] This principle is obviously being taken here in its logical sense, in which it asserts that every proposition has its ground or reason. The notion of "real actuality," or as Kant puts it, "existence at a determinate time," is therefore the correlate of the logical conception of groundedness. Common to both is the thought of fixedness or determinateness. In the one case it applies to propositions, considered in connection with other propositions that provide its reasons or grounds; in the other case it applies to states of affairs or events, considered in connection with other states of affairs or events in a single time.

More serious problems arise concerning the schema of necessity, which Kant defines as "the existence of an object at all times" (*das Dasein eines Gegenstandes zu aller Zeit*). First, it seems to be manifestly false that when we say of some object or state of affairs that it is necessary, what we really mean or presuppose is that it exists at all times. Second, existence at all times (permanence or sempiternity) is the schema of substance, and in the Postulates Kant says explicitly that "it is not the existence of things (substances) that we can know to be necessary, but only the existence of their state" (A227 / B279). Finally, in connection with the same point, Kant links the "material necessity in existence," which he contrasts with the "merely logical necessity in the connection of concepts," with the principle of causality. Thus he writes:

> Necessity concerns only the relations of appearances in conformity with the dynamical law of causality and the possibility grounded upon it of inferring *a priori* from a given existence (a cause) to another existence (the effect). [A227–28 / B280]

These considerations suggest that the only way to make any sense of Kant's characterization of the schema of necessity is to assume that he does not mean quite what he appears to mean. The same holds for his cryptic identification of *necessitas phaenomenon* and *aeternitas* (A196 / B186). I therefore propose to follow Paton, who does not explicitly raise the difficulties noted above, and characterize the schema of necessity as "existence in relation to the whole of time."[44] This is certainly a vague formula, but it captures some of the vagueness of Kant's *zu aller Zeit*.[45] More important, it enables us to make Kant's position comprehensible, as well as compatible with what he says in the Postulates and elsewhere about necessity. Given this reading, we can take Kant to be claiming that the existence of a state of affairs is determined "in relation to the whole of time" in the sense that, *qua* effect, it is the product of a causal chain, which, since it can have no first member, must itself exist throughout all of time. The important point, however, is that membership in a causal nexus defines "real" or "material" necessity. This may not be exactly what Kant meant by his characterization of the schema of necessity, but it is certainly what he ought to have meant.

C. Substance, Causality, and Their Schemata

The "deduction" of the schemata of the relational categories is based upon the same principle that was used in the case of the modal categories: the schema must provide a translation into temporal terms of the purely judgmental or conceptual sense that pertains to the pure concept. We have already seen that the pure concept of substance is the concept of something that must always be considered as subject and never as predicate of something else. Thus our first concern is to determine how such a thought can be specified in temporal terms. In other words, we must specify the conditions under which we can say of something temporal that it is such a subject. This condition will be the schema of the concept. In Kant's syllogistic language, it will be the "condition of the rule."

Not surprisingly, the analysis here parallels in temporal terms the previous analysis of the pure concept. We thus begin by asking for the necessary condition under which we can say of something temporal that it is a real subject or owner of properties rather than a merely logical subject of predicates. The most obvious candidate for such a necessary condition is reidentifiability; only something that is reidentifiable throughout a change of states can be distinguished from one or more of these states and considered to be their "real subject," that is, as something to which these states pertain as modifications or in which they "inhere" as accidents. But in order to be reidentifiable throughout a given period of time, the subject must continue to exist throughout that period. We thus arrive at the result that at least a relative permanence is a necessary condition for something temporal that is to function as a "real subject." Such an analysis can provide the basis for the refutation of an atomistic impressionism or sense-data theory of experience of the Humean sort.[46]

This, however, is still not quite what is needed here. The schema that Kant assigns to the pure concept of substance is not relative permanence, but real permanence or sempiternity. The problem, therefore, is to see if it is possible to justify this stronger claim. The key to the solution lies in the distinction, introduced in the discussion of the Metaphysical Deduction, between the strictly judgmental concept of something that is fixed as the subject of a given judgment and the "pure" ontological concept of substance, which is the concept of something that for every judgmental context must be conceived always as subject and never as predicate or property of anything else. The basic point is that the schema of substance (permanence) is required for the conception in temporal terms of the latter (the ontological concept), but not the former. The argument here is relatively simple, consisting of nothing more than the extension of the line of reasoning sketched in the preceding paragraph. Just as reidentifiability throughout a certain period of time, and thus relative permanence, is a condition that must be met by anything temporal that is to serve as a "real subject" to which properties are attached, so reidentifiability throughout *all* time, and thus absolute permanence, is a condition that must be met by anything temporal that is *always* to be conceived as subject and never as property of anything else. In other words, the concept of something existing in time that must always be regarded as subject and never as property or state is equivalent to the concept of something that is reidentifiable throughout all change. But to be reidentifiable throughout all change is to be permanent. Permanence is, therefore, the schema of the concept of substance. As Kant himself puts the matter:

> If I leave out permanence (which is existence in all time), nothing remains in the concept of substance save only the logical representation of a subject—a representation which I endeavor to realise by representing to myself something which can exist only as subject and never as predicate. But not only am I ignorant of any conditions under which this logical pre-eminence may belong to anything; I can neither put such a concept to any use, nor draw the least inference from it. For no object is thereby determined for its employment, and consequently we do not know whether it signifies anyting whatsoever. [A242–43 / B300–01]

Kant equates the pure concept of causality with the relation of ground and consequent. As we have seen, this is the concept of the logical sequence of thoughts in a judgment, and it is connected with the hypothetical form of judgment. Specifically, it is a rule for the sequential ordering of thoughts (themselves problematic judgments) that are connected together in a hypothetical judgment. The schema of causality is defined as "the succession of the manifold, insofar as that succession is subject to a rule" (A144 / B187). Simply put, the schema is rule-governed succession. Our final task in this section is thus to determine whether the notion of rule-governed succession is a plausible translation into temporal terms of the logical conception of the relation of ground and consequent.

Given the preceding analysis, this should not be too difficult to accomplish. The essential point here is that the pure concept serves as an ordering rule; it determines the sequence of thoughts in a judgment as a necessary sequence. The schema must, therefore, provide the representation of a temporal sequence which exhibits the same or an analogous necessity. But to represent a sequence of states of affairs or events in time as necessary is simply to think of it as governed by a rule of the form: if A at t_1 then B at t_2. Equivalently, it is to think of the order as irreversible. Rule-governed succession or irreversibility is, therefore, the schema of the pure concept of causality. It is the condition under which alone the pure concept has any applicability to the data of human sensibility. Again, it is the "condition of the rule." As we shall see in chapter 10, Kant's answer to Hume consists in the demonstration of the claim that this schema is also the condition under which alone we can experience objective succession.

IV. THE SCHEMATA AND THE PRINCIPLES

The transcendental schemata are not only the sensible conditions which give "real" significance to, and restrict the scope of, the pure concepts, they are also conditions of the determination of appearances in time, and thus of the possibility of experience. In fact, it is precisely because of this dual function as "conditions" that they can be said to mediate between the pure concepts and appearances. As we have already seen, both the syllogistic model of subsumption and the much-derided characterization of a transcendental schema as a "third thing" are intended to capture this duality of function.

The first sense of 'condition' is the main focus of the Schematism chapter, the first chapter of the Transcendental Doctrine of Judgment. The assertion that a schema furnishes a meaning condition for a corresponding pure concept is expressed in each of the synthetic a priori schema judgments discussed in the previous section. The second sense of 'condition' is operative in the Principles of Pure Understanding. With the obvious exception of the modal Principles,[47] each of these Principles can be characterized as a synthetic a priori judgment which asserts that a particular schema functions as a necessary condition of the possibility of experience. For example, the Axioms of Intuition and the Anticipations of Perception assert, respectively, that everything intuited has an extensive magnitude and is therefore numerable (the schema of quantity), and that every sensation has an intensive magnitude, that is, a degree (the schema of quality). Again, each of the Analogies of Experience claims that the schema of one of the relational categories functions as a condition of empirical time determination.

Kant himself emphasizes this intimate connection between the schemata and the Principles. Thus, near the end of his general discussion of the Analogies of Experience, he suggests that in these Analogies appearances are subsumed "not simply under the categories, but under their schemata" (A181/B224). Although Kant is explicitly discussing only the Analogies here, it is clear that this claim is equally applicable to all the Principles.[48] The same can be said of his significant closing remarks in the general discussion:

> By these principles, then, we are justified in combining appearances only according to what is no more than an analogy with the logical and universal unity of concepts. In the principle itself we do indeed make use of the category, but in applying it to appearances we substitute for it its schema as the key to its employment, or rather set it alongside the category, as its restricting condition, and as being what may be called its formula. [A181/B224]

In addition to its clarification of the connection between the schemata and the Principles, this passage is noteworthy because of the manner in which it construes the term 'analogy'. Ostensibly, this is still part of

Kant's account of why the Principles involving the schemata of the relational categories are termed Analogies of Experience. Nevertheless, it has frequently been recognized that Kant is here introducing a second sense of the term, and that, taken in this sense, the reference of the term is not limited to the Analogies of Experience.[49]

The first sense of 'analogy', which is clearly applicable only to the Principles designated by that name, is equivalent to the mathematical terms 'ratio' and 'proportion'. Kant justifies his choice of this term on the grounds that the schemata involved in these Principles correspond to the relational categories (each of which expresses a two-term relation) and that the specific function of these Principles is to determine the relation of appearances to one another in a single time. The "analogy" is thus between the two-term relation expressed in the category and its schema on the one hand, and the presumed relation of a given appearance to some unspecified *relatum* on the other. For example, in the case of the causal relation, the "analogy" enables us to determine a priori that for any given event y, there must be some antecedent event x from which y follows in accordance with a rule. In Kant's own terms, "the relation yields a rule for thinking the fourth member in experience, and a mark whereby it can be detected" (A180/B222). Kant notes that the fact that the "analogy" provides only a rule or decision procedure for finding the fourth member in experience, rather than the fourth member itself, differentiates "analogies" in philosophy from those in mathematics.[50] It is also the reason why he characterizes these Principles as "regulative" rather than "constitutive."

In contrast to the reasonably well developed (by Kantian standards) analysis of the first sense of 'analogy', the cryptic discussion of the second sense seems like a mere afterthought on Kant's part. Nevertheless, it is of considerable significance for the understanding of the synthetic a priori character of the Principles. As the passage cited above makes clear, the basic analogy that Kant has in mind is between the pure concepts and their schemata. I take the claim that there is an analogy between them to be equivalent to the contention that the schemata provide translations into temporal terms of what is thought in the pure concepts. The ensuing analogy between category and principle is thus attributable to the fact that the Principles all make use of the schemata: namely, they subsume appearances under them. This is precisely what makes these judgments both synthetic and a priori.

To begin with, that category and schema (and therefore Principle) are *merely* "analogous" to one another, rather than being identical, is a direct consequence of Kant's transcendental distinction between sensibility and understanding. To deny the transcendental nature of the distinction is to deny the basis for any real distinction between the pure concept and its sensible counterpart (the schema). This denial underlies the conflation, typical of rationalistic philosophy, of the temporal relation of cause and effect with the logical relation of ground and consequent. More generally, it also leads to the "transcendental illusion" by means of which these pure concepts are seen as themselves the source of metaphysical principles that are applicable to "real objects." Since such principles would be based on nothing more than an analysis of what is logically necessary for the unity of thought, they would be analytic. An example of such an analytic principle is the Leibnizian principle of sufficient reason, especially in its Wolff-ian form, where it is derived from the principle of noncontradiction.[51] Moreover, as we have seen in the first part of this study, the "objects" to which such analytic principles purportedly apply are noumena. This is a direct consequence of the fact that they would have to be defined in purely conceptual terms, as "objects of a mere understanding," without any reference to sensibility or conditions of sensible intuition. In short, the characterization of the relation between pure concept and schema as one of "analogy" rather than identity is crucial for the syntheticity of the Principles that make use of these schemata, as well as for the limitation of the scope of these Principles to phenomena.

Equally significant for Kant's position is the claim that, because of the "analogy" between pure concept and schema, *there is* an "analogy" between pure concept and Principle. The claim that there is an "analogy" between the pure concepts and the Principles entails that the latter contain a categorial element (because of the schemata), in virtue of which they can function as universal and necessary rules for the unification of appearances. The denial of this "analogy" is, therefore, tantamount to a denial of the apriority of the Principles. It leads directly to the interpretation of them as mere generalizations from experience. Consequently, it is as necessary for Kant to affirm that there is an "analogy" between the unity of experience produced by the Principles and the "logical and universal unity" of the pure concepts, as it is to deny that it is more than an "analogy." Moreover, the key to this "analogy" is the more fundamental one between pure concept and schema.

Given this interpretation of the Principles, there can be little remaining doubt concerning their synthetic a priori character. Unlike judgments which predicate pure concepts of "objects in general," those which subsume appearances under schemata cannot be regarded as even "covertly analytic," because the formal conditions of sensibility (schemata) under which objects (appearances) are subsumed in these judgments are not themselves contained in the mere concept of an object. Nor can it be argued that these judgments become analytic as soon as we characterize the objects being subsumed under these schemata as themselves temporal. The determination of the essential, that is, universal and necessary, properties of objects qua temporal is itself only possible through synthetic judgments which link such objects with their temporal conditions.[52] Indeed, the Principles are precisely such judgments. I have also tried to argue here, however, that the possibility of these judgments, and, therefore, the possibility of a "metaphysic of experience," rests upon the prior possibility of specifying the temporal "analogues" of the categorial rules provided by the pure concepts of the understanding. This specification is the systematic task of the Schematism chapter in the *Critique of Pure Reason*. It explains why, in his letter to Reinhold, Kant suggests that it is here that we find the real beginning of the account of synthetic a priori knowledge.

9

The First Analogy

The initial problem for any interpretation of the First Analogy is to determine just what the argument is intended to prove. Unfortunately, this is not as simple a matter as one might suppose. For instance, in his summary statement at the conclusion of his discussion of all three Analogies Kant writes:

> These, then, are the three analogies of experience. They are simply principles of the determination of the existence of appearances in time, according to all its three modes, viz., the relation to time itself as a magnitude (the magnitude of existence, that is, *duration*), *the relation in time as a successive* series, and finally the relation in time as a sum of all *simultaneous* existence. [A215 / B262]

Kant here seems to link the First Analogy directly with the problem of determining duration, that is, with providing conditions of the possibility of answering questions of the form, How long has x existed (or been in state $A)$? and, How long is the interval between events y and z? Since the Analogy speaks of the permanent or, more precisely, of the "permanence of the real in time" (the schema of the concept of substance), the implication is that the goal of the argument is to prove that the presence of something permanent in experience (objects that can function as clocks) is a necessary condition of the possibility of answering such questions and, therefore, of "measuring time."

But even if we disregard the problems raised by Kant's conception of "modes of time" and the claim that duration is such a mode,[1] it is quite clear that the true picture is considerably more complex than this relatively simple account suggests. The First Analogy is really concerned with the necessary conditions of all time determination, and not merely with the conditions of the possibility of time measurements.[2] What Kant must show is that only some thing or things that are really permanent, that is, sempiternal, can provide the requisite condition for the unification of all things and events (phenomena) in a single time, and thus in a single experience.[3] Given such a result, it certainly follows that this permanent in experience must be relevant to the measurement of time. In fact, in the First Edition version of the argument, Kant does affirm that apart from the existence of the permanent we would have no consciousness of duration.[4] This claim, however, can hardly be taken as the main thrust of Kant's argument.[5]

The situation is further complicated by Kant's combining this general thesis about the necessity of the permanent as a condition for all time determination (duration, coexistence, and succession) with a thesis about change. He argues that all "change" (*Wechsel*) among appearances must be conceived and experienced as an alteration (*Veränderung*) of a substance that endures. In fact, in the First Edition the Principle states: "All appearances contain the permanent substance as the object itself, and the transitory [*das Wandelbare*] as its mere determination, that is, as a way in which the object exists" (A182). Moreover, he insists that this requires absolute and not merely relative permanence. Finally, in the Second Edition Kant goes even further, asserting that the quantum of substance remains constant in the universe. Because of this latter claim many critics have assumed that Kant is engaged in the *Critique* in the manifestly futile project of trying to provide a transcendental proof of the principle of the conservation of matter.

These, then, constitute the basic issues with which the present chapter deals. My basic strategy is to concentrate on the argument which Kant added to the text at the beginning of the Second Edition. By means of a step-by-step analysis of this argument (suitably supplemented by other materials), I hope to show that Kant is not guilty of the silly mistakes and confusions he is all too often accused of making. In particular, I argue that the move from relative to absolute permanence is sound and that the claim about the permanence of the quantum of substance in the *Critique* is in order and must be distinguished sharply from the principle of the conservation of matter with which Kant deals in the *Metaphysical Foundations of Natural Science.*All this is the task of the first section. In a second section, I briefly consider the question of the coherence of Kant's conception of substance, which has been challenged by numerous critics.

I. THE SECOND EDITION ARGUMENT

The First Analogy in the Second Edition states: "In all change [*Wechsel*] of appearance substance is permanent; its quantum in nature is neither increased nor diminished" (B224). Since Kant holds that the proposition that substance is permanent is a tautology,[6] it is clear that what is really claimed in the first part of the Principle is that something permanent, that is, substance, underlies all change of appearances. The basic argument for both parts of this Principle is contained in the first paragraph of the text in the Second Edition. For the sake of convenience I shall first cite the entire argument and then comment upon each step.

[1] All appearances are in time; and in it alone as substratum (as permanent form of inner intuition), can either coexistence or succession be represented.

[2] Thus the time in which all change of appearances has to be thought remains and does not change; for succession or coexistence can only be represented in it as its determinations.[7] [3] Now time cannot by itself be perceived. [4] Consequently there must be found in the objects of perception, that is, in the appearances, the substratum which represents time in general; and all change or coexistence must, in being apprehended, be perceived in this substratum, and through relation of the appearances to it. [5] But the substratum of all that is real, that is, of all that belongs to the existence of things, is *substance;* and all that belongs to existence can be thought only as a determination of substance. [6] Consequently the permanent, in relation to which alone all time relations of appearances can be determined, is substance in the [field of] appearance, that is, the real in appearance, and as the substrate of all change remains ever the same. [7] And as it is thus unchangeable in its existence, its quantity in nature can be neither increased nor diminished. [B224–25]

As can be seen, the argument consists of seven distinct steps.[8] These steps, in turn, can be grouped into four parts, each of which constitutes a subargument. The first part, steps 1 through 4, contends that something at least relatively permanent is required as a substratum or backdrop in relation to which change can be experienced. I term this the Backdrop Thesis. The second part, step 5, argues that every "change" (*Wechsel*) of appearances must be regarded as the change of state of this substratum. The third part, step 6, asserts that this substratum must be absolutely, not simply relatively, permanent. The final part, step 7, maintains that the quantity of this permanent substratum remains constant throughout all change. It should be clear from this outline that the argument has a progressive structure: each step presupposes and builds upon the preceding. Moreover, this structure is reflected in the increasingly controversial nature of Kant's claims.

A. The Backdrop Thesis

[Step 1.] All appearances are in time; and in it alone as substratum (as permanent form of inner intuition), can either coexistence or succession be represented.

The initial step of the argument reaffirms the temporality of all appearances, thereby merely reiterating the contention of the Transcendental Aesthetic that "time is the formal *a priori* condition of all appearances whatsoever," and therefore that "all appearances whatsoever, that is, all objects of the senses, are in time and necessarily stand in time-relations" (A34 / B50–51). The foundational role of time for all appearance is now expressed by characterizing it as 'substratum'. This is a key term in the overall argument, and its appearance here serves to prepare the way for the eventual introduction of the concept of substance. At this stage of the argument, however, all that Kant can legitimately claim is that in general the representation of time must be presupposed in order to represent either coexistence or succession. Obviously, by "representation of time" must here be understood time as form of intuition (the indeterminate pure intuition), not formal (determinate) intuition.

[Step 2.] Thus the time in which all change of appearances has to be thought remains and does not change; for succession or coexistence can only be represented in it as its determinations.

It is frequently argued against this claim that, while it is true to say that time does not change, but rather that things change in time, it is equally true that time does not remain or endure. As Caird expresses it:

It may be objected that to say that "time itself does not change" is like saying that passing away does not itself pass away. So far the endurance of time and the permanence of the changing might even seem to mean only that the moments of time never cease to pass away, and the changing never ceases to change. A perpetual flux would therefore sufficiently "represent" all the permanence that is in time.[9]

Caird's contention, which is reiterated by Robert Paul Wolff,[10] is true enough, but it is largely irrelevant as a criticism of Kant. The essential point is that the constant flux occurs in a single time.[11] The claim that time is unchangeable or permanent is really equivalent to the claim that it retains its identity as one and the same time (temporal framework) throughout all change. The most that Kant can be charged with here is a lack of clarity, although it is difficult to imagine what else he could have meant by this claim. Moreover, as we shall soon see, this is precisely the sense in which substance is said to be unchangeable or permanent. That is why the thesis of the unity of time, that is, its identity through all change, is central to the whole argument: it makes it possible to link substance directly to time and to argue that the concept, or better, the schema of substance is necessary for a determinate representation of time.

[Step 3.] Now time cannot by itself be perceived.

The unperceivability of time, or of "time itself," is a common and essential premise of the argument of each of the Analogies. Like the preceding two steps, it is a consequence of the analysis of the Transcendental Aesthetic; specifically, it is derived from the doctrine that time is a form or mode of representing objects rather than itself an object that is represented. For the very reasons already noted in chapter 5 with respect to space, this is not incompatible with the claim that "we can quite well think time as void of appearance" (A31 / B46). In any case, this premise is significant because it both defines the problem to be resolved and points to the direction in which the solution is to be found. It accomplishes the former by eliminating the possibility of determining the objective temporal relations of appearances by referring them to "time itself." Since this manner of determining time-relations rests on the assumption that time is some sort of experientially accessible object or quasi object, it is ruled out by this premise.[12] It accomplishes the latter because it makes clear that the temporal relations of appearances can be determined only by considering the appearances themselves and the rules for their connection in consciousness.

[Step 4.] Consequently there must be found in the objects of perception, that is, in the appearances, the substratum which represents time in general; and all change or coexistence must, in being apprehended, be perceived in this substratum, and through relation of the appearances to it.

This makes explicit the obvious and already noted implication of the preceding step: that the unperceivability of time makes it necessary to presuppose some perceptually accessible model for time itself as a condition of the possibility of determining the temporal relations of appearances. In the First Edition, Kant identifies this model or, as he terms it, "substratum," with the "object itself" (A182–83/B227). The basic point is that this model or object must somehow embody the unchangeableness or permanence that has already been attributed to time itself. If there were nothing that endures, if everything were in constant flux, then we could not even be aware of succession as such, not to mention coexistence. Consequently, an enduring, perceivable object (or objects) is required to provide the backdrop or frame of reference by means of which the succession, coexistence, and duration, of appearances in a common time can be determined.

This is the 'Backdrop Thesis', which I take to be the result of the first four steps of the argument. Although itself not a trivial result, the argument for it involves little more than a spelling out of the implications of the analysis of time in the Transcendental Aesthetic. Consequently, the major interest of the First Analogy centers around Kant's efforts to go beyond this result. This occurs in the next three parts of the argument, each of which is compressed into a single sentence in the text.

B. From Substratum to Subject, or the "All Change is Alteration" Thesis

[Step 5.] But the substratum of all that is real, that is, of all that belongs to the existence of things, is *substance;* and all that belongs to existence can be thought only as a determination of substance.

The expression "all that belongs to existence" (*alles was zum Dasein gehört*), which Kant here uses to characterize the real, is highly obscure, but it seems reasonable to follow Paton in taking it to refer to changing appearances which have determinate positions in time.[13] On this reading, then, Kant is claiming that all these appearances must be regarded as states or determinations of substance. At this stage of the argument there is certainly no warrant for taking 'substance' in the full-blown ontological sense, as referring to something absolutely permanent (what Jonathan Bennett calls "substance$_2$"). But even if we understand the term to refer merely to relatively permanent phenomenal entities ("substance$_1$" in Bennett's terminology),[14] the claim still takes us considerably beyond the Backdrop Thesis. Whereas that thesis asserts only that the presence in experience of some relatively permanent entity or entities is a necessary condition of the possibility of the experience of the succession or coexistence of appearances in time, the present claim is that all changes (*Wechseln*) of appearances (where one appearance is succeeded by another) must be experienced as alterations (*Veränderungen*) in the states of these entities. This is clearly a new step in the argument, and it stands in need of a separate justification.

Kant's most explicit formulation of this claim is at the beginning of the Second Analogy, where he remarks that one way of expressing the result of the First Analogy is in terms of the principle "All change (succession) of appearance is merely alteration" (B233). In the more precise reformulation of James Van Cleve, this becomes the proposition "For any x, if x changes, there is a y such that y alters in respect of x."[15] Admittedly, Kant misdescribes the situation somewhat by suggesting that this principle is itself the final conclusion of the argument; nevertheless, it is certainly an essential step (perhaps *the* essential step) in this argument. Our present concern, therefore, is to see if it is possible to find an argument capable of supporting this claim.

First, however, it is crucial to become clear about the meaning of *Wechsel,* which Kemp Smith usually translates simply as "change." Since Kant frequently uses the term to refer to a "coming to be" (*Entstehen*) or a "ceasing to be" (*Vergehen*), it might be thought that Kant means by it a radical change akin to the Aristotelian notion of substantial change. But it would be extremely misleading to render *Wechsel* as "substantial change" because Kant's main thesis is that only states or determinations of substances *wechseln,* not the substances themselves. His own example of *ein Wechsel* is the change that occurs when a piece of wood is burned. In ordinary parlance we might say that the wood "becomes" smoke and ashes, just as we might say of a successful experiment in alchemy that the base metal "becomes" or is "changed into" gold. But since neither the wood nor the base metal themselves survives the process, it is obvious that what is really meant is that what initially appeared in the form of wood or base metal (the matter) is transformed in the process into smoke and ashes in the one case and gold in the other. This is, of course, precisely what the argument must show; but for the present the main point is simply that *ein Wechsel* is the kind of change in which one item is replaced by another. In order to capture this, I propose to translate *Wechsel* as "replacement change."

Admittedly, this is a somewhat awkward expression, and it is not without a certain ambiguity of its own. Nevertheless, it is more helpful than Kemp Smith's "change," which totally fails to indicate the *kind* of change at issue and, therefore, fails to indicate what the argument is about.[16] For reasons which should be clear from the above, I also regard this as considerably less misleading than Bennett's rendering of *Wechsel* as "existence-change."[17] Thus, given this reading, it is at least apparent that what must be shown is that every replacement of a given state of affairs (x) at t_1, by some contrary state of affairs (non-x) at t_2, must be conceived and experienced as the alteration (change of state) of some entity (y) that endures throughout the process. Correlatively, as the combustion and alchemy examples indicate, x and non-x must be thought as successive determinations of y.

Unfortunately, since Kant is ultimately concerned in the First Analogy with the demonstration of the necessity of something or things that are absolutely permanent or sempiternal, it is difficult to locate an argument devoted specifically to this subordinate but essential principle. Perhaps the closest thing to it is buried in the folowing passage (also cited by Van Cleve):

> A coming to be or ceasing to be that is not simply a determination of the permanent but is absolute, can never be a possible perception. For this permanent is what alone makes possible the representation of the transition from one state to another, and from not-being to being. These transitions can be empirically known only as changing determinations of that which is permanent. If we assume that something absolutely begins to be, we must have a point of time in which it was not. But to what are we to attach this point, if not to that which already exists? For a preceding empty time is not an object of perception. But if we connect the coming to be with things which previously existed, and which persist in existence up to the moment of this coming to be, this latter must be simply a determination of what is permanent in that which precedes it. [A188/B231]

Since much of this passage is concerned with the question of absolute permanence, which is the subject of the next section (step 6), we now need consider only two sentences:

> For this permanent is what alone makes possible the representation of the transition from one state to another, and from not-being to being. These transitions can be empirically known only as changing determinations of that which is permanent.

The references in these sentences to the representation of transition and to empirical knowledge indicate that the required argument must turn on an appeal to the condition of the possibility of the conception or experience of a replacement change. It is perhaps not immediately evident that there is any such argument; nevertheless, following a suggestion of D. P. Dryer, I believe that it is possible to provide at least the sketch of one.[18]

Like the argument for the Backdrop Thesis, the present argument requires the premise that time cannot be perceived: "For a preceding empty time is not an object of perception." Since this is the case, a single observation is never adequate to determine that a change of any sort has taken place, and a fortiori not a replacement change. Any such experience requires two successive observations and the noticing of some difference between what is observed in each case. One cannot, however, infer from a difference in two successive observations that a replacement change has in fact occurred. Despite all that can be determined from the two observations alone, one could simply be having successive observations of coexisting states of affairs. For example, I perceive my desk at t_1 and my bookcase at t_2, but I do not infer from the succession of perceptions that a replacement change has occurred; that is, I do not assume that the desk has somehow "become" or been changed into the bookcase. Again, let us suppose that during the interval between t_1 and t_2 the desk was removed and the bookcase put in its place. I would certainly experience this as a change, but not as a replacement change (at least not in the sense in which the term is being used here). If, by contrast, I experience or believe that I experience a genuine replacement change (as in the cases of combustion and alchemy), then I am constrained to refer the successive states of affairs to some common subject and to view this occurrence as an alteration in this subject. Only by so doing can I represent through my successive perceptions or observations the replacement of one state of affairs or determinations by its contrary.

The crucial point here, which admittedly is somewhat obscured by the empirical examples and the talk about observations, is that the assignment of the successively represented states of affairs to an enduring substratum (as its successive states) functions as the rule through which we think a replacement change. It can also be described as the form of the thought of a replacement change in the sense that to think such a change (as an object of possible experience) is just to connect one's perceptions according to the rule. This, in turn, makes it into a transcendental condition of the experience of a replacement change. (Keep in mind here the definition of 'experience' as "knowledge by means of connected perceptions.")[19] Behind this lies the general principle of the Analogies, which, in the First Edition, states that "all appearances are, as regards their existence, subject a priori to rules determining their existence in one time" (A176–77). Unfortunately, Kant himself contributed to the almost universal misunderstanding of the argument of the First Analogy by his failure to spell out any of this. He does make it perfectly explicit, however, in a key passage at the beginning of the Second Analogy, which we shall consider in the next chapter.

C. From Relative to Absolute Permanence

[Step 6.] Consequently the permanent, in relation to which alone all time relations of appearances can be determined, is substance in the [field of] appearance, that is, the real in appearance, and as the substrate of all change remains ever the same.

Up to this point, the argument has shown only that one must include in one's ontology ("metaphysic of experience") enduring, reidentifiable entities which function as substrata of change. The next and decisive step must demonstrate that some of these entities, or perhaps something more fundamental, are absolutely permanent. Only by so doing can Kant establish the objective reality of the schema of the pure concept of substance. It is precisely at this point, however, that virtually all of the commentators draw the line; the recurring criticism is that Kant's argument is at best only capable of proving the need for relative permanence and that the move to absolute permanence is, therefore, totally unwarranted.[20]

At first glance at least this criticism seems well founded. There are many places where Kant appears simply to assume that anything that functions substantivally in experience, that is, anything that serves as a substratum of change, must for that very reason be sempiternal. For example, he equates the Principle of Permanence with the thesis of the "ever-abiding existence, in the appearance of the subject proper" (A185/B228); and he further claims that "only the permanent (substance) is altered" (A187/B230–31). Moreover, once again the situation is not helped by Kemp Smith's translation. In an important passage in which Kant contends that the unity of experience would be impossible if *neue Dinge (der Substanz nach)* could come into or go out of existence (A186/ B229), Kemp Smith renders this into English as "new things, that is, new substances." This gives the impression that Kant is simply equating things with substances. In reality, however, what he is saying here, albeit somewhat awkwardly, is that the unity of experience would be impossible if *what is substantial* in things could come into or go out of existence. This leaves completely open the question of what it is that is "substantial" in things.

What must, therefore, be proven is that there is something substantial in things, something that does not come into or go out of existence. By construing the problem in this way it becomes clear that there is no need to take Kant to be arguing that substantiality in this sense is assignable to everything that can serve as a subject of change or a bearer of properties. Kant was undoubtedly well aware that the sorts of things that normally function in this way, such as tables, trees, horses, mountains, and plants, themselves come into and go out of existence. Consequently, it seems more reasonable, as well as more in accord with the text, to construe him to be claiming that such changes can be experienced as alterations only of something truly substantial that persists throughout all change.

The argument that is required at this stage turns on the necessary unity or identity of time as a condition of the unity of experience. It proceeds by applying the "all replacement change is alteration" principle to the enduring entities or substance candidates whose necessity has been established in the preceding step. Thus, far from assuming that *these* entities are sempiternal, it assumes that they are not and considers the conditions of the possibility of the experience of their coming-into or passing-out of existence. Since any such occurrence involves the replacement of one state of affairs by its contrary (*x* by non-*x*, and vice versa), it would count as a replacement change. We have already seen, however, that the conception or experience of any such change requires that both states of affairs be linked to an identical subject ("the object itself") as its successive determinations. But an absolute coming-into or passing-out of existence would be an occurrence in which, *ex hypothesi*, these conditions would not pertain. Moreover, since there would be no way in which the emergence of this new state of affairs could be connected empirically with the preceding time (in which the contrary state of affairs existed), such an occurrence would cause a rupture in the unity of time, and therefore in the unity of experience.[21] Kant sums up the matter at the end of the Analogy:

> Substances, in the [field of] appearance, are the substrata of all determinations of time. If some of these substances could come into being and others cease to be, the one condition of the empirical unity of time would be removed. The appearances would then relate to two different times, and existence would flow in two parallel streams—which is absurd. There is only one time in which all different times must be located, not as coexistent but as in succession to one another. [A188–89 / B231–32]

The point can be clarified by a brief consideration of Kant's own well-known illustration of the principle; namely, the Lavoisier-inspired example of the burning of a piece of wood.

> A philosopher being asked how much smoke weighs, made reply: "Subtract from the weight of the wood burnt the weight of the ashes which are left over, and you have the weight of the smoke." He thus presupposed as undeniable that even in fire the matter (substance) does not vanish, but only suffers an alteration of form. [A181 / B228]

Clearly, the piece of wood which was burnt must be assumed to have existed for a period of time prior to its destruction by fire and to have been capable of being altered in any number of ways during that period without losing its identity as a particular piece of wood. Equally clearly, its destruction by fire cannot be regarded as just another alteration of the wood, since it is no longer identifiable as wood at the end of the process. Nevertheless, and this is the main point, in spite of the radical nature of the change, we are still required to regard the process of combustion as an alteration. The difference is that instead of treating the piece of wood as the subject that alters, we are constrained to presuppose some matter, which at one stage of its career assumed the form of a piece of wood, and at a later stage was transformed into smoke and ashes. In other words, in order to conceive of such a transformation in time, it is necessary to consider the piece of wood as the temporary form, state, or determination of some enduring matter. Correlatively, this matter of which things are composed is the "ultimate subject" of predication or, equivalently, "the substantial" in things. As such, it must be presupposed to endure throughout all change, including the coming-into and passing-out of existence of its particular configurations or determinations.

Kant's basic claim goes back at least to Aristotle, who asserted the necessity of presupposing prime matter as the "material cause" of "substantial change." Moreover, Kant himself insists that the idea (if not its philosophical articulation) is recognized by the "common understanding." The issue, then, is simply how we are to establish the "obviously synthetic proposition" that "in all appearances there is something permanent, and that the transitory is nothing but a determination of its existence" (A184/ B287). Herein lies Kant's originality. As in the preceding steps, he gives this principle an epistemic rather than a logical or an ontological grounding. Thus, he does not claim that there is anything self-contradictory in the thought of something simply coming into or passing out of existence. The claim is rather that such an "event" (like an "event" without a cause) could not be an object of possible experience.[22] Ultimately, this is because, if such an "event" were to occur, "we should lose that which can alone represent the unity of time, namely, the identity of the substratum" (A186/B229). In such a hypothetical situation, Kant suggests, "The appearances would then relate to two different times, and existence would flow in two parallel streams" (A188/B231–32). Although Kant goes on to note that this latter supposition is absurd (*ungereimt*), it cannot be a question of logical impossibility. As we saw in the discussion of the transcendental synthesis of the imagination, there is no contradiction in the thought of a number of times (or spaces) that are not parts of a single time (or space). The impossibility is grounded in the nature of human sensibility, our form of intuiting.

The key to this argument for absolute permanence lies in the identification of substance, or what is "substantial" in things, with the matter of which the things are composed. This identification is necessary in order to have a subject or "substratum" of which one can predicate the changes which occur when enduring physical objects (the first-order subjects of predication) come into or pass out of existence. Moreover, if it is to function as the ultimate subject of predication, this matter must obviously be regarded as sempiternal. It should be kept in mind, however, that this is a strictly transcendental claim, which tells us nothing about the nature of this matter. That remains a question for empirical investigation.

D. The Quantity of Substance

[Step 7.] And as it is thus unchangeable in its existence, its quantity in nature can be neither increased nor diminished.

Kant here goes beyond what has been established so far by asserting, in effect, that the permanence of substance entails the conservation of its quantity in the universe. In spite of the fact that Kant explicitly makes this claim only in the Second Edition, the discussion of the philosopher's answer to the query regarding the weight of smoke makes it clear that the thought is already implicit in the First Edition. It therefore seems appropriate to regard it as an essential aspect of Kant's theory of substance, and not as a mere afterthought that can be summarily dismissed. At the same time, however, it is also an aspect of the theory that is widely rejected. The usual and obvious objection here is that Kant is making an illicit move from transcendental to empirical considerations; in particular, that he is attempting to "deduce" the principle of the conservation of mass as it is understood within Newtonian mechanics.[23]

This objection, however, is completely misguided, for it stems from a failure to distinguish the transcendental-level argument of the First Analogy from the parallel argument of the *Metaphysical Foundations of Natural Science,* where Kant does affirm the principle of the conservation of matter, but only by "applying" the transcendental principles of the *Critique* to the empirical concept of matter. In order to underscore the difference, I shall briefly consider each argument in turn.

In the *Critique,* Kant does not actually offer an explicit argument to take us from step 6 to step 7, but it is easy enough to provide one on the basis of materials contained in the text. We have just seen that substance, the ultimate subject of predication, must be identified with the matter of which things are composed and that this matter must be conceived as permanent (in order to function as such a subject). Given this result, the next question is how we are to characterize this matter in a transcendental account, that is, an account which does not make use of any empirical assumptions. Fortunately, Kant himself answers this question for us in the Architectonic of Pure Reason, where he characterizes matter, so conceived, as "impenetrable, lifeless extension" (A848/B876). The point, I take it, is that the only property that can be legitimately assigned to matter in a transcendental account is the occupation of space or spatiality.

Matter so conceived, or equivalently, "the object itself," is completely indeterminate. Unlike Aristotelian prime matter, however, which is indeterminate in the metaphysical sense that it is a pure stuff, literally without properties, this matter is indeterminate in the strictly methodological sense that no properties other than the occupation of space can be legitimately assigned to it in a transcendental account. If matter is conceived in this way, however, then clearly the only category available for its conceptualization is quantity. Consequently, the permanence of matter, which is established in step 6, must be conceived as the permanence of its quantity, which is just what is claimed in step 7.[24]

In contrast to this perfectly general conceptual claim, which cannot be equated with either a specific law of nature or a conservation principle, Kant does attempt in the *Metaphysical Foundations of Natural Science* to derive a conservation principle which he there terms the First Law of Mechanics. The law states: "With regard to all changes of corporeal nature, the quantity of matter taken as a whole remains the same, unincreased and undiminished."[25] Kant gives to it the status of an a priori law of nature, but the main point is that its derivation, as well as those of other a priori laws considered in that work, requires the introduction of empirical, or at least quasi-empirical, premises. Specifically, it appeals to the concept of matter as the "movable in space." Movability, therefore, is the "empirical" feature which differentiates this definition from that of the *Critique,* and which supposedly makes possible the derivation of specific laws of nature.[26]

In the case of the principle of the conservation of matter, the key move is the determination of the nature of material substance or, equivalently, of what is substantial with respect to matter. Kant attempts to accomplish this by combining his definition of matter with the pure concept or nominal definition of substance as "the ultimate subject of existence, i.e., that which does not itself in turn belong merely as predicate to the existence of another."[27] The point seems to be that only matter, defined as the movable in space, satisfies the definition of substance. This is because apart from matter (so defined) no real subject for the properties or accidents of the objects of outer sense can be thought except for space itself. The Transcendental Aesthetic has shown, however, that space is not itself an object of outer sense, but rather the form or condition of our representation of such objects. The movable in space is thus the only available candidate for substantial status.[28]

As a direct consequence of this thesis, Kant further contends that the independently movable parts of material substance are themselves substances, and that by the 'quantity of matter' is to be understood the number of such substances of which a given portion of matter is composed. The argument here seems to be that any such particle of matter, insofar as it is capable of moving independently of the other particles, is likewise capable of functioning as a subject to which properties or accidents can be attached.[29] One might also argue in this connection that something that is movable in space independently of other things cannot be regarded as a property or accident of these other things. Any such object, therefore, fits the definition of substance offered in the *Critique.* The upshot of this, then, is that a capacity for independent motion replaces the ontological independence of traditional metaphysics as a criterion of substance. Finally, it should be noted here that this analysis enables Kant to speak of a plurality of substances, in spite of the identification of substance with matter, which suggests a monistic conception.[30]

Given this conception of material substance, it is quite easy for Kant to derive the principle of the conservation of matter. It requires only the combination of this conception with the doctrine of the First Analogy that substances cannot be created or destroyed. Since the quantity of matter is defined in terms of the number of substances (independently movable particles of matter) of which matter is composed, this quantity can be changed only through the addition or subtraction of substances. But this would require the creation or annihilation of substances, and that is ruled out by the First Analogy. Consequently, the quantity of matter in nature as a whole must remain constant throughout all time.[31]

As Van Cleve points out, this argument works only for the conservation of the quantity of matter as Kant defines it. Since Kant fails to show that the quantity of matter, so construed, can be equated with mass, he fails to establish the principle of the conservation of mass.[32] This point is certainly well taken, but whether it can be regarded as a serious objection against Kant depends on whether or not we take Kant's project in the *Metaphysical Foundations of Natural Science* to be that of providing a priori proofs of the specific principles of Newtonian physics (as opposed to merely accounting for the possibility of such principles).[33] Without entering into that issue here, however, it should at least be clear that we cannot accuse Kant of attempting any such thing in the *Critique,* where the argument proceeds at a higher level of generality.

II. KANT'S CONCEPTION(S) OF SUBSTANCE

The preceding analysis of the argument of the First Analogy makes it easy to understand why commentators frequently have accused Kant of conflating distinct conceptions of substance. Indeed, we can even see why these same commentators disagree about the specific conceptions of substance which Kant allegedly conflates. For example, we have already seen that Jonathan Bennett accuses Kant of sliding from substance conceived of as something that can function as a subject or bearer of attributes (s_1) to substance conceived of as something sempiternal (s_2). By contrast, Robert Paul Wolff accuses Kant of operating with two distinct conceptions of permanence. One is an essentially Aristotelian conception of the permanent as the substratum of change, "an unchanging base in which attributes succeed one another." The other is a modern, scientific conception of a closed system in which the "stuff" is conserved.[34] More recently, Gordon Brittan has developed essentially the same point by locating both an Aristotelian and a Cartesian conception of substance in Kant. He also follows Wolff in suggesting that the former is characteristic of the First and the latter of the Second Edition version of the argument of the First

Analogy. In Brittan's terms, the Aristotelian conception regards "substance as the substratum of change, that of which properties can be predicated but which cannot be predicated of anything else"; and the Cartesian conception regards substance as "that which exists in its own right, depending for its existence on itself alone."[35]

Although clearly related and perhaps inspired by similar considerations, these ways of distinguishing between conceptions of substance are not equivalent. The s_1-s_2 distinction relates specifically to the duration that can be ascribed to substances. Presumably, instances of both s_1 and s_2 are enduring physical objects. The difference between them consists entirely in the fact that the former are relatively and the latter absolutely permanent. The Aristotelian-Cartesian distinction concerns the nature of that which is to be regarded as substance, and thus as permanent. Roughly put, the former equates substance with determinate things to which properties can be assigned, while the latter equates it with the stuff or matter of which these things are composed. If we consider these distinctions in light of the argument analyzed in the previous section, we can say that a proponent of the s_1-s_2 distinction would tend to locate the source of Kant's difficulty in the move from step 5 to step 6. Correlatively, the proponent of the Aristotelian-Cartesian distinction would locate it in the move from step 6 to step 7.

The question then is whether Kant can be judged guilty of conflating the senses of 'substance' that are involved in either of these two distinctions; and this is a question which takes us beyond the text of the First Analogy. In fact, the problem can be traced back to the Metaphysical Deduction, where Kant is sometimes thought to jump from the concept of a subject of predication or owner of properties, which is required for the exercise of the categorical function of judgment, to the full-fledged ontological concept of substance; namely, that which must be conceived always (in *every* judgmental context) as subject and never as property or predicate of anything else. I have, however, attempted in chapter 6 to explain this jump on the grounds that the ontological concept can be regarded as a hypostatization of the judgmental concept. On this interpretation Kant is not engaged in the Metaphysical Deduction in the misguided project of attempting to "deduce" the ontological concept by claiming that it is itself a necessary condition for judgment. On the contrary, Kant's goal is to show how the ontological concept arises from the concept which is such a necessary condition.

We have also seen that, in the same way, a two-step analysis is required to make any sense out of the schema of substance. First we noted that reidentifiability throughout a given period of time (relative permanence) is a necessary condition for anything in time that is to function as the real subject of a categorical judgment. But this is not sufficient to establish the schema of substance, which requires absolute permanence or sempiternity. In order to arrive at this schema, which corresponds to the ontological concept, it was necessary to raise the further question: What need be assumed about something in time that must always be regarded (in *every* experiential context) as subject and never as property or determination of anything else? The answer, it will be recalled, was that such a subject must be assumed to be reidentifiable throughout all change, which is equivalent to being permanent.

Both of these cases, but particularly the two-step analysis of the schema judgment of the concept of substance, certainly suggest Bennett's distinction between s_1 and s_2. Moreover, as already suggested, step 5 of the argument of the First Analogy can be read as an attempt to demonstrate the necessity for s_1, while step 6 can be taken as an attempt to do the same for s_2. This does not, however, entail that there is any confusion or conflation of these two conceptions on Kant's part. On the contrary, it seems clear that s_2 (the really permanent) is the conception of substance Kant is arguing for, and that s_1 plays only a provisional, dialectical role in this argument. Thus, in spite of some texts which suggest the contrary, Kant cannot be accused of simply conflating the two conceptions.

The issue of the Aristotelian-Cartesian distinction is more complex. We can begin by noting that if there is any slide from the one conception to the other by Kant it cannot be correlated with a change from the First to the Second Edition. Against this view it suffices to recall that the account of the burning of the wood, which might be taken to reflect a Cartesian or "stuff" conception of substance, is already contained in the First Edition. It is also worthy of noting here that the contrast between the Aristotelian and the Cartesian conceptions of substance is not as sharp as those who apply the distinction to Kant tend to assume. Both Aristotle and Descartes (as well as many other thinkers) regard substance as a subject of predication or bearer of attributes that cannot itself be borne by anything else. Again, both Aristotle and Descartes regard substance as an enduring substratum of change.[36] These two characterizations are, of course, not equivalent. The property of being a subject of predication is not identical to that of being a substratum of change. Nevertheless, they can be said to constitute two sides of a conception of substance that is more or less common to the Western philosophical tradition, to which Kant is obviously an heir. Indeed, the subject aspect of the conception is reflected in his nominal definition of substance, and the enduring substratum aspect is reflected in his characterization of the schema. A significant modification of the traditional conception, to which reference has already been made, is Kant's replacement of ontological independence with the physical property of independent mobility. It is in connection with this property that one must understand Kant's elliptical reference to action as the empirical criterion of substance.[37]

The question, however, is whether Kant's argument involves any conflation of a "thing" with a "stuff" conception of substance. Seen in this context, 'Aristotelian' and 'Cartesian' are to be taken merely as convenient labels used in referring to these conceptions, not as actually held theories. If we consider Kant's thought as a whole, it is clear that he does sometimes appeal to a "thing" conception. In addition to the Metaphysical Deduction, perhaps the best-known example of Kant's use of this conception is in the Third Analogy, where he appears to treat 'thing' and 'substance' as if they were interchangeable terms, and to understand by 'substance' enduring physical objects. A similar treatment of substance, albeit in a metaphysical context, is also found in Kant's *Lectures on Metaphysics,* especially in connection with his critique of Spinoza. Indeed, it is precisely by equating the concept of substance with that of a thing that Kant attacks Spinoza's dictum that there is only one substance of which all particular things are modes or accidents.[38]

Within the First Analogy, however, this conception of substance is only present at a preliminary stage of the argument (step 5), where, as already noted, it functions in a provisional or dialectical manner. Moreover, there is no basis for attributing to Kant a "stuff" conception of substance, whether this be understood in terms of the model of either Aristotelian prime matter or Cartesian *res extensa.* The former must be rejected because, as we have already seen, it rests upon a failure to distinguish between the purely methodological sense in which Kant regards substance as indeterminate (in a transcendental account) and the metaphysical indeterminateness of Aristotelian prime matter. The latter must be rejected because it involves the importation into the First Analogy of certain scientific doctrines which are not called for by the argument. Thus, while I do not pretend to be able to reconcile Kant's treatment of substance in the First Analogy with everything that he has to say about it elsewhere, I do not think that there is any basis for the charge that he conflates different conceptions within the First Analogy itself.

10

The Second Analogy

The argument of the Second Analogy is the culmination of the Transcendental Analytic. In the eyes of Kant himself, as well as those of most of his commentators and critics, the whole project of establishing a "metaphysic of experience" stands or falls with the success of this argument. Once again, however, Kant formulates the Principle differently in the First and Second Editions. In the First Edition it is called the Principle of Production, and it states: "Everything that happens [*geschieht*], that is, begins to be, presupposes something upon which it follows according to a rule" (A189). In the Second Edition it is termed more elaborately the Principle of Succession in Time, in Accordance with the Law of Causality, and it states: "All alterations take place in conformity with the law of the connection of cause and effect" (B232).

Although it is generally agreed that Kant did not read the *Treatise,* the First Edition formulation is certainly reminiscent of Hume's characterization of the causal principle as the maxim that "whatever begins to exist must have a cause of its existence."[1] It thus suggests that the target of the Second Analogy is Hume's challenge to the general principle of causality in the *Treatise,* rather than his challenge in the *Enquiry* to the quite different principle that similar causes produce similar effects. Following Lewis White Beck, I shall call the former the "every-event-some-cause" principle and the latter the "same-cause-same-effect" principle.[2] The reformulation in the Second Edition is obviously intended to bring the argument into closer connection with the First Analogy. This is also borne out by the first paragraph of the Second Edition text, which contains a summary of the results of the First Analogy. Just as the First Analogy argues that all change, including "replacement change," is merely the alteration of substance, so the Second Analogy will argue that all alterations are governed by the "law of the connection of cause and effect." In reality, however, the difference between the two formulations is merely cosmetic. Since the "law of the connection of cause and effect" in the Second Edition is equivalent to what is called the Principle of Production in the First, the two versions are equivalent. We can thus safely say that in both editions the goal is to establish the every-event-some-cause principle.

The basic concern of this chapter is to analyze and evaluate Kant's argument in support of this principle. A second, closely related concern is to delineate the connection between this argument and Kant's transcendental idealism. The chapter is divided into three parts. The first deals with Kant's general reflections on the conditions of the representation of an objective temporal order. This prefaces the actual argument, and provides what I term a "transcendental setting" for it. It is here that we shall see the inseparability of Kant's argument from his transcendental idealism. The second analyzes the main line of argument for the every-event-some-cause principle. The third considers the precise nature and scope of Kant's claim, and analyzes one of the most significant objections that has been raised against it: the Lovejoy-Strawson non sequitur charge.

I. THE TRANSCENDENTAL SETTING

In the incredibly dense and confusing first paragraph of the First Edition (the third paragraph in the Second Edition), Kant raises the general problem of explaining how knowledge of an objective temporal order is possible. Much of the confusion is caused by Kant's tendency to shift unannounced from the empirical to the transcendental senses of such key terms as 'appearance' and from talk about the manifold of representations to the manifold of items represented.[3] For all its obscurity, however, the paragraph does make it abundantly clear that the argument for the causal principle cannot be separated from the transcendental perspective from which the problem is posed. The paragraph seems to fall fairly neatly into four parts. The first raises the problem of explaining the possibility of knowledge of an objective temporal order. The second argues that transcendental realism cannot explain the possibility of such knowledge. The third formulates the problem in terms of the language and assumptions of transcendental idealism. The fourth sketches the "critical" or transcendentally idealistic solution.

A. The Problem of Knowledge of an Objective Temporal Order

By an "objective temporal order" is meant simply an order of occurrences in the world. The general problem with which all the Analogies are concerned is the possibility of the knowledge of such an order. Thus the general account which Kant prefaces to the argument of the Second Analogy really serves as an introduction to the Analogies as a whole.[4] The specific problem of the Second Analogy is the possibility of knowledge of an order of successive states of an object, that is, the possibility of judgments of the form, state A precedes state B in object x. Such a succession of states can also be called an "objective succession."

It is, however, by no means apparent that there is any real problem here. Moreover, Kant's own explanation serves more to obscure than to clarify the issue:

The apprehension of the manifold of appearance is always successive. The representations of the parts follow upon one another. Whether they also follow one another in the object is a point which calls for further reflection, and which is not decided by the above statement. [A189/B234]

This suggests that the problem is that, since apprehension is always successive, an inspection of the order of apprehension or, equivalently, of the "subjective order" in which representations occur in consciousness (the order of represent*ing*) does not provide adequate evidence for forming reliable judgments about the quite different order of occurrences in the world. Thus, from the succession of representations *a-b* in the mind (from the fact that I apprehend *a* before *b*), I cannot infer anything about the order of the object. To cite Kant's own notorious example: I apprehend the parts of a house successively, yet I judge them to be coexisting parts of an enduring object. How is such a judgment possible?

It is frequently claimed that Kant finds a problem here only because of his highly dubious psychological assumption that all apprehension is in fact successive. Against this objection it is sometimes argued that Kant does not really need this assumption, for all that is required to generate the problem is the noncontroversial claim that the order of apprehension or subjective order is not a reliable indicator of the objective order. The two orders may, but need not, coincide.[5] This response is correct as far as it goes; the trouble is that it shares with the original objection the erroneous assumption (admittedly suggested by Kant's formulation) that the problem lies in having to make a judgment about the objective order on the basis of the subjective order.

If we are to understand the problem that concerns Kant in the Analogies we must first reject the assumption that the subjective order is a datum or bit of evidence from which we must somehow make inferences about an objective order. This becomes clear once we recognize that the subjective order corresponds to what is called in the Transcendental Deduction a "subjective unity of consciousness." As such, it can be made into a "subjective object" through introspection (we shall be concerned in chapter 12 with the nature of the process through which this occurs), but it is not itself given to the mind as such an object. The key point here is that to speak transcendentally about this order (as Kant is presumably doing here) is not to consider it as something introspected or actually represented; it is rather to regard it as the indeterminate preconceptualized material for sensible representation.[6] In other words, it is what would remain if (*per impossibile*) we could remove the determinate structure imposed on the sensibly given (the manifold of inner sense) by the understanding. Thus, what Kant is trying to say here is that if all we had were this indeterminate subjective order, we would not be able to represent any temporal order at all (whether "objective" or "subjective").[7] The problem, then, is to explain how time-consciousness, and with it the consciousness of objective succession, is possible. In Kant's terms, it is to provide the "formal conditions of empirical truth." Not only is this a significant problem, it is also the very problem that was left unresolved by the Transcendental Deduction.

B. The Inadequacy of Transcendental Realism

I have suggested that the second part of the paragraph can be taken to be arguing that transcendental realism is incapable of accounting for the possibility of knowledge of an objective temporal order. Admittedly, this is a somewhat free reconstruction that goes beyond what Kant actually says. To cite only the most obvious objection to this interpretation, Kant does not explicitly refer to transcendental realism at all. Nevertheless, this interpretation of Kant's intent is not without a basis in the text. Let us first consider Kant's own characterization of this problem in terms of his transcendental distinction:

> If appearances were things in themselves, then since we have to deal solely with our representations, we could never determine from the succession of the representations how their manifold may be connected in the object. How things may be in themselves, apart from the representations through which they affect us, is entirely outside our sphere of knowledge. [A190/B235]

Kant is here maintaining that if empirical, that is, spatiotemporal, objects are regarded as things in themselves rather than as appearances, then it is impossible to understand how we could have any knowledge of an objective temporal order of such objects. This is because "we have to deal only with our representations," while the order in question is, by definition, distinct from the order in which the representations occur in consciousness. Since transcendental realism does regard what for Kant are "mere appearances" (in the transcendental sense) as things in themselves (again in the transcendental sense), it follows that transcendental realism will not be able to account for the possibility of knowledge of an objective temporal order.

This "argument" is nothing more than an application of the general point made in the First Edition version of the Fourth Paralogism to the specific problem of the knowledge of a temporal order: "If we treat outer objects as things in themselves, it is quite impossible to understand how we could arrive at a knowledge of their reality outside us, since we have to rely merely on the representation which is in us" (A378). Consequently, the argument certainly applies to empirical idealism, that is, the Cartesian-Lockean version of transcendental realism which is under attack in the Paralogisms. One might ask, however, whether it can be made applicable to *all* forms of transcendental realism, including those which for one reason or another might reject empirical idealism.

I believe that it can, although doing so requires making explicit a premise that is merely implicit in the present argument. The needed premise is Kant's familiar claim that "time in itself" or "absolute time" cannot be perceived.[8] We saw in the last chapter that this precludes the possibility of directly comparing our representations with a pregiven temporal order or, more generally, of being aware of such an order (even assuming that it exists; that is, even assuming that time is transcendentally real). I take this premise to be acceptable to all versions of transcendental realism, including Newton's.[9] If "time itself" cannot be perceived, it follows that the only way to determine an objective temporal order is through the ordering of "appearances" (here taken in an ontologically neutral sense). But at this point the transcendental realist will have to admit that the only order that is actually "given" to the mind is the order of the occurrence of its own representations. This subjective order, then, will be the only "object" to which the mind, on a transcendentally realistic account, has any access. Thus, the problem of access, which empirical idealism raises about material objects and which leads to a skepticism about the "external world," recurs in the case of an objective temporal order for all versions of transcendental realism. Moreover, it can be seen from this that it is the transcendental realist (not Kant) who is in the impossible situation of having to make inferences about an objective temporal order on the basis of a subjective order.

C. The Idealistic Reformulation

Given the way in which the problem of explaining the possibility of knowledge of an objective temporal order has been presented, it is by no means obvious that the transcendental idealist is in any better position to resolve it than the transcendental realist. Thus, while the transcendental realist has the problem of explaining the possibility of access to an objective temporal order of things in themselves, the transcendental idealist has the problem of explaining the possibility of distinguishing between an objective and a subjective temporal order *within* the realm of appearance.

After introducing the previously cited example of the perception of a house, which is designed to illustrate the point that we do not identify the order of the representing of the parts (the subjective order) with an order of successive states in the object represented (the objective order), Kant poses the problem in explicit terms. "Now immediately," he writes, "I unfold the transcendental meaning of my concepts of an object, I realize that the house is not a thing in itself, but only an appearance." This realization, in turn, gives rise to a question:

> What am I to understand by the question: how the manifold may be connected in the appearance itself, which yet is nothing in itself? That which lies in the successive apprehension is here viewed as representation, while the appearance which is given to me, notwithstanding that it is nothing but the sum [*Inbegriff*] of these representations, is viewed as their object; and my

concept, which I derive from the representation of apprehension, has to
agree with it." [A191/B236]

The key to understanding this difficult passage lies in recognizing the
progressive, dialectical nature of Kant's procedure in the entire discussion. He begins by raising the question of the conditions of the possibility
of making judgments about an objective temporal order, which can also
be expressed as a question regarding the grounds or legitimating conditions for such judgments. That we make such judgments is taken as
unproblematic; the question is how it is possible to do so. This question is
relevant to both the transcendental realist and the transcendental idealist,
although the former is incapable of answering it. But the transcendentally
idealistic analysis of the general problem leads to a new question about
the very concept of an objective temporal order of appearances. This
question is unique to the transcendental idealist.
  Further reflection, however, suggests that these two questions are
really equivalent for the transcendental idealist. As we have already seen,
it is the very essence of Kant's "transcendental turn" that the meaning of
'object' must be explicated in terms of the conditions of the representation of objects. This is the basic principle underlying the "Copernican"
conception of an object as something $= x$ that conforms to our mode of
cognition. All that Kant is really doing here is applying this principle to a
special sense of 'object'; namely, an objective temporal order. Since it is
only in and through judgment that we can represent objects, determining
the conditions or grounds for making judgments about an objective temporal order (an account of its possibility) also explains what is represented in the thought of such an order. In other words, the answer to the
first of the questions referred to in the preceding paragraph will also be
an answer to the second.

D. The "Critical" Solution

In the remainder of the paragraph Kant gives the gist of his solution to
the problem. He thus explains how, through successive representations,
we can represent to ourselves an object (in the "weighty" sense), "not-
withstanding that it [the object] is nothing but the sum of these representations." Kant's answer, of course, is that we represent appearance as an
object, that is, a temporal order of appearances as objective, by subjecting our representations to a rule. Correlatively, the "object" here is just
the temporal order of given appearances that is thought as the result of
the subjection of the representations to a rule. As Kant himself puts it at
the conclusion of the paragraph:

  that appearance, in contradistinction to the representations of apprehension,
  can be represented as an object distinct from them only if it stands under a
  rule which distinguishes it from every other apprehension and necessitates

some one particular mode of connection of the manifold. The object is *that* in the appearance which contains the condition of this necessary rule of apprehension. [A191/B236]

Kant also expresses the same point in a somewhat clearer fashion later in the argument of the Analogy:

> If we enquire what new character *relation to an object* confers upon our representations, what dignity they thereby acquire, we find that it results only in subjecting the representations to a rule, and so in necessitating us to connect them in some one specific manner; and conversely, that only in so far as our representations are necessitated in a certain order as regards their time-relations do they acquire objective meaning. [A197/B242–43]

Both passages make the same point, but the second is to be preferred because it does not contain the misleading suggestion that the rule in question is one that determines apprehension. It is rather a rule for conceptualization or judgment, which expresses how the given representations are to be connected in the "objective unity of apperception." The representation of an objective succession involves a determinate manner of conceiving the manifold of representations that are referred to the "object" in the judgment. To anticipate for a moment the main theme of the next section, in the representation of an objective succession *A-B* (where *A* and *B* stand for successive determinations or states of some object), the order of perceptions *a, b* (where *a* stands for the perception of *A* and *b* for the perception of *B*) is thought as determined. In other words, it is thought as $AB \cdot \sim BA$. The "necessity" here actually consists only in the conceptual constraint on the thought of this order, through which this thought becomes objectively valid (the thought of an objective succession). As always for Kant, this necessity, and with it the objective validity of the thought, is produced by the imposition of an a priori rule. The argument of the Second Analogy consists largely in the application of this general principle to the special case of the succession of states of an object.

II. THE ESSENTIAL ARGUMENT

Following Kant's lead, "let us now proceed to our problem," which is to locate and analyze Kant's basic argument in support of the every-event-some-cause principle. In so doing, I propose to abstract from the fact that commentators have found as many as six different "proofs" of the principle in the text of the Second Analogy, including one that is added in the Second Edition.[10] Such abstraction is possible because it is generally recognized that at least five of these proofs are really varieties of a single line of argument. The remaining one, the so-called argument from the nature of time, does seem to stand apart from the rest and to involve peculiar difficulties.[11] Nevertheless, I believe that it is possible to present the basic structure of the Kantian defense of the causal principle without appealing to any of the unique and especially problematic features of that argument.

Before proceeding to the argument, however, we must first consider how Kant construes the two key terms, 'cause' and 'event'. It is frequently noted that the essential feature of the Kantian conception of causality is the element of necessity.[12] Kant claims that "this concept makes strict demand that something, A, should be such that something else, B, follows from it *necessarily and in accordance with an absolutely universal rule*" (A91/B124); and again, that "the concept of cause involves the character of necessity which no experience can yield" (A112–13). Although Kant does not explain just what he means by 'necessity' in this context, the way in which he uses it suggests that here, as in the introduction to the *Critique,* it must be taken as essentially equivalent to 'strict universality' or 'invariability'.[13] Thus to claim that A is the cause of B is to claim that given A, together with certain presupposed "standing conditions" which Kant ignores, B will invariably (*jederzeit*) follow. This is equivalent to the claim that B follows from A "in accordance with an absolutely universal rule." This shows that the characterization of causality on page A91/B124 is somewhat misleading. Kant's use of the conjunction *and* suggests that following "necessarily" and following "in accordance with an absolutely universal rule" are two distinguishable properties which are assigned to every effect considered in relation to its cause. In reality, however, they come to the same thing. Both locutions express merely the thought that a particular effect must be conceived to follow in every case or without exception from its cause[14] (again assuming the relevant "standing conditions"). Similarly, the claim that every event has some cause is equivalent to the claim that for every event there is some unspecified antecedent condition to which it is related in this way. This is precisely what Kant must show to be the case.

The second key term is 'event' (*Begebenheit, Ereignis, Wirklichkeit*), which Kant generally treats as synonymous with 'happening' or 'occurrence' (*Geschehen*), and even at times in the Second Analogy with 'alteration' (*Veränderung*). This is indeed confusing, but the main point to keep in mind is that all of these terms refer to the coming to be of a state or determination of some object.[15] To cite one of Kant's own examples, the freezing of water is an event because it involves the coming into existence of a new state (solidity) of the water. It is, therefore, the *becoming* and not the *being* solid that constitutes the event. An event thus involves an alteration, which is just the point that Kant emphasizes in his Second Edition reformulation. In the most famous example, the ship moving downstream, it is presumably the change of spatial position of the ship that constitutes the event.[16]

So much for the preliminaries. The actual argument begins with an account of the essential features of event perception: "That something happens, i.e., that something, or some state which did not previously exist, comes to be, cannot be perceived unless it is preceded by an appearance that does not contain in itself this state" (A191/B236–37). In other words, I cannot be aware that "something has happened" unless I can contrast the present state of some object or substance with its preceding state. This much is already clear from the argument of the First Analogy, and so is the consequence that "every apprehension of an event is a perception that follows upon another perception" (A192/B237). But this is only a necessary and not also a sufficient condition of event perception. Since all apprehension is successive, *every* perception follows upon a preceding perception. The problem, therefore, is to determine the conditions under which a succession of perceptions can be taken as the perception of a succession of states in the object.

The example of the perception of a ship sailing downstream is introduced by Kant in order to clarify the problem. His point is simply that in contrast to the perception of the house, where I do not regard my successive perceptions as perceptions of a change or succession in the object itself, in the perception of a ship I do regard my perceptions in just this way. Kant concludes from this that in the latter case I am constrained to regard the order of my perceptions as determined or irreversible. In other words, if I judge that I am perceiving a change in the position of the ship from point A at t_1 to point B at t_2, then I must also think the order of my perceptions as determined; that is, I must think this order as $AB \cdot \sim BA$. This is not to say that I cannot imagine a different order of perceptions; that is certainly possible. In doing so, however, I am imagining a different event; for example, a ship sailing in the opposite direction.[17]

Unfortunately, Kant's manner of formulating the irreversibility thesis is very misleading. Thus in one key place he writes: "The order in which the perceptions occur in apprehension is determined, and to this order apprehension is bound down" (A192/B238). This, and similar passages, have often led commentators to take Kant to be claiming that in event perception the actual subjective order of perceptions (the order of apprehension) is rendered necessary by the successive order of the states perceived. In other words, the claim that "apprehension is bound down" is taken to mean that *its* order is causally determined, and that this is what makes it impossible for the perception to occur in the reverse order.[18] This would indeed be a strange line of argument for Kant to invoke. First, it amounts to an appeal to a causal theory of perception in order to justify the principle that every event (which presumably includes perceptual events) has a cause. Such a line of argument would seem to be an obvious begging of the question. Second, if Kant's claim is really about the necessity of the subjective order of perceptions *a-b* (the order in which they occur in empirical consciousness) in the perception of the sequence *A-B*, then it is manifestly false. As Robert Paul Wolff points out:

> It is not true that we must perceive the boat at B after we have perceived it at A. We might hear its whistle at A after we see its smoke from B. Or, to be somewhat more fanciful, the light from A might be reflected back and forth between mirrors enough times to make it arrive after the light from B. By the same token the accidents of my perceptual situation might make it objectively impossible for me to view the house in more than one order. In general, by manipulating the physical and physiological setting of a perceptual situation, a particular succession of representations, $p1, p2, p3, \ldots, pn$ can be made compatible with any of the $n!$ alternative objective successions of the states represented by the perceptions. Kant is apparently led to the contrary position by an oversimplified identification of perception with sight, although even with regard to sight his conclusion is unwarranted.[19]

We need not speculate, however, about the accuracy of Wolff's conjecture that Kant identifies perception with sight. The main point is simply that if irreversibility is understood in this way (as pertaining to the order in which perceptions appear in "empirical consciousness"), then Kant must be taken as claiming that it somehow functions as an "inference ticket," licensing judgments about the objective temporal order. But if this is the case, then Kant is, indeed, hopelessly confused; for this interpretation commits him to the very empirical idealism which, as we have seen, he adamantly rejects.[20] Thus, although it is suggested by some of Kant's language, particularly when he speaks loosely of apprehension being "bound down," this reading of the irreversibility thesis is clearly wrong: we cannot regard the irreversibility of the perceptions *ab* in the perception of an objective succession *AB* as either a property which these perceptions have in "empirical consciousness" or as a datum from which we can somehow infer that an objective succession has occurred. It could not be a property because the recognition of any such "property" presupposes that the order of perceptions is already conceptualized and made into a "subjective object," and, as we shall see in chapters 12 and 14, this itself presupposes "objective experience." Moreover, no such "property" of perceptions could possibly justify any claims about the temporal properties or relations of objects distinct from them.

How, then, are we to understand the irreversibility thesis? The answer is that it characterizes the way in which we connect perceptions in thought (the objective unity of apperception) if we are to experience *through* them an objective succession.[21] To put the same point somewhat differently, irreversibility does not refer to a given perceptual order, which we can inspect and then infer that it is somehow determined by the object; it refers rather to the conceptual order*ing* of the understanding (by subsumption under a rule) through which the understanding determines the thought of an object (in this case objective succession). Prior to the conceptual determination there is no thought of an object at all and, a fortiori, no experience. Similarly, in the Third Analogy, where the concern is with the representation of coexistence, the claim is that we think the order of perceptions as reversible and by this means represent *through* them the coexistence of objects and of their states.[22]

The task is, therefore, to determine the condition under which we think the order of perceptions as irreversible. Given Kant's transcendental analysis, such a condition can be supplied only by an a priori rule. Moreover, since the order in question is temporal, the rule must have the status of a transcendental schema. We need, then, only ask which schema is involved in the thought of such an order. When the problem is posed in this way, however, the answer is obvious. It can only be the schema of the pure concept of causality, which, as we have seen, is characterized as rule-governed succession, or "the succession of the manifold insofar as it is subject to a rule." Consequently, it is only by subjecting our perceptions to this rule or, equivalently, subsuming them under the schema of causality, that we can regard them as containing the representation of an event. But in that case the event itself, qua object represented, that is, qua object of possible experience, is likewise subsumed under the schema. In other words, it is presupposed that there is something antecedent to the event "on which it follows according to a rule" (A195 / B240).

The move from the subjection of the perceptions to the rule to the subjection of the perceived event is clearly the key step in the argument. It might seem that the most that the line of argument sketched above can establish is the necessity of subjecting the perceptions to the rule, and that it can have no bearing at all on the rule-governedness of the object. In that case the only expedient is, in phenomenalistic fashion, to reduce judgments about objects to judgments about our *perception* of objects. In fact, Kant is frequently assumed to be arguing in just this way.[23] It should be clear by now, however, that this cannot be an acceptable reading. The whole problematic of the Second Analogy is grounded in the assumption of the impossibility of simply identifying the order of perceptions with the order of the successive states of the object perceived. Once again, then, the subjection of perceptions to a rule cannot be construed as the means for making the perceptions themselves into objects, but rather as the basis for conceiving of a distinct, objective temporal order in and through these perceptions. But in so doing we are necessarily thinking the objective order in accordance with the rule, that is, applying the rule to it. The principle at work here is one that is fundamental to Kant's whole philosophy: "the conditions of the *possibility of experience* in general are likewise conditions of the *possibility of the objects of experience*" (A158 / B197). Moreover, in the present case the whole function of the rule is to determine the order as objective. As Kant succinctly puts it:

> I render my subjective synthesis of apprehension objective only by reference to a rule in accordance with which the appearances in their succession, that is, as they happen, are determined by the preceding state. [A195/B240]

Again, in another passage, Kant contrasts the merely subjective synthesis of the imagination (the "play of representations") with the objectifying synthesis:

> But if this synthesis is a synthesis of apprehension of the manifold of a given appearance, the order is determined in the object, or, to speak more correctly, is an order of successive synthesis that determines an object. [A201/B246]

This, in essence, is the central line of argument of the Second Analogy. It is not an argument from the nature of time, although it is concerned with the conditions of the representation of a succession in time. As I have sketched it above, the argument falls into the following five steps: (1) All event perception requires successive perceptions of an object. (2) But this is merely a necessary and not a sufficient condition of event-perception. The latter also requires the perception of successive states of the object, and (since all apprehension is successive) this can never be determined on the basis of the successiveness of the perceptions themselves. (3) In order to consider a succession of perceptions as perceptions of successive states of an object, it is necessary to regard their order as irreversible. (The irreversibility thesis, however, does not pertain to the order in which perceptions are apprehended in "empirical consciousness," but rather to the order in which they are conceptualized in a judgment concerning objective succession.) (4) To regard perceptions in this way is just to subject them to an a priori rule, which in this case must be the schema of causality. (5) As a condition of the possibility of the experience of an objective succession, the schema is also a condition of the succession itself (as an object of possible experience). The schema thus has "objective reality," which is just what the argument is intended to prove.

It should be clear from this summary, as well as from the preceding analysis, that the argument of the Second Analogy cannot be neatly separated from Kant's transcendental idealism. On the contrary, it is grounded in the transcendental analysis of objectivity, and it consists largely in the application of the results of this analysis to the problem of the experience of objective succession. Nevertheless, it does not involve a phenomenalistic reduction of claims about objects, or an objective order, to claims about an order of perceptions considered as such. Moreover, although it certainly presupposes the argument of the Transcendental Deduction, it goes beyond it precisely because it establishes the function of the schema as a condition of experience in contrast to mere apprehension. This, as we have seen, is something that the Deduction itself was not able to accomplish for any category (whether pure or schematized). For the same reason it also makes a vital contribution to a "metaphysic of experience" in the Kantian sense.

Finally, a word is certainly in order about the question of whether the argument provides an adequate answer to Hume's skeptical challenge to the causal principal in the *Treatise*. As Lewis White Beck points out, the notorious difficulty with many of the familiar versions of "Kant's answer to Hume" is, to use Kant's own words, that they "took for granted that which Hume doubted, and demonstrated with zeal, and often with impudence that which he never thought of doubting."[24] Beck also makes it clear that in order to demonstrate that the argument of the Second Analogy constitutes a successful response to Hume, it must be shown that it is based upon a premise (or premises) that Hume accepts, and that its conclusion expresses a necessary condition of this premise.[25] I believe that the argument as outlined above meets these criteria, at least in part. The premise which Hume cannot doubt is that we do, in fact, distinguish between a mere sequence of perceptions and the perception of an objective sequence. He cannot doubt this because the possibility of event awareness is presupposed by his own well-known account of how we come to form the belief that future sequences of events will resemble past sequences. Correlatively, the argument shows that it is only by the application of the schema of causality that we can experience such succession. The premise which Hume would not accept is transcendental idealism or, more accurately, the transcendental perspective from which the problem is approached. Since Hume is a transcendental realist he could hardly be expected to accept this mode of analysis. Nevertheless, it must be kept in mind that the argument also contains an analysis of the inability of the transcendental realist to explain the possibility of the experience of objective succession. In this respect it presents an even more fundamental challenge to the Humean position, albeit one that can be evaluated only in terms of an overall consideration of transcendental idealism.

III. INTERPRETATION AND DEFENSE

The question that inevitably arises at this point is just what the preceding line of argument is supposed to establish. The more or less traditional interpretation is that Kant's real goal is to establish the lawfulness or uniformity of nature. By this is meant roughly the necessary conformity of nature to universal laws of the type found in Newtonian physics. Another way of putting the same point is to claim that Kant endeavored to reply to Hume in the Second Analogy by demonstrating a "law of causality" or "principle of induction" that would guarantee particular generalizations or laws.[26] The obvious failure of Kant's argument to establish anything like this result is then taken as the basis for its complete rejection. This whole line of interpretation culminates in the non sequitur objection of Lovejoy and Strawson. I have already claimed, following Lewis White Beck, that Kant's argument is intended merely to establish the more modest thesis that every event has some cause, and I believe that only such a reading of Kant's intent is compatible with the argument which he provides. Even granting this, however, it is still not clear how much is built into Kant's claim and what it entails about the "lawfulness of nature," in the sense of its conformity to empirical laws. Accordingly, in this final section I propose first to answer this question and then to show that, properly construed, Kant's claim is not susceptible to the non sequitur objection.

A. The Nature of Kant's Claim

The first point to note here is that Kant's argument attempts to prove that the concept or schema of causality is a necessary condition of the experience of the succession of the states in an object, that is, of *an event,* not that it is a condition for the ordering of distinct events. One might think this too obvious to mention, were it not for the fact that the opposite is so frequently assumed to be the case. Some Kant interpreters make this assumption because they realize that the appeal to causal laws can be used to fix the temporal location of given events or types of events vis à vis one another. Thus, given a causal law linking events of type A (as cause) with events of type B (as effect), we can fix the temporal location of events of these types with respect to one another. And, since time cannot be perceived, it is only by appeal to such laws that we can determine the temporal order of distinct events. By extension of this principle we arrive at the idea that the determinability of the location of all events in a single time presupposes their connectibility according to causal laws.[27] There may very well be something to this line of argument, and it is certainly Kantian in spirit. The problem is that it is not the argument which Kant advances in the Second Analogy. The notion of the complete or thoroughgoing (*durchgängig*) determinability of the temporal position of events is, for Kant, a regulative Idea; as such, it expresses a requirement of reason, not a transcendental condition of the possibility of experience.[28]

In order to determine how much is built into the claim that every event has a cause, it is crucial to keep in mind the meaning of 'event'; namely, the change of state of an object. As we have already seen, it is a necessary condition of the experience of a change of state of an object that the object was perceived to be in an opposite state at a prior time. In other words, every event must have a perceptual antecedent. Given this, I believe that the central exegetical question is, Just what does the argument of the Second Analogy require us to assume about the connection between an event and its perceptual antecedent? The main lines of interpretation can be classified in terms of their answer to this question. Assuming that by 'cause' is meant something like "initiating condition," that is, the factor to which primary responsibility for a change of state is to be assigned,[29] three possibilities suggest themselves: (1) the initial state A (the perceptual antecedent) must itself be regarded as the cause of the change to state $B;$ (2) the sequence of states A-B must be "lawlike" in the sense that, given some initiating condition ("the condition of the rule," in Kant's terminology), the transition from A to B is necessarily subsumable under a "covering law" (presumably this requirement would hold even if we were not in fact capable of discovering the law); and (3) the sequence can (but need not) be "contingent," in the sense that it is not necessarily characterizable in either of the two previous manners, but the event is still subject to the principle of causality as a transcendental condition.

The first way of interpreting Kant's argument leads directly to the famous reductio objection of Schopenhauer. He took Kant to be arguing that the only succession which we can regard as objective is that of cause and effect. Against this, Schopenhauer quite correctly pointed out that appearances can perfectly well follow after one another without following from one another. Thus his classical example of a person walking out of his house at t_1, which is followed by a brick falling on his head at t_2. Since Kant (on this interpretation) must deny that there can be any such non-causal succession, Schopenhauer contended that he falls into the error opposite to Hume's. Just as Hume falsely took "alles Erfolgen für blossen Folgen," so Kant maintains "dass es kein andres Folgen gebe, als das Erfolgen."[30] Although this consequence is obviously absurd, it is not an absurdity to which Kant is committed. Kant claims only that without the appeal to the schema of causality we could not distinguish between the representation of successive states of a changing object and the successive representations of coexisting parts or properties of an enduring object. This does not at all entail that the only succession which we can experience is that of cause and effect. In fact, there are relatively few cases in which the preceding state of an object can itself be regarded as the cause, or "initiating condition," of its subsequent state.[31]

Most versions of what can be called the "strong" interpretation of the Second Analogy construe Kant to be arguing for something like the second of the three possibilities outlined above. In other words, they take Kant to be claiming that all succession of states in an object must be "lawlike" in the sense that for every object x that changes from state A at t_1 to state B at t_2, there must be some "initiating condition" C, which may or may not have anything to do with A. This condition being given (together with certain unspecified "standing conditions"), states of A's *type* will necessarily be followed by states of B's *type* in all objects of x's *type*. It is obvious that many cases of objective succession do fit this model. For instance, we need consider only Kant's own example of the freezing of water. Here the succession of states, fluidity-solidity, is subsumable under an empirical law which tells us that, given a drop in temperature to zero degrees centigrade, the former state will invariably be succeeded by the latter. The question, however, is whether Kant's argument requires us to assume that all objective succession is necessarily lawlike in this sense or whether it is compatible with the existence of "contingent sequences" as described by the third possibility.

Now, as Buchdahl points out, Kant's own example of the ship moving downstream is a good example of a "contingent happening," that is, one that is not "lawlike" in the abovementioned sense. As he puts it, "clearly we are not to imagine that the ship's sailing downstream is necessarily, if ever, an instance of a law-like happening, or that it is *as such* determined by preceding or underlying causes."[32] Although this suggests the disanalogy between the successive positions of the ship and the successive states of the water in the previous example, I believe that the point can be brought out more forcefully by an example of a succession that is explicitly unlawlike. Let us consider the case of Jones, who is perceived at t_1 to be in a state of blissful inebriation, and immediately thereafter, at t_2, is observed to pass out. At first this would no doubt be regarded as a familiar instance of a "lawlike" succession: we simply subsume the successive states of Jones under an empirical law regarding the effects of alcohol. Suppose, however, that we learn subsequently that Jones's passing out was really due to a slow-working drug ingested hours before the event, and thus that it had nothing to do with the amount of alcohol in his system. In that case the perceptual antecedent, drunkenness at t_1, does not stand in any causal or "lawlike" connection with the event. Nevertheless, it is obvious that the succession of states is itself objective and "necessary" in precisely the same sense as it would be if it did. The objectivity of the sequence is thus not a function of its lawlikeness.

Examples of this type, which can easily be multiplied, express what I take to be the correct intuition behind Buchdahl's characterization of the sequence with which the Second Analogy is concerned as "contingent." For that very reason they also support what can be called the "weak" interpretation. The basic point is that judgments about objective temporal succession do not presuppose that the elements of the succession are connected by empirical laws. All that is presupposed is that there is some antecedent condition (presumably roughly contemporaneous with x's being in state A at t_1), which being given, state B necessarily ensues for this particular x at t_2. There are no additional assumptions regarding the repeatability of the sequence and its relevance to other objects of x's type that are either required or licensed by this presupposition. Nor is the situation changed by the fact that in the example cited above an actual lawful connection was established between the event and a different antecedent condition (the ingestion of a drug). The latter makes possible the explanation of the event, and the search for such conditions is a requirement of reason in its regulative capacity. This, in turn, requires the assumption of the uniformity of nature or the affinity of appearances. It is not, however, in any sense part of the task of the Second Analogy to provide a justification for this requirement of reason.

B. The Non Sequitur Objection

Of all the objections that have been raised against the argument of the Second Analogy, the claim that it involves a non sequitur is perhaps the most fundamental and potentially damaging. It is also the kind of objection that seems to arise naturally at any number of crucial points in Kant's philosophy. Nevertheless, I believe that the preceding considerations have put us in a position to dispose of it in relatively brief fashion. This objection was first formulated by Arthur Lovejoy and later reiterated, apparently without any awareness of Lovejoy's analysis, by P. F. Strawson.

According to Lovejoy, the bulk of the Second Analogy contains nothing more than a restatement of Wolff's proof of the principle of sufficient reason. In spite of Kant's claims to the contrary, it is thus analytic and dogmatic rather than synthetic and critical. The only exception which Lovejoy will allow to this is the step where Kant moves from the reflection that in every instance of event perception the order of perceptions is determined and thus irreversible, to the conclusion that every event follows from a preceding state of affairs in accordance with a universal and necessary law. Lovejoy acknowledges the originality of this step, but he proceeds to dismiss it as "one of the most spectacular examples of the *non sequitur* which are to be found in the history of philosophy."[33] Lovejoy does not find fault with Kant's contention that in the perception of an event the order of perceptions is determined by "something in the object"; nor does he object to the claim that this order must be regarded as irreversible in *that instance*. Thus, in connection with Kant's example of the ship moving downstream, he admits the impossibility of the perceptions occurring in reverse order. Nevertheless, he maintains,

all this has no relation to the law of universal and uniform causation, for the manifest reason that a proof of the *irreversibility* of the sequence of my perceptions in a *single instance* of a phenomenon is not equivalent to a proof of the necessary *uniformity* of the sequence of my perceptions in *repeated instances* of a given *kind* of phenomenon. Yet, it is the latter alone that Hume denied and that Kant desires to establish.[34]

Strawson makes much the same point, calling the move "a *non sequitur* of numbing grossness."[35] Like Lovejoy, he is willing to acknowledge Kant's claims that in the experience of an event the order of perceptions is determined or irreversible and "in this sense necessary." He takes this to be a more or less legitimate way of articulating the denial of "order indifference" that is characteristic of event perception. Consequently, Strawson admits that, apart from obvious exceptions of the kind suggested by the previously cited criticism of Robert Paul Wolff, in the perception of a succession *A-B* it is "necessary that the perception of the second state *B* follows and does not precede the perception of the first state *A*." Kant's problem, however, is that he erroneously believes that

> to conceive this order of perception as necessary is equivalent to conceiving the transition or change from A to B as *itself* necessary, as falling, that is to say, under a rule of law of causal determination; it is equivalent to conceiving the event of change or transition as preceded by some condition such that an event of that type invariably and necessarily follows upon a condition of that type.[36]

Here, according to Strawson, lies the non sequitur, which he traces to Kant's illicit and unwitting shift from a conceptual to a causal notion of necessity. It is conceptually necessary that in the perception of the sequence of states *A-B* the observer's perceptions should follow the order: perception of *A*, perception of *B*. Nevertheless, he insists,

> the necessity invoked in the conclusion of the argument is not a conceptual necessity at all; it is the causal necessity of the change occurring, given some antecedent state of affairs. It is a very curious contortion indeed whereby a conceptual necessity based on the fact of a change is equated with the causal necessity of that very change.[37]

There are two points to be made about this line of criticism, and they apply to its exposition by both Lovejoy and Strawson. The first is its complete neglect of the transcendentally idealistic thrust of Kant's argument. The objection presupposes a transcendentally realistic standpoint and, in effect, treats Kant as if he were an empirical idealist. More specifically, it assumes that Kant's argument rests on an inference from a feature of our perceptions (their irreversibility) to a conclusion regarding the causal relations of ontologically distinct entities or states of affairs that supposedly correspond to these perceptions. This would indeed be a non sequitur of "numbing grossness," but we have already seen that it is not Kant's. Moreover, as Lewis White Beck correctly points out, Kant could very well respond to Lovejoy and Strawson that, given *their* conception of an object, we could not infer anything about the objective order *A-B* from the order of our perceptions.[38] The result would thus be a skepticism that not even Hume could accept, because he assumes that we do experience events.

One should not, however, jump from this to a "subjectivistic" or "phenomenalistic" reading of the argument, according to which the successive states of affairs are either simply identified with the representations or construed as complexes of actual and possible representations.[39] To do so is to ignore the *transcendentally* idealistic nature of Kant's position. As we have seen in the analysis of the "transcendental setting," the argument assumes the Copernican or transcendental conception of an object as the correlate of a certain mode of representation. Such an "object" is "distinct from our representations," but not in the way in which this is understood by the transcendental realist. This is because the very concept of an object in the "weighty" sense (here an objective temporal order) must be characterized in terms of the conditions of our representation of it. Given this conception, the argument of the Second Analogy maintains that the schema of causality (succession in accordance with a rule) is the condition to which our perceptions must be subjected if they are to yield the experience of an objective temporal order. As a condition of the possibility of the experience of such an order, the schema is also a condition of the possibility of the order itself.

The second point about the non sequitur objection is that it rests upon a "strong" interpretation of the argument of the Second Analogy. Obviously, both Lovejoy and Strawson take it for granted that Kant is claiming that in order to determine the objectivity of the sequence A-B, it must be subsumed under a causal law which specifies that, given certain conditions, states of A's type are invariably followed by states of B's type, and not vice versa. On this interpretation, then, Kant does move from the contention that the sequence is irreversible, and in this sense necessary in a particular instance (which both Lovejoy and Strawson allow), to the conclusion that it is irreversible in all relevantly similar instances, and thus necessary in the very different sense of being law-governed. Once again, this move is a non sequitur, but it is not one which we need attribute to Kant.[40] As we have seen, the "weak" interpretation of the argument requires that we assume only that in the succession of states A-B of some object x, there must be some antecedent condition that determines the x, which was in state A at t_1, to enter into or assume state B at t_2. Since this neither implies anything about the connection between the new state B and its perceptual antecedent A, nor requires that we assume anything about all objects of x's type, there is no non sequitur. By the same token, the argument does not establish anything about the uniformity of nature, the "affinity of appearances," or their conformity to necessary laws. As Buchdahl has shown, Kant's views on these and similar topics cannot be understood apart from his account of the regulative functions of reason and reflective judgment. This, however, is a subject which is beyond the scope of the present study.

PART FOUR
THE PHENOMENAL, THE NOUMENAL, AND THE SELF

11

The Thing in Itself and the Problem of Affection

Of all the criticisms that have been raised against Kant's philosophy, the most persistent is that he has no right to affirm the existence of things in themselves, noumena, or a transcendental object, much less to talk about such things as somehow "affecting" the mind. Any account of Kant's transcendental idealism must, therefore, include an analysis of this issue, and this is the task of the present chapter. Building upon the discussion of transcendental idealism in the first part of this study, I hope to show that talk about things considered as they are in themselves, including the claim that things so considered "affect us," does not violate the doctrine of the unknowability of things as they are in themselves.

This chapter is divided into three parts. The first deals with the general problem of finding a justification for referring, in a transcendental context, to things as they are in themselves. The second traces the relationship between the concept of the thing in itself and the associated yet distinct concepts of a noumenon and a transcendental object. The third attempts to provide a solution to the notorious problem of affection, by suggesting a sense in which Kant can consistently maintain that things as they are in themselves affect us.

I. THE PROBLEM OF THE THING IN ITSELF

Given the analysis of transcendental idealism in the first part of this study, the problem of the thing in itself can be described as the problem of having to provide a legitimate, nonpolemical use for the concept. The polemical use is justified by the critique of transcendental realism; it enables Kant to explain the errors of his precedessors and to show how the objects of human cognition are *not* to be considered in a philosophical account. This does not, however, justify any positive use for the concept within the "critical philosophy" itself: the claim that certain philosophers erroneously treat mere appearances as if they were things in themselves no more entails that there are things in themselves than the claim that a certain person acts "as if he were God" entails the existence of a deity. Moreover, in those places in the *Critique* where Kant is most concerned with the concept of the thing in itself and the related concepts of the noumenon and the transcendental object (in the Ground of the Distinction of all Objects in General into Phenomena and Noumena and the

Amphiboly of Concepts of Reflection), his primary intent seems to be either to articulate his critique of Leibnizian noumenalism or to correct some of the excesses of his own position in the Inaugural Dissertation.[1] For example, although Kant does admit noumena in "the purely negative sense," he goes on to insist that the whole force of this admission is to underscore the limitation of "our kind of intuition" to objects of our senses, and thus to allow for the (logical) possibility of "some other kind of intuition, and so for things as its objects" (A286/B342–43).

Passages like this, together with Kant's frequent insistence upon the unknowability of things in themselves, would appear to rule out the possibility of finding any positive, nonpolemical use for the concept. Nevertheless, there are numerous places in which Kant does speak affirmatively and unproblematically about things in themselves. The following are among the best-known and most widely discussed passages in which this occurs:

> The Transcendental Aesthetic, in all its teaching, has led to this conclusion; and the same conclusion also, of course, follows from the conception of an appearance in general; namely, that something which is not in itself appearance must correspond to it. For appearance can be nothing by itself, outside our mode of representation. Unless, therefore, we are to move constantly in a circle, the word appearance must be recognized as already indicating a relation to something, the immediate representation of which is, indeed, sensible, but which, even apart from the constitution of our sensibility (upon which the form of our intuition is grounded), must be something in itself, that is, an object independent of sensibility. [A251–52]

> And we indeed, rightly considering objects of sense as mere appearances, confess thereby that they are based upon a thing in itself, though we know not this thing as it is in itself but only know its appearances, namely, the way in which our senses are affected by this unknown something. The understanding, therefore, by assuming appearances, grants the existence of things in themselves also; and to this extent we may say that the representation of such things as are the basis of appearances, consequently of mere beings of the understanding, is not only admissible but unavoidable. [*Prolegomena*, 314–15]

> But our further contention must also be duly borne in mind, namely, that though we cannot *know* these objects as things in themselves, we must yet be in a position at least to think them as things in themselves otherwise we should be landed in the absurd conclusion that there can be appearance without anything that appears. [Bxxvi–xxvii]

> At the same time, if we entitle certain objects, as appearances, sensible entities (phenomena), then since we thus distinguish the mode in which we intuit them from the nature that belongs to them in themselves, it is implied in this distinction that we place the latter, considered in their own nature, although we do not so intuit them, or that we place other possible things, which are not objects of our senses but are thought as objects merely through

the understanding, in opposition to the former, and that in so doing we entitle them intelligible entities (noumena). [B306]

The doctrine of sensibility is likewise the doctrine of the noumenon in the negative sense, that is, of things which the understanding must think without this reference to our mode of intuition, therefore not merely as appearances but as things in themselves. [B307]

The first thing to note about these passages is that they speak of the "thing in itself," the "noumenon," or the "non-sensible object" (for the present these will be regarded as equivalent) in two different ways. For the most part these terms clearly refer to the object that appears, considered as it is in itself; that is, as it is "apart from the constitution of our sensibility." There are, however, places where they refer to an entity or entities ontologically distinct from the sensible objects of human cognition. This second conception is implicit in the second passage and fully explicit in the fourth. In fact, the fourth passage makes it apparent that Kant takes the concept of a noumenon to encompass both kinds of non-sensible object.[2]

It should not be inferred from this, however, that Kant is confused about his own transcendental distinction. As we have already seen, the appearance-thing in itself, phenomenal-noumenal distinctions indicate a contrast between two ways in which the objects of human experience can be considered in transcendental reflection. The conception of a noumenon as an ontologically distinct entity is required only in order to allow for the possibility of conceiving of God (and perhaps rational souls). This conception is, therefore, important for Kant's metaphysics, including his metaphysics of morals, but it does not enter directly into a transcendental account of the conditions of the possibility of human knowledge. Accordingly, the task of a transcendental justification of the concept of the thing in itself (and its associated concepts) is to explain the possibility and significance of considering "as they are in themselves" the same objects which we can know only as they appear; it is not, as is frequently assumed, to license the appeal to a set of unknown entities distinct from appearances.

Unfortunately, the search for such a justification in the Kantian texts does not appear to meet with much initial success. There seem to be intimations of two distinct lines of argument in "defense" of the thing in itself, each of which has advocates among Kant interpreters, but neither of which is capable of doing the job. According to one line, which finds its strongest textual support in the second passage quoted above, the reference to things in themselves is not only admissible but necessary because of the need to acknowledge a "cause" or "ground" of appearances. This can be termed the "causal interpretation," since it construes the relationship between an appearance and a thing in itself to be that of an effect and its cause or ground.³ An obvious problem with this interpretation is that it requires that we take the appearance and the corresponding thing in itself as two distinct entities. But even if we ignore this, as well as the notorious difficulties associated with the notion of a "noumenal causality," it is clear that this move cannot provide the needed justification. After all, if things in themselves are taken as causes, or grounds of appearance, then it is presupposed that we can refer to things in themselves, and this is the very point at issue.

Other passages suggest that Kant's claim is semantic. On this reading, Kant is affirming a relation of logical implication between the *concept* of an appearance and the *concept* of a thing as it is in itself, rather than a causal connection between the entities falling under these concepts.⁴ The basic thought here is that the expression 'appearance' is parasitic upon, or at least correlative with, the expression 'thing in itself': to use the former expression is already to presuppose the legitimacy of the latter. Such an interpretation seems to find textual support in the contention in the first passage that the affirmation of "something which is not an appearance," that is, a thing in itself, "follows from the concept of an appearance in general." Similarly, in the same passage Kant contends that "the word appearance" must be taken as already indicating a relation to some such thing. Finally, in the third passage, Kant suggests that the denial of things in themselves would lead to the "absurd conclusion that there can be appearance without anything that appears."

While it cannot be denied that these passages suggest some such argument, it is also clear that the straightforward semantic approach is no more successful than the causal argument. First, on the most natural reading, it assumes that the expressions 'appearance' and 'thing in itself' refer to two distinct entities, the claim being that reference to entities of the former sort presupposes the possibility of reference to those of the latter sort. As such, it is not even applicable to the transcendental distinction between two ways of considering one and the same thing. Second, the attempt to modify the argument so as to make it relevant to the transcendental distinction seems to lead to incoherence. The problem here is that the notion of considering a thing as it is in itself is presented by Kant in essentially negative terms: to consider a thing in this way is just to consider it as it is apart from the conditions under which it appears to us, and thus as *not* being an appearance. Consequently, if we apply the semantic argument to *this* distinction, we arrive at the claim that the designation of a thing as an 'appearance' requires that we also designate the very same thing as a 'nonappearance'. On this interpretation, then, Kant is requiring us to contradict ourselves.⁵

Fortunately, the last difficulty can be avoided by means of a somewhat more precise specification of the nature of the transcendental distinction. In spite of what Kant's language sometimes suggest, the distinction is not between a thing considered as an appearance and the same thing considered as a thing in itself; it is rather between a *consideration* of a thing as it appears and a *consideration* of the same thing as it is in itself.[6] In other words, the relevant terms function adverbially to characterize *how* we consider things in transcendental reflection, not substantivally to characterize what it is that is being considered or reflected upon. To consider things as they appear, or as appearing, is to consider them in their relation to the sensible conditions under which they are given to the mind in intuition. Correlatively, to consider them as they are in themselves is to think them apart from all reference to these conditions. But clearly, in order to consider things as they appear, or as appearing, it is necessary to distinguish the character that these things reveal as appearing (their spatiotemporal properties, and so forth) from the character that the same things are thought to possess when they are considered as they are in themselves, independently of the conditions under which they appear. This means that to consider something as it appears, or as appearing, we must also consider it as it is in itself. These contrasting ways of considering an object are simply two sides of the same act of transcendental reflection, an act which Kant describes as "a duty from which nobody who wishes to make any *a priori* judgments about things can claim exemption" (A263 / B319).

The perplexing aspect of this account is that, according to Kant's own analysis, in considering an object as it is in itself we cannot gain any knowledge of the real nature of that object. But although we cannot know things as they are in themselves, we can nonetheless know how they must be conceived in transcendental reflection, when they are considered as they are in themselves. Thus, as we have seen in chapter 5, we can assert the nonspatiality and nontemporality of things considered as they are in themselves without violating the principle of "critical" agnosticism. We can do so because such claims do not involve any synthetic a priori judgments about how things *really are* in contrast to how they merely *seem* to us. On the contrary, they involve merely analytic judgments or, perhaps more accurately, methodological directives, which specify how we must conceive things when we consider them in abstraction from their relation to human sensibility and its a priori forms. These directives serve to undermine the "common assumption" of transcendental realism: that objects can be taken under their empirical description, that is, regarded as spatiotemporal entities, when they are considered in this manner.

This admittedly extremely abstract account can perhaps be clarified somewhat by means of an empirical analogy. As is well known, within Newtonian physics bodies can be said to have weight only insofar as they stand in a relation of attraction and repulsion to other bodies. Hence, only insofar as a given body is "considered" in such a relation is a description which includes a reference to weight applicable to it. The intelligibility of this claim is in no way affected by the fact that bodies are always found to be in a relation of interaction with other bodies, so that "body as such" can never be an object of experience. The point is simply that bodies can very well be *conceived* although not *experienced* apart from their relation to other bodies (Newton's First Law of Motion is precisely about bodies so conceived). Making allowance for the shift from the empirical to the transcendental level, much the same can be said about the distinction between things as they appear and the same things as they are in themselves. In this case also what we have is the distinction between a thing considered in a certain relation, in virtue of which it falls under a certain description, and the same thing considered in abstraction from this relation, and therefore not falling under this description.

But this analogy obviously cannot be pushed too far. The basic difference is that in the Newtonian context we are dealing with a determinate, empirical concept (body). This makes it possible to recognize marks in the concept which apply to bodies even when they are considered apart from their relation to one another; for example, extension or divisibility. These are then said to be "analytically contained" in the concept. The transcendental context, however, explicitly rules out such a possibility. Here the relation in question is between the object and the cognitive capacity of the human mind. When one abstracts from *this* relation, one abstracts from everything empirical, leaving with nothing more than the completely indeterminate concept of a "something in general = x" (an object for which no description is available). Nevertheless, the fact remains that the transcendental context does involve a genuine instance of "considering." In fact, our ability to consider objects in this way is precisely what is meant by the claim that we can "think" things as they are in themselves; while the unique features of the transcendental context (the fact that it involves an abstraction from everything empirical) explains why we cannot *know* them as such. In this respect there is a strong parallel between the reflection on things as they are in themselves and the procedure of traditional negative theology (the *via negativa*), which combines the assertion of the unknowability of God with a series of dicta regarding how He is not to be conceived.

II. THE NOUMENON AND THE TRANSCENDENTAL OBJECT

We are now in a position to treat the concepts of the noumenon and the transcendental object, which are both intimately connected with the concept of a thing considered as it is in itself. The concept of a noumenon has already been encountered in several places in the first part of this study. It is the epistemological concept *par excellence,* characterizing an object, of whatever ontological status, considered qua correlate of a nonsensible manner of cognition. Since sensibility is an essential characteristic of the cognitive structure of the human mind, to know an object in this manner is to know it as it is independently of its relation to this structure, and this is equivalent to knowing it as it is in itself.[7] This explains why Kant frequently simply identifies the noumenon with the thing as it is in itself. To consider an object as it is in itself is just to treat it as a noumenon. Although Kant denied the possibility of knowledge of noumena on the grounds that such knowledge would require intellectual intuition, he did not totally reject the concept of a noumenon. On the contrary, he sought to reinterpret it in such a way that it could be incorporated into his transcendental account. This is accomplished by giving it the function of a limiting concept.

Kant develops this thesis in the the Grounds of the Distinction of all Objects in General into Phenomena and Noumena. At the heart of his position lies the contention that, despite its problematic status, the concept of a noumenon is "no arbitrary invention" (A255 / B311). This should be taken to mean that it has a basis in transcendental reflection and is, therefore, not a merely fictitious concept.[8] In other words, the "understanding" which, according to Kant, must think noumena (in the negative sense) is the critical understanding, or, equivalently, the human understanding qua engaged in transcendental reflection. The point here is essentially the same as that made in the preceding section in connection with the concept of the thing considered as it is in itself. The critical understanding must think noumena because this concept is a correlate of the transcendental concept of appearance (or phenomenon) and is thus intimately connected with the doctrine of sensibility. In fact, it is just this connection with sensibility that enables it to function as a limiting concept. Its specific task is to "curb the pretensions of sensibility" (A255 / B311); it accomplishes this by referring, albeit in a completely indeterminate way, to a different manner of knowing (intellectual intuition), with respect to which the objects that appear to us as subject to sensible conditions would be known as they are in themselves, independently of these conditions. An object known in this way is, by definition, a noumenon.

In his initial treatment of the problem in the Inaugural Dissertation, Kant used the "limitation of sensibility" brought about by the introduction of the concept of the noumenon to provide the basis for a positive theory of the non-sensible. In the *Critique,* by contrast, he notes that by limiting sensibility, which is accomplished by "applying the term noumenon to things in themselves (things not regarded as appearances)," the understanding also limits itself. It does so because it recognizes "that it cannot know these noumena through any of the categories, and that it must therefore think them only under the title of an unknown something" (A256 / B312).

The "unknown something," into which the rich concept of the noumenon at work in the Inaugural Dissertation is transmuted is now called the "transcendental object." Unfortunately, the task of explicating the Kantian conception of the transcendental object is greatly complicated by the fact that Kant uses the term in at least two apparently quite distinct ways. For the most part the transcendental object seems to be equated with the thing in itself, and there is even one passage (A366) in which they are explicitly identified. There are some places, however, where this is obviously not the case. For example, Kant grants to the "pure concept of the transcendental object" the function of conferring "upon all our empirical concepts in general relation to an object, that is, objective validity" (A109). Such a claim made with respect to the thing in itself would lead immediately to transcendental realism. In a similar vein, he later refers to the transcendental object as the "correlate of the unity of apperception," and claims that it can "serve only for the unity of the manifold in sensible intuition" (A250). Once again, this appears to be an inappropriate task for Kant to assign to the thing as it is in itself.

The situation has led to an ongoing debate in the literature regarding the nature and function of the concept of the transcendental object. Since our concern here is mainly with the transcendental object insofar as it is equated with the thing in itself, it is not necessary to enter into the details of this debate, or even to provide a full-scale analysis of the concept.[9] Here it must suffice to note that the two ways in which Kant uses the notion of the transcendental object correspond to the two distinct ways in which one can speak transcendentally about an object distinct from our representations. Somewhat confusingly, in the First Edition of the *Critique* at least, Kant uses the term 'transcendental object' to refer to the object spoken about in both of these ways.

First, there is the object in the "weighty" sense, or as Kant himself characterizes it, the object "corresponding to, and also distinct from our representations." In the Transcendental Deduction Kant argues that, since we cannot, so to speak, stand outside of our representations in order to compare them with some transcendentally real entity, such an object "can be thought only as something in general $= x$" (A104). This is, of course, just the concept of the transcendental object. In this context, then, the concept functions as a kind of transcendental pointer, which serves to indicate that the common-sensical and transcendentally realistic concern with the "real" nature of objects must be replaced by a "critical" analysis of the conditions of the representations of an object. This leads to the recognition of the transcendental unity of apperception as the ultimate transcendental condition of the representation of an object, which provides the basis for the whole transcendental account of objectivity in terms of the necessary, rule-governed, synthetic unity of the representations themselves.

Second, there is the object considered as it is in itself. This provides us with a very different sense in which it is possible to speak of an object as distinct from our representations. In fact, here the object is not simply considered as distinct from our representations, but also as distinct from, or independent of, the sensible conditions under which an object can alone be intuited by the human mind. As such, it is distinct from our capacity to represent objects. For that very reason, however, the object, so considered, can only be characterized as a completely indeterminate "something in general = x," that is, as a "transcendental object." Here the reference to the transcendental object serves to underscore the point that the consideration of an object as it is in itself does not yield the determinate concept of a knowable object.

Given this account of the transcendental object, it should be clear that insofar as the concept of a noumenon is taken in the rich sense as the concept of a genuinely knowable object, it must be distinguished from that of the transcendental object. Thus, after Kant acknowledges that the object to which one refers appearance in general (the correlate of the transcendental concept of appearance) is "the transcendental object, that is, the completely indeterminate thought of *something* in general," he proceeds to point out, "This cannot be entitled the *noumenon;* for I know nothing of what it is in itself, and have no concept of it save as merely the object of a sensible intuition in general, and so as being one and the same for all appearances" (A253). Admittedly, it is strange to find Kant denying that the transcendental object is the noumenon on the grounds that he knows "nothing of what it is in itself," as if he *could* know what the noumenon is in itself! His point, however, is simply that the object to which I refer my representations must be described merely as a transcendental object, not as a noumenon, because I am lacking a faculty of nonsensible intuition. The underlying assumption is that if I had such a faculty, the object would be a genuine noumenon, and I would know it as it is in itself. Moreover, in light of this assumption, Kant can even acknowledge the legitimacy of referring to this object as a noumenon, as long as this is done merely to point out that this object is something nonsensible. As he puts the matter in the Note to the Amphiboly of Concepts of Reflection, in connection with the analysis of the function of the noumenon as limiting concept:

> Understanding accordingly limits sensibility, but does not extend its own sphere. In the process of warning the latter that it must not presume to claim applicability to things-in-themselves but only to appearances, it does indeed think for itself an object in itself, but only as transcendental object, which is the cause of appearance and therefore not itself appearance, and which can be thought neither as quantity nor as reality nor as substance, etc. (because these concepts always require sensible forms in which they determine an object). . . . If we are pleased to name this object noumenon for the reason that its representation is not sensible, we are free to do so. But since we can apply to it none of the concepts of our understanding, the representation remains for us empty, and is of no service except to mark the limits of our sensible knowledge and to leave open a space which we can fill neither through possible experience nor through pure understanding. [A288–89 / B344–45][10]

The account offered so far has been based upon the First Edition texts, although it quite naturally includes references to passages that are retained in the Second Edition. The situation is somewhat complicated, however, by the fact that Kant substantially revised the Ground of the Distinction of all Objects in General into Phenomena and Noumena chapter in the Second Edition. Moreover, in the revised version he not only dropped all references to the transcendental object, but also introduced the distinction between a positive and a negative sense of the noumenon.[11] By the former is to be understood "an *object* of a nonsensible intuition," and by the latter "a thing so far as it is *not an object of our sensible intuition*" (B307). The former is the rich concept of the noumenon, and Kant's point is once again that we cannot operate with this concept because we have no faculty of nonsensible intuition and are not even able to conceive of its possibility. Thus he notes: "That, therefore, which we entitle 'noumenon' must be understood as being so only in a negative sense" (B309). When we take the term in this sense, we do operate with the concept; for, as we have already seen, "the doctrine of sensibility is likewise the doctrine of the noumenon in the negative sense." The thought expressed here is the by now familiar one that the concept of a nonsensible correlate of appearance is necessary to the very formulation of the Kantian theory. The noumenon in the negative sense is the Second Edition's candidate for this required concept.

But it should be clear that this terminological shift does not reflect any significant doctrinal change. The distinction between the positive and the negative senses of the noumenon, which is the essential feature of the Second Edition account, is really only a more explicit and somewhat clearer reworking of the contrast between the noumenon and the transcendental object drawn in the First Edition. Thus, the noumenon in the negative sense is not really a noumenon at all, except in the attenuated sense that it is something nonsensible. Moreover, since it refers merely to the nonsensible as such, it is completely indeterminate; in this respect it is not distinguishable from the transcendental object of the First Edition.[12] The real point of all of this, however, is that these seemingly diverse and conflicting formulations reflect Kant's abiding concern to articulate the sense which the consideration of a thing as it is in itself can have for the finite transcendental philosopher, who is not in possession of intellectual intuition. In the First Edition this is expressed mainly by characterizing a thing so considered as "the transcendental object = *x*." This is then contrasted with the concept of a noumenon derived from the precritical standpoint of the Inaugural Dissertation. Although Kant abandoned this formula in the Second Edition, he certainly did not abandon the thought which it expresses.[13]

III. AFFECTION

The acid test of any interpretation of the thing in itself and the related concepts of the noumenon and the transcendental object is its ability to deal with what has been aptly termed *"die heikle Frage der Affektion"*;[14] that is, with the question of how we are to characterize the nature of the object which Kant claims affects the mind and thereby provides it with the matter of sensible intuition. The question is important since, despite everything that Kant says about the unknowability of things as they are in themselves and the completely indeterminate nature of the concept of the transcendental object, there are numerous passages in which he characterizes the thing as it is in itself or the transcendental object as the nonsensible "cause" or "ground," either of appearances or of our sensible representations.[15] Moreover, it can be assumed that the thing in itself or the transcendental object can only be thought to function in this way if it can also be thought to affect the mind. Accordingly, our present task is to examine such assertions and the whole conception of a transcendental affection in light of the interpretation of the thing as it is in itself and the transcendental object that has just been presented.

The problem of affection has been given its classical formulation by F. H. Jacobi. Starting with the uncontroversial premise that the Kantian theory of sensibility requires that the human mind be somehow affected by objects if it is to have any material for thought, he points out that there are only two possible candidates for the affecting object: an appearance and the transcendental object (which he equates with the thing in itself). Although Jacobi believes that Kant himself actually regarded the latter as the affecting object, his own strategy is to show that neither can do the job. The former, he argues, cannot do it because it is defined by Kant as a mere representation in us; the latter cannot do it because of its unknowability, which precludes the application to it of any of the categories, including causality.[16] Idealistically oriented followers and "improvers" of Kant have tended to respond to this line of criticism by denying that the *Critique* contains any doctrine of affection through things in themselves.[17] This ploy, however, encounters two difficulties: (1) it is apparently contradicted by those passages in which it seems quite clear that Kant does recognize some sort of transcendental affection; and (2) it does not explain how empirical affection, that is, affection through empirical objects or appearances, can provide the necessary ground of our representations. Vaihinger has summarized the results of the whole post-Jacobi debate in the form of a trilemma:

1. Either one understands by the affecting objects the things in themselves; in which case one falls into the contradiction discovered by Jacobi, Aenesidemus and others that one must apply beyond experience the catego-

ries of substantiality and causality which are only supposed to have meaning and significance within experience.

2. Or one understands by affecting objects the objects in space; but since these are only appearances according to Kant, and thus our representations, one falls into the contradiction that the same appearances, which we first have on the basis of affection, should be the source of that very affection.

3. Or one accepts a double affection, a transcendent through things in themselves and an empirical through objects in space. In this case, however, one falls into the contradiction that a representation for the transcendental ego should afterwards serve as a thing in itself for the empirical ego, the affection of which produces in the ego, above and beyond that transcendental representation of the object, an empirical representation of the very same object.[18]

Although the theory of double affection, which was developed in great detail by Adickes,[19] still has some support among Kant commentators as a statement of what Kant actually maintained,[20] it has been decisively repudiated from a number of quite different perspectives.[21] The basic problem is that the attribution of such a theory to Kant, with its postulation of two distinct yet parallel activities, one of which is in principle unknowable, renders absurd his claim to be offering a "critical" philosophy. According to Prauss, who develops his analysis with great subtlety, the whole problematic is grounded in a false "transcendent-metaphysical" as opposed to genuinely transcendental conception of the thing as it is in itself. Prauss argues that once it is realized that this conception merely characterizes a manner in which empirical objects can be considered in transcendental reflection, it becomes obvious that nothing other than these same empirical objects affects us.[22] We thus return, albeit from a new perspective, to the old idealistic claim that the *Critique* admits only of an empirical affection; although Prauss readily acknowledges that this conception is itself not without difficulties.[23]

Unfortunately, the problem of affection cannot be dismissed quite so easily. In fact, the preceding analysis shows only that the problem has been misconstrued, not that it is a pseudo-problem. As traditionally understood, the issue is whether the affecting object is an appearance, a thing in itself, or perhaps both. This formulation is based, at least tacitly, on the assumption that the distinction between appearances and things in themselves is between two kinds of entity.[24] Obviously, once this assumption is repudiated, this way of stating the problem loses all meaning. It does not follow from this, however, that the problem itself is dissolved; it is still meaningful to ask whether Kant's statements about objects affecting the mind and producing sensations involve a reference to objects considered in their empirical character as appearances, or, rather, to these same objects considered in abstraction from their empirical character, and thus as they are in themselves. If the former is the case, affection is to be construed in an empirical, and if the latter, in a transcendental sense.

Before addressing the problem in this new formulation, it is necessary to dismiss the Jacobi-inspired objection that the very notion of an empirical affection is incompatible with the Kantian philosophy because empirical objects are appearances, and appearances are "mere representations in us." This objection rests upon a simple conflation of Kantian appearances with Berkeleian ideas. Kant not only can but does speak about the mind as affected by empirical objects. For example, he speaks unproblematically of colors as "modifications of the sense of sight which is affected in a certain way by light" (A28); of a sensation of red which is incited by cinnabar (*Prolegomena*, §13); and of a degree of influence on the sense that must be ascribed to all perceptual objects (A166/B208). He also states that "the light, which plays between our eye and the celestial bodies, produces a mediate community between us and them . . ." (A213/B260). Kant can perfectly well characterize human sensibility in this way because, on the empirical level, the human mind is itself considered as part of nature, just as the objects that affect it are considered as things in themselves.[25] The question, therefore, is not whether affection can be considered empirically, that is, whether, on the phenomenal level, Kant can legitimately regard the human mind as affected by spatiotemporal objects; it is rather whether there is ever any warrant for assuming that a statement about an object (or objects) affecting the mind involves a reference to the object considered as it is in itself, or, equivalently, to the transcendental object. To provide such a warrant is to provide a "critical" justification for the transcendental consideration of affection.

Such a warrant is provided by the fact that affection is taken, as it is in the beginning of the Transcendental Aesthetic, as a necessary (material) condition of the possibility of experience, and in this sense as part of a "transcendental story." One must be very careful here, however, if one is to avoid saddling Kant with a gross confusion. The temptation is to argue against Kant that, even if one grants that the assertion "something must affect the mind (or its faculty of representations)" has a transcendental status in that it expresses a necessary (material) condition of the possibility of experience, this does not require us to construe the expression 'something' or its equivalents as doing anything other than referring indifferently to one or more of the members of the class of empirical objects. In other words (so the objection goes), all that has been established by this is the entirely general claim that some (empirical) object or other must affect the mind, if the mind is to have any experience. Consequently, if *this* is the Kantian warrant for the injection into the transcendental story of a reference to the transcendental object (a "something in general = *x*"), then the whole account rests on a failure to distinguish between 'something', construed as having an indefinite reference, with 'a something in general', construed as a name or referring expression.

The problem with this line of criticism, which I take to be implicit in the endeavor to reject as unintelligible the very concept of a transcendental affection,[26] is that it ignores one half, indeed, the most important half, of the transcendental story. Let us recall that the Kantian theory of sensibility not only requires that something be "given to" or "affect" the mind; it also maintains that this something becomes part of the content of human knowledge (the "matter" of empirical intuition) only as the result of being subjected to the a priori forms of human sensibility (space and time). It certainly follows from this that this something which affects the mind (thereby functioning as the cause or ground of its representations) cannot be taken under its empirical description (as a spatiotemporal entity). To do so would involve assigning to that object, considered apart from its relation to human sensibility, precisely those features which, according to the theory, it only possesses in virtue of this relation. Consequently, the *thought* of such an object is, by its very nature, the thought of something nonsensible, nonintuitable, and hence "merely intelligible." But to consider an object in this way is, as we have seen, to consider it as it is in itself. Any reference to an object (in a transcendental context) as the cause or ground of our representations must, therefore, involve the thought (although certainly not the knowledge) of the object as it is in itself. Moreover, since the thought of the object remains completely indeterminate, containing nothing more than the idea of "something in general $= x$" regarded as a mere "substrate of sensibility," it also follows that the object can be aptly termed the "transcendental object."

If, therefore, it is a necessary (material) condition of human experience that something affect the mind, it is a necessary condition of a *transcendental account* of such experience that this something be viewed as a "something in general $= x$," that is, as the transcendental object. But this does not commit Kant to the illegitimate postulation of any superempirical, unknowable entities. On the contrary, there is in this entire account of affection no reference to any entities other than those which are describable in spatiotemporal terms. The point is only that insofar as such entities are to function in a transcendental context as material conditions of human cognition, they cannot, without contradiction, be taken under their empirical description. This means that, in a purely methodological sense, they must be considered as they are in themselves, or, equivalently, referred to collectively, as 'the transcendental object'.[27]

This analysis provides the key to the interpretation of a number of the murkiest passages in the Kantian corpus. For illustrative purposes, however, it should suffice to apply it to two of these, one which does and one which does not contain any mention of the transcendental object. Of those which do contain such a mention, the following is perhaps the most interesting:

> The faculty of sensible intuition is strictly only a receptivity, a capacity of being affected in a certain manner with representations, the relation of which to one another is a pure intuition of space and of time (mere forms of our sensibility), and which, in so far as they are connected in this manner in space and time, and are determinable according to laws of the unity of experience, are entitled *objects*. The non-sensible cause of these representations is completely unknown to us, and cannot therefore be intuited by us as object. For such an object would have to be represented as neither in space nor in time (these being merely conditions of sensible representations), and apart from such conditions we cannot think any intuition. We may, however, entitle the purely intelligible cause of appearances in general the transcendental object, but merely in order to have something corresponding to sensibility viewed as a receptivity. To this transcendental object we can ascribe the whole extent and connection of our possible perceptions, and can say that it is given in itself prior to all experience. But the appearances, while conforming to it, are not given in themselves, but only in this experience, being mere representations, which as perceptions mark out a real object only in so far as the perception connects with all others according to the rules of the unity of experience. Thus we can say that the real things of past time are given in the transcendental object of experience; but they are objects for me and real in past time only in so far as I represent to myself (either by the light of history or by the guiding-clues of causes and effects) that a regressive series of possible perceptions in accordance with empirical laws, in a word, that the course of the world, conducts us to a past time-series as condition of the present time—a series which, however, can be represented as actual not in itself but only in the connection of a possible experience. [A494–95/B522–23]

This well-known passage falls naturally into two parts, each of which assigns a different role to the transcendental object. In the first part the context is the familiar one of the theory of sensibility. Here we note immediately the reference to the "non-sensible" and thus "unknowable" cause of our representations, which is apparently equated with the "purely intelligible cause of appearance in general." As such, it is characterized as the "transcendental object" and assigned the function of providing "something corresponding to sensibility viewed as receptivity."

One noteworthy feature of the first part of the passage is the shift from "representation talk" to "appearance talk," which is a frequent and at times discomforting feature of Kantian analysis. Nevertheless, insofar as 'appearance' is taken to refer to an object qua sensibly represented, we can allow Kant to talk indifferently about either the cause of representations or the cause of appearances. The really important point is the reference to "appearances in general." This underscores the transcendental nature of the account; for it makes it clear that the concern is not with the

cause of a given appearance or representation, which is always an empirical matter, but rather with the cause or ground of the "matter" of human
knowledge taken as a whole (the sensible manifold). Kant characterizes
this cause as "non-sensible" and hence "unknowable" precisely because it
must not be represented as being in either space or time. We note that
Kant does not say that such an object (cause) cannot *be* in space or time,
but merely that it may not be *represented* as in either. This prohibition
has a strictly transcendental status; it stipulates how an object must be
conceived if it is to function in a transcendental account as "something
corresponding to sensibility viewed as receptivity." As such, the prohibition does not bring with it any ontological assumptions about the real
nature of things or about a supersensible realm. On the contrary, Kant
frequently introduces the concept of the transcendental object in order to
underscore the emptiness of such "transcendental questions."[28]

In the second part of the passage, Kant seems to expand the role of the
transcendental object. Thus he allows us to ascribe to it "the whole extent
and connection of our possible perceptions," and even to say that "the
real things of past time are given in the transcendental object of experience." Expressions such as these have led to the suggestion that the
concept of the transcendental object actually functions as a kind of "conceptual repository" for our way of referring to the remote past or to
distant regions of space.[29] On such an interpretation, the concept of the
transcendental object is simply a high-order empirical concept, one which
refers to experience as a whole. The strategy behind such an interpretation is obviously to undercut the standard objections to Kant's purported
appeal to nonempirical objects. If it can be shown that Kant makes no
such appeal, then these objections can be dismissed out of hand. The
problem, however, is that here, as elsewhere, the transcendental object is
explicitly characterized in nonempirical terms. It is regarded as the nonempirical ground of appearances, and this conception is a product of
transcendental reflection rather than empirical generalization. But to say
this is not to commit ourselves to the view that Kant is here offering some
kind of metaphysical explanation which, in the manner of Berkeley's
appeal to the divine mind, allows us to "save" the reality of unperceived
objects and events. The truth is just the opposite: once again the characterization of this ground as the transcendental object serves to repudiate
any such metaphysical explanation, thereby enabling us to see that we
must define the reality of past events in terms of their connection with the
present "in accordance with the laws of the unity of experience."

The second passage dealing with a transcendentally considered cause or
ground of representation or appearance is contained in Kant's reply to
Eberhard. In pursuit of his avowed goal of demonstrating the superiority
of Leibnizian rationalism to Kantian criticism, which involves the demonstration of the knowability of things as they are in themselves, Eberhard

claims, supposedly, in opposition to the *Critique,* that things in themselves must be viewed as the source of the matter of sensibility. To this Kant replies:

> Now this is precisely what the *Critique* constantly asserts. The only difference is that it places this ground of the matter of sensible representations not itself again in things as objects of the senses, but in something super-sensible, which *grounds* the sensible representations, and of which we can have no knowledge. It says the objects as things in themselves *give* the matter to empirical intuition (they contain the ground of the determination of the faculty of representation in accordance with its sensibility), but they *are not* the matter of these intuitions.[30]

Unlike the first passage, this one does not mention the transcendental object. Nevertheless, the conception of a supersensible ground, which we find here, is in all essentials identical to the one which we have just seen to be at work in the *Critique.*[31] This can be seen with only minimal attention to the polemical context. The key point to bear in mind is that the passage reflects the continuing debate concerning the Kantian theory of sensibility and its relation to the Leibnizian theory advocated by Eberhard. Kant himself poses the issue quite sharply when he notes that, on his view, sensibility is understood to be "only the mode in which we are affected by an object which in itself is entirely unknown to us." This is contrasted with the Leibnizian doctrine, according to which "we intuit things as they are in themselves" and, correlatively, "sensibility consists merely in the confusedness which is inseparable from such in all inclusive intuition."[32] The contrast drawn here is between their respective views on the relation between sensibility as a faculty (and, therefore, sensible knowledge) and things as they are in themselves. Here, as in the *Critique,* Kant's claim is that we cannot know the affecting object (or any object) as it is in itself, because we can know an object only if it is given in intuition, and it can be given only in accordance with the mind's a priori forms of sensibility (space and time). Since Leibniz does not acknowledge these a priori forms, he is committed to the transcendentally realistic doctrine that we sensibly apprehend things as they are in themselves. All of this is, of course, familiar from our previous discussions of these same points. It is, however, worth reiterating that for Kant, but not for Leibniz or Eberhard, what is given in intuition is sensible, regardless of its clearness or distinctness, while whatever cannot be so given but is merely thought is nonsensible, intelligible, or, equivalently, supersensible.

This conception of the sensible and its opposite, here characterized as supersensible, underlies the distinction between the *matter* of sensible representation or empirical intuition and its *ground* (which Kant elsewhere terms 'transcendental matter').[33] Because he is confused about the nature of sensibility, Eberhard confuses these two concepts. It is also on the basis of this same confusion that he affirms, against Kant, the knowability of things as they are in themselves, considered as the grounds of the matter of our sensible representations.[34] The point of Kant's distinction between "ground" and "matter" is just to indicate the supersensible nature of the former, in contrast to the sensible nature of the latter. The reason for characterizing the ground as supersensible is precisely the same as in the previous passage; namely, its nonrepresentability in space and time. Moreover, as supersensible, Kant naturally assigns this ground to "the objects as things in themselves" (*Die Gegenstände als Dinge an sich*), rather than to "things, as objects of the senses" (*Dinge, als Gegenstände der Sinne*). Since 'as' in both cases is obviously short for 'considered as', Kant can be taken to be merely affirming the by now familiar contention that the thought of an object as such a ground requires the consideration of the object in abstraction from its empirical character, and thus as it is in itself. Once again, Kant can say this because it is a merely analytic claim, based upon the concept of an object that is conceived within a transcendental context as the ground of our representations.

The analysis sketched above can easily be applied to a great many other passages in which Kant appears to be making illicit claims about the nature and function of things as they are in themselves or the transcendental object. So interpreted, these passages can be seen to accord with the principle of "critical" agnosticism with respect to things as they are in themselves. Far from providing a metaphysical story about how the mind or noumenal self is somehow mysteriously affected by the transcendental object, they merely stipulate how the affecting object must be conceived in the transcendental, or nonempirical, account of the affection required for the explication of the Kantian theory of sensibility. To be sure, these claims involve the use of the categories, especially causality. This is only to be expected, given the function of the categories as a priori rules of judgment and concepts of an object in general. It should be clear by now, however, that this does not justify the frequently voiced criticism that Kant is guilty of an illicit application of the categories to things as they are in themselves. The point here is simply that the function of the categories in these transcendental contexts is purely logical, and does not carry with it any assumptions about their objective reality with respect to some empirically inaccessible realm of being.

12

Inner Sense, Self-Knowledge,
and the Phenomenal Self

Few writers on Kant would find cause to quarrel with Paton's lament that "unfortunately Kant's doctrine of self-knowledge is the most obscure and difficult part of his philosophy."[1] The reasons for both the obscurity and the difficulty are not hard to find. Ultimately, they stem from the fact that Kant's account of self-knowledge is rooted in his theory of inner sense, according to which we can know ourselves only insofar as we affect ourselves and, therefore, only as we appear to ourselves. Not only is this theory of the sensory nature of self-knowledge inherently paradoxical—indeed, it is so presented by Kant—but his scattered discussions of the topic are exceedingly fragmentary and unsatisfactory. Moreover, much of what might be regarded as of central interest in any discussion of self-knowledge—questions about intentions, desires, dispositions, beliefs, and so forth—are not even touched upon in Kant's official discussions. What is interesting and important in these discussions is simply Kant's attempt to show that self-knowledge is subject to the same transcendental conditions as the knowledge of objects distinct from the self. It is this general thesis that I propose to examine in the present chapter. This will involve: (1) an analysis of the claim that time is the form of inner sense; (2) a determination of the nature of the object of inner sense and inner experience; and (3) an examination of Kant's argument for the phenomenality of this object.

I. TIME AS THE FORM OF INNER SENSE

In the Transcendental Aesthetic Kant links time specifically with inner sense. Although Kant does connect time with the mind's representation of its own thoughts in the Inaugural Dissertation,[2] this is one aspect of the doctrine of the Aesthetic that goes far beyond the treatment of the topic in the earlier work. In the *Critique* the claim is not only that we intuit ourselves, that is, our thoughts, or our inner states in time, but also that time cannot be outwardly intuited. As he expressly puts it in the second conclusion following the Metaphysical and Transcendental Expositions of the "concept of time,"

> Time is nothing but the form of inner sense, that is, of the intuition of ourselves and of our inner state. It cannot be a determination of outer

255

appearances; it has to do neither with the shape nor position; but with the relation of representations in our inner state. [A33/B49-50]

Taken in connection with other aspects of Kant's position, the contention that time cannot be a determination of outer appearances seems doubly paradoxical. First, Kant repeatedly insists that we must appeal to outer intuition and its form, space, in order to represent time. In fact, he makes this very point immediately after the passage just cited when he remarks, "And just because this inner intuition yields no shape, we endeavor to make up for this want by analogies" (A33/B50). These analogies, of course, all turn out to be spatial. For example, we are constrained to represent time in terms of a line. Again, as we saw from the First Analogy, it is only by referring to outer intuition and, therefore, to objects in space that we can represent to ourselves the "permanence" of time. Similarly, we shall see in chapter 14 that it is only with reference to outer, that is, spatial, objects that we can determine our own existence in time. Second, we have seen that the Analogies of Experience are concerned with the conditions of the experience of an objective temporal order of appearances. These appearances certainly include objects in space. How, then, one is led to ask, can Kant talk about the experience of such an order if time cannot be a "determination" of outer appearances?

Apart from the cryptic remark that time has nothing to do with either shape or position, Kant himself is silent on the whole topic. So too, for the most part, are the commentators.[3] Nevertheless, it may be possible to shed some light on the problem by considering the observation, frequently made by philosophers working in the areas of tense logic and grammar, that individual objects, including both things and persons (objects of outer sense for Kant), do not themselves have temporal parts, extension, or even location. In a word, these objects are spatial but not temporal. Temporal properties are all predicated of the histories, processes, and events connected with things and persons, but not *directly* of the things and persons themselves.[4] This feature of our conceptual scheme is reflected in ordinary language. For example, I cannot say that the table on which I am now writing has a temporal beginning and end analogous to its spatial parameters. I can say this about the existence ("history") of the table but not about the table itself. Again, we can ask how long a game lasted, but not how long a player did, unless we mean by this simply how long he played or lived. Finally, we ask *where* John is, not *when* he is; although we do, of course, ask when he lived.

Unfortunately, there is no direct textual evidence to support the claim that this, or anything like it, is what Kant actually had in mind when he denied that time can be outwardly intuited. Indirect evidence, however, is provided by the fact that it enables us to understand a good deal of what Kant has to say about time. At the very least, then, it has some value for a reconstruction of Kant's position. The first point to note here is that it does not follow from the fact that I cannot represent time except by drawing a line that the line itself is to be thought of as temporal. Indeed, Kant's claim is that we arrive at the representation of time by attending to the *successive* nature of the act of drawing or generating the line in the imagination.[5] Even here, therefore, time is connected with the act and not with the thing. If we consider a line simply as something given or intuited, we are not able to arrive at any conception of temporality or temporal properties. In addition, it must not be forgotten that the objective temporal order with which Kant is concerned in the Analogies, is a thought and not an intuited order. To be sure, it is an order of outer appearances (things and persons) and, therefore, of items that are intuited. It is also, however, an order that pertains only to these items insofar as they are subsumed under the schemata of the relational categories. Presumably, this is the point of Kant's contention that time is the "mediate condition of outer appearances" (A34 / B51).

Finally, and perhaps most significantly, this interpretation enables us to understand a feature of Kant's doctrine that is frequently regarded as totally mysterious: why, in his general discussion of the Analogies, he distinguishes between the mere intuition and the existence of appearances, and why he connects the Analogies with the latter and not with the former.[6] First, Kant's distinction between intuition and existence seems to parallel the distinction between things or persons and their histories. In Kantian terms, it is the outer appearance (thing or person) that we intuit and its existence (history) that we conceive. The fact that existence cannot be intuited can perhaps be regarded as part of the force of Kant's contention that it is not a real predicate or determination. It is also connected with his claims in the Analogies regarding the unperceivability of time. The main point, however, is that, as rules for the determination of appearances in time, the Analogies only apply to appearances qua existing, that is, as objects of possible experience. They do not apply to appearances, at least not to *outer* appearances, qua intuited, that is, as apprehended in empirical consciousness. Thus the whole argument of the Analogies rests not only on the distinction between things and their histories or existence, but also on the assumption that temporal properties pertain directly to the latter and only indirectly to the former. This also serves to underscore the point that there is considerably more agreement between the doctrines of the Aesthetic and the Analytic than is generally assumed.

Let us now consider briefly inner intuition and inner appearances, that is, the contents of inner sense. These contents are all mental items or "representations" in the broad Cartesian sense that encompasses feelings and other mental states as well as representations proper. In contrast to things or persons which are outwardly intuited (represented in space), such items do, qua intuited, have temporal parts, extension, and duration. Thus, I can say of my headache that it began immediately after the occurrence of the thought that I should try to explicate Kant's theory of inner sense; that it was mild in the beginning (its first "part"), but that it got progressively worse; that it lasted for two hours; and finally, that it came to an end immediately after I decided to abandon such a hopeless project and go to the beach. Similarly, I can say that it was at exactly 11:45 A.M. that the thought of using the example occurred to me. All of this is, of course, rather obvious, but it does indicate that what we inwardly intuit is immediately temporal, that is, temporal qua intuited.

At bottom, the manifest difference between outer and inner intuition stems from the fact that what we outwardly intuit are appearances with spatial forms and properties, while what we inwardly intuit is the appearing of these very appearances, along with mental states such as feelings, in consciousness. This appearing is a temporal process with the temporal properties already noted. That is why Kant contends that time is "the immediate condition of inner appearances (of our souls)" (A34/B51). Another way to put the same point is to note that in the case of the mental we cannot make the distinction between a thing or its intuition and its existence that we make in the case of objects of outer intuition. Since what we intuit is the appearing, and since apart from its appearing it is nothing, Berkeley's principle here holds: the *esse* of a mental content is its *percipi*. The existence of a headache consists of its being felt; a sensation in its being sensed; an appearance in its appearing; and so forth. One cannot say the same of a thing or person, which is why they are only temporal in a secondary or "mediate" sense, that is, with respect to their existence.

II. THE OBJECT OF INNER SENSE

According to Kant's official theory, the object of inner sense is the soul, just as the object of outer sense is body (including one's own).[7] Inner experience is thus supposed to yield empirical knowledge of the soul and its states. By 'soul' Kant means a separate immaterial substance with the capacity to think, feel, and so on.[8] It does not, however, appear to do any great violence to Kant's doctrine to consider 'mind' and 'self' as synonymous with 'soul'. In the *Anthropology* Kant also claims that the soul can be regarded as the "organ" of inner sense. Its function is viewed as analogous to the five special senses which, taken collectively, constitute outer sense.[9] The picture suggested by all of this is that of a strict parallelism between outer and inner sense. The former provides outer intuitions, which are representations of outer, that is, spatial, objects, and which are referred to these objects in the empirical judgments that constitute outer experience. The latter provides inner intuitions, which are representations of the unique inner object, the soul, mind, or self, and which are referred to it in the empirical judgments that constitute inner experience. Unfortunately, this general picture is grossly oversimplified, and serious difficulties arise as soon as one turns to the details of Kant's theory.

The difficulties are many, and we shall be concerned with them throughout the remainder of the chapter. At the heart of the problem, however, is the fact that, according to Kant's own account, inner sense has no manifold of its own. This means that inner sense does not have any data that can be regarded as representations of the soul in the way in which outer intuitions are regarded as representations of body. Kant's position is that the only manifold available for inner intuition is that of outer sense and this, as we have seen, contains data only for the representation of outer objects. As he succinctly puts it, "The representations of the *outer senses* constitute the proper material with which we occupy our mind" (B67). In accordance with this position, Kant explicitly rules out what would appear to be the most obvious candidates for representations of the soul and its states; namely, feelings.[10] These are denied any cognitive role because, although they belong to the subject as its feelings, they are not themselves representations of the subject and its states. Kant's clearest and most explicit statement of this doctrine is in the *Critique of Judgment,* where he remarks:

> When a modification of the feeling of pleasure or displeasure is termed sensation, this expression is given quite a different meaning to that which it bears when I call the representation of a thing (through sense as a receptivity pertaining to the faculty of knowledge) sensation. For in the latter case the representation is referred to the Object, but in the former it is referred solely to the Subject and is not available for any cognition, not even for that by which the Subject *cognizes* itself.[11]

Given this, the problem is simply to understand how Kant can talk about inner sense as representative and, therefore, as a sense. Perhaps the most interesting attempt to deal with the problem is by T. D. Weldon,[12] who is followed closely by Robert Paul Wolff.[13] According to Weldon, the key to understanding Kant's doctrine of inner sense lies in its connection with that of his contemporary, the psychologist Johann Nicholas Tetens. The relevant features of Tetens's work are the distinctions which he makes between an act of awareness of a given datum and an awareness of that awareness, and between the times of the two awarenesses. Tetens insists that the second, reflexive awareness always occurs after, not simultaneously with, the initial awareness. Moreover, he assigns the second awareness to inner sense.[14] Weldon's hypothesis, then, is that Kant borrowed this conception of inner sense from Tetens; thus, inner sense for Kant contains an awareness of past acts of awareness, while the initial awarenesses are always of objects in space. By interpreting Kant in this way, Weldon believes that he has found a specific job for inner sense to do, in spite of the fact that it has no content that belongs uniquely to it.

Unfortunately, this again paints too simple a picture. While there is no doubt that Kant was very much influenced by Tetens, one cannot, without significant modifications, assign the latter's theory of inner sense to Kant. One problem with such a view is that it ignores the sharp contrast that Kant draws between apperception and inner sense. Particularly relevant here is the *Anthropology,* where Kant characterizes apperception as a "consciousness of what we are doing" and states that it "belongs to the power of thinking," while inner sense is described as "a consciousness of what we undergo insofar as we are affected by the play of our own thoughts."[15] We shall deal with the difficult notion of self-affection and the question of its role in Kant's theory of inner sense in the next section; for the present we need only note the incompatibility of this account with Weldon's suggestion that inner sense provides an awareness of past *acts* of awareness. Indeed, one of the few relatively clear aspects of Kant's theory of self-knowledge is that the consciousness of the act of thinking is assigned to apperception and not to inner sense. Another problem with Weldon's account is that there is absolutely no textual evidence for the claims that Kant viewed awareness and the awareness of the awareness as temporally successive acts, and that he identified inner sense with the consciousness of *past* acts of awareness. On the contrary, the latter claim seems flatly to contradict Kant's distinction between sense (presumably including both inner and outer sense), defined as "the power of intuiting when the object is present," and imagination, defined as the power of intuiting "even when the object is not present."[16] Finally, even if we were to accept Weldon's account, we still would not understand how Kant can claim that inner sense provides us with sensible representations of the soul, mind, or self. In short, Weldon's interpretation locates a job for inner sense, but it is not the job that Kant assigns to it.

Instead of assuming a borrowing from Tetens or any other thinker, I believe that Kant's theory of inner sense is best understood in terms of the account of the subjective unity of consciousness which we have already considered. As such, it is to be regarded as a theory to which Kant was led by the full working out of the implications of his analyses of judgment and of objectivity in the Second Edition of the *Critique.* Thus the theory, although certainly not the notion of an inner sense, is very much a product of the Second Edition of the *Critique.* At the same time, however, I do not believe that this theory can be said to fulfill completely the task which Kant set for it. At best it explains how one can have sensible knowledge of one's own representations; what it does not explain is how we can have sensible knowledge of the soul, mind, or self, considered as the empirical subject to which these representations belong. In this respect, then, Weldon is not to be faulted for the failure of his interpretation to explain this claim of Kant's. The fault lies rather with Kant's own account.

Let us recall that by a "subjective unity of consciousness" is to be understood a unity, or collection, of representations in a single consciousness through which nothing is represented, not even the subject's own mental states. The point is that instead of functioning as representations which can be referred to objects in a judgment of inner sense, the representations contained in a subjective unity are themselves represented as "determinations of the mind." Inner sense enters the picture as the means through which these representations are given to the mind as its representations. It must be emphasized that this account of inner sense is not incompatible with Kant's denial that feelings, here included among the contents of inner sense, have a representative function. The claim is not that we somehow represent or "come to know" our inner states through feelings; it is rather that feelings, together with other mental items such as desires and volitions, can be represented as "subjective objects." In fact, Kant assumes that we are aware of all of these through inner sense.[17]

We are now in a position to understand the full implications for Kant's theory of self-knowledge of the claim that inner sense has no manifold of its own. Quite simply, this means that there are no sensible representations which we can recognize as representations of the soul, mind, or self. Insofar as we concern ourselves only with inner sense and ignore apperception, Kant's position turns out to be very close to Hume's; namely, that there is no "impression of the self." The problem, for Kant at least, is that this tends to undermine the parallelism between outer and inner sense upon which he puts such great emphasis. According to this presumed parallelism, just as outer sense provides the sensible data for the thought of outer objects, so inner sense provides sensible data for the thought of soul, mind, or self. If, however, inner sense has no manifold of its own, if its data include only outer intuitions, which can be used only to represent outer objects, and mental states such as feelings, which do not represent anything at all, then this parallelism breaks down. To put the point another way, Kant's account of inner sense explains how the mind can become aware of its own representations as "subjective objects," but it does not explain how it can represent *itself* as object. In fact, it seems that the whole parallelism thesis ultimately rests on an equivocation concerning 'my representations' and equivalent expressions. This can mean either representations *of me* or representations *belonging to me*. The parallelism thesis requires the former, but Kant's theory allows only for the latter.

Not surprisingly, the lack of parallelism between outer and inner sense is reflected in the contrast between outer and inner experience. Although Kant defines 'experience' in a number of different ways, not all of which are compatible, we have seen that the main thrust of his thought is to equate it with empirical knowledge. Typical in this regard is the characterization of it as "knowledge by means of connected perceptions," which we have considered in connection with the analysis of the arguments of the Transcendental Deduction and the Analogies of Experience. This characterization is, of course, intended to apply to both outer and inner experience; and since knowledge for Kant is judgmental, this means that both outer and inner experience should consist of judgments in which representations (perceptions or intuitions) are synthesized so as to be referred to an object. The problem is that this general formula obscures the difference between the kinds of predication involved in the judgments of inner and of outer experience.

In judgments of outer experience, and therefore in outer experience itself, representations are taken as representations of the object and are predicated of the object in the judgment. The object itself, however, qua object of outer experience, is not regarded as a "bare particular" or "substratum" to which properties are attached.[18] It is rather a determinate object, taken under some description; and it is of this determinate object that additional properties are predicated in the judgment. Moreover, this is exactly what one would expect, given the account of Kant's theory of judgment sketched in chapter 4. To be sure, Kant does frequently refer to the object as a "something in general $= x$," and this certainly suggests a "bare-particular" theory of predication; but this characterization applies only to the transcendental object or, perhaps better, the object considered transcendentally, not to the object qua object of outer experience.

But since inner experience has no manifold of its own, there are no sensible representations (intuitions) by means of which the self can represent itself to itself as object. Consequently, in referring its representations to itself in judgments of inner sense, it does not conceive of them as representations of itself in the way outer intuitions are regarded as representations of outer objects. Instead, it conceives of these representations as belonging to itself, as its own "subjective objects." Correlatively, the self regards itself as the substratum or subject in which these representations inhere. Thus, in spite of his theory of judgment, Kant is led to what amounts to a "substratum" or "bare-particular" theory of predication when he deals with judgments of inner sense. Moreover, Kant himself admits as much in an important Reflexion, where he writes:

> All inner experience is (has) a judgment in which the predicate is empirical and the subject is I. Independently of experience, therefore, there remains merely the I for rational psychology; for the I is substratum of all empirical judgments.[19]

In addition to the explicit characterization of the I as substratum of empirical judgments (presumably Kant means those of inner experience), the most noteworthy feature of this Reflexion is its clear implication that this I, as subject of the judgments, is nonempirical. Since this I is the I of apperception, this is, indeed, Kant's position; and we shall see in the next chapter that the merely formal nature of this I underlies the critique of rational psychology to which he here alludes. For present purposes, however, the important point is simply that, as nonempirical, the I cannot know itself through the empirical predicates (representations) which it refers to itself in judgments of inner experience in the same way in which it knows outer objects through the predicates which it attributes to such objects in judgments of outer experience. In fact, the I (soul, mind, or self) is not itself an object of inner experience or inner sense. These objects are rather the representations (in the broad sense) which it attributes to itself as "subjective objects."

III. INNER SENSE AND TRANSCENDENTAL IDEALITY

One of the apparent consequences of the preceding analysis is that the application of the transcendental distinction to the object of inner sense becomes, to say the least, extremely problematic. If this object is regarded as the substratum or owner of its representations, which seems to be the view to which Kant is committed, then it cannot be said to appear to itself at all. Consequently, we cannot draw a distinction between this substratum as it appears and as it is in itself. Nor does it seem to help matters very much if we take the object of inner sense and inner experience to be the representations themselves. The problem here is that representations, as mental entities, are themselves ideal in the empirical sense. Once again, then, we seem to be without any basis for distinguishing between such an object as it appears and as it is in itself.

Nevertheless, Kant does insist upon the transcendental ideality of the object of inner sense and, therefore, upon the doctrine that we know ourselves only as we appear to ourselves. Underlying this doctrine is the distinction between inner sense and apperception, and Kant's tendency to connect the latter, considered as a mode of consciousness, with the consciousness, although not the knowledge, of the I as it is in itself. We shall deal with that aspect of Kant's position and the difficulties which it involves in the next chapter. Our present concern is only with the doctrine of the phenomenality of the knowledge gained through inner sense. Here it is important to distinguish between two lines of argument which Kant offers in support of the ideality or phenomenality thesis. For convenience' sake, I shall call them the "materials argument" and the "self-affection argument," respectively. We shall see that while neither of these arguments is itself capable of establishing the desired conclusion, the second at least points us in the right direction.

A. The Materials Argument

The main statement of this argument, such as it is, is embedded in an overall argument for the transcendental ideality of both outer and inner sense, which Kant added to the Transcendental Aesthetic in the Second Edition. This new argument is presented as a "confirmation" of the main ideality argument, which we have examined in chapter 5. It consists simply of the conjunction of the claim that the content of intuition consists of nothing but mere relations with the essentially Leibnizian premise that a "thing (*Sache*) in itself cannot be known through mere relations." Kant first applies this to outer sense. His conclusion is that the content of outer sense, consisting as it does of mere relations, can yield a representation of the object only in its relation to the subject, not as it is in itself, independently of this relation. He then continues:

> This also holds true of inner sense, not only because the representations of the *outer senses* constitute the proper material with which we occupy our mind, but because the time in which we set these representations, which is itself antecedent to the consciousness of them in experience, and which underlies them as the formal condition of the mode in which we posit them in the mind, itself contains [only] relations of succession, coexistence, and of that which is coexistent with succession, the enduring. [B67]

Kant's extreme crypticness once again makes any interpretation hazardous, but the language of the passage clearly suggests that he construes these considerations to constitute two independent arguments for the ideality of inner sense. The first of these is what I have called the materials argument. Reduced to its essentials, it seems to have the following form: (1) since the materials of outer sense are also the materials of inner sense, that is, since inner sense has no manifold of its own; and (2) since these representations contain nothing but relations; and (3) since a thing in itself cannot be known through mere relations; it (4) follows that we cannot represent (know) ourselves as we are in ourselves through inner sense.

So formulated, the argument is obviously inadequate. In fact, it involves not one but two distinct non sequiturs. The first pertains to the overall ideality argument. The problem here is that even if we assume that sensible intuition contains only relations and nothing "absolutely inner," it still does not follow that such intuition yields a representation of the object only as it is in relation to the subject and not as it is in itself. Kant appears here to conflate two quite distinct theses about the relational character of that which is sensibly intuited. The first is that we can sensibly intuit only the *relational properties* of things (because of the spatiotemporal form of sensible intuition); the second is that we can sensibly intuit objects only *in their relation to the subject*. Moreover, this is correlated with an additional conflation between two senses of 'thing in itself': one is the Leibnizian conception of a simple substance or monad, which serves as the nonsensible ground of relations, but which presumably does not itself contain any relational properties; the other is the transcendental conception of the thing as it is apart from its epistemic relation to the knowing subject.[20]

The second non sequitur occurs in the application of the conclusion, which is affirmed first in the case of outer sense, to inner sense. Even if, for the sake of argument, we accept the claim that through outer sense we can know objects only as they appear, it does not follow that inner sense yields a representation of the self only as it appears. Nor is anything changed by the introduction of the premise that the materials of inner sense are all derived from outer sense. This is because, as we have already seen, outer intuitions, by definition, are not representations of the self. In fact, if this argument establishes anything, it is that we cannot know ourselves at all, at least not through sensible intuition, not that we can know ourselves only as we appear to ourselves.

B. The Self-Affection Argument

Although the difficult notion of self-affection is obviously crucial to Kant's whole account of self-knowledge, it is only discussed in two places in the Second Edition. The first is in connection with the previously cited passage from the Transcendental Aesthetic. The second is in §24 of the Transcendental Deduction. In both places Kant's concern is to link this notion with his doctrine of the transcendental ideality of the objects of inner sense. We have seen that in the passage cited from the Aesthetic Kant speaks mysteriously of the "positing" (setzen) of representations in the mind and of time as the "formal condition" of the "mode" of this positing. Later in the same paragraph he explicitly equates this positing first with self-affection and then with the more familiar notion of apprehension. Very roughly, the basic idea is that the mind must somehow affect itself in the act of apprehending, or intuitively representing, its own contents to itself as these contents appear in inner sense. From this, taken in connection with the doctrine of the ideality of time, it is inferred that the mind can know itself only "as it appears to itself, not as it is" (B69).

This account in the Aesthetic does not provide very much enlightenment about the nature of the act of self-affection, but it does indicate the line of argument through which Kant attempts to connect it with the ideality thesis. The argument presupposes Kant's general theory of sensibility, particularly the connection between sensibility and affection. As we have seen, Kant maintains that affection by "external objects" (transcendentally considered) is the source of the matter of empirical intuition and, therefore, of the materials of our knowledge. Since the mind can receive these materials only insofar as it is affected by objects, the mind is to that extent passive. Nevertheless, the materials which the mind receives through affection are, qua received, subject to the mind's own mode or condition of receptivity, that is, its "form of sensibility." Kant infers from this that anything known through sensible intuition and, a fortiori, on the basis of affection, is known only as it appears. Given all of this, Kant argues in the present context that, since the mind allegedly must affect itself in order to know itself, that is, apprehend its contents, the knowledge which the mind has of itself is sensible in nature, and concerns only the way in which it appears to itself.

As the above sketch indicates, the real crux of Kant's position is that self-knowledge requires sensible intuition and, therefore, an inner sense.[21] This, in turn, is presented as a consequence of the "fact" that self-knowledge involves self-affection. In other words, the argument is from the "fact" of self-affection to the sensible nature of self-knowledge, and from this to the ideality of what is known. So construed, this argument is obviously no stronger than the presumed analogy between self-affection and affection by external objects on which it rests. Once again, however, the analogy does not seem to be very strong, at least not strong enough to bear the heavy transcendental weight which Kant places upon it. The disanalogy is clearly pointed out by Paton, who remarks that the function of affection by external objects is to supply the sensible data or raw materials for knowledge, while the function of self-affection is to combine this data in consciousness in accordance with the conditions of time.[22] The original connection that Kant asserts between affection and sensibility, however, rests upon the conception of affection as the source of sensible data; that is to say, it rests upon an understanding of affection as outer affection. Consequently, it hardly seems to follow that a comparable connection with sensibility must be assigned to self-affection. In fact, it is easy to see that the disanalogy is simply a reflection of the same difficulty that we have considered previously; namely, that inner sense has no manifold of its own. If this is the case, then, clearly, self-affection cannot, like outer affection, be regarded as the source of sensible data. But if this be denied, how are we to understand the connection between self-affection and sensibility?

Kant's position becomes even more problematic if we consider the much fuller account of self-affection given in §24 of the Transcendental Deduction. Kant there explicitly states that by "self-affection" or, equivalently, the "affection of inner sense" is meant the determination of inner sense by the understanding "under the title of the transcendental synthesis of the imagination" (B153). In other words, it is equivalent to the figurative synthesis. Since we have already dealt at length with this synthesis and its transcendental function, it is not necessary to explicate the conception here. Nevertheless, two points must be noted which relate directly to our present concern. The first is simply that the identification of self-affection with the transcendental synthesis serves to accentuate the disanalogy between the two modes of affection. There is, indeed, little in common between the influence of objects upon outer sense, which is outer affection, and the "synthetic influence of the understanding" (B154), which is one of the ways in which Kant characterizes self-affection. Here, perhaps as much as anywhere in the *Critique*, it is difficult to resist the impression that Kant has been victimized by his own jargon. The second point is that the figurative synthesis is a transcendental condition of *all* experience, not merely of inner experience. As we have seen, the main thrust of the argument of the second part of the Transcendental Deduction is to show that the determination of inner sense by the understanding ("under the title of the transcendental synthesis of the imagination") is necessary in order to provide a determinate intuition for consciousness. This claim is independent of the issue of whether the intuition is of inner or outer objects because all appearances, as modifications of the mind, belong to inner sense. Consequently, the mere appeal to self-affection, construed as transcendental synthesis, hardly explains how such synthesis could serve as a specific condition of self-knowledge. In fact, this suggests that there may be a fundamental incoherence in Kant's whole account of self-affection. The problem is that in the Aesthetic self-affection is presented as if it were equivalent to the synthesis of apprehension, while in the Deduction it is equated with the transcendental synthesis of the imagination. At the same time, however, Kant explicitly distinguishes between these two types of synthesis on the grounds that the latter is empirical and is conditioned by the former.[23]

C. The Ideality Thesis of Another Attempt

Fortunately, Kant's position is not as hopelessly confused or incoherent as the preceding remarks might suggest. The difficulties alluded to are real enough, but they can be attributed mainly to the extremely cryptic and inadequate way in which Kant presents his doctrine. First, it is clear that what Kant needs here is a distinction between two senses of "self-affection," one connected with the transcendental synthesis and serving as a condition of all experience, the other connected with the empirical synthesis of apprehension and serving as a condition of a specifically inner experience. Admittedly, Kant never presents this distinction in so many words, but Michael Washburn has shown that it is implicit in the account of self-affection in the Transcendental Deduction.[24] The key text is Kant's characterization of the transcendental synthesis as the "first application" of the understanding to sensibility, "and thereby the ground of all of its other applications to the objects of our possible intuition" (B152). As we have already seen, this "first application," or, as he also calls it, "action" (*Wirkung*), determines the representation of a single universal time in which all appearances, as objects of possible experience, have a determinate location. Accordingly, this application functions as a transcendental condition of all experience. The importance of this text for our present purposes is its clear suggestion that there may be a second application or action (also describable as self-affection), which is conditioned by, and yet distinct from, the first in the same way in which the empirical synthesis of apprehension is conditioned by, and distinct from, the transcendental synthesis of the imagination. Presumably, this "second application" would be directly involved in inner experience.

This is confirmed by Kant's subsequent appeal to the phenomenon of attention in a footnote in §25. To be sure, Kant once again manages to confuse matters by suggesting that attention is simply a convenient empirical illustration of the apparently paradoxical claim that the mind affects itself. In spite of this, however, it is clear that the real significance of Kant's appeal to the phenomenon of attention is not that it renders intelligible an otherwise mysterious notion of self-affection; it is rather that it indicates the specific kind of self-affection required for the institution of inner experience. The main point here is that, in attending to its representations, the mind makes these representations into objects represented. Thus, instead of perceiving a house by means of a succession of perceptions, all of which are referred to the house as representations thereof, I might take this sequence itself as my object. As a second-order reflective act, this presupposes a prior "outer experience," in this case the experience of the house. Consequently, it presupposes the transcendental synthesis of the imagination (the "first application"). By the same token, this reflective act must be distinguished from the original and acknowledged as a "second application." It involves an active seeking out by the mind of the representations which it endeavors to make into objects of inner sense. This also requires a change of epistemic focus, and with this change comes a fresh act of conceptualization. The initial conceptualization is the act whereby the given representations are referred to an object. The second conceptualization is the act whereby the same representations become themselves objects. In the last analysis, Kant's claim that self-knowledge requires self-affection boils down to the claim that the mind must reconceptualize its representations in order to grasp them as objects.

We are finally in a position to deal with the question of the connection between self-knowledge and transcendental ideality. The key to understanding this connection, and with it Kant's whole account of self-knowledge, lies partly in the preceding account of self-affection and partly in the previously noted dual status of time, as at once the form of the appearing of representations in the mind and the universal condition of the existence of phenomenal objects. The account of self-affection enables us to see how this activity is involved in the determination of the objects of inner sense. Such objects are products of this activity in the sense that it is only in and through it that the given contents of the mind (its representations) can be represented as objects. This activity is thus constitutive of inner experience, just as the transcendental synthesis is constitutive of experience in general.

But since time is the form of the appearing of representations in inner sense, it follows that time must also be the form in which the products of its own activity appear to the mind in inner experience. Notice that it is not that time or a temporal form is imposed upon the manifold of representations by the conceptual activity of attention; it is rather that this activity is itself constrained or conditioned by the temporal form of the appearing of these representations in consciousness. In this regard at least, the role which time plays in inner experience is analogous to that which space plays in outer experience. Just as space, the form of outer sense, is the form according to which the mind (through its conceptual activity) represents objects as outer, so time, as the form of inner sense, is the form according to which it represents (through a subsequent conceptual activity) something inner (its own representations) as an object. This means that the objects of inner experience, which qua objects are the products of this conceptual activity, are sensibly represented. Such objects, however, are for Kant appearances in the transcendental sense. Consequently, Kant can claim that the objects of inner experience are appearances, represented according to the form of their appearing in consciousness.

Moreover, insofar as the self knows itself in inner experience, it conceives itself as a conditioned object in the world, that is, as a phenomenon. The fact that we are here concerned with *inner* experience must be emphasized. Kant is not arguing that the self knows itself only as phenomenon because, in Strawsonian fashion, he understands by "self" or "person" a subject to which both outer (material) and inner (mental or psychological) predicates pertain. The phenomenality of the self, qua object of inner experience, is not a function of the corporeality of the person. Quite apart from the question of what Kant really means by "self" or "person,"[25] it is clear that the phenomenality thesis, as it stands in connection with Kant's theory of inner sense, refers specifically to the mind's knowledge of itself and its representations. Similarly, this phenomenality cannot be explained as a simple consequence of the thesis of the Refutation of Idealism that inner experience is impossible apart from the experience of objects in space. The two claims are obviously closely connected; nevertheless, as we shall see when we come to consider the argument of the Refutation of Idealism, its thesis must itself be understood in light of the doctrine presently under consideration.

The key to understanding this doctrine, which is the real thrust of Kant's whole account of self-knowledge, lies in the previously noted dual status of time. Time, it will be recalled, functions both as the form of the appearing of representations in inner sense (the form of inner intuitions) and as the condition of phenomenal existence. By the latter is meant simply that everything that exists in this single universal time exists in the phenomenal world, and vice versa. Strictly speaking, then, time can be characterized as both a necessary and a sufficient condition of phenomenal existence. This is the point that Kant first endeavors to express in the Inaugural Dissertation when he characterized time as a "form" of the sensible world. It also underlies the importance given to time in the Schematism. Now, since time is the form of appearing, and since there is only a single universal time in which all particular times are contained, it follows that by attending to the appearing of its own representations, the mind or self must place ("posit") these representations in this time. In other words, it must regard the "subjective" succession of its representations in inner sense as an occurrence in "objective time." Moreover, in so doing it must also conceive of its own existence as determined, or fixed, in this same time. In attending to its own representations, the mind or self can, therefore, be said to "inject" both them and itself into "objective time." Kant makes this point in yet another important Reflexion, when he remarks that not only is time in the self (as form of inner sense), but also that the self is in time (as object of inner experience).[26]

Now, insofar as the self exists in time, it, together with its "inner determinations" (its successive representations), also exist in the phenomenal world. This follows directly from the status of time as a condition of phenomenal existence. Consequently, in inner experience the self must experience the succession of its own representations as a conditioned event (or sequence of events) in the phenomenal world. Correlatively, it must also experience itself as a conditioned object or thing (*Sache*) in this world. The situation here should be compared with the one suggested by the argument of the Analogies of Experience. As we saw when considering that argument, Kant's concern there is to explain how, on the basis of a succession of representations, the mind is capable of representing a succession of states of an enduring object. Here, by contrast, the problem is to explain how the mind can regard this subjective succession as itself objective. Given the operative meaning of 'objective', this is equivalent to explaining how this succession can be experienced at all. Clearly it follows from the basic principles of the Transcendental Analytic, and especially the Second Analogy, that this must involve representing the succession as conditioned by antecedent events in the phenomenal world. In other words, through inner experience the mind can encounter itself and its states only as a causally conditioned part of the universal order of nature, which is coextensive with the phenomenal world. In this way, then, the transcendental conditions of the possibility of experience also serve as conditions of inner experience and of the objects of such experience.

The position sketched in the preceding paragraphs is one to which I take Kant to be committed in virtue of the general thrust of the argument of the Transcendental Analytic. It comes to the fore in the Second Edition of the *Critique,* particularly in connection with the theory of inner sense, the account of the subjective unity of consciousness, and the Refutation of Idealism. The key to it is the principle that self-knowledge is governed by the same transcendental conditions as other kinds of empirical knowledge. In light of this account, we can understand Kant's cryptic claim in the General Note on the System of the Principles (added in the Second Edition) that although outer intuition is required to establish the objective reality of the categories and Principles, they can subsequently or mediately be applied to inner intuition.[27] The point is that this second application occurs through self-affection construed as attention (the "second application" of the understanding to sensibility), and that it results in the injection of the contents of the mind into the phenomenal world.

Unfortunately, any attempt to go beyond this very general result soon runs into grave difficulties. First, not everything that Kant has to say about self-knowledge or, as it is sometimes called, "subjective experience" is readily reconcilable with this account. The treatment of judgments of perception is a case in point; another, to be considered later, is the account of practical freedom. Second, Kant has next to nothing to say about *how* the categories and Principles are applied in inner experience. Presumably, this neglect is justified by the principle, articulated in the footnote in the preface of the *Metaphysical Foundations of Natural Science,* that the general result of the Transcendental Deduction stands secure, even if it proves to be impossible to give an adequate account of how the categories make experience possible.[28] The problem, however, is that in the case of inner experience it is not at all clear whether certain categories and Principles are applicable. Moreover, these include the key categories of substance and causality. To a limited extent at least, we shall be discussing the possible role of these categories in inner experience in the ensuing chapters. Nevertheless, anything like an adequate treatment of the general topic of the function of the categories of inner experience is beyond the scope of this study. Indeed, given the paucity of texts relating to the topic, I venture to say that it is beyond the scope of Kantian exegesis.[29]

13

Apperception, Rational Psychology, and the Noumenal Self

The account of inner sense sketched in the preceding chapter constitutes only one half of the Kantian view of self-knowledge. The second, equally important half is his analysis of apperception. Inner sense and apperception, for Kant, are two distinct, yet complementary forms of self-consciousness. Together they are supposed to yield a two-fold consciousness of a single I or subject.[1] As we have seen, Kant seems to work with two distinct conceptions of an object of inner sense. According to his official doctrine, based on the parallelism between inner and outer sense, the object is the phenomenal self (the soul, mind, or self as it appears to itself.) According to the actual account of inner sense, however, this object is more properly described as the succession of representations as they occur in consciousness. As we have also seen, the consciousness of this succession requires a reflective act (attention), whereby these representations are made into "subjective objects" and, as it were, "injected" into the phenomenal world. Since it is only by means of this act that we can gain any empirical knowledge of the contents of our own minds, it follows (according to the argument of the Transcendental Analytic) that we can experience our own mental lives only as a series of conditioned occurrences in the phenomenal world. Apperception, by contrast, is supposed to yield a consciousness, although not an experience, of the activity of thinking. Kant further contends that this involves a consciousness, or at least a "feeling," of existence.[2] In this respect Kant's conception of apperception stands in an interesting connection with Descartes's conception of the *cogito*.

The roots of this conception of apperception are contained in the Transcendental Deduction. Although for the most part Kant there treats apperception, or perhaps better, the unity of apperception, as a formal or transcendental condition of experience, expressing the "necessity of a possibility," he also insists that all unity for the understanding is the product of a unifying act and that apperception involves an actual consciousness of this act. Indeed, the possibility of such self-consciousness is itself held to be a condition of the possibility of the consciousness of an object.[3] Even in the Transcendental Deduction, then, apperception is something more than a transcendental principle or reference point. It is, as Kant himself suggests in a quite different context, "something real" (B419); namely, it is a real mode of self-consciousness. This is the point on which the ontologically oriented interpreters of Kant rightly insist.[4] The problem, however, is to explain how such consciousness is possible, and how it is linked to the consciousness of existence. Finally, it must be determined to what extent this account of apperception is compatible with Kant's project of applying the transcendental distinction to the self.

The above problems constitute the main concern of the present chapter, which is divided into four parts. The first analyzes Kant's account of apperception as a nonexperiential consciousness of the activity of thinking. As an essential step in this analysis and, indeed, in the entire discussion of Kant's doctrine of apperception, it attempts to formulate a viable distinction between empirical and transcendental apperception. The second deals with the alleged connection between apperception and the consciousness of existence. The third considers the main features of Kant's critique of the misuse of the conception of apperception by "rational psychology" in the Paralogisms. The fourth considers some of the difficulties inherent in the attempt to correlate the inner sense-apperception distinction with the phenomenal-noumenal distinction.

I. APPERCEPTION AS THE CONSCIOUSNESS OF SPONTANEITY

A. Empirical and Transcendental Apperception

Insofar as apperception is "something real," it clearly contains an empirical dimension. What I can be said to apperceive is always an act of thinking with a determinate content; for example, my act of thinking a line by drawing it in thought. This suggests a need to distinguish between empirical apperception, as an actual consciousness (even when the object thought is not itself empirical), and transcendental apperception, as a transcendental condition of experience (or perhaps as the consciousness of such a condition). Now Kant does, in fact, occasionally distinguish between empirical and transcendental or pure apperception. The problem is that in doing so he tends to equate the former with inner sense, thereby effectively undermining the distinction between two kinds of apperception.[5] The discussion in the *Anthropology* is typical in this regard. Kant there contrasts a "pure consciousness of the activity that constitutes thinking," which is assigned to logic, with an empirical consciousness of the determinate contents of the mind, which is assigned to psychology.[6] The former is, of course, identified with transcendental apperception; but Kant identifies the latter with both empirical apperception and inner sense, thereby treating the two notions as equivalent.[7]

Kant, however, is far from consistent in this matter. For example, in the First Edition version of Transcendental Deduction he distinguishes between sense and apperception as "faculties," and suggests that each of them can be considered both empirically and transcendentally.[8] Empirical apperception is here characterized as the "empirical consciousness of the identity of the reproduced representations with the appearances whereby they were given, that is, in recognition" (A115). This characterization, which is certainly not applicable to inner sense, is closely connected with the First Edition doctrine of the three-fold synthesis, more particularly, with the "synthesis of recognition in a concept." Correlatively, transcendental apperception is equated with the recognition of the identity of the 'I think' that accompanies diverse representations.

This formulation is promising in that it suggests that the empirical-transcendental contrast pertains to two ways in which apperception can be considered, rather than to two distinct activities. Unfortunately, this promise is not borne out by the manner in which Kant actually presents the contrast. Moreover, neither the empirical nor the transcendental version described above accord very well with the characterization of apperception as a consciousness of the activity of thinking. Given this characterization, together with the empirical-transcendental distinction, it would seem that the contrast that Kant really needs to draw is between a consciousness of the activity as it functions determinately with a given content and a thought of the same activity, considered in abstraction from all content. To regard apperception in the first way is to consider it empirically, and thus as "something real"; to consider it in the second way is to consider it transcendentally, and thus as a transcendental condition of experience. Empirical apperception is achieved through ordinary reflection or introspection. It always occurs in connection with inner sense, which is perhaps why Kant sometimes identifies them. By contrast, transcendental apperception is a product of philosophical or transcendental reflection. In what follows I propose to construe the distinction in this manner. My claim is not that there are passages in which Kant unambiguously draws the distinction in these terms; it is rather that this is how the distinction ought to be drawn, if one is to make any sense out of Kant's account of apperception as an actual mode of self-consciousness.

B. Apperception and Spontaneity

Since we are now concerned with apperception insofar as it is "something real," we can confine our attention to the consciousness which we have of ourselves as knowers, engaged in the activity of thinking. As a consciousness of this activity, it is also a consciousness of spontaneity. Consequently, it is to be distinguished from the consciousness which we have of the conditioned succession of our own representations in inner experience. But even limiting ourselves to the consciousness of thinking, thereby ignoring the consciousness which we have of ourselves as free agents (which is the subject of chapter 15), it seems possible to distinguish between two senses of spontaneity.[9] The first of these should be sufficiently familiar from the previous account of the nature of thought. It is simply the spontaneity that pertains to discursive thought *per se*. As we have seen, to think is to judge, and this consists in the combination of given representations in accordance with categorial principles derived from the very nature of the understanding. Behind this conception lies the contrast between judging and associating, which is central both to the critique of Hume and to the overall argument of the Transcendental Deduction. As previously indicated, the main point is that, insofar as the mind is merely associating its representations, it is passive; the connections which it makes between these representations are all determined by extrinsic and empirical factors, such as past experience. By contrast, insofar as the mind is judging, that is, connecting its representations in a manner that is "objectively valid," it is combining them in accordance with categorial principles which it derives from its own resources.

The second epistemic sense of spontaneity is attributed to the mind when it exercises an actual power over its representations. This power is exercised in voluntary intellectual activities such as attention, abstraction, and concept formation. In these activities the mind self-consciously objectifies or determines a given content. Spontaneity in this sense can thus be attributed to the reflective capacity of the mind. Kant also suggests that this same kind of spontaneity is manifested at a higher level in the activity of reason, that is, in the mind's use of Ideas which have no corresponding object in the sensible world. The claim is that reason's power to form such Ideas demonstrates its total independence of sensibility (something that cannot be said of the understanding). Underlying all of this is the notion that the spontaneity of reason is at work in the process of enquiry, which is itself regulated by these Ideas and directed toward self-imposed goals. In other words, reason, in its theoretical function, is spontaneous in the sense that it exhibits an inherent purposiveness. It is self-directed, self-determining. Kant analyzes this purposive activity at length in the *Critique of Judgment,* in the context of his treatment of reflective judgment.[10] A discussion of this topic obviously lies outside the scope of this study, but it should at least be noted that this activity is the expression *par excellence* of the spontaneity of reason in its theoretical capacity.

C. Consciousness but Not Experience

There is nothing particularly problematical in Kant's claim that we can be aware of ourselves as thinking. Also, given Kant's account of discursive thought, we cannot quarrel with his characterization of this awareness as a consciousness of spontaneity. What does seem questionable, however, is the claim that this consciousness must be distinguished from inner experience and thus from self-knowledge. Kant states this explicitly in §20 of the Transcendental Deduction, immediately after the account of inner sense. Behind this claim lies the familiar Kantian thesis that knowledge requires intuition as well as thought. The point, then, is that we can have no intuition of ourselves as spontaneous, or "self-active," beings. As Kant puts it in a key footnote in this section, "I do not have another self-intuition which gives the *determining* in me (I am conscious only of the spontaneity of it) prior to the act of *determination* [*vor dem Aktus des Bestimmens*]" (B158 n.). The conclusion which he draws from this is that one's consciousness of the spontaneity of one's thought must be regarded as a nonempirical or intellectual consciousness.

Kant develops this thought in a number of significant passages in the Paralogisms, which we shall consider later in the chapter. For the present it should prove instructive to consider Kant's attempt to deal with this very problem in a well-known Reflexion: "Is it an Experience that we Think?"[11] Kant's treatment of the issue reflects the conception of inner experience delineated in the previous chapter. The underlying assumption is that inner as well as outer experience involves a judgment expressing the empirical knowledge of an object. In the case of inner experience, the object is a determinate temporal order of representations or mental states. Kant begins his discussion by contrasting the thought of a geometrical figure such as a square with the recognition or apprehension of the product of this thought. The claim is that the former does not while the latter does count as an experience. As is often the case, 'thought' (*Gedanke*) is here ambiguous. It can mean either the content (the concept of a square) or the act of thinking.[12] By the 'product' of the thought, regarded as an object of inner experience, is presumably meant the image of the figure sketched in the imagination, that is, the image that one actually has "before the mind" when engaged in geometrical reasoning.

> This thought [the thought of a square] produces an object of experience or determination of the mind which can be observed, namely, insofar as it [the mind] is affected by the faculty of thought. I can, therefore, say: I have experienced what is involved in comprehending in thought a figure with four equal sides and right angles in such a way that I can demonstrate its properties. This is the empirical consciousness of my state in time by thought; thought itself, though it happens in time, makes no reference to time in the thinking of the properties of the figure.[13]

The argument as it stands is puzzling. The crucial second half of the last sentence suggests that the point is simply that although the mental process of thinking the square takes place in time, the thought itself (the content) does not involve any reference to time. This is certainly true. For Kant at least, the thought, in contrast to the image, of a square consists of a certain rule or procedure for constructing the figure. The actual construction, whether in the imagination or in some physical medium, is, of course, an occurrence in time; nevertheless, this has no bearing on the properties of the figure.[14] The problem, however, is that it does not follow from the fact that the thought of a square does not involve any reference to time that the consciousness of the act of thinking a square is not an experience. Moreover, even if we were to grant this inference, Kant's general thesis would not follow. There are, after all, situations in which the thought *does* involve a reference to time, for example, when one is thinking about one's own inner experience. Clearly, even here it is necessary to distinguish between the act of thinking and the object thought, and, therefore, between the consciousness of the former and of the latter. What Kant must show, then, is that the consciousness of the act of thinking (apperception) is not an experience even when one is thinking about a temporal process.

Interestingly enough, Kant seems to deal with just this point in the incredibly obscure last paragraph of the Reflexion. Here the focus shifts explicitly to inner experience *per se,* and the contrast with which Kant operates is between the consciousness that arises when one "institutes" such an experience ("Das Bewusstsein wenn ich eine Erfahrung anstelle") and the consciousness of the act of instituting. Since the first is characterized as the consciousness of one's existence insofar as it is determined in time, it can be assumed that Kant is here talking about the consciousness of one's mental state (the sequence of representations) which arises through attention. This consciousness is empirical, and the goal of the argument is to show that the same cannot be said of the consciousness of the act of instituting. The argument, such as it is, takes an indirect or reductio form and relies heavily on the status of time as a condition of inner experience. The basic point is that if the latter consciousness were likewise empirical, it would have to be a consciousness of something that is determined in time. This follows from the abovementioned status of time, but it also generates an absurdity.

> If this consciousness (the consciousness of the act of thinking), were itself in turn empirical, then the same time determination would again have to be represented as contained under the conditions of the time determination of my state. It would, therefore, be necessary to conceive of another time under which (not in which) the time which constitutes the formal condition of my inner experience is contained. Consequently, there would be a time in which and simultaneously with which a given time flows, which is absurd. However, the consciousness of instituting an experience or, in general, of thinking, is transcendental consciousness, not experience.[15]

The supposition of an absurdity involved in the thought of two times that are not themselves parts of a single universal time rests upon the intuition argument of the Transcendental Aesthetic and recalls the indirect argument of the First Analogy. Nevertheless, the argument here is somewhat different from that of the Analogy. Its nerve is the contention that the "objects" of the two modes of consciousness could not be experienced together in a single time frame. If they were, then the act of thinking would itself have to be conceived as a determinate and determined occurrence in objective time. In that case, however, it would lose its character as a determining act (of thinking). The implication seems to be that in order to preserve the determining, spontaneous character of the act of thinking, while at the same time attributing an empirical character to the consciousness of this act (as is required by the assumption under consideration), it would be necessary to posit a distinct "meta-time" in which the determining act occurs, which itself somehow determines or conditions the objective time of human experience. It is this consequence which generates the absurdity to which Kant alludes.

Fortunately, it seems possible to express Kant's basic point in a much less convoluted way. Reduced to its simplest terms, it is that the conceptual activity through which the mind represents an object, including itself as object, cannot itself be given to it as an object. Insofar as one objectifies thinking, that is, treats it merely as a psychological occurrence, one *eo ipso* destroys its character as thinking. Moreover, this objectified thought is always objectified by and for another consciousness that does the objectifying. Consciousness (the act of thinking) is thus incapable of grasping itself as object precisely because it must always be presupposed as already on the scene, doing the objectifying. As we shall see in the last section of this chapter, this has important consequences for the Kantian project of applying the transcendental distinction to the self, considered qua knower or epistemic subject.

II. APPERCEPTION AND EXISTENCE

In many of those places in which Kant characterizes apperception as a consciousness of the spontaneity of thought he also maintains that it involves an awareness of existence. Moreover, just as he denies to this consciousness the status of an experience (empirical knowledge) of one's spontaneity, so he denies that this awareness of existence can be equated with the knowledge of oneself as a thinking being. Thus, he begins the discussion of apperception in §25 of the Transcendental Deduction by remarking that "in the transcendental synthesis . . . , and therefore in the synthetic original unity of apperception, I am conscious of myself, not as I appear to myself, nor as I am in myself, but only that I am" (B157). Again, in the footnote in the same section he states: "The '*I think*' expresses the act of determining my existence. Existence is already given thereby, but the mode in which I am to determine this existence, that is, the manifold belonging to it, is not thereby given" (B158 n.). The same line of thought is further developed in the Second Edition version of the Paralogisms, particularly in a notoriously obscure footnote, which also contains the gist of Kant's critique of Descartes's *cogito* inference.

The 'I think' is, as already stated, an empirical proposition, and contains within itself the proposition 'I exist'. But I cannot say 'Everything which thinks, exists'. For in that case the property of thought would render all beings which possess it necessary beings. My existence cannot, therefore, be regarded as an inference from the proposition 'I think', as Descartes sought to contend—for it would then have to be preceded by the major premise 'Everything which thinks, exists'—but is identical with it. The 'I think' ex-presses an indeterminate empirical intuition, i.e., perception (and thus shows that sensation, which as such belongs to sensibility, lies at the basis of this existential proposition). But the 'I think' precedes the experience which is required to determine the object of perception through the category in re-spect of time; and the existence here [referred to] is not a category. The category as such does not apply to an indeterminately given object but only to one of which we have a concept and about which we seek to know whether it does or does not exist outside the concept. An indeterminate perception here signifies only something real that is given, given indeed to thought in general, and so not as appearance, nor as thing in itself (*noume-non*), but as something which actually exists, and which in the proposition, 'I think', is denoted as such. For it must be observed, that when I have called the proposition, 'I think', an empirical proposition, I do not mean to say thereby, that the 'I' in this proposition is an empirical representation. On the contrary, it is purely intellectual, because belonging to thought in general. Without some empirical representation to supply the material for thought, the *actus*, 'I think', would not, indeed, take place; but the empirical is only the condition of the application, or of the employment, of the pure intellec-tual faculty. [B422 n.]

Taking this note as our main text for the discussion of Kant's view on the connection between apperception and existence, it is clear that we must distinguish between three closely related aspects of the Kantian position: (1) the claim that existence is already given in the '*I think*', or equivalently, that it "contains within itself the proposition 'I exist' "; (2) the claim that '*I think*' is an empirical proposition; (3) the critique of the Cartesian infer-ence, *cogito, ergo sum*. In what follows I propose to treat each of these separately, although of necessity there will be some overlap.

A. 'I Think' and 'I Exist'

Kant's account of the nature of the connection between these two propo-sitions is obviously related to his critique of Descartes, but the logical point he is trying to make is worthy of being considered independently of this critique. In the First Edition he makes the point with specific refer-ence to Descartes by declaring that "what is referred to as the Cartesian inference, *cogito, ergo sum,* is really a tautology, since the cogito (*sum cogitans*) asserts my existence immediately*"* (A355). In the Second Edi-tion footnote cited above, he indicates that his point is simply that the propositions 'I think', 'I am thinking', and 'I exist thinking' are all equivalent. Kant's claim, then, seems to be that the existential assumption or presupposition is already built into the proposition 'I think' and, therefore, cannot appropriately be regarded as an inference from it.

In an interesting discussion of Kant's cryptic remarks concerning the cogito, Bernard Williams has suggested as a possible source for Kant's view the dictum of Spinoza: " 'I think, therefore, I am' is a proposition equivalent to 'I am thinking.' "[16] Williams is certainly correct in his claim that this expresses Kant's view. Nevertheless, given Kant's extremely negative attitude toward Spinoza, this does not appear to be a very likely source. Far closer to home is Leibniz, who makes the same point in the *New Essays*, when he writes, "To say *I think therefore I am* is not really to prove existence from thought, since *to think* is already to say *I am*."[17] Since Kant was a keen student of the *New Essays*, he was undoubtedly familiar with this remark of Leibniz. There is, however, really no need to assume any external source for Kant's view of the cogito. The main point is simply that his claim about existence follows directly from the conception of apperception as a consciousness of the activity of thinking. There can be no activity without an agent, and to acknowledge the existence of an activity is to acknowledge the existence of something that acts.

B. 'I Think' as an Empirical Proposition

This claim is more difficult, particularly if one tries to connect it with the contention that the I that functions as the subject of the proposition is not itself empirical. Moreover, it is precisely at this point that Kant's account suffers from the failure to distinguish clearly between empirical and transcendental apperception. Certainly, part of what Kant means here is that the proposition expresses a contingent rather than a necessary truth. In this respect he is again in agreement with Leibniz, who contends that it is a "proposition of fact, founded on immediate experience, and is not a necessary proposition whose necessity is seen in the immediate agreement of ideas."[18] The text, however, also indicates that part of what Kant means is that some given sensible representation must function as the occasion for the act of thought and, therefore, for the awareness of existence. Without something given to sensibility, that is, without sensation, there would be no *cogitatio* or, better, no *ergo sum cogitans*. In other words, the apprehension of some sensible content (as modification of inner sense) is a necessary condition of the awareness of existence that is presumed to be inseparable from the consciousness of thinking. Thus Kant maintains parenthetically that "sensation, which as such belongs to sensibility, lies at the basis of the existential proposition" and, again, at the very end of the note, that "the empirical is only the condition of the application, or of the employment of the pure intellectual faculty." The relevant point here is not that the empirical is *only* the condition but rather that it *is* the condition. It follows from this that apperception as an actual consciousness of thinking ("something real") always involves an empirical element.

The situation is complicated by Kant's insistence that the sensation that provides the occasion for apperception, and therefore for the apprehension of existence, is not itself an empirical representation of the subject. In fact, it is not a representation of the subject at all. Moreover, since in pure or transcendental apperception one explicitly abstracts from everything empirical, including sensation, and since there is no determinate nonempirical representation of the subject (no intellectual intuition), it follows that the thinking subject, whose existence is given or "contained" in the consciousness of thinking, can be characterized only as a "something in general = x." This is clearly a nonempirical, "purely intellectual" representation; indeed, it is nothing more than the empty thought of a logical subject. Consequently, it does not follow from the fact that the thought of an existing subject of thought is nonempirical that we can have any nonempirical knowledge of the "real," or noumenal, nature of this subject. Kant makes the same point in the Transcendental Deduction, when he remarks that, through apperception, "I am conscious of myself, not as I appear to myself, nor as I am in myself, but only that I am" (B157).

This puts us in a position to make some sense out of Kant's mysterious remark that the notion of existence involved in the cogito cannot be equated with the category of existence. Kant justifies this on the grounds that we are dealing with an "indeterminately given object," and "the category as such" does not apply to such an object, but only to one of which we have a concept and about which we seek to know "whether it does or does not exist outside the concept." Behind this lies Kant's claim that existence, unlike the other categories (at least the nonmodal categories), is not a real predicate or determination of a thing, but merely involves the positing of an actual object corresponding to a given concept.[19] Given this doctrine, it follows that the category of existence is called into play only when we have a determinate concept and wish to determine whether there is an actual object answering to that concept. But this is precisely what is lacking in the case of the I of the 'I think'. Instead of a determinate concept of a thinking subject, we have only an "indeterminate perception" or, as Kant elsewhere puts it, a "bare consciousness" (A346/B404) that is inseparable from, or "contained in," the act of thought. Since it is not connected with a determinate concept or definite description of an individual thinker, 'I think' cannot issue in a genuine existential judgment, which would be the case if it involved the category.

C. Cogito, ergo sum: The Kantian Critique

Kant's critique of the Cartesian cogito inference is embedded in his general critique of rational psychology, but it is more convenient to treat it separately. The critique itself falls rather nicely into two parts. The first is based upon Kant's interpretation of the inference as a syllogism. His claim is that, so construed, it generates the unpalatable conclusion that whatever thinks exists necessarily. The second, which is closely connected with the general argument of the Paralogisms, is directed against the Cartesian project, as it is manifest in the whole program of radical doubt. Seen through Kantian spectacles, this project can be described as the attempt to arrive at certainty about the existence of the noumenal self as *res cogitans* by simply reflecting upon what must be presupposed as a condition of thinking.

The basic problem with the first part of Kant's critique lies in his syllogistic reading of the cogito inference, a reading which is widely rejected by Descartes's interpreters.[20] Kant's critique of the Cartesian project, however, is based entirely upon his own account of apperception. It is, therefore, independent of his interpretation of the logical form of the cogito inference. His central claim is that the cogito, which survives the program of radical doubt, is nothing more than the 'I think', which must be able to accompany all of my representations, and which, for that very reason, cannot be removed by even the most radical doubt. Correlatively, our conception of this cogito must be characterized as the "bare representation" or "purely intellectual consciousness" of an abiding subject of thought. Given this position, Descartes's mistake is clear: he identifies this formal or transcendental I with the real, or noumenal, self. As a result of this illicit identification, Descartes erroneously believed that he had arrived by means of the cogito inference at a certainty with respect to his own existence as a particular thinking substance (*res cogitans*). This is a clear example of what Kant means by "transcendental illusion." It is also closely connected to the basic error of rational psychology to which we shall turn shortly.

First, however, it is worth noting that the same point has been made in somewhat different terms by Bernard Williams, who remarks that in the solipsistic universe produced by the Cartesian doubt, where the I is ubiquitous, 'I' cannot fulfill its normal referring function, because there is no particular content to which it can be attached to the exclusion of anything else.[21] Kant does not deal explicitly with the problem of reference, but instead tends to pose the issue in straightforwardly epistemological terms. Thus he insists upon the need for sensible intuition as that through which alone a particular thinking subject can be given to the mind (itself) as object. Nevertheless, it is clear that these two ways of characterizing the problem with the Cartesian cogito come to very much the same thing. In fact, if anything Kant's account cuts deeper because it shows that the reason why there is no particular, individuating content to which the I can be attached is that the representation of it is "purely intellectual." Because of this, 'I' designates only "something in general," which is to say that it does not refer to anything at all. Moreover, the ubiquity of the I to which Williams alludes is explained in Kantian terms by the fact that it must be able to accompany all my representations.

III. THE CRITIQUE OF RATIONAL PSYCHOLOGY

By 'rational psychology' Kant means a metaphysical theory of the soul, mind, or self which is based solely upon an analysis of its capacity to think or, equivalently, its presumed nature as a "thinking being." As rational, such a psychology must abstract from or ignore everything that can be learned about the mind and its contents by empirical means. Kant describes the situation by remarking that 'I think' is "the sole text of rational psychology, and from it the whole idea of its teaching has to be developed" (A343 / B402). On the basis of this "text" alone, one is supposed to be able to demonstrate that the soul is a simple, immaterial, and enduring substance. This, in turn, is intended to provide a basis for the demonstration of its immortality, which is the ultimate goal of this "science."

Although it incorporates theses and arguments advanced by a number of other philosophers, most notably Leibniz, rational psychology as a whole is obviously a systematic extension of the Cartesian project.[22] It should, therefore, come as no surprise to find that Kant's critique of this "science" is very much of a piece with his critique of the cogito inference. The essence of the matter is contained in the proposition "Through this I or he or it (the thing) which thinks, nothing further is represented than a transcendental subject of the thoughts $= x$" (A346 / B449). The transcendental subject is the counterpart of the transcendental object. Just as the latter is the concept of the bare form of an object (the concept of an "object in general"), which is all that remains for thought when abstraction is made from the sensible content through which an actual object can be represented, so the former is the concept of the bare form of a thinking subject (a logical subject of thought or "subject in general"), which is all that remains when abstraction is made from the content of inner sense. The claim, then, is that the rational psychologist conflates this empty or formal concept with the concept of a real, or noumenal (in the positive sense), subject to which nonsensible predicates can be synthetically attached. In a word, the rational psychologist hypostatizes this merely logical or transcendental subject; and this hypostatization generates the pseudo-inferences of rational psychology, just as the hypostatization of the Idea of an absolute totality of conditions generates the Antinomies.

The key to Kant's argument in the Second Edition (which, in the interest of brevity, I shall focus upon) lies in the claim that the conflation or hypostatization and, therefore, the Paralogisms themselves are based upon the following invalid syllogism:

That which cannot be thought otherwise than as subject does not exist otherwise than as subject, and is therefore substance. A thinking being, considered merely as such, cannot be thought otherwise than as subject. Therefore it exists also only as subject, that is, as substance. [B410–11]

The syllogism commits the fallacy of an ambiguous middle term (*a sophisma figurae dictionis*). In his analysis of this syllogism, Kant suggests that the term used ambiguously is 'thought'. It would be more accurate, however, to locate the ambiguity in the whole expression: 'That which cannot be thought otherwise than as subject'. In the major premise this refers to an object or entity in general, and thus (supposedly) to something that can be given in intuition. To say of such an entity that it cannot be thought otherwise than as subject is just to say that it is a substance. This is a synthetic judgment in which an object is subsumed under a category. By contrast, in the minor premise it is simply the thinking subject, which cannot think itself otherwise than as a subject, insofar as it regards itself as the subject of thought. The key expression here is 'merely as such'. This is clearly elliptical for 'merely as the subject of thought', which is the only way in which the rational psychologist claims to consider the self. Here the "thought" reduces to the tautology that the subject of thought must consider itself as the subject of thought. As such, it does not license the conclusion that this self-conscious subject of thought is an actual thinking substance.

This schema applies to each of the inferences of rational psychology. By appealing to it Kant is able to show in each case that a merely analytic claim about how a subject of thought must conceive itself is mistakenly taken for a synthetic a priori claim about the nature of an actual thinking being. This is clearly illustrated by the First Paralogism, which deals with the substantiality of the soul. Kant's analysis of the argument begins with the characterization of the I as the "determining subject of that relation which constitutes judgment" (B407). The point is the same as before: the I that thinks (the judging subject) must be able to regard itself as the logical subject of thought. The claim is "logical" in the sense that it is grounded in an analysis of the formal conditions of thought. This is reflected in Kant's own description of the proposition as "apodeictic and indeed identical." In opposition to the rational psychologist, however, Kant also insists that this does not mean "that I, as *object,* am for myself a self-subsistent being or substance." The latter is a synthetic a priori claim, which must be distinguished from the former analytic claim.

The Second Paralogism, which concerns the unity or simplicity of the subject of thought, receives a similar treatment. Kant remarks: "That the 'I' of apperception, and therefore the 'I' in every act of thought is *one* [*ein Singular*], and cannot be resolved into a plurality of subjects, and consequently signifies a logically simple subject, is something already contained in the very concept of thought, and is therefore an analytic proposition" (B407). But this does not license the conclusion (drawn by the rational psychologist) that the subject, whose unity is a condition of the unity of thought, and thus of thought itself, exists as a simple substance. Once again, the latter claim is synthetic. As such, it can be established only by an appeal to intuition, which in this case is unavailable.

The Third Paralogism affirms the numerical identity of the thinking subject, which Kant equates with its personality.[23] The analysis is virtually identical to that of the preceding Paralogism. Once again, the basic point is that the rational psychologist conflates an analytic proposition about the identity of the logical subject of thought with a synthetic proposition about the identity of a person.

The Fourth Paralogism marks the point at which the general critique of rational psychology is linked to the specific critique of Descartes. Interestingly enough, this is true of both editions, even though the doctrine under attack is completely changed in the Second Edition. In the First Edition, the subject of the Paralogism is Descartes's problematical or skeptical idealism. In the Second Edition, the Paralogism deals with Descartes's doctrine that the soul, qua thinking substance, can exist independently of its body. Unlike its First Edition counterpart, the issue discussed here is directly related to the problem of immortality, and, therefore, to the central concerns of rational psychology.

The specific argument under attack infers the ontological distinctness of the soul or mind, qua thinking substance, from the body on the grounds that the subject can distinguish its own existence as thinking being from that of other things "outside" it, including its own body. Although Kant does not refer to Descartes here, this is readily recognizable as the well-known argument of the Second and Sixth Meditations. In the Second Meditation, Descartes contends that the mind is assured of its existence as a thing that thinks, even in the face of the methodological denial (on the assumption of the Evil Genius) of the existence of the body. Descartes recognizes that this does not of itself establish the distinctness of the mind from the body, but he does contend that this is established in the Sixth Meditation, where an appeal is made to the veracity of God. This more or less official Cartesian argument involves a combination of the claim that the mind can be clearly and distinctly conceived apart from the body (presumably established in the Second Meditation) with the principle that "all things which I apprehend clearly and distinctly can be created by God as I apprehend them." On the basis of this, Descartes concludes:

> It suffices that I am able to apprehend one thing apart from another clearly and distinctly in order to be certain that the one is different from the other, since they may be made to exist in separation at least by the omnipotence of God; and it does not signify by what power this separation is made in order to compel me to judge them to be different: and, therefore, just because I know certainly that I exist, and that meanwhile I do not remark that any

other thing necessarily pertains to my nature or essence, excepting that I am a thinking thing, I rightly conclude that my essence consists solely in the fact that I am a thinking thing [or a substance whose whole essence or nature is to think].[24]

Kant's cryptic reformulation of this line of argument does not contain any reference to the familiar Cartesian notions of clear and distinct ideas and divine veracity. It does, however, capture the essential move from separate conceivability to separate existence. Moreover, Kant characterizes the move in such a way that it becomes clear that the error which it involves is identical to the error committed in the cogito argument, as well as in the other Paralogisms. Thus Kant insists upon the analyticity of the claim that I can distinguish my existence as a thinking being from the existence of other things outside me, including my own body. The weight here falls on 'other things'. Since this refers to whatever is distinct from myself qua thinking being, it obviously includes within its scope my own body. In this sense, then, it is an analytic truth that my body is "other" than, and thus distinct from, my mind. Nevertheless, the key point is that I cannot determine from this (as Descartes attempted to do) whether self-consciousness is possible "apart from things outside me through which representations are given to me, and whether, therefore, I could exist merely as a thinking being (i.e., without existing in human form)" (B409). Although Kant does not say so explicitly, the latter is obviously a synthetic proposition, which, as such, could be based only upon an intuition of the thinking subject.

The Second Edition version of the Paralogisms has a conciseness and clarity that Kant achieves only rarely, if ever, in the rest of the *Critique*. In each case the Paralogism is seen to arise from the attempt to arrive at substantive metaphysical claims about the mind merely by reflection on the act of thinking. This project is doomed to failure because, given its meager resources (the 'I think' is "the sole text of rational psychology"), it can provide only an entirely vacuous characterization of the nature of the mind: "a thing which thinks."[25] Problems arise, however, as soon as we move from this purely critical result to a consideration of Kant's effort to link his analysis of apperception with his transcendental distinction. It is to this issue that we now turn.

IV. APPERCEPTION AND THE NOUMENAL SELF[26]

The *Critique* contains two distinct and incompatible doctrines about the relation between the subject of apperception and the noumenal self. According to one, which is Kant's official position, the subject of apperception is identified simply with the noumenal or "real" self. Kant succinctly expresses this view in a frequently cited Reflexion when he remarks, "The soul in transcendental apperception is *substantia noumenon,* hence it has no permanence in time, since this belongs only to objects in space."[27] Although this view makes the phenomenal-noumenal distinction directly relevant to the analysis of self-knowledge (which is undoubtedly its attraction for Kant), it turns out to be both incoherent and in conflict with the critical thrust of the argument of the Paralogisms. According to the other, which I take to express Kant's deepest view, the subject of apperception is distinguished from the noumenal self, indeed, from any kind of intelligible *object.* This view is both coherent and compatible with the critique of rational psychology. The problem with it is that it makes the application of the transcendental distinction to the problem of self-knowledge extremely problematic. In what follows I shall discuss each of them in turn.

A. The Official View and Its Incoherence

This view is very much of a piece with Kant's official position regarding inner sense. Both rest upon an assumed parallelism between outer and inner sense, and both prove to be untenable for that very reason. The essential feature of this view is that the subject of apperception or the transcendental subject ("the I or he or it [the thing] which thinks") is treated as a special kind of object; namely, as a "transcendental object of inner sense."[28] Such a doctrine is implicit in those places where Kant insists that inner sense and apperception yield a two-fold consciousness of a single I,[29] but it can be found throughout the *Critique* and in both editions. For illustrative purposes, I shall cite three passages, one from each of the three main divisions of the *Critique,* in which this view is contained either implicitly or explicitly.

The first is from the Second Edition addition to the Transcendental Aesthetic, which was discussed in the last chapter. In the portion of the text that is relevant to our present concerns, Kant writes:

> Everything that is represented through a sense is so far always appearance, and consequently we must either refuse to admit that there is an inner sense, or we must recognize that the subject, which is the object of the sense, can be represented through it only as appearance, not as that subject would judge of itself if its intuition were self-activity only, that is, were intellectual. The whole difficulty is as to how a subject can inwardly intuit itself; and this is a difficulty common to every theory. [B68]

The second is from §24 of the Transcendental Deduction. Kant here attempts to deal with the "paradox," which appears to him to be generated by the account of inner sense given in the Transcendental Aesthetic:

> this sense represents to consciousness even our own selves only as we appear to ourselves, not as we are in ourselves. For we intuit ourselves only as we are inwardly *affected*, and this would seem to be contradictory, since we should then have to be in a passive relation (of active affection) to ourselves. It is to avoid this contradiction that in systems of psychology *inner sense,*

which we have carefully distinguished from the faculty of *apperception*, is commonly regarded as being identical with it. [B152–53]

The third is from the account of transcendental idealism in the Antinomies. In an effort to show how the notion of transcendental ideality is applicable to inner sense as well as to outer sense Kant states:

> Even the inner and sensible intuition of our mind (as object of consciousness) which is represented as being determined by the succession of different states in time, is not the self proper, as it exists in itself—that is, is not the transcendental subject—but only an appearance that has been given to the sensibility of this, to us unknown, being. [A492/B520]

The assumption underlying all of these passages is that the problem of self-knowledge is to explain how the subject of apperception can know itself as object. As the first passage indicates, this is taken as something that must be accounted for by any theory of self-knowledge. All that Kant's theory does is to maintain that such knowledge is subject to the same epistemic conditions and constraints as other species of knowledge. It follows from this that the subject of apperception can only know itself as it appears to itself through inner sense, not as it is in itself or, equivalently, not in the manner in which it could know itself if its intuition were intellectual. Given this way of posing the problem of self-knowledge, the identification of the subject of apperception, which is thought only as a transcendental subject $= x$, with the real, or noumenal, self becomes unavoidable.

This line of thought has been subject to constant criticism since the time of its initial, precritical appearance in the Inaugural Dissertation.[30] In the recent literature it has been subjected to a particularly sharp criticism by Strawson, who contends that it is crucial for Kant to establish a connection "by way of identity" between the natural or empirical subject and the "real" or supersensible subject. Basing his account solely on one text in the Antinomies, Strawson also suggests that the point of contact (for Kant) is to be found in "the man's consciousness of his own possession and exercise of the power of thought, of the faculties of understanding and reason."[31] In other words, it is through apperception that the empirical subject is supposed to recognize its identity with the transcendental subject that it "really" is. Apperception, on this view, is therefore not only a consciousness of the "real," or noumenal, self but also of its identity with the empirical self.

This doctrine, according to Strawson, is incoherent on two counts. First, both the consciousness of the activity of thinking (the apperceiving) and the thinking which is apperceived take place in time. Consequently, both this consciousness and its "object" must be assigned to a being which, in Strawson's terms, "*has* a history and hence is not a supersensible being, not the subject in which the representation of time has its original ground."[32] Second, by identifying the empirically self-conscious subject which has a history with a supersensible, transcendental subject, Kant commits himself to the absurd doctrine that the empirical self both *appears to* and *is an appearance of* the "real," supersensible self. Once again, the problem stems from the presumed atemporal nature of such a subject. Since it is atemporal, the appearing to it of the successive states of the empirical subject (with which it is supposed to be identical) cannot itself be regarded as an occurrence in time; but any attempt to put a nontemporal construction on the verb 'to appear' lands us immediately in unintelligibility. For similar reasons, it does not make any sense to talk about the succession of states in the empirical subject as the appearing *of* the supersensible subject. From this Strawson concludes:

> The reference to myself as I (supersensibly) am in myself drops out as superfluous and unjustified: and with it goes all ground for saying that, in empirical self-consciousness, I appear to myself as other than I really am.[33]

While there is certainly much to quarrel with in the details of Strawson's account, particularly with his complete failure to deal with the inner sense–apperception distinction, it cannot be denied that his analysis strikes a nerve. The fact of the matter is simply that Kant's language, as it is found in the previously cited passages as well as many other texts, does lend itself to such an interpretation and critique. As already indicated, the key point is the identification of the subject of apperception with the "real," or noumenal, self. Given this identification, it does seem as if we are constrained to conceive of the empirical subject as both appearing to and as an appearance of the transcendental subject, and such a view is incoherent for the very reasons which Strawson cites.

The incoherence of this view can also be brought out in another manner, indeed, in one which is much more in accord with Kant's own thought. The problem lies in Kant's contention that if the subject of apperception had intellectual intuition it could somehow intuit and, therefore, know itself in its capacity as spontaneous, determining self. Such a contention is just what one would expect, given the identification of the subject of apperception and the noumenal self. Unfortunately, it is also self-contradictory because it requires the assignment of contradictory predicates to such a subject. *Ex hypothesi,* it would have to be at one and the same time both an intuitive intellect (in order to know itself in this manner) and a discursive intelligence (in order to be known as spontaneous, determining, and so forth). Each of these conceptions or models of mind, however, is defined by Kant in contrast to the other. The thought of a mind that embodies both is self-contradictory. Thus, while I can coherently, if vacuously, claim that if I had an intuitive *instead* of a discursive intellect, I could know *other* things (objects) as they are in themselves, I cannot similarly claim that I could know myself as object in my capacity as a spontaneous, thinking subject. Nor is the situation really helped very much by stipulating that this intuitive knowledge is possessed by God (or some other "intelligence"). The difficulty here stems from the productive, archetypal nature of intellectual intuition. In conceiving of myself as known by such a mind, I would be constrained to regard the spontaneity of my own thought as itself a product of something else. This is again a contradiction.

B. Kant's Alternative View

Just as Kant's official view about the subject of apperception is of a piece with his official designation of the soul (mind, or self) as the object of inner sense, so his alternative view goes together with his second way of characterizing the object of inner sense. The essential feature of apperception on this alternative view is that it is a consciousness of the activity of thinking, not of a thinker. This parallels the view that the objects of inner sense are the contents of the mind (its *cogitationes*), not the mind itself. Taken as a whole, then, this position maintains that the contrast between inner sense and apperception is between a consciousness of the contents of the mind (taken as "subjective objects") and a consciousness of the activity of thinking. There is no room for any additional consciousness of a mind or thinker who owns these thoughts and is engaged in this activity.

Clearly, the second view of apperception is the one that is at work in the critique of rational psychology. As we have seen, the characterization of the subject of apperception as a "transcendental subject = x" is not intended to assign the act of thinking to some inaccessible noumenal entity, which is nonetheless to be identified with one's "real" self. On the contrary, it is to underscore the uniformativeness of the only possible answer available to rational psychology to the question, What is the I which thinks? To be sure, one can always find a perfectly good *empirical* answer to this question; for example, Henry Allison. The problem, of course, is that such an answer is based upon my conception of myself as a subject in the world with a body, memory, and history (in Kantian terms, as a being whose "existence is determined in time"), and this is just what is precluded by the method of rational psychology. This "science" is committed to providing a nonempirical answer to the question, one based solely upon a reflection on the activity of thinking. Such an answer, however, is shown by Kant to be impossible. Once again, the reason for this is simply that such reflection yields only the bare thought of a subject that must be presupposed as a condition of thinking. Thus, far from himself advocating the identification of the subject of apperception with the real, or noumenal, self, the whole thrust of Kant's critique of rational psychology is to show that this identification is illiicit.

It is instructive to compare Kant's position here with Wittgenstein's treatment of a similar issue in the *Tractatus*. As Wittgenstein puts it,

"There is no such thing as the subject that thinks or entertains ideas" (Das denkende, vorstellende, Subjekt gibt es nicht).[34] And again, "The subject does not belong to the world: rather, it is a limit of the world."[35] Finally, more expansively, "The philosophical self [*Das philosophische Ich*] is not the human being, not the human body or the human soul, with which psychology deals, but rather the metaphysical subject, the limit of the world—not a part of it."[36] Although Wittgenstein was motivated by quite different philosophical concerns, more particularly, by the problem of solipsism, it seems reasonable to regard his "philosophical self" or "metaphysical subject" as equivalent to Kant's transcendental subject of apperception; it is the knowing subject considered qua knower or, in the English rendering of Wittgenstein's expression, "the subject that thinks or entertains ideas." Thus, to say with Wittgenstein that there is no such subject or that it is a limit and not a part of the world is just to say that it is a transcendental presupposition and, therefore, unlike "the human soul with which psychology deals," not an object in the world. But if the metaphysical subject or transcendental subject of apperception cannot be regarded as an object in the world, then it cannot be equated with the noumenal self, for the concept of the latter is the concept of an object in the world (the "transcendental object of inner sense"), albeit one that can be known only in a unique, nonsensible manner.

Although this view underlies the whole argument of the Paralogisms, there are three passages in which it is especially clear. Accordingly, a consideration of these passages should help us to underscore the contrast between it and the first view. The first is contained in a brief introductory section common to both editions. It is intended as an explanation of why the "I or he or it (the thing) which thinks" is characterized as a "transcendental subject of the thoughts = x."

> It is known only through the thoughts which are its predicates, and of it, apart from them, we cannot have any concept whatsoever, but can only revolve in a perpetual circle, since any judgment upon it has already made use of its representation. And the reason why this inconvenience is insepara- bly bound up with it, is that consciousness in itself is not a representation distinguishing a particular object, but a form of representation in general, that is, of representation in so far as it is to be entitled knowledge; for it is only of knowledge that I can say that I am thereby thinking something. [A346/B404]

The second is a closely related passage from the conclusion to the First Edition account. In a summary statement of the outcome of the argument Kant writes:

> Self-consciousness in general is therefore the representation of that which is the condition of all unity, and itself is unconditioned. We can thus say of the thinking 'I' (the soul) which regards itself as substance, as simple, as numeri- cally identical at all times, and as the correlate of all existence, from which

all other existence must be inferred, that it does *not* know *itself through the categories*, but knows the categories, and through them all objects, in the absolute unity of apperception, and so *through itself.* Now it is, indeed, very evident that I cannot know as an object that which I must presuppose in order to know any object, and that the determining self (the thought) is distinguished from the self that is to be determined (the thinking subject) in the same way as knowledge is distinguished from its object. [A402]

Finally, in the Second Edition version he states simply:

The subject of the categories cannot by thinking the categories acquire a concept of itself as an object of the categories. For in order to think them, its pure self-consciousness, which is what was to be explained, must itself be presupposed. [B422]

The common theme running through all of these passages is the impossibility of even thinking (much less knowing) the I of apperception as an object through the categories. Since the categories are the concepts of an object in general, this is equivalent to the impossibility of thinking it as an object at all. The main thing to be noted here is that this is different from and stronger than the familiar noumenal ignorance thesis, even though Kant himself constantly seems to confuse the two. The latter is always based upon a presumed lack of the proper intellectual equipment; namely, intellectual intuition. Since we lack the capacity for such an intuition, Kant holds that our thought of an object as it is in itself is doomed to vacuity. It can be thought only as a "something in general = x" or, equivalently, a "noumenon in the negative sense." Nevertheless, we can at least form the problematic idea of the sort of equipment that would be required in order to know such an "intelligible object." This, in turn, suffices to license the regulative use of the concept of such an object as a "critical reminder."

Here, by contrast, Kant's claim is that we are lacking a concept, even a problematic one, of the subject of apperception.[37] We have seen that Kant makes precisely the same point about the cogito of Descartes. Moreover, the reason for this should be apparent from the analysis of the Reflexion "Is it an Experience that we Think?" It is that the subject of apperception, or more simply, consciousness, cannot grasp itself as an object because, first, in the endeavor to do so it succeeds only in negating its character as subject,[38] and second, as that through which alone there can be objects (whether of mere thought or of experience), it must be thought as already on the scene, doing the conceptualizing. This has nothing to do with a lack of intellectual intuition. Indeed, the situation can be nicely illustrated by means of the very analogy to which Wittgenstein appealed to make essentially the same point; namely, that of the eye and its visible field.[39] Thus, following Wittgenstein's suggestion, we can say that just as the eye cannot see itself because it is not part of its own visible field, so the subject of apperception cannot think itself as object because it is not itself part of its "conceptual field." Finally, since the subject of apperception cannot think itself (or be thought) as an object at all, it cannot think itself (or be thought) as a noumenal object.[40]

This alternative view, which requires the distinction between the I or subject of apperception and the noumenal self, would clearly seem to be superior to the official view and to represent the deepest strand of Kant's thought on the topic. At the same time, however, it does raise serious problems for the accommodation of the inner sense–apperception to the phenomenal-noumenal distinction. Moreover, as we have seen, these problems extend in both directions. Just as the object of inner sense (on the alternative view) turns out to be something phenomenal, which yet cannot be identified with an appearance of the soul, so the subject of apperception turns out to be something "intelligible," or nonsensible, which nonetheless cannot be identified with the noumenal self. We shall return to the general problem of the applicability of the transcendental distinction to the self in chapter 15 in connection with the analysis of the acting subject and its practical freedom. In the meantime, we must still deal with Kant's refutation of Cartesian idealism, which is an essential aspect of this overall account of self-knowledge.

14

The Refutation of Idealism

The Refutation of Idealism contained in the Second Edition of the *Critique* is frequently regarded as an appendage to the Transcendental Deduction. On this interpretation, which was given currency by Strawson, it forms with the Deduction a single transcendental argument. The goal of the argument is to refute the skeptic by demonstrating that the reality of "objective experience" or, equivalently, the applicability of the concept of an object in the "weighty" sense is a necessary condition of the consciousness of one's identity through time as a subject of experience (the self-ascription of experience).[1] Here, by contrast, the Refutation of Idealism will be regarded as an integral part of the critique of Cartesian subjectivism which Kant developed in the Second Edition. As such, it stands in a close connection with the critique discussed in the previous chapter.

The analysis of Kant's argument is divided into three parts. The first introduces some general considerations in support of this line of interpretation. The second analyzes the argument itself. The third deals with a possible skeptical response that Kant's argument does not explicitly address; namely, a skepticism about self-knowledge. It argues that such a skepticism does not constitute a significant challenge either to Kant's anti-Cartesian argument or to his own account of self-knowledge.

I. SOME GENERAL CONSIDERATIONS

The dominant line of interpretation, which links the Refutation of Idealism closely to the Transcendental Deduction, derives virtually all of its plausibility from the fact that both arguments turn on a presumed correlation between self-consciousness and the consciousness of objects. Both texts can, therefore, be described as arguing that the latter is in some sense a condition of the possibility of the former. The problem with this line of interpretation is that it neglects the fact that the terms of the correlation are quite different in the two cases. We have already seen that the correlation for which Kant argues in the first part of the Second Edition Deduction is between the transcendental unity of apperception and an object in the judgmental or logical sense (*Objekt*). He does so by claiming that this transcendental unity is itself objective, that is, a unity which inherently involves, indeed constitutes, the representation of an object. Just as the concept of object involved here is logical or judgmental, so the unity of consciousness or self-consciousness with which it is correlated is purely formal. It is simply the unity which allows for the possibility of the consciousness of an identical 'I think' accompanying all my representations. Moreover, although the second part of the Deduction does attempt to establish the necessity of the categories for objects in the "weighty" sense, it neither asserts nor implies that the experience of objects in this sense is a necessary condition of the possibility of self-consciousness.

In the Refutation of Idealism, by contrast, Kant's concern is to establish a correlation between empirical self-consciousness, described as the "consciousness of one's existence as determined in time," or "inner experience," and the experience of objects in space, or "outer experience." The thesis for which he argues is that "the mere, but empirically determined, consciousness of my own existence, proves the existence of objects in space outside me" (B275). There are, according to Kant, two forms of "material idealism" which deny this thesis by denying the possibility of experiencing objects in space. One, the "dogmatic" variety, attributed to Berkeley, does this by denying the very possibility of spatial objects. Somewhat mysteriously, Kant connects this denial with what he takes to be Berkeley's misguided views about space, and he contends that this form of idealism has already been disposed of in the Transcendental Aesthetic.[2] The other, the "problematic idealism" of Descartes, which is the real target of the Refutation of Idealism, merely denies that we can have immediate experience, and therefore certainty, regarding the existence of such objects. Its basic claim is that "there is only one empirical assertion that is indubitably certain, namely, that 'I am' " (B274). Given this, it follows that the existence of anything distinct from the mind and its contents can be established only by inference. The problem is that any such inference can itself be called into question. Since this line of reasoning leads with equal cogency to a skepticism about other minds, "problematic idealism" could also be described as "problematic solipsism." Kant, however, completely ignores the problem of other minds and focuses only on a skepticism about an external, physical world.

Kant's analysis of the logic of the Cartesian position shows that the root of the problem lies in its assumption regarding self-knowledge. In fact, the problem is precisely the same as in the cogito inference: the Cartesian skeptic conflates the consciousness of the completely indeterminate, nonindividuated I of apperception, the existence of which is given (through an "indeterminate perception") in the very act of thought, with the determinate awareness of a particular existing subject, which is given in empirical self-consciousness. In short, this skepticism conflates apperception and inner sense. This conflation is the source of whatever plausibility Cartesian skepticism appears to possess, because it underlies its governing assumption that it is possible to have secure knowledge of the existence of the self as a thinking being, while remaining in doubt about the existence of anything external to this self. Once the distinction between these two forms of self-consciousness is clearly drawn, and it is seen that the certainty which presumably survives the Cartesian project of radical doubt is properly attributable only to the former ("intellectual" or "transcendental consciousness"), which does not itself count as genuine self-knowledge, then the doctrine that self-knowledge is possible independently of a knowledge of things in space loses its main support. And since the Cartesian will not deny the reality of self-knowledge, he is forced to give up his skepticism. Kant dwells on this point at some length in several of the Reflexionen dealing with the Refutation of Idealism,[3] but he also expresses it clearly in the *Critique* itself. Thus, in the preface he writes:

> If, with the *intellectual consciousness* of my existence, in the representation 'I am' which accompanies all my judgments and acts of understanding, I could at the same time connect a determination of my existence through *intellectual intuition,* the consciousness of a relation to something outside me would not be required. [Bxl n.]

And again, in the text of the Refutation of Idealism:

> Certainly, the representation 'I am', which expresses the consciousness that can accompany all thought, immediately includes in itself the existence of a subject; but it does not so include any *knowledge* of that subject, and therefore also no empirical knowledge, that is, no experience of it. [B277]

The fact that Kant explicitly locates the source of the Cartesian's mistake in the failure to distinguish between these two forms of self-consciousness provides strong support for the interpretation of the Refutation of Idealism advocated here. Taken together with the fact that Kant argues that *empirical,* not "intellectual" or "transcendental," self-consciousness (transcendental apperception) presupposes the actual experience of objects in space, it shows that Kant did not regard such experience, or more generally, the consciousness of objects in the "weighty" sense, as a necessary condition of apperception. If he did, the distinction between the two forms of self-consciousness would be irrelevant to his argument; the Cartesian position could be refuted simply by appealing to the doctrine of apperception. In that event, the Refutation of Idealism would be in truth nothing more than a trivial addendum to the Transcendental Deduction, where the doctrine of apperception is established. But since the Transcendental Deduction does not (because it cannot) establish any such result, a distinct argument is needed to refute the Cartesian skeptical idealist. Moreover, the argument must be grounded in a premise about empirical self-consciousness that the Cartesian will accept. Consequently, it must also take a reductio form, showing that the Cartesian cannot accept this premise while at the same time denying that we have outer experience. We shall see that, for the most part at least, Kant's argument takes just such a form, although it is intertwined with a quite different and dogmatic argument, which involves premises that the Cartesian need not accept.

II. KANT'S ARGUMENT

The argument of the *Critique* consists of five steps. I shall discuss each in turn, introducing material from elsewhere in the Kantian corpus, particularly the *Reflexionen,* when relevant.

A. Step 1

I am conscious of my own existence as determined in time.

This is the premise that must be accepted by the Cartesian skeptic and that is supposed to generate the reductio. Questions immediately arise, however, concerning its proper interpretation. One question, which has received some attention in the literature, is whether this consciousness (empirical self-consciousness) should be identified with the mere awareness or with the actual empirical knowledge of the self (mind) and its states.[4] Equally important, although not so frequently discussed, is the question of what exactly one is supposed to be conscious of when one is conscious of one's existence as determined in time. The first question concerns the epistemic status of this form of consciousness, and the second its actual content.

It seems relatively clear that the kind of consciousness that Kant has in mind involves actual self-knowledge rather than mere self-awareness. Textual support for this is provided by the fact that Kant identifies this consciousness with inner experience (B275).[5] Moreover, the argument requires that the premise be taken in this way, or more precisely, that it be taken to involve the assumption of the real possibility of empirical self-knowledge.[6] This does not mean, however, that Kant, in proto-Wittgensteinian fashion, is concerned with the conditions of the justification or verification of particular knowledge claims about the self and its states. His concern is rather with the conditions of the possibility of making such judgments (judgments of inner sense) at all. It is this possibility which the Cartesian simply assumes, without any consideration of its necessary (epistemic) conditions.

The answer to our first question provides us with the key to answering the second. If the consciousness of one's existence in time is equated with inner experience, then, given the previous account of inner sense, it must consist in the mind's knowledge of its own representations taken as "subjective objects." As we saw in connection with the account of inner sense, these "subjective objects" are experienced as they "exist objectively in time." In other words, they are experienced as mental occurrences, which are nonetheless all datable in the single objective time of the phenomenal world. Moreover, the mind or self on this view is conscious of itself just as the owner of this sequence of representations, the subject of this particular mental history. This gives the subject its own identity as an empirical subject. Consequently, insofar as it is conscious of the determinate sequence of its own representations in time, it is likewise conscious of its own existence as determined in time. Indeed, given the Cartesian assumptions with which the argument operates, wherein the existence of objects in space, including one's own body, is just the point in question, this is *all* that such consciousness could mean.

B. Step 2

All determination of time presupposes something *permanent* in perception.

This premise refers to the Backdrop Thesis of the First Analogy. It will be recalled that this thesis maintains that, because of the unperceivability of time, it is necessary to presuppose some (at least relatively permanent) perceptual surrogate for time itself as a condition of the possibility of determining the temporal relations of phenomena. If there were nothing that endured, then we could not become aware of either the coexistence or the succession of phenomena in a common, objective time. We also saw that this permanent must be something that occupies space. The present step merely extends this principle to the domain of inner experience. Kant does not produce any additional argument here, but it can be assumed that this extension is warranted by the generality of the claim of the First Analogy (it refers to *all* succession and coexistence), and by the fact that the content of inner experience is "objective" in the relevant sense.

C. Step 3

But this permanent cannot be an intuition in me. For all grounds of determination of my existence which are to be met within me are representations; and as representations themselves require a permanent distinct from them, in relation to which their change; and so my existence in time wherein they change may be determined.

In the footnote in the preface dealing with the Refutation of Idealism, Kant remarks that the above passage is to replace the sentence from the text which reads, "This permanent, however, cannot be something in me, since it is only through this permanent that my existence in time can itself be determined." Although the reason given for this apparently last-minute emendation is the obscurity of the original version, a more likely explanation is that Kant realized that the failure to mention intuition left open an obvious move for the Cartesian: claiming that the thinking subject (*res cogitans*) is itself the required permanent entity, and that the existence of its states can be determined in time by being referred to it.

As we have seen repeatedly, Kant acknowledges that we have the thought but not the intuition of such a subject, and that it must be conceived always as subject and never as predicate of anything else. We do, therefore, have the representation of something "in us" that is permanent; namely, the I itself. Once again, however, the point is that because this representation is a thought and not an intuition, it does not refer to anything determinate which can itself serve to determine the existence of the self and its states in time. Kant makes this explicit in his subsequent discussion of the argument:

> The consciousness of myself in the representation 'I' is not an intuition, but a merely *intellectual* representation of the spontaneity of a thinking subject. This 'I' has not, therefore, the least predicate of intuition, which, as a permanent, might serve as correlate for the determination of time in inner sense— in the manner in which, for instance, impenetrability serves in our empirical intuition of matter. [B278]

The situation is remedied in the revised version of the premise. Not only is there a reference to intuition, there is also an attempt to explain why the required intuition cannot be "in me." Since *all* intuitions, qua representations or modifications of inner sense, are "in me" (in the empirical sense), it is clear that the term must here refer to the object intuited (*das Angeschaute*) and not to the intuition (*die Anschauung*). In other words, Kant's claim is that the required permanent cannot be something inwardly intuited, and this is equivalent to the claim that it cannot be an object of inner sense. This follows from Kant's essentially Humean view of inner intuition or experience and its object. Once again, all that we inwardly intuit is the appearing (to ourselves) of our own representations. There is no additional intuition of a subject to which they appear (no impression of the self). Since each of these appearings is a fleeting occurrence, inner intuition or experience does not provide anything capable of determining the existence of the subject in time. The function of the third step in the argument is to make this purely negative point. It shows that we cannot "look within" for the permanent that is required in order to determine our existence in time.

D. Step 4

> Thus perception of this permanent is possible only through a *thing* outside me and not through the mere *representation* of a thing outside me; and consequently the determination of my existence in time is possible only through the existence of actual things which I perceive outside me.

Having eliminated inner intuition or experience as a possible source of this permanent, Kant here turns to the only remaining candidate; namely, outer intuition. Since 'outside me' must be taken in the empirical sense in order to characterize something intuited, and since space is the form of outer sense, the implication is that permanence must pertain to an object or objects in space. It certainly follows from this that the capacity to represent such objects is a necessary condition of the possibility of determining my existence in time. But if he is to refute the Cartesian skeptic, Kant cannot rest content with this rather modest conclusion. Instead, he must show that I actually experience or perceive, not merely imagine or believe that I perceive, such objects. This is precisely what Kant claims in the passage cited above. To be sure, he is careful to point out in the last of the three scholia attached to the argument that this claim does not entail that all my perceptions of outer objects must be veridical. In any given case I could be imagining rather than actually experiencing such objects. The essential point, however, is that whether in a particular instance I am experiencing or merely imagining is itself an empirical question, which can be intelligibly raised only against a presupposed background of actual experience. It is the latter that the skeptic denies and that Kant's argument attempts to establish. According to his own formulation of the project: "All that we have sought to prove is that inner experience in general is possible only through outer experience in general," (B278–79).

But has he proven it? This claim is obviously the crucial step in the argument, yet it confronts us in the text as a bald assertion without a trace of justification. The Cartesian skeptic might very well be willing to accept a weaker claim about an entailment relation between beliefs, and thus acknowledge the necessity of outer *representations*. What he would not grant is the key contention that this licenses a conclusion about actual *experience* or real *existence*. Moreover, it is clear from the note in the preface that Kant was well aware of this fact.

> To this proof it will probably be objected, that I am immediately conscious only of that which is in me, that is, of my *representation* of outer things; and consequently that it must still remain uncertain whether outside me there is anything corresponding to it, or not. [Bxl n.]

Perhaps the most important task confronting any interpretation of the argument of the Refutation of Idealism is to present the Kantian answer to this obvious retort. Unfortunately, this is not as easy as it might appear. In fact, if one considers the official argument of the *Critique,* the note from the preface, and the relevant sections of the Reflexionen, it seems possible to find two distinct lines of argument, which Kant himself never carefully distinguishes. Moreover, only one of these provides the basis for an adequate response to the skeptic, and even this one must be developed well beyond the point at which Kant leaves it. In what follows I shall sketch and discuss each of these in turn, beginning with the manifestly inadequate one.

This line of argument turns on the nature of outer sense. Its basic premise, which Kant formulates in the note in the preface, is that "outer sense is already a relation of intuition to something actual outside me." Since no one will deny that we at least seem to have an outer sense, that is, that we have representations of outer (spatial) objects, all that is necessary to refute the Cartesian skeptic is to demonstrate the incoherence of the suggestion that we might merely believe or imagine ourselves to have an outer sense. Kant regards this as equivalent to the claim that we have merely an outer imagination but not an outer sense. He expresses his basic response to such a claim in a footnote to the main text:

> It is clear, however, that in order even to imagine something as outer, that is, to present it to sense in intuition, we must already have an outer sense, and must thereby immediately distinguish the mere receptivity of an outer intuition from the spontaneity which characterizes every act of imagination. For should we merely be imagining an outer sense, the faculty of intuition, which is to be determined by the faculty of imagination, would itself be annulled. [B276–77]

This claim seems to be implicit in the actual argument of the *Critique* (in the move from *representation* to *thing* represented), and it reappears explicitly, in slightly different form, in the third scholium attached to the argument. In commenting on the possibility of merely imagining outer things (as in dreams or illusions), Kant remarks: "Such representation is merely the reproduction of previous outer perceptions, which, as has been shown, are possible only through the reality of outer objects" (B278). In addition, variations of the same basic theme are scattered throughout the Reflexionen.[7] Although these various formulations differ from one another in detail, at bottom they all reduce to the assertion of the incapacity of the imagination, either of itself or with the assistance of inner sense, to produce the representation of space or of things in space. Behind this assertion lies the doctrine of the total heterogeneity of inner and outer sense, from which Kant infers the incapacity of the former to produce the data of the latter.[8] Consequently, the mere fact that we have outer representations is taken as proof that we have an outer sense. Given the previously noted characterization of outer sense, this entails that the mind is affected by, and perceives, actually existing objects.

It is not necessary to pursue any further the details of this line of argument in order to recognize its inadequacy as the basis for an answer to the Cartesian skeptic. For one thing, the contention that we could not even imagine or dream about outer objects unless we had an outer sense is similar to one which Descartes himself entertains and rejects in the First Meditation. For another, it seems to be hopelessly intertwined with Kant's faculty psychology: it rests upon some dubious claims about the capacity (or lack thereof) of particular faculties to produce particular species of representations. There simply is no reason for the skeptic to accept these claims. But even if, for the sake of argument, they are accepted, the possibility still remains open that our representations of outer things are the results of some unknown "hidden faculty." It will be recalled that Descartes raises this very possibility in the Third Meditation in connection with his argument for the existence of God. Although Descartes denies that such a faculty could be the source of the Idea of God as a most perfect being, the Cartesian skeptic could easily respond to Kant at this point by suggesting the possibility that some such faculty might be the source of our representations of outer things.[9] In short, because of its dogmatic assumptions, the argument from the nature of outer representations cannot undermine the possibility raised by the skeptic that the contents of consciousness, that is, the sequence of "outer" representations, might be precisely as they in fact are, without there being anything external to the mind corresponding to these representations. The same can be said, *mutatis mutandis,* for contemporary versions of Cartesian skepticism, where the demon hypothesis is replaced by the brain in the tank and similar philosophical fantasies.

Fortunately, the second line of argument provides a more promising basis for a critique of such a position. It is also the one to which Kant refers when he claims that in it "the game played by idealism has been turned against itself, and with greater justice" (B276). This is so because, unlike the first, it is based upon a premise to which the idealist is presumably committed: I am conscious of my existence as determined in time, or equivalently, that I have inner *experience.* Perhaps Kant's most explicit statement of the essentials of this line of argument is contained in the note from the preface, immediately after the presentation of the anticipated retort to the claim about an actual permanent. In response to this object Kant writes:

> But through inner *experience* I am conscious of *my existence* in time (consequently also of its determinability in time), and this is more than to be conscious merely of my representation. It is identical with the *empirical consciousness of my existence,* which is determinable only through relation to something which, while bound up with my existence, is outside me. This consciousness of my existence in time is bound up in the way of identity with the consciousness of a relation to something outside me, and it is therefore experience not invention, sense not imagination, which inseparably connects this outside something with my inner sense. [Bxl n.]

Kant's main point here is that the consciousness of one's existence as determined in time is a genuine bit of empirical knowledge: it involves the knowledge of the existence of a particular thinking subject (oneself) and of the temporal order of its states. The subject is conscious of these states as its own, and through the consciousness of the determinate temporal order of these states it can determine its own existence in a single, universal time. Once again, it is assumed that the Cartesian skeptic accepts the genuineness of such consciousness, that he does not raise the possibility that one might merely imagine having inner experience. But since the skeptic does not doubt the reality of inner experience, it follows that he cannot doubt the reality of whatever can be shown to be a necessary condition of the possibility of this experience. We have seen in step 2, however, that the determination of time, and therefore the determination of the existence of anything in time, presupposes the perception of something permanent in space. The skeptic, therefore, cannot consistently doubt the reality of this perception; more precisely, he cannot, without contradicting his assumption about self-knowledge, doubt that he actually intuits, not merely imagines or believes that he intuits, enduring objects in space.

Admittedly, this is more of a sketch for a possible argument than a fully worked out argument, capable of answering the Cartesian skeptic. Considerable development and spelling out of details are necessary, if it is to become an adequate refutation. In particular, I think that the development, which Kant barely hints at in the Reflexionen and which I will not attempt here, would involve showing that one's body functions as the enduring object, with reference to which one's existence is determined in time.[10] Put roughly, the temporal order of one's mental states is determined by their correlation with one's bodily states, and through this connection one's existence is determined with respect to that of other objects in the "field of experience." I do not, however, wish to insist upon any of this here. The important point is only that, even in its embryonic form, this second line of argument is both distinct from and vastly superior to the first. Whereas the former involves a questionable claim about what must be presupposed in order to account for some of the representations that we do possess (outer representations), this one contends that a mode of experience or knowledge that is accepted by the skeptic is conditioned by, and inseparable from, another mode, which the skeptic does not accept. It thus provides us with a genuine reductio of the skeptic's position. Clearly, this is Kant's intent.

E. Step 5

Now consciousness (of my existence) in time is necessarily bound up with consciousness of the (condition of the) possibility of this time-determination; and it is therefore necessarily bound up with the existence of things outside me, as the condition of the time-determination. In other words, the consciousness of my existence is at the same time an immediate consciousness of the existence of other things outside me.

This marks the final step of the argument. In spite of appearances, it really does little more than make explicit the conclusion already arrived at. The reason one might think that something new is being claimed here is that Kant speaks of the consciousness of one's existence as determined in time as being "bound up with" (*verbunden mit*) and even as being "at the same time an immediate consciousness of the existence of other things outside me." Similarly, in the previously cited passage from the note in the preface, Kant contends that this consciousness is "bound up in the way of identity with the consciousness of a relation to something outside me." These remarks suggest that the two modes of consciousness are two poles or aspects of a single experience. In other words, Kant now seems to be claiming that there is no purely inner experience, which is surely different from claiming that outer experience is a necessary condition of the possibility of inner experience. While it is true that these claims are distinct, it is also the case that what appears here as a fresh claim is already implicit in the preceding analysis. Once again, the key point is that inner experience involves not merely a bare awareness of one's representations, but also the consciousness of one's existence as determined in time. The argument has shown that this consciousness requires a reference to something permanent, and that this permanent must be located in space. It therefore not only shows in a general way that the possibility of inner experience is conditioned by outer experience, it also shows that inner experience is, in fact, always correlated with outer experience. This is because the objects of both forms of experience exist in a single, universal time. It should also be noted, however, that the converse does not hold; that is, the possibility of outer experience is not, in a similar way, conditioned by inner experience. Since it provides the data necessary for the determinate representation of time, outer experience can be said to "wear the trousers." Thus, the Cartesian is in error in granting epistemic priority to inner experience or, as he would put it, to self-knowledge.

III. THE RETURN OF THE SKEPTIC

In addition to its schematic nature, the line of argument just presented seems to suffer from at least one major defect: it rests on the premise that we are conscious of our existence as determined in time, or equivalently, it presupposes the reality of inner experience. Since the Cartesian skeptic likewise accepts the premise, and since the argument is specifically directed against this form of skepticism, Kant cannot be criticized for making this assumption. Nevertheless, the fact that he does so raises the obvious question about the relevance of the argument to a more radical form of skepticism.[11] Such a hyper-skepticism would not only, like the Cartesian variety, doubt the reality of outer experience, it would also raise similar doubts about the whole sphere of inner experience and self-knowledge. Unless this form of skepticism can be refuted, the most that can be claimed for Kant's argument is that it shows that one cannot both assume the reality of inner experience and doubt that of outer experience.[12] This is not a trivial result in its own right, but it is somewhat less than one might hope for from an argument that is designed to remove "the scandal to philosophy and to human reason in general that the existence of things outside us . . . must be accepted merely on *faith,* and that if anyone thinks good to doubt their existence, we are unable to counter his doubts with a satisfactory proof" (Bxxxix n.).

It is not immediately apparent just what kind of criticism this premise is actually vulnerable to, but one intriguing possibility is an attack on the reality of time. This could take either a dogmatic or a skeptical form, depending on whether the reality of time is denied or simply made subject to doubt. We can, however, limit ourselves to the skeptical form. Clearly, if I could not know with certainty that time exists, then I could not attach any certainty to my consciousness of my existence as determined in time. The most that I could say is that I believe that I exist in time; but this belief would be just as dubitable as my belief that I have a body or that I perceive an external world.

The Kantian response to this line of attack turns on the distinction between transcendental and empirical reality. We have seen that Kant himself denies that time is real in the former sense; consequently, he has no quarrel with any philosopher making a similar claim. From this point of view, the problem with the skeptical position is that a mere doubt (as opposed to denial) of the reality of time is too weak. The situation is far different, however, with regard to the empirical reality of time. Even if one could deny or doubt that spatial objects, including one's own body, exist in time by denying or doubting that there are any such objects (the idealist's move), one cannot do the same with respect to "inner objects." If I am conscious of a succession of representations or mental states (a subjective succession), then, by that very fact, these items really do succeed one another in my consciousness. In other words, my consciousness of such a succession is, at the same time, a succession in my consciousness. But it is precisely the latter that is claimed to be known with certainty and that is sufficient to establish the empirical reality of time. Here, as in the usually discussed cases of incorrigibility, which involve one's present consciousness of being in a mental state, there is no room for doubt because the consciousness is self-certifying.

Interestingly enough, the same considerations also apply to the consciousness of coexistence. Suppose, for example, that I am having a pain-sensation during the time in which I am perceiving a strong light. I can perhaps doubt the existence of a physical source for my light perception and the existence of the body with which the pain sensation seems to be associated. I cannot, however, doubt the coexistence in my consciousness of these two mental states, any more than I can doubt the existence of either of them taken individually. Nor is this incompatible with Kant's thesis regarding the successive nature of apprehension. Once again, the point is that even in the case of a temporal order of "subjective objects," it is necessary to distinguish between the order of apprehension and the order apprehended. Thus, in reflecting upon the contents of my consciousness, I may first apprehend either the pain sensation or the light perception; nevertheless, in inner experience (which involves judgment) I am conscious of their coexistence. Moreover, this consciousness is both "objectively valid" (in the sense previously indicated) and self-validating. Insofar as I am conscious of their coexistence, they really coexist in my consciousness.

A skepticism about time might, however, be regarded as a rather extravagant tack to adopt against Kant's premise. A more likely strategy would be to raise doubts about the reliability of memory. This move gains plausibility from the fact that my consciousness of having a past history, which is itself based on memory, seems to be an essential component in my consciousness of my existence as determined in time. In fact, Kant is sometimes taken to be arguing in the Refutation of Idealism that it is *this* consciousness that requires outer experience.[13] But if this were Kant's position, he could hardly have regarded the premise in question as one that would be accepted as unproblematical by the Cartesian skeptic. Such a skeptic would find a claim about the reliability of memory just as dubitable as one about outer experience. On this interpretation, then, the reductio would never get off the ground. Admittedly, this does not prove that Kant did not construe the premise in this way. It does, however, suggest that such a reading should be accepted only as a last resort, after all other interpretations have been shown to fail.

Fortunately, this is not necessary. Clearly, my "recollection" of the past is part of my present consciousness: I am now conscious of myself as a person with certain "memories" and, more generally, with a determinate history. But it does not follow from this that I must be certain about these "memories" and this history in order to be certain about my present existence. After all, it is one thing for me to doubt whether my "recollection" of a past experience is veridical and quite another for me to doubt that I (Henry Allison) am now "recollecting" such an experience. Moreover, this present consciousness is itself a consciousness of my existence as determined in time. To put the same point somewhat differently: suppose, perchance, that I have just been created, together with my full complement of "memories" and beliefs about my past experience, by some contemporary analogue of the Cartesian demon. In that case all my judgments about my past would be manifestly false. Nevertheless, it would remain certain that I am conscious of myself as the presently existing subject who has these pseudo-memories and this pseudo-history. But this certainty is all that is required by the argument of the Refutation of Idealism.

Even granting this, however, the skeptic might still appeal to the dubitability of memory claims in order to undermine the certainty that presumably pertains to immediate self-awareness. An extreme view of this sort constitutes the first of four forms of skepticism distinguished by G. E. Moore in his well-known essay by that name. According to Moore's succinct formulation of the position, this form of skepticism asserts that "I never know with complete certainty anything whatever about *myself*. I do not know with certainty even that I am 'having a white percept', and I never have known any such thing."[14] In fact, all that can be asserted with certainty on this view are propositions of the form 'There is a white percept'.

Moore attributes this, as well as the other forms of skepticism distinguished in the essay, to Russell, and he judges it to rest essentially on Russell's contention that "the meaning of the word 'I' evidently depends on memory and expectation."[15] The point is that in making a claim about oneself as the subject of a present experience, one is implicitly assuming one's identity with a past and future self. But since there can be no certainty about the past, not to mention the future, there can be no certainty with respect to any judgment about oneself, even one concerning present experience. Underlying this entire analysis is an atomistic conception of consciousness, according to which the only contents of consciousness are a series of evanescent percepts or sense data, each of which is the object of a distinct, momentary awareness. This naturally gives rise to the question about the identity of the subject or subjects of these awarenesses. The answer forthcoming is that this identity must be inferred and that this inference relies essentially on memory. It is as if the subject of a white percept at t_2 must "remember" having also been the subject of a blue percept a moment earlier at t_1. Since the subject cannot be certain about this, it cannot be certain about its own identity.

Insofar as it raises doubts about the referent of the word 'I', this line of attack is reminiscent of the one which we have seen to be implicit in Kant's own critique of Descartes's cogito argument. Nevertheless, since it denies the possibility of any certainty with respect to the identity over time of the subject of experience, it constitutes a direct challenge to the joint Cartesian-Kantian premise of the Refutation of Idealism. It is, however, also a challenge that is easy to dismiss. In order to do so, we need only note that minimally, that is, under the hypothesis of a purely inner experience, consciousness involves not only a succession of representations (percepts or sense data), but also an awareness of this succession. In other words, it must contain the temporal dimension that Kant accounts for by characterizing time as the form of inner sense. We have seen that a consciousness of succession (even of "subjective objects") requires the unification of the successive items in a single consciousness, and that this entails the numerical identity of the I that is successively aware of the items unified in this consciousness. Consequently, the numerical identity of the I that is aware of the blue percept at t_1 with the one that is aware of the white percept of t_2 is not established by a fallible inference based on memory; it is, rather, recognized as a necessary condition of the possibility of the awareness of the succession of these two percepts.[16]

The misguided nature of a putative doubt about the ownership of present mental states can also be shown without appealing to any specifically Kantian doctrines. In fact, it is frequently argued that the only doubts that can be intelligibly raised about the ownership of mental states concern past, or "remembered," states, and these must be taken as doubts about whether a past mental state actually existed.[17] Thus, I can be uncertain whether I really had the headache yesterday, which I now recall having had while working on an earlier version of this argument. What I cannot be uncertain about is that I was the one who had that headache (assuming that it really existed). The fundamental point here is that I cannot be aware of a representation or mental state without also being aware of it as mine. That is to say, there are not, as the skeptic must assume there to be, two acts of awareness involved, one through which I become aware of a mental state, the other through which I recognize it as mine. To return to the example of the headache: I do not first perceive, or feel, that there is a headache, and then infer that it is mine (as if it could have been anyone else's). Rather, to become aware of the headache is to become aware of it as mine. Moreover, the same principle applies to a succession of mental states. Insofar as I am conscious of such a succession, for example, a headache followed by a white percept, I am aware of them both as pertaining to my numerically identical self. There is, therefore, no inference involved, no judgment of identity. To cite Sydney Shoemaker's apt dictum, "A judgment of identity can be made only when a question of identity can be sensibly asked."[18]

In spite of all this, Kant himself is sometimes thought to have entertained, if not advocated, a skepticism similar to the one just discussed. The relevant text is the First Edition version of the Third Paralogism. As usual, his target is the rational psychologist, this time the latter's assumption that one can infer the identity (personality) of a thinking substance from the necessary identity of the 'I think'. Kant attacks this thesis by sketching a logically possible scenario in which successive states of consciousness are somehow transferred from one substance to another, much as an elastic ball communicates its entire motion to a similar ball when it impinges upon it.[19] The idea is presumably that in such a situation the necessary identity of the I would be preserved, but there would be no identical person or thinking substance. This seems to support the skeptic because if, as the scenario stipulates, states of consciousness could be transferred from subject to subject, without any discernible difference, then there would be no certainty with respect to the identity of the subject.[20]

Nevertheless, it is highly implausible to construe the argument in this way, which assumes that the only alternatives open to Kant are dogmatism and skepticism. An essential feature of Kant's analysis is his caveat that such doubts can be raised only by an external observer, for whom I am an object of outer intuition; I cannot raise them about myself: "In my own consciousness, therefore, identity of person is unfailingly met with" (A362). The fact that a hypothetical observer can raise such doubts about my identity is enough to block the move to any metaphysical conclusions about the identity, or permanence, of the noumenal self, which is just what the rational psychologist affirms. Given our present anti-skeptical concerns, however, the main interest of the argument lies in the contention that these doubts can never affect the way in which the self is for itself. In order to grasp the full import of this, two points must be kept in mind. First, the kind of radical skepticism currently under consideration assumes a solipsistic standpoint, and thus cannot make use of any doubts that are generated only by supposing the existence of an outside observer, not to mention one equipped with outer intuition. Indeed, any such doubts would be self-defeating, for they would concede the main point at issue in the Refutation of Idealism. Second, although Kant is making a conceptual claim here, it is not a claim about "transcendental consciousness" or the merely "logical I." On the contrary, Kant refers specifically to "self-consciousness in time," which is equivalent to empirical self-consciousness. The claim is that my numerical identity throughout the time in which I am conscious of myself, that is, the identity of my phenomenal self, is not inferred, as the skeptic maintains, but is a "completely identical proposition of self-consciousness in time" (A362). From this it follows that I cannot intelligibly doubt (at least not without going beyond the resources of self-consciousness) my identity as the enduring subject of a determinate set of representations or mental states; for example, as the subject who has a blue percept at t_1, followed by a white percept and a pain sensation at t_2. To be conscious of my identity as such a subject, however, is precisely to be conscious of my existence as determined in time. Consequently, this consciousness is immune to the skeptical challenge.

In conclusion, I have argued in this section that the key first premise of the Refutation of Idealism is not subject to the typical skeptical challenge to the reliability of memory, because it does not itself rest upon any assumptions about the self's knowledge of its past states. I have further argued that attempts to undermine it by raising doubts about the reality of time or the ownership of mental states are to no avail. Finally, I have tried to show that Kant himself adumbrates a similar anti-skeptical line of argument in a controversial text where he is frequently thought to be doing precisely the opposite. Admittedly, this does not amount to a defense of the premise in question against any conceivable skeptical challenge. It does, however, at least require the skeptic to find a fresh basis for an attack on this premise.

15

Between Cosmology and Autonomy: Kant's Theory of Freedom in the *Critique of Pure Reason*

One of the most perplexing aspects of Kant's treatment of the problem of freedom is the radical gulf separating the cosmological context of the Third Antinomy, in which the problem is initially posed, from the moral context in which the significance of freedom is fully realized. According to Kant's own retrospective account of the situation in the *Critique of Practical Reason,* the First Critique establishes the possibility of transcendental freedom through the resolution of the Third Antinomy, while the Second Critique establishes its reality by showing its necessary connection with the moral law, which itself has the status of a "fact of reason." The moral law thus becomes the *ratio cognoscendi* of freedom, since it is through the consciousness of this law that one becomes aware of one's freedom, while freedom functions as the *ratio essendi* of the moral law.[1]

This account, however, reflects a moral philosophy that differs considerably from the one to which Kant himself adhered in 1781. In particular, it reflects Kant's "discovery" of the principle of autonomy, that is, the presumed capacity of the will to be a law to itself and to act for the sake of the law, which he first clearly articulates in the *Groundwork of the Metaphysic of Morals* in 1785.[2] Accordingly, if one were to limit oneself to the *Critique of Pure Reason,* assuming by way of a thought experiment that the subsequent ethical works were never written, a considerably different picture of Kant's conception of freedom would emerge. This conception would, of course, still be linked to the cosmological dispute of the Third Antinomy, but it would also be connected to a view of human agency in general rather than merely to moral agency.

It is just such a thought experiment which I propose to conduct in the present chapter. In so doing, I hope to show that the *Critique of Pure Reason* contains at least the outlines of a theory of human agency (practical freedom) that does not rest upon an appeal to any specifically "moral" facts and that constitutes an essential ingredient in the overall Kantian treatment of self-knowledge. We are not only conscious of ourselves as epistemic subjects, the owners of representations, we are also conscious of ourselves as agents, capable of resisting inclinations and of choosing between alternative courses of action. Kant, therefore, must elucidate this consciousness, and this, I contend, is precisely what the account of practical freedom in the *Critique of Pure Reason* is designed to do.

This chapter is divided into four parts. The first discusses the argument of the Third Antinomy and its relevance to the problem of human freedom. The second argues that, in spite of a good deal of opinion to the contrary, Kant adheres to the same conception of freedom in the Dialectic and the Canon. The third analyzes this conception of freedom and its connection with transcendental idealism. The fourth examines Kant's controversial claim that the predictability of actions on the basis of causal laws is compatible with the imputation of these same actions to agents as products of practical freedom.

I. FREEDOM AND THE THIRD ANTINOMY:
THE COSMOLOGICAL CONTEXT

The cosmological conception of freedom with which Kant is initially concerned in the Third Antinomy is characterized as "transcendental freedom," which is defined as "the power [*Vermögen*] of beginning a state *spontaneously* [*von selbst*]" (A533/B561). This is contrasted with "causality according to laws of nature" or, more simply, mechanistic causality, which governs the connection of events in time.[3] According to this conception, familiar to us from the Second Analogy, every occurence has an antecedent cause; but this cause, or, as Kant sometimes terms it, the "causality of the cause," is itself an occurrence in time. Consequently, it too must be determined by an antecedent cause, ad infinitum. Since both parties to the antinomical dispute assume the exclusive reign of mechanistic causality within the world, the point at issue is whether it is also necessary, or even possible, to appeal to the other mode of causality (transcendental freedom) in order to conceive a first beginning of the world. In other words, the question is whether or not there can be a first cause or prime mover;[4] and this is surely a cosmological question, distinct from the question of the reality of human freedom. The thesis affirms the necessity of appealing to such a cause in order to find the required resting place for reason (the Idea of the unconditioned). Correlatively, the antithesis denies both the necessity and the possibility of doing so. It affirms instead that all causation (without exception) must be of the mechanistic type; in so doing it commits itself to the assumption of an infinite causal chain.

Fortunately, the remoteness of the dispute from the main concern of this chapter relieves us of the need to examine the arguments for the thesis and antithesis in any detail. Very roughly, then, the argument for the thesis goes as follows: (1) According to the assumption to be repudiated, "everything which *takes place* presupposes a preceding state upon which it invariably follows according to a rule." This is simply a restatement of the causal principle. (2) Since, *ex hypothesi*, this applies to every state, it must also apply to the "causality of its cause." In other words, every cause must be construed as an occurrence in time, which, as such, requires its own cause. (3) On this assumption, then, there would never be a first or absolute beginning, which means that there would be no completeness in the series of conditions. (4) But if this were so, then there would be no cause or ground sufficient to determine the whole, that is, no adequate explanation of the totality of appearances. This, however, contradicts the principle of sufficient reason.[5] (5) Consequently, in addition to "causality according to laws of nature," or mechanistic causality, it is also necessary to assume a "causality through freedom," or transcendental freedom, at least with respect to a first cause.

Just as with the other Antinomies, the argument for the antithesis is verificationist in nature. Moreover, it rests almost entirely on the argument of the Analytic, specifically the First and Second Analogies. Again, very roughly, it goes as follows: (1) Let us assume that there is freedom in the transcendental sense, that is, "a power of absolutely beginning a state, and therefore also of absolutely beginning a series of consequences of that state." (2) It follows from this that a series of occurrences has its first or absolute beginning in this spontaneous cause, but this spontaneous cause itself must have an absolute beginning; that is to say, "there will be no antecedent through which this act, in taking place, is determined in accordance with fixed laws." This, of course, follows from the very definition of transcendental freedom. (3) But the problem is that we have learned from the Analytic that "every beginning of action presupposes a state of the not yet existing cause." Here is where the "all change is alteration" principle of the First Analogy comes into play. The point is that in the case of an absolute beginning, we have, *ex hypothesi,* an act which cannot be connected to the antecedent condition of an agent. (4) This, however, violates the conditions of the unity of experience in just the way in which the notion of a creation *ex nihilo* was shown to do in the discussion of the First Analogy. (5) Consequently, there can be no transcendental freedom, that is, no spontaneous act, and all causality is in accordance with laws of nature.

Of greater significance than the arguments themselves is the manner in which Kant endeavors to resolve the Antinomy. In contrast to the first two, or mathematical, Antinomies, where both thesis and antithesis are shown to be false, Kant suggests that here and in the Fourth, the so-called Dynamical Antinomies, it is possible for both thesis and antithesis to be true.[6] The difference stems from the manner in which the regress from conditioned to condition occurs in the two cases. In the Mathematical Antinomies the conditioned and its conditions are always homogeneous; that is, they are all members of the same spatiotemporal series. Thus, it seems necessary to assume that this series has either a finite or an infinite number of members, which means that the opposing claims are regarded as contradictories.

In the Third Antinomy, by contrast, the regress is from effect to cause or ground. Here the elements can, but need not, be homogeneous, for it is at least conceivable that there is a cause or ground of an event that is not itself sensible, that is, not part of the series of appearances. As nonsensible, such a cause or ground would have to be called "intelligible." The spontaneous, transcendentally free cause affirmed in the thesis is a cause of precisely that sort. Correlatively, the argument of the antithesis, with is verificationist appeal to the conditions of possible experience, really rules out the possibility of such a cause only within the phenomenal world. The possibility is, therefore, left open that both sides may be correct: the thesis, with its assertion of an intelligible, transcendentally free first cause of the whole series of appearances; the antithesis, with its refusal to admit such a cause within the series. This does not prove that the thesis claim is correct; Kant, however, does not claim that it does. All that he claims to have shown is that causality through freedom is not incompatible with mechanistic causality. Presumably, this suffices to resolve the Antinomy because it shows that the conflict rests on an illusion.[7]

It seems obvious, however, that by analyzing the dispute in this way Kant effectively undermines his claim to have presented a genuine antinomy. To be sure, here, as well as in the Mathematical Antinomies, we begin with an apparent contradiction and end up by seeing that it is merely apparent. To that extent the two situations are parallel. Nevertheless, in the case of the Mathematical Antinomies, the thesis and antithesis are in direct conflict because they make incompatible claims about the same "object." Here, by contrast, the two sides are shown to be merely arguing at cross purposes.[8] In fact, since the thesis admits the role of mechanistic causality within nature and insists only on its supplementation by causality through freedom in order to "think the whole," the actual outcome of Kant's analysis is that the antithesis is unjustified in its move from the denial of the possibility of the latter mode of causality within the sensible world to the denial in general. It is here rather than in the thesis that we find the locus of the "illusion."

The illusion, of course, rests upon the "common assumption" that appearances are things in themselves; the acceptance of this assumption leads directly to the denial of freedom. As Kant puts it, "If appearances are things in themselves, freedom cannot be upheld. Nature will then be the complete and sufficient determining cause of every event" (A536/B564). Although transcendental realism remains the villain, the situation differs radically from that of the Mathematical Antinomies, since it does not allow for an analogous, indirect argument for transcendental idealism.[9] One cannot, after all, contend that transcendental idealism is true simply because, in contrast to transcendental realism, it allows us to regard transcendental freedom and mechanistic causality as compatible with one another. Since the reality of mechanistic causality is not in dispute, that argument requires an independent guarantee of the reality, or at least the real possibility, of transcendental freedom. Kant does argue in this way in the *Critique of Practical Reason;* and he can do so because he there contends that the reality of transcendental freedom is "deduced" from the moral law as a "fact of reason."[10] No such claim is forthcoming, however, in the *Critique of Pure Reason.*

This brings us to the question of what the Third Antinomy really has to do with human freedom and with the problem of reconciling *this* freedom with the mechanism of nature. The issue is introduced in a preliminary way in the observation on the thesis, which begins by remarking that transcendental freedom or, more properly, the transcendental Idea of freedom, constitutes part, but not all, of the ordinary, or "psychological," concept of freedom. The basic point seems to be that the act of choice is commonly thought to involve an element of spontaneity, similar to the spontaneity affirmed in the thesis in connection with a first cause. In other words, the transcendental Idea provides a model for conceiving of human choice or agency. It is further suggested that once this conception of causality is allowed in connection with a first cause of the world, "it is now also permissible for us to admit within the course of the world different series as capable in their causality of beginning of themselves, and so to attribute to their substances a power of acting from freedom" (A450/B478). This claim is justified by the introduction of a distinction between a "beginning in time" and a "beginning in causality." By the former is meant simply a first event, or an event not preceded by another event, and by the latter the institution of a new causal series, or a series which does not stand in any causal connection with an antecedent state of affairs. The point here is that since an act of transcendental freedom, which constitutes an "absolute beginning," is thought as a beginning only in the latter sense, there is no contradiction in assuming the possibility of a number of such acts within the world. Moreover, it is suggested that ordinary cases of voluntary action, such as my "free" decision to rise from my chair, are to be conceived in just this way.

Although some aspects of this preliminary account, particularly the modeling function assigned to the transcendental Idea of freedom, are central to Kant's own position, the general tenor of these remarks reflect the dogmatic standpoint of the thesis more than they do Kant's own critical view. Lest there be any doubt about this, we need only note that the observation on the antithesis quite correctly points out that the move from the extra- to the intramundane appeal to transcendental freedom is a non sequitur. Given this, it would seem as if we must look elsewhere than the Antinomy itself for an accurate picture of Kant's own view on the matter. In fact, we must look to Kant's account of the connection between transcendental and practical freedom. It is to this topic that we now turn.

II. TRANSCENDENTAL AND PRACTICAL FREEDOM: THE TWO ACCOUNTS

Kant discusses the connection between transcendental and practical freedom in two distinct places in the *Critique*. The first and best known of these accounts is in the Dialectic. The second and frequently ignored account is in the Canon of Pure Reason. The situation is further complicated by the fact that these two accounts seem to differ from one another in significant ways. This, in turn, raises doubt about the coherence of Kant's whole treatment of freedom in the *Critique of Pure Reason*.

In the Dialectic, transcendental freedom is described in the manner previously noted: as the "power [*Vermögen*] of beginning a state spontaneously [*von selbst*]." As already noted, Kant also contends that freedom, so construed, is a "pure transcendental Idea," neither derivable from nor referable to any object that can be given in experience. By contrast, practical freedom, the sense of freedom that is directly relevant to the understanding of human action and agency, is defined as the "will's independence of coercion through sensuous impulses" (*die Unabhänglichkeit der Willkür von den Nötigung durch Antriebe der Sinnlichkeit*) (A534/B562). Kant attempts to clarify this by means of a distinction between a *pathologically affected* and a *pathologically necessitated* will. The former includes any will that is affected by sensuous motives (*Bewegursachen der Sinnlichkeit*), and this includes all finite wills. The point is that not every will that is pathologically affected is also necessitated, or determined; this applies only to the animal will (*arbitrium brutum*), not to the human will, which is characterized as an *arbitrium sensitivum,* but none the less *liberum*. About the connection between these two senses of freedom Kant writes: "It should especially be noted that the practical concept of freedom is based on this *transcendental* Idea, and that in the latter lies the real source of the difficulty by which the question of the possibility of freedom has always been beset" (A533/B561). In an apparent reinforcement of this point, he later adds, "The denial of transcendental freedom must, therefore, involve the elimination of all practical freedom" (A534/B562).

As the further discussion of practical freedom makes clear, the defining characteristic of an *arbitrium liberum* is its rationality; such a will is capable of choosing a course of action on the basis of general rules or principles, rather than merely responding in a quasi-mechanical fashion to stimuli. Moreover, it is precisely in virtue of this rational capacity that such a will is able to resist determination by inclination. The capacity to act on the basis of reasons and the freedom from determination by inclination can thus be construed as the positive and negative aspects of the concept of a practically free will. Although this account is reminiscent of the well-known distinction which Kant later draws between a positive and a negative concept of freedom,[11] it is important not to be misled by the similarity. First, in the later version, the positive concept of freedom is equated with autonomy, that is, "the property which the will has to be a law to itself,"[12] not simply rationality. Second, rationality here must be taken in a very broad sense; even a person who acts on the basis of "irrational," that is, imprudent, self-defeating, or morally pernicious, principles is rational in the sense that is relevant to the notion of practical freedom.

The reason why this point is so frequently lost sight of is that Kant develops his account of a rational, practically free will in terms of the role of an imperative in determining choice. His doctrine is that a practically free will is one that is capable of deciding in virtue of the recognition of an "ought," that is, in virtue of the consciousness of some general rule or principle of action, which is then applied to a given situation. It is crucial to realize, however, that "ought" here does not have an exclusively ethical connotation. On the contrary, it encompasses prudential as well as moral rules for action. In the language of Kant's fully developed moral philosophy, it includes hypothetical as well as categorical imperatives.[13]

In the Canon, Kant describes practical freedom in substantially the same terms. As before, he introduces the conception by distinguishing between animal and human (free) will. The former is characterized as one that can be "pathologically determined," and the latter as one that can be "determined independently of sensuous impulses, and therefore through motives which are represented only by reason." He further adds that "everything which is bound up with this will, whether as ground or consequence, is entitled practical" (A802/B830). Similarly, practical freedom is regarded positively as the capacity to act on the basis of the recognition of an "ought"; and once again, this is not construed in exclusively moral terms. In fact, this aspect of Kant's position is much clearer in the Canon, where he explains how practical freedom is manifested in nonmoral contexts.

> For the human will is not determined by that alone which stimulates, that is, immediately affects the senses; we have the power to overcome the impressions on our faculty of sensuous desire, by calling up representations of what, in a more indirect manner, is useful or injurious. But these considerations, as to what is desirable in respect of our whole state, that is, as to what is good and useful, are based on reason. [A802/B830]

The only hint of a discrepancy between these two accounts of practical freedom concerns Kant's claim in the Canon that "(the fact of) practical freedom can be proved through experience" (*Die praktische Freiheit kann durch Erfahrung beweisen werden*) (A802/B830). And again, "we thus through experience know practical freedom to be one of the causes in nature, namely to be a causality of reason in the determination of the will" (A803/B831). These claims have no precise parallel in the Dialectic. Moreover, as we shall see in the next section, since Kant holds that practical freedom includes an element of spontaneity, he cannot, strictly speaking, claim that we "experience" ourselves as practically free. Nevertheless, it is also clear from both accounts that he regards the capacity of the will to resist inclination and to act on the basis of imperatives as a "fact" of which we can become conscious in much the same way as we can become conscious of our capacity to think.[14] Even if it does not count as "experience" in the technical Kantian sense, such consciousness can be regarded as sufficient to establish the reality of practical (but not transcendental) freedom; and this is the main point of the passages from the Canon. Consequently, it seems reasonable to conclude that there is no substantial conflict between the accounts of practical freedom contained in the two texts.

The same can be said about their respective characterizations of transcendental freedom. In the Dialectic, transcendental freedom is defined as absolute spontaneity, and this is understood in essentially negative terms as a causal power that is itself independent of determination by antecedent causes. Since his concern in the Canon is exclusively with practical freedom, he does not define transcendental freedom at all; but he does remark in passing that "Transcendental freedom demands the independence of this reason in respect of its causality in beginning a series of appearances from all determining causes in the sensible world" (A803/B831). This suggests that the absolute spontaneity and independence from everything sensible, which is the defining characteristic of transcendental freedom, is regarded specifically as the spontaneity and independence of reason in determining the will. In other words, the Canon contains an application or specification of the conception of transcendental freedom contained in the Dialectic, not an alternative conception.

The compatibility question does arise, however, regarding the connection between transcendental and practical freedom in the two accounts. The Dialectic explicitly affirms the dependence of practical on transcendental freedom: it states that "the practical concept of freedom is based on this transcendental Idea," and even that "the denial of transcendental freedom must, therefore, involve the elimination of all practical freedom." By contrast, the Canon explicitly divorces these two conceptions. Since Kant is there concerned only with practical freedom, he states that he will simply leave aside "that other transcendental meaning which cannot be empirically made use of in the explanation of appearances, but is itself a problem for reason" (A801–02/B829–30). And, after claiming that reason provides imperatives which can be made into objective laws of freedom and which tell us "what ought to happen," he remarks:

> Whether reason is not, in the actions through which it prescribes laws, itself again determined by other influences, and whether that which, in relation to sensuous impulses, is entitled freedom, may not, in relation to higher and more remote operating causes, be nature again, is a question which in the practical field does not concern us, since we are demanding of reason nothing but the *rule* of conduct; it is a merely speculative question, which we can leave aside so long as we are considering what ought or ought not to be done. [A803 / B831]

This passage, which is followed immediately by the claim that "we . . . through experience know practical freedom to be one of the causes in nature," is the locus of the difficulty. Kant's main point here is obviously that from the practical standpoint, where the question is simply what one ought to do, the concerns are solely with the rule of action and with reason, as the source of rules and imperatives. Thus, theoretical questions about what might be termed the "transcendental status" of our practically free acts do not arise. So far there is nothing particularly problematical. The problem arises, however, with the further suggestion that the reality of practical freedom is not threatened by the possibility that the rules of action and the incentives for following these rules might be traceable to our sensuous nature, and, therefore, that "that which in relation to sensuous impulses, is entitled freedom, may . . . in relation to higher and more remote operating causes, be nature again." Since, if the latter were the case, we would not be free in the transcendental sense, it is difficult to avoid the conclusion that Kant is here maintaining that practical freedom would remain in place even if there were no transcendental freedom. Such a conclusion, however, seems to stand in blatant contradiction to the doctrine of the Dialectic.

Interestingly enough, Kant also seems to maintain in the Canon that the ultimate reducibility of freedom to nature is compatible with morality, which must be the case if the question of transcendental freedom is of no practical, or moral, relevance. To be sure, he does distinguish between moral and pragmatic laws, and he does maintain that the former, but not the latter, are "pure and determined completely *a priori*" (A800 / B828). This, however, need mean only that the moral laws themselves, qua laws, are not derived from a consideration of what will yield happiness. In this strictly epistemic sense they are independent of sensibility; but this is quite distinct from the claim that the will, in acting in light of such laws, must (or can) be motivated by respect for law as such. The latter doctrine, which is the keystone of Kant's fully developed ethical theory, is incompatible with the reducibility of freedom to nature and, therefore, with the denial of transcendental freedom. Nevertheless, far from maintaining any such doctrine in the Canon, Kant asserts instead that, apart from the postulation of God and a future life, "reason would have to regard moral laws as empty figments of the brain" (A811/B839). And again, in a notorious passage, "Thus without a God and without a world invisible to us now but hoped for, the glorious ideas of morality are indeed objects of approval and admiration, but not springs of purpose and action" (A813/B841).[15] Given such an ethical position, it is not surprising to find that Kant is not concerned about the reality of transcendental freedom.[16]

These considerations have led many of the interpreters who have concerned themselves with the Canon at all to find two distinct and incompatible theories of freedom at work in the *Critique of Pure Reason*. A version of the "patchwork thesis," long familiar to the students of the Transcendental Deduction, is thus introduced into the discussion of freedom. According to this thesis, the Canon account is "precritical," containing a theory of freedom which reflects an early stage in the development of Kant's moral philosophy. Correlatively, the Dialectic account is regarded as fully "critical," and so as in accord with the moral philosophy articulated in the *Groundwork of the Metaphysics of Morals* and the *Critique of Practical Reason*.[17] By this means the *Critique of Pure Reason* is brought into harmony with the later ethical writings, but only at the cost of admitting a fundamental contradiction within the *Critique* itself.

It must be emphasized, however, that this interpretation rests almost entirely upon a particular reading of Kant's contention that "the denial of transcendental freedom must . . . involve the elimination of all practical freedom." Kant, on this reading, is taken to be saying that the human will is free in the practical sense if and only if it is also free in the transcendental sense. Such a reading might very well be the natural one; it certainly agrees with what Kant says in the *Critique of Practical Reason*.[18] Nevertheless, it is not the only possible reading. It is also possible to take Kant to be affirming a necessary connection between the *concept* of practical freedom and the transcendental Idea, rather than between the reality of the two types of freedom. In fact, this is precisely what Kant does say when he remarks that "the practical concept of freedom is based on this *transcendental* Idea." If we take this seriously, then Kant's point is that the conceivability of practical freedom necessarily involves a reference to the transcendental Idea. In Kantian terms, the Idea of transcendental freedom has a regulative function with respect to the conception of practical freedom. This is in accord with the modeling function assigned to the Idea in the observation of the thesis of the Third Antinomy. It is also compatible with the Canon, since it leaves open the possibility that we are free in the practical, but not the transcendental, sense. In what follows I intend to argue that this is, in fact, Kant's position in the Dialectic, and that this provides the key to the understanding of the First Critique's conception of practical freedom.

III. IDEALITY AND SPONTANEITY:
THE DOCTRINE OF THE DIALECTIC

If we are to understand the account of the relationship between practical and transcendental freedom contained in the Dialectic, we must begin with a further consideration of the metaphysical framework in which the whole discussion is enmeshed. As already noted, this framework is transcendental idealism, and Kant's treatment of the topic reflects his concern to establish a connection between the problem of human freedom and the cosmological dispute dealt with in the Third Antinomy. His general strategy is to suggest that just as transcendental idealism makes it possible to resolve the Antinomy by finding a "transcendental location" for the concept of intelligible causality or transcendental freedom in the noumenal world,[19] so, too, it establishes the conceivability (although not the actuality) of human freedom. This extraordinary step is deemed necessary because, even though the ordinary concept of human freedom (psychological or practical) is for the most part empirical, it contains an essential nonempirical or transcendental component; namely, spontaneity. Accordingly, room must be found for this spontaneity alongside mechanistic causality; and, so the argument goes, this can be accomplished only by means of an appeal to the transcendental distinction. The distinction resolves the problem by making it conceivable that the very same actions, which when considered as appearances are connected to other appearances according to empirical laws, might, when considered from another point of view, be thought to have grounds that are not appearances.[20]

Kant relates this very general and abstract point to the specific issue of the conceivability of human freedom by contrasting an empirical and an intelligible character. Exactly how this contrast is to be understood, both here and in the other texts in which it appears, is undoubtedly one of the more perplexing questions of Kant interpretation.[21] For present purposes, however, it should suffice to regard it simply as the causality or agency version of the phenomenal-noumenal distinction. Since Kant intends the term 'character' to designate a universal property of efficient causes, that is, "a law of its causality, without which it would not be an efficient cause" (A539/B568), the contrast between an empirical and an intelligible character is between two distinct ways in which the causal activity of an agent can be considered or, if one prefers, between two descriptions under which it can be taken. As such, the distinction is completely general and has no specifically psychological or anthropological sense.[22] To be sure, Kant also applies this distinction to the causal agent (the subject of causality), and talks about this subject as having both an empirical and an intelligible character. Once again, however, there is no indication, at least in the initial discussion, that this subject is to be conceived of in psychological terms, that is, as a person.

To consider a subject and its causality according to its empirical character is to consider it as part of the phenomenal world. Not surprisingly, Kant insists that when a subject is considered in this way, there is no possibility of ascribing freedom to it. Considering a subject in its intelligible character, which is required if one is to conceive of it as a free agent, turns out to be a much more complex and mysterious procedure, but the general idea is that we proceed just as we do when "we are constrained to think a transcendental object as underlying appearances, though we know nothing of what it is in itself" (A540 / B563). Given what we have already learned about Kant's conception of the transcendental object, this can mean only that we form our conception of the putative intelligible character of an agent by stripping away all those features which pertain to its empirical character. Since considered in this way the subject would not "stand under any conditions of time," it follows that we could no longer speak meaningfully of something happening in or to this subject, and thus of its being determined by antecedent conditions. Kant expresses this in cryptic terms:

> In this subject no *action* would *begin* or *cease,* and it would not, therefore, have to conform to the law of the determination of all that is alterable in time, namely, that everything *which happens* must have its cause in the *appearances* which precede it. [A540 / B568]

By means of this *via reductionis*[23] we arrive at the notion of a causal activity not subject to the conditions of time, which is precisely what is required by the transcendental Idea of freedom. This whole line of analysis, however, raises two obvious and closely related problems. One is that this account of an intelligible character is purely analytic. It tells us, in negative terms, how such a character must be conceived by contrasting it with the familiar thought of an empirical character, but it does not provide an alternative positive characterization. The other is that the distinction can be applied to every action or event, and, therefore, to every subject. After all, given the generality of the transcendental distinction, every occurrence can, in principle at least, be considered in relation to its transcendental ground. Consequently, the appeal to this distinction does not make it possible to delimit a class of actions or events which, in some determinate sense, are characterizable in terms of a free or intelligible causality. On the contrary, the analysis seems to lead to the absurd result that in order to conceive of freedom anywhere we must be ready to conceive of it everywhere.[24]

Fortunately, this objection is not as damaging as it appears, for Kant was perfectly aware of the problem and addressed himself specifically to it. Thus, while admitting that in principle every occurrence can have some unspecified transcendental ground, he insists that this consideration becomes relevant only when we are actually constrained to think of a kind of causality which cannot be characterized in empirical terms. Then, and only then, does the transcendental distinction come into play.

> Whatever in an object of the senses is not itself appearance, I entitle *intelligible*. If, therefore, that which in the sensible world must be regarded as appearance has in itself a faculty which is not an object of sensible intuition, but through which it can be the cause of appearances, the *causality* of this being can be regarded from two points of view. Regarded as the causality of a thing in itself, it is *intelligible* in its *action;* regarded as the causality of an appearance in the world of sense, it is *sensible* in its *effects.* We should therefore have to form both an empirical and an intellectual concept of the causality of the faculty of such a subject, and to regard both as referring to one and the same effect. [A538 / B566]

Although he does not mention it, it is clear that what Kant has in mind here is the human will with its practical freedom. As the causal power of a sensible being (man), the effects of the will are manifested in the phenomenal world; but the power itself, as involving spontaneity, is non-sensible. The basic idea behind this has already been discussed: in willing, as in thinking, we have an activity of which we can become conscious, but which, since it involves spontaneity, cannot be "experienced" in the strict Kantian sense of the term. Rather than spelling this out, Kant introduces the previously noted contrast between an empirical and intelligible character. The result is that the analysis remains at the same high level of abstraction, creating the impression that it has no specific application to human agency. Kant, however, finally gets to the point in an important and well-known passage:

> Let us apply this to experience. Man is one of the appearances of the sensible world, and in so far one of the natural causes the causality of which must stand under empirical laws. Like all other things in nature, he must have an empirical character. This character we come to know through the powers and faculties which he reveals in his actions. In lifeless, or merely animal, nature we find no ground for thinking that any faculty is conditioned otherwise than in a merely sensible manner. Man, however, who knows all the rest of nature solely through the senses, knows himself also through pure apperception; and this, indeed, in acts and inner determinations which he cannot regard as impressions of the senses. He is thus to himself, on the one hand phenomenon, and on the other hand, in respect of certain faculties the action of which cannot be ascribed to the receptivity of sensibility, a purely intelligible object. We entitle these faculties understanding and reason. The latter, in particular, we distinguish in a quite peculiar and special way from all empirically conditioned powers. For it views its objects exclusively in the light of ideas, and in accordance with them determines the understanding, which then proceeds to make an empirical use of its own similarly pure concepts. [A546–47 / B574–75]

The most striking feature of this passage is the claim that man "*knows* himself also through pure apperception" (italics mine). This suggests that through apperception we somehow obtain knowledge of ourselves as spontaneous, noumenal beings, or at least as beings with an intelligible character. The obvious problem is that this stands in blatant contradiction to Kant's official account of self-knowledge. But, really, we need not take Kant to be doing anything more than making the by now familiar point that apperception provides a consciousness of the spontaneity of thought (both of understanding and reason). This, we have seen, involves an awareness of something nonsensible, or nonexperienceable, which cannot be accounted for in terms of the mechanism of nature or the empirical character of the subject; and this suffices to provide a foothold in self-consciousness for the notion of an intelligible character. Man is now seen to be for himself (not merely for the transcendental philosopher) a "purely [blosse] intelligible object." As the German term suggests, however, this 'purely intelligible object' is better described as a "merely intelligible object," that is, one which can be thought but which cannot be given in intuition. Consequently, the upshot of the matter is that while we can indeed become aware of something intelligible, namely, the spontaneity of thinking, which we connect with the idea of an intelligible character, we cannot lay claim to any knowledge of this character or of the noumenal subject to which it belongs.

The connection between the thinking and the acting subject is made in the next paragraph, which begins with the sentence, "That this [diese] reason has causality, or that we at least represent it to ourselves as having causality, is evident from the *imperatives* which in all practical matters [allein Praktischen] we impose as rules upon our executive powers [ausübenden Kräften]" (A547 / B575).[25] There are several things to be said about this sentence, which touches upon virtually every aspect of Kant's theory of practical freedom. First, the suggestion that we impose imperatives in "all practical matters" and that this imposition is always regarded as an expression of the "causality" of reason underscores the previously emphasized point that Kant's conception of practical freedom is not simply a conception of moral agency. The "practical matters" to which Kant refers include but are not limited to moral decisions, just as the rules include but are not limited to moral rules.

Second, the sentence indicates that although Kant identifies theoretical and practical reason (diese Vernunft) and holds that one and the same spontaneity is operative in both thinking and acting, he nevertheless distinguishes between the consciousness which we have of ourselves as thinking subjects (apperception) and the consciousness of ourselves as agents. Thus, in spite of the fact that Kant sometimes seems to suggest that our freedom can be established simply by reflection on our rationality,[26] this freedom cannot be identified with the practical freedom which we assign ourselves in our status as agents. Agency includes, but involves more than, a capacity to think.[27] It also includes a capacity to set goals, to adopt a course of action on the basis of these goals, and to resist the pull of inclinations which lure us in directions opposed to these goals. In short, it involves not merely reason, but a "causality of reason." We cannot, however, infer from the mere fact that a subject has reason, that this reason has any causal power or executive force; that is to say, we cannot infer that the subject has an *arbitrium liberum.*

A similar point is made by Sellars when he remarks that for all that can be gleaned from the spontaneity of conceptualizing mind (the activity of synthesis), it is perfectly possible to construe the human mind as a complex computer. So construed, the mind would be thought of as a kind of "noumenal mechanism," which is programmed to follow a set routine (conceptualization in accordance with the categories) whenever the appropriate "input" (sensible data) is received. Such a capacity would still count as "spontaneity," but only in a very limited and relative sense. Certainly, the possession of spontaneity in this sense would not suffice to characterize the subject as a free agent, much less a person. Moreover, Sellars also suggests, and I think correctly, that this fact explains why Kant refers to the thinking subject as the "I or he or it (the thing) which thinks." His point is that the consciousness of thinking does not suffice to establish that the thinking subject is anything more than an *automaton spirituale* or *cogitans,* that is, a thing which thinks.[28]

For our purposes, however, the most significant aspect of the sentence is Kant's weakening of the straightforward claim that reason has causality by the interjection of the caveat "or that we at least represent it to ourselves as having causality." Kant here seems to be entertaining the possibility that our consciousness of agency or practical freedom might somehow be illusory, and this *would* conflict with the Canon as well as with most of what he has to say on the topic in the Dialectic.[29] The conflict can be avoided, however, if we take Kant to be suggesting that even though reason is capable of setting goals and determining action in the sense already indicated, it might still be the case that reason is governed in the goals which it sets by our sensuous nature. Such a possibility obviously calls to mind Hume's well-known dictum, "Reason is and ought to be the slave of the passions."[30] Even in 1781, Kant would undoubtedly have rejected the latter part of this claim, but it is by no means certain that he would have ruled out the possibility that the former is true. On the contrary, an agnosticism about this feature of our "intelligible character" represents the authentic critical position, at least if one abstracts from the appeal to the moral law as a "fact of reason." But even in the face of such an agnosticism, it can still be maintained that the will is free in the practical sense.

What is needed here is a distinction between an absolute and a merely relative or conditioned spontaneity of the will. Kant himself does not explicitly draw such a distinction in the *Critique,* but there are clear intimations of it elsewhere in the Kantian corpus.[31] Absolute spontaneity is, of course, precisely what is thought in the transcendental Idea of freedom, and is presupposed by the principle of autonomy. It is the spontaneity of a will for which pure reason is practical. This is the kind of spontaneity toward which Kant assumes an agnostic stance in the Dialectic. Relative spontaneity characterizes the will of a rational agent for whom reason is the "slave of the passions." In the language of Kant's later moral philosophy, the will of such an agent would be ineluctably heteronomous. As Sellars, who introduces a version of the same distinction, suggests, such an agent would be called a *practical automaton spirituale*.[32] The point, however, is not that Kant in 1781 believed that man is such an automaton, possessed of only this limited kind of spontaneity. It is rather that he regarded it as unproblematic that the human will is spontaneous in *at least* that sense; that this suffices to establish the reality of *practical* freedom; and that we neither know nor need to know whether it is *also* spontaneous in the former sense.

IV. PRACTICAL FREEDOM AND PREDICTABILITY: THE PROBLEM OF COMPATIBILISM

The above interpretation of Kant's First Critique theory of practical freedom not only resolves the apparent contradiction between the Dialectic and the Canon, but also puts us in a position to deal with the difficult issue of compatibilism. As Kant characterizes the situation in the First Critique: "if we could exhaustively investigate all the appearances of men's wills, there would not be found a single human action which we could not predict with certainty, and recognize as proceeding necessarily from its antecedent conditions" (A550/B578). At the same time, however, he also insists that this does not prevent us from considering the same actions "in relation to reason," that is, as products of practical freedom. From this perspective we can impute the actions to an agent and claim that they ought or ought not to have been performed. This, Kant suggests, is because in viewing actions in this manner we are considering them in relation to "something intelligible," which stands outside of the temporal order of the phenomenal world. This is, of course, the agent's practical spontaneity, his capacity to act on the basis of reason, which is assigned to his intelligible character.[33]

Unfortunately, even Kant's most sympathetic interpreters find this doctrine unacceptable as it stands. The common retort is that if an action can be explained or predicted by being subsumed under a covering law, then one can no longer properly characterize that action as free or hold an agent responsible for its performance. Nor is Kant's distinction between an empirical and an intelligible character thought to resolve the difficulty: since the agent's intelligible character is, by definition, empirically inaccessible, the appeal to it neither helps to explain a free action nor provides a workable criterion for assigning responsibility.[34]

As a first step in response to this line of criticism, it is important to note that Kant has neither the need nor the right to assert dogmatically (as he appears to do in the passage cited above) that, given sufficient knowledge, we could infallibly predict human actions. This claim presupposes the principle of the uniformity or lawfulness of nature (Hume's "like causes–like effects" principle), but this is itself merely a regulative Idea of reason, not a constitutive, transcendental condition of the possibility of experience. In fact, we have seen that no such result is established, or even argued for, in the Second Analogy. Accordingly, what Kant should have said here is that the thought of the complete explicability and predictability of human actions (their subsumability under covering laws) is merely a regulative Idea, required for the scientific investigation of human behavior. As merely regulative, this principle leaves room for the possibility of an appeal to a different regulative Idea (transcendental freedom) for the conception of agency and the imputation of actions. In short, the way seems open for a solution to the conflict between causal determinism and freedom in the First Critique analogous to the solution which Kant provides in the Third Critique to the conflict between mechanism and teleology.[35]

This is, however, only a first step, for even if we grant a merely regulative status to the covering law model and all that it involves, the fact still remains that the Second Analogy contends that every event has a cause or antecedent condition from which it invariably follows "according to a rule." Thus the concept of practical freedom seems to be threatened by the Second Analogy, even when it is given the "weak" interpretation advocated in chapter 10. In order to deal with this objection, we must look more closely at Kant's conception of practical freedom. The essential point here is that this conception does not preclude the assignment of causes to practically free actions; rather, it requires us to construe the connection between such actions and their causes differently than we do when we connect effects with their causes according to the mechanistic model.

By the "cause" of a practically free act is meant its incentive (*Triebfeder*). Kant, of course, recognizes that other causal factors and "standing conditions," such as environment and education, enter into the explanation and prediction of human actions. These factors, however, play a subordinate role, since their function is to explain why a given incentive, such as the desire for wealth or fame, could have led a particular individual to act in a certain way in a given situation. Thus the direct or primary cause of an action, the factor first appealed to in its explanation, is its incentive. To give its incentive is to give the reason for the action. Kant does not deny that free actions have incentives. On the contrary, he insists that they do throughout his career, even in the *Critique of Practical Reason*. The relevant difference between the two Critiques on this issue is only that in the Second Critique the question is whether the moral law can itself serve as an incentive or, equivalently, whether pure reason can be practical, while in the First Critique the question is simply how the connection between an incentive (whatever it may be) and an *arbitrium liberum* is to be conceived.

Kant deals with this issue at the very beginning of his account in the Dialectic, where he remarks that, in viewing an action as free, we are constrained to consider its "cause" as "not . . . so determining that it excludes a causality of our will" (A534/B562). Admittedly, this characterization of the cause as "not . . . so determining" is highly obscure. Nevertheless, I think it reasonable to take Kant to be appealing here to an essential aspect of his theory of agency: the principle that an incentive can only determine an agent to act insofar as the agent incorporates that incentive into his rule or maxim of action.[36] Consequently, when we consider an act to be free, that is, when we impute it to an agent, we do not deny that this act has an antecedent cause, or incentive; but we also assume that the incentive leads to the act only through the adoption by the agent of a rule of action according to which the incentive can serve as a reason for the act in question.[37] This act of incorporation is what Kant means by the "causality of reason." It is also the element of spontaneity that constitutes the essential (nonempirical) ingredient in the conception of practical freedom and that requires an appeal to the transcendental Idea of freedom (in its regulative function as "model").

Since this conception of practical freedom denies neither the necessity of an antecedent cause for a free action (its incentive) nor the possibility of explaining the action in terms of this cause (which is assigned to the agent's "empirical character"), it does not conflict with the Second Analogy. It simply requires an additional factor (the act of incorporation), which does not enter into an empirical account of human behavior. To be sure, this additional factor is "nonsensible" and, therefore, is thought in connection with the agent's "intelligible character." This does not, however, involve any dogmatic claims about the "real" nature of some inaccessible noumenal agent. First, as in the case of apperception, we have a consciousness, although not an experience, of this capacity. Second, while this consciousness suffices to establish our practical freedom and, therefore, at least relative spontaneity, it does not establish our absolute spontaneity or transcendental freedom; although it does require us to use the transcendental Idea of freedom as a "model."

The main thrust of this interpretation can be clarified and reinforced by a brief glance at Kant's notorious account of the "malicious lie," which, interestingly enough, he describes as an empirical illustration of the "regulative principle of reason." The operative assumption here is that the empirical character of the action can be adequately explained in terms of conditions such as "defective education, bad company, . . . the viciousness of a natural disposition," as well as other "occasional causes that may have intervened" (A554/B582). The precise nature of these conditions and "occasional causes" is, of course, irrelevant; the important point is only that "although we believe that the action is thus determined, we none the less blame the agent." Moreover, Kant continues, we do this because, for the purpose of imputation,

> we presuppose that we can leave out of consideration what the way of life may have been, that we can regard the past series of conditions as not having occurred, the act as being completely unconditioned by any preceding state; just as if the agent in and by himself began in this action an entirely new series of consequences. [A555/B583]

Kant's language here requires careful consideration. The remark that "we presuppose that we can leave out of consideration" the factors noted above strongly suggests a methodological rather than an ontological claim. In other words, it suggests that he is here merely characterizing the "logic" or "language game" of imputation, not providing it with an ontological grounding in the noumenal world. I believe that this is exactly how Kant is to be understood. Nevertheless, it is important to distinguish this interpretation from the familiar fictionalist reading of transcendental freedom, which might seem to be suggested by the remark that in doing this, that is, "playing the language game," we proceed "just as if," etcetera. The "as if" is here intended to capture the problematic nature and merely regulative function, not the fictional status, of the transcendental Idea of freedom. In other words, it is not that the reality of transcendental freedom is denied; it is rather that it is not necessary to establish this reality in order to "save" practical freedom. All that this requires is the conceivability of transcendental freedom, which makes is possible to use the transcendental Idea in a regulative fashion as a "model" for the conception of agency and the imputation of actions to agents. Once again, the essential point in all of this is that the reality of practical freedom is not affected by the possibility that what we call freedom "may . . . in relation to higher and more remote operating causes be nature again."

This, in all essentials, is what I take to be the theory of practical freedom or agency contained in the *Critique of Pure Reason*. At least it is the theory that must be attributed to Kant if one is to reconcile the Dialectic with the Canon. Admittedly, this interpretation cannot be reconciled with every line of the text, especially not with some of the passages added in the Second Edition, which make specific reference to the *Critique of Practical Reason*.[38] Also, it cannot be reconciled either with the doctrine of the Second Critique itself, which links the consciousness of freedom directly to the moral law and which regards anything less than transcendental freedom as nothing more than the "freedom of a turnspit," or with Kant's attempts outside of the two Critiques to establish the reality of transcendental freedom by appealing to our spontaneity as thinking beings.[39] Nevertheless, it is compatible with the great bulk of what Kant does have to say about freedom in the *Critique of Pure Reason,* as well as with the previously discussed account of apperception and spontaneity added in the Second Edition. More important, it is the theory of freedom appropriate for a "critical" philosophy that does not appeal to any specifically "moral facts," such as the principle of autonomy.

Conclusion

The main task for any interpretation of Kant's idealism, indeed, for any interpretation of his theoretical philosophy as a whole, is to explicate and analyze its transcendental dimension. It is only after attaining some clarity about what makes Kant's philosophy transcendental that one can begin to understand his criticisms of his predecessors, which often seem capricious, and to evaluate the central doctrines of the *Critique of Pure Reason*. As obvious as this point is, it is completely missed by the standard picture of Kant's idealism, with the inevitable result that this idealism is regarded as an incoherent blend of phenomenalism and skepticism, and his main arguments dismissed as the products of gross confusions and elementary blunders.

In the preceding pages I have tried to provide a corrective to this picture, one which is better able to bring into focus the transcendental thrust of Kant's thought. To this end I have introduced the conception of an epistemic condition in order to clarify Kant's claims about the transcendental ideality of the objects of human experience. The underlying intuition is that Kant's claim that human knowledge has its own a priori conditions, which determine what can count as an object or as objective for the human mind, is his distinctive and "revolutionary" contribution to philosophy. It is what makes his philosophy a "critical" or transcendental philosophy. If we interpret Kant in light of this conception, we can make good sense of the transcendental distinction between things as they appear and the same things as they are in themselves, and of Kant's "Copernican" assumption that objects "conform to our knowledge." We can also see why Kant could regard all noncritical philosophies (including the phenomenalistic theories of Berkeley and Hume) as species of transcendental realism, as well as why he could find in the Antinomies an indirect proof of transcendental idealism. Correlatively, without this conception, or something very similar, the standard picture and the criticisms that stem from it become unavoidable.

These considerations suffice to show the inadequacy of the standard picture and the potential fruitfulness of the conception of an epistemic condition as an interpretive device; but they do not of themselves constitute a defense of transcendental idealism. This larger project requires a detailed examination of Kant's claims in the Transcendental Aesthetic and the Metaphysical Deduction about the sensible and intellectual conditions of human knowledge, of his endeavor in the Transcendental Analytic as a whole to show how these conditions conjointly function as conditions of the possibility of experience, and of his attempt (largely in the Second Edition) to prove that the transcendental conditions of knowledge and experience are also conditions of self-knowledge and "inner" experience. These, together with Kant's treatment of the concept of the thing in itself and of the problem of freedom, have been the topics of the final three parts of this study. My aim throughout has been to present Kant's arguments in their strongest form, without ignoring the obscurities of the text and the difficulties that emerge at virtually every step. The difficulties are real, and I have no wish to minimize them. In fact, I believe that I have pointed to a number of serious problems which have not been generally recognized in the secondary literature. By the same token, however, the genuine difficulties must be distinguished from a host of imaginary ones, which are largely the result of a failure to grasp the transcendental nature of Kant's claims. One of my concerns in this study has been to show that a good many of the stock criticisms of Kant fall into the second category.

There are, of course, a number of other significant criticisms, mainly of a methodological nature, that have been raised against Kant from within a transcendental perspective by thinkers such as Hegel and Husserl.[1] The common thrust of these criticisms is that Kant's philosophy is insufficiently transcendental because it rests upon a number of unexamined "dogmatic" assumptions concerning such issues as the nature of our cognitive faculties. This type of criticism also underlies the frequently expressed demand for a "metacritique," that is, an account of the possibility of transcendental philosophy itself; and many critics have pointed out that such an account is lacking in Kant.[2] Although I have not dealt explicitly in this study either with these criticisms or with the problem of a metacritique, I believe that a good deal of what has been said here is relevant to both issues.[3] In any event, my neglect of these issues in the present work is not due to a denial of their importance, but rather to a recognition of their complexity (and therefore their demand for separate treatment), and to my conviction that the fundamental task is to define and (where possible) defend Kant's own transcendental approach in the *Critique of Pure Reason* against a prevalent type of criticism which simply refuses to take this approach seriously. This is the task to which I have devoted myself in the present study.

Notes

CHAPTER 1

1. All references to the *Critique of Pure Reason* are to the standard First and Second Edition pagination and are included in the text following the citation. I usually follow Norman Kemp Smith's translation of the *Critique of Pure Reason*. Where my departure from Kemp Smith is significant and reflects a difference in interpretation I call attention to it in the notes. Apart from some passages from the *Reflexionen* and various versions of the *Vorlesungen,* all other references to Kant's works are to the standard edition: *Kants gesammelte Schriften,* ed. Königlich Preussischen Akademie der Wissenschaften (hereinafter cited as *Ak.*). Where possible, I also include a reference to the standard English version of the work in question.

2. These include Pistorius, Eberhard, Jacobi, Maimon, and Aenesidemus-Schulze. Perhaps the clearest contemporary expression of this kind of interpretation, however, is to be found in the notorious Garve-Feder review to which Kant himself replied in the *Prolegomena* (*Ak.* IV, 372–80). For an account of many of these interpretations and criticisms of Kant, see H. Vaihinger, *Commentar zu Kants Kritik der reinen Vernunft,* vol. 2, pp. 494–505.

3. P. F. Strawson, *The Bounds of Sense,* p. 38.

4. Ibid., p. 16.

5. For a critical discussion of some of these attempts, see Ralph S. Walker, *Kant,* esp. pp. 14–23.

6. The above is admittedly an oversimplified account of Strawson's position, based largely upon his introductory account, *The Bounds of Sense,* pp. 38–42. He also discusses transcendental idealism in several other places in the work, most notably pp. 235–62, and he distinguishes among various possible interpretations. My present concern, however, is not to examine the details of Strawson's interpretation and critique, but merely to use it as a clear and well-known illustration of what I take to be the standard picture. I have dealt at length with Strawson's views in my "Transcendental Idealism and Descriptive Metaphysics," *Kant-Studien* 60 (1969): pp. 216–33. For a similar line of criticism, see H. E. Matthews, "Strawson on Transcendental Idealism," *Philosophical Quarterly* 19 (1969): 204–20. I shall also return to Strawson's interpretation in chapter 3.

7. The most extreme expression of this view in the recent literature is by Colin Turbayne, "Kant's Refutation of Dogmatic Idealism," *Philosophical Quarterly* 5 (1955):225–44. Strawson goes only so far as to remark that "Kant, as transcendental idealist is closer to Berkeley than he acknowledges" (*Bounds of Sense,* p. 22).

8. Cf. Strawson, *Bounds of Sense,* pp. 235–39.

9. H. A. Prichard, *Kant's Theory of Knowledge,* pp. 71–100. A rigorous and sensitive critique of Prichard's Kant-interpretation has been provided by Graham Bird in *Kant's Theory of Knowledge,* esp. pp. 1–17. Although I differ from him on many issues, the strategy of this chapter, and also the overall direction of my interpretation, owes much to his work. To my mind, he deserves credit for being the first English-language Kant commentator of this generation seriously to challenge the standard picture.

10. Cf. Strawson, *Bounds of Sense,* pp. 91–92 and passim.

11. Prichard, *Kant's Theory,* esp. pp. 78–79.

12. As already noted, my strategy of contrasting the empirical and the transcendental versions of these distinctions is very close to Bird's. I differ from Bird mainly in my account of the transcendental versions. For a comparison, see Bird, *Kant's Theory,* pp. 36–51.

13. '*Realität*', as one of the pure concepts of the understanding under the general heading of '*Qualität*', is contrasted with '*Negation*'. Presumably, then, when Kant uses the term in a contrast with '*Idealität*' it must be taken in a noncategorical sense. In this regard, it should also be noted that Kant distinguishes between *realitas phenomenon* and *realitas noumenon* (A264–65/B320–21).

14. Cf. A28–30/B44–45, A45–46/B62–63, A368–73.

15. At one point in the Transcendental Aesthetic Kant suggests that this is the only genuine sense of ideality. Thus, in contrasting the ideality of space with that of other representations (sensations) he claims: "With the sole exception of space there is no subjective representation, referring to something *outer,* which could be entitled (at once) objective (and) *a priori.* For there is no other subjective representation from which we can derive *a priori* synthetic propositions as we can from intuition in space. Strictly speaking, therefore, these other representations have no ideality, although they agree with the representation of space in this respect, that they belong merely to the subjective constitution of our manner of sensibility" (B44). The ideality of space is thus connected here specifically with its status as a source of a priori truths. It should be noted that this is a Second Edition replacement for a passage in which the ideality of space is explained in terms of its function as a "condition of outer objects" and, more specifically, as a necessary condition "under which alone objects can be for us objects of the senses" (A28–29). The original passage, more so than its replacement, suggests the conception of space as an "epistemic condition" for which I wish to argue.

16. This would be a noumenon "in the negative sense," by which Kant means simply the concept of "a thing so far as it is *not* an *object of our sensible intuition*" (B307). I shall deal systematically with the concepts of the noumenon, the transcendental object, and the thing in itself in chapter 11.

17. *Ak.* XX, 269. Other relevant texts include the *Critique of Pure Reason,* A45–46/B62–63, and *Prolegomena,* §13, remark II, *Ak.* IV, 289–90.

18. Gerold Prauss, *Kant und das Problem der Dinge an sich,* pp. 20 ff. Prauss also points out that the short forms, such as we find in the Transcendental Aesthetic, can generally be seen as abbreviations of the long forms.

19. It should be noted that I am not here claiming that Kant has an adequate answer to the skeptic. A consideration of that issue must await discussion of the central argument of the Transcendental Analytic, including the Refutation of Idealism. My present concern is only to counter the charge that transcendental idealism is itself a form of skepticism, as Prichard and many others seem to assume.

20. I do not know of another use of this term or the precise notion that I associate with it in the literature. The closest thing to it of which I am aware is Arthur Melnick's characterization of the pure concepts of the understanding as "epistemic concepts" in *Kant's Analogies of Experience,* pp. 37–42.

21. Especially notable in this regard are Reflexionen 4900 and 4901, which have been cited by numerous commentators, including Bird, (*Kant's Theory,* pp. 10–11). In the first of these Kant writes: "I concerned myself not with the evolution of concepts, like Tetens (actions through which concepts are generated) nor with the analysis of them, like Lambert, but merely with their objective validity. I am no rival to these men." In the second: "Tetens investigated the concepts of human reason merely subjectively (human nature), but I investigated them objectively. The former analysis is empirical, the latter transcendental" (*Ak.* XVIII, 23).

22. *Ak.* IV, 258.

23. Kant makes essentially the same point about Berkeley in connection with the Refutation of Idealism (B274–75).

24. I have dealt with this topic in some detail in "Kant's Critique of Berkeley," *Journal of the History of Philosophy* 11 (1973): 43–63.

CHAPTER 2

1. Two examples of this view are Colin Turbayne, "Kant's Refutation of Dogmatic Idealism," *Philosophical Quarterly* 5 (1955): 228, and Sadik J. Al-Azm, *The Origins of Kant's Argument in the Antinomies,* p. 148.

2. In the *Critique of Pure Reason* (B53) Kant seems to equate "absolute" with "transcendental" reality. The notion of absolute reality goes back at least as far as the Dissertation, where Kant criticizes the conception of time as something "posited in itself and absolutely" (*in se et absolute positum*) (*Ak.* II, 401 ff.). For a discussion of some of these terminological points see Norbert Hinske, *Kants Weg zur Transzendental-philosophie,* esp. p. 49.

3. *Ak.* XX, 287.

4. *Ak.* XX, 335.

5. After developing his formal principle of autonomy in the *Critique of Practical Reason,* Kant proceeds to group systematically all previous moral philosophies under a number of labels which characterize the various aspects of heteronomy (*Ak.* V, 40–41).

6. Cf. Turbayne, "Kant's Refutation," and Norman Kemp Smith, *A Commentary to Kant's "Critique of Pure Reason,"* pp. 301 ff.

7. For a different interpretation of this claim, which relies upon the contention that Kant's idealism essentially involves an imposition theory, see Jonathan Bennett, *Kant's Dialectic,* p. 55.

8. *Ak.* V, 53.

9. The entire treatment of this passage is greatly indebted to the analysis of Lewis White Beck, *A Commentary on Kant's Critique of Practical Reason,* pp. 181–82.

10. Cf. Spinoza, *Ethics* II, prop. XLIV, Corollary II. Spinoza there claims that "it is in the nature of reason to perceive things under a certain form of eternity" (*sub quâdam aeternitatis specie*). I discuss this aspect of Spinoza's epistemology in *Benedict de Spinoza,* pp. 107–17, and Kant's overall criticism of Spinoza in "Kant's Critique of Spinoza," pp. 199–227.

11. In this regard a comment of Kant cited by Bird is of particular interest. According to Kant, "Berkeley found nothing constant, and could find nothing so, which the understanding conceived in accordance with *a priori* principles, so he had to look for another intuition, namely the mystical one of God's ideas, which required a two-fold understanding, one which connected phenomena in experience, and another which knew things in themselves. I require only one sensibility and one understanding" (*Ak.* XXIII, 58; Bird, p. 37).

12. The fullest discussion of this point is by Aron Gurwitsch, *Leibniz, philosophie des panlogismus,* esp. pp. 23–31, 142–51, 450–54. It is also brought out in connection with Kant by Gottfried Martin, who refers to it as the "theological foundation of truth." *Kant's Metaphysics and Theory of Science,* trans. P. G. Lucas, p. 62.

13. G. W. Leibniz, *New Essays On Human Understanding,* trans. Peter Remnant and Jonathan Bennett, book 4, chap. 2, §14, p. 447.

14. This is shown nicely by Gurwitsch in his discussion of the "Affinität des menschlichen und göttlichen Geistes" (*Leibniz,* pp. 142–44).

15. G. W. Leibniz, *Discourse on Metaphysics,* trans. G. R. Montgomery, §8, p. 13.

16. Cf. *Critique of Pure Reason,* A43–44/B61–62; *Prolegomena, Ak.* IV, 290–91; "On a Discovery," in *The Kant-Eberhard Controversy,* p. 133; and *Ak.* VIII, 219.

17. *Critique of Pure Reason,* A271–76/B327–32; "On a Discovery," pp. 156–60; *Ak.* VIII, 246–50.

18. John Locke, *An Essay Concerning Human Understanding,* ed. A. C. Fraser, vol. 2, p. 57.

19. See ibid., pp. 57–58.

20. Ibid., vol. 1, p. 30.

21. Ibid., pp. 29, 402.

22. Cf. Kemp Smith, *Commentary,* pp. 591–92.

23. Locke, *An Essay,* vol. 1, p. 403.

24. Cf. James Gibson, *Locke's Theory of Knowledge and its Historical Relations,* pp. 164 ff.

25. *Ak.* I, 391. English translation, "A New Exposition of the First Principles of Metaphysical Knowledge," by F. E. England in *Kant's Conception of God,* p. 219.

26. *Ak.* I, 395–96; "A New Exposition," p. 225.

27 *Ak.* I, 413; "A New Exposition," p. 248.

28. The most important of these consequences concern the alleged nonspatiality and nontemporality of things as they are in themselves. The whole issue is dealt with at length in chapter 5.

29. *Ak.* IV, 375.

30. Implicit in all of this is the equivalence of 'form' and 'condition'. This point is discussed in chapter 5 and elsewhere. For a detailed account of Kant's conception of form, see Robert B. Pippin, *Kant's Theory of Form.*

31. Cf. Arthur Melnick, *Kant's Analogies of Experience,* esp. p. 164. Melnick here develops what I take to be a substantially similar argument in terms of the notion of formality. This turns on the incoherence of construing an element that functions as a form of our cognitive relation to the world as a feature of the world in itself, that is, a feature which pertains to the world in abstraction from our cognitive relation to it.

32. I am here anticipating the discussion of chapter 7, where it is argued that the distinction between two senses of 'object' noted in this paragraph is the key to the distinction between the two parts of the Transcendental Deduction in the Second Edition. At present, however, I wish only to insist upon the fact that Kant does use 'object' in these two senses, and that this is reflected in his use in the Deduction of the two German terms *Objekt* and *Gegenstand.* It is perhaps also worth noting here that the failure to recognize these two senses of 'object' vitiates Melnick's otherwise perceptive account of the connection between judgment and the transcendentally idealistic conception of an object. Thus he argues (ibid., p. 145) that in order to understand Kant's idealism it is necessary to see that "he is making a point about the dependence of the *concept* of an object on the notion of a (judging) subject, not on any point about the dependence of the existence of objects upon the existence of a subject." This interpretation, which is in many ways reminiscent of the views of Kant's follower and sometime critic Jakob Sigismund Beck, certainly moves in the right direction. The basic problem with it is that it fails to do justice to the role of Kant's theory of sensibility in his idealism. This role becomes apparent when we move from the first to the second sense of 'object'. Although he is not concerned with the issue of the two senses of 'object', a somewhat similar criticism of Melnick's interpretation of transcendental idealism is given by Karl Ameriks, "Recent Work on Kant's Theoretical Philosophy," *American Philosophical Quarterly* 19 (1982): 1–24, esp. 2–3.

33. For a discussion of this point see Gerold Prauss, *Kant und das Problem der Dinge an sich,* pp. 184 ff. The passages in which Kant describes transcendental ideality in this way include A129 and Bxxvii–xxix.

34. For a discussion of the relevant literature on the topic see S. Morris Engel, "Kant's Copernican Analogy: A Re-examination," *Kant-Studien,* 59 (1963): 243–51. Moreover, Norwood Russell Hanson, "Copernicus' Role in Kant's Revolution," *Journal of the History of Ideas* 20 (1959): 274–81, points out that Kant himself nowhere uses the expression "Copernican revolution" to characterize his own thought, and that the explicit comparison

of his own procedure to that of Copernicus consists simply in noting that they both tried an alternative hypothesis when existing theories proved unsatisfactory. I am, however, here concerned neither with the appropriateness of the analogy nor with textual questions about the precise use that Kant makes of it. My concern is rather with the understanding of the nature and significance of this "changed point of view." I here refer to it as Kant's "Copernican revolution" simply because this is the expression that is commonly used in the literature.

35. *Prolegomena,* §14, *Ak.* IV, 294.

36. It is interesting to note that in the preface Kant suggests that this "supposition" or "experiment" is confirmed by its success in dealing with the Antinomies (Bxx–xxi). We shall see in the next chapter why Kant thought this to be the case.

37. Jonathan Bennett, *Locke, Berkeley, Hume,* pp. 136–37.

38. George Berkeley, *The Principles of Human Knowledge,* §6, in *The Works of George Berkeley, Bishop of Cloyne.*

39. Ibid., §3.

40. Cf. ibid., §132, and *An Essay Towards a New Theory of Vision,* §§79–87, in *Works of George Berkeley.*

CHAPTER 3

1. *Ak.* XII, 258; *Kant's Philosophical Correspondence, 1759–99,* ed. and trans. A. Zweig, p. 252.

2. *Ak.* IV, 260.

3. *Ak.* IV, 338.

4. For a discussion of this see Allison, *The Kant-Eberhard Controversy,* pp. 95–96, 112–16.

5. Norman Kemp Smith, *A Commentary to Kant's "Critique of Pure Reason,"* p. 479.

6. Sadik J. Al-Azm, *The Origins of Kant's Arguments in the Antinomies.* I think, however, that Al-Azm goes a bit far by treating the arguments as essentially nothing more than restatements of the views of Newton and Leibniz.

7. See Al-Azm, *Origins of Kant's Arguments,* pp. 5–7.

8. See Pierre Bayle, *Historical and Critical Dictionary,* s.v. "Zeno of Elea."

9. See *Critique of Pure Reason,* A529–32/B557–60, and *Prolegomena,* §53, *Ak.* IV, 443–47. I discuss the issues raised by this distinction in chapter 15.

10. It should be clear from the context that 'v' is here taken in the exclusive sense. I have symbolized the antithesis position as *I* (for infinite) rather than as ~*F* (for not finite) because the antithesis argues for an actual infinite, rather than claiming merely that the world cannot be considered as finite in relevant respects. In fact, we shall see that this is precisely what is wrong with the position.

11. This is clearly stated by Al-Azm, *Origins of Kant's Arguments,* p. 8.

12. *De Mundi Sensibilis atque Intelligibilis Forma et Principiis,* §2, *Ak.* II, 390. This work will henceforth be referred to as the Inaugural Dissertation. English translation by G. B. Kerferd and D. E. Walford, in *Selected Pre-Critical Writings and Correspondence with Beck,* p. 51.

13. Cf. "Die Metaphysik," according to H. L. A. Dorra, 1792/93. In *Die Philosophischen Hauptvorlesungen Immanuel Kants,* ed. Arnold Kowalewski, p. 575.

14. Kemp Smith, *Commentary,* p. 485.

15. Bertrand Russell, *Our Knowledge of the External World,* pp. 160–61.

16. Ibid., p. 161.

17. Ibid.

18. P. F. Strawson, *The Bounds of Sense,* p. 176.

19. G. E. Moore, *Some Main Problems of Philosophy,* p. 179.

20. Ibid.; and Jonathan Bennett, *Kant's Dialectic,* pp. 118–19.

21. Moore, *Some Main Problems,* p. 181.

22. Such an argument was offered by Martin Knutzen. For a discussion of this issue see Jonas Cohn, *Geschichte des Unendlichkeitsproblems in abendländischen Denken bis Kant*, p. 215.

23. We can see from this the inappropriateness of a criticism such as that of Richard Swinburne, *Time and Space*, p. 282. According to Swinburne, the meaningfulness of the infinitistic thesis can be defended on the grounds that we can understand what it means to say that there is no limit to the succession of events, even if we cannot count them. This is quite correct but irrelevant, for the question still arises whether we are to understand this thesis with Kant, as expressing a regulative Idea to the effect that we can always conceive of further conditions, or with the "dogmatist," as asserting the existence of an actual infinity of conditions (past events).

24. I am indebted to William McKnight for this formulation. This concept of the infinite can be formally defined in the following way: S contains infinitely many members iff for every n, S contains more than n members (where n is a natural number).

25. As William McKnight has also noted, the definition of the infinite given in the preceding note is equivalent to the Cantorian definition according to which S has infinitely many members iff there is a proper subset of S, S', and a relation R, such that R sets up a one-to-one correlation between S and S'. The issue is also discussed with specific reference to Russell's formulation by Moltke S. Gram, "Kant's First Antinomy," *The Monist* 51 (1967): 499–518, esp. p. 514. As before, the key is to take 'number' in the Kantian characterization of the mathematical infinite as equivalent to 'natural number'. For to say, with Kant, that the infinite is greater than any (natural) number is to say that it is reflexive and noninductive; in short, that it cannot be arrived at by a process of counting which begins with the natural numbers.

26. The expressions *totum analyticum* and *totum syntheticum,* as well as the claim that space and time are the former and bodies the latter occur in Reflexion 393, *Reflexionen Kants zur kritischen Philosophie,* ed. by Benno Erdmann, p. 121. Although he does not refer to this Reflexion, an account of this distinction and its relevance to Kant's argument is found in Al-Azm, *Origins of Kant's Arguments*, pp. 9–22.

27. In another passage (*Critique of Pure Reason,* A428 / B456 n.), Kant remarks that an indeterminate quantum could be intuited as a whole (*als eine Ganzes*), if it were given or enclosed within limits. In that case, Kant suggests, the limits themselves determine the totality, so that the totality can be grasped without having to be constituted in thought. The point, however, is that the proponent of the infinitistic position cannot claim this of the world. As infinite (*ex hypothesi*) it is neither indeterminate nor limited. Consequently, in this case, a synthesis would be both necessary and impossible.

28. An interesting misinterpretation of Kant on this point is found in Swinburne, *Time and Space,* pp. 282–83. Although he recognizes that the difficulty which Kant is raising involves talking about the universe as a whole, he mistakenly assumes this to be a worry about the general impossibility of making a claim about all of the members of a class. Having construed it in this way, he is obviously able to dismiss it easily, simply by pointing out that we can talk about, for example, all swans. Clearly, however, this has nothing to do with Kant's argument, for talk about the universe as Kant construes it is about a high-order individual, not about the members of a class.

29. In Kantian terms, it is a "synthetic definition," that is, one through which the concept to be defined is itself "made" or "synthesized." The definition of 'world' differs, of course, from the "causal" or genetic definitions that can be provided for geometrical figures in that the latter are "real," that is, they establish the real (as opposed to merely logical) possibility of the object and, therefore, the objective reality of the concept, while the former is merely "nominal." The difference is crucial for the overall argument, but it does not affect the present point. For a discussion of the various conceptions of definition which Kant recognizes see Lewis White Beck, "Kant's Theory of Definition," in *Kant: Disputed Questions,* ed. by Moltke S. Gram, pp. 215–27.

30. Cf. *Critique of Pure Reason,* A410–11/B437. The issue is discussed by A. C. Ewing, *A Short Commentary on Kant's "Critique of Pure Reason,"* p. 210.

31. Cf. *Prolegomena* §52, *Ak.* IV, 340.

32. Strawson, *Bounds of Sense,* pp. 177–79.

33. Keith S. Donnellan, "Reference and Definite Descriptions," *Philosophical Review* 75 (1968): 281–304.

34. Bennett, *Kant's Dialectic,* p. 160.

35. Ibid., p. 161.

36. Ibid.

37. Ibid.

38. See chapter 10 for a detailed treatment of this topic.

39. Although Kant does not draw precisely this distinction, he does remark in his *Vorlesung über Rationaltheologie, Ak.* XXVIII, 1095, that the creation of the world cannot be regarded as an event in time, since time first began with creation.

40. Kant seems to acknowledge this in the note to A521/B549, where he distinguishes his "critical" resolution of the Antinomy from the "dogmatic" proof of the antithesis.

41. This line of criticism is sketched by Moltke S. Gram, "Kant's First Antinomy," pp. 509–12.

42. For want of a better alternative, I am here using the expression 'state of affairs' in an extremely broad sense to encompass antecedent moments of time and surrounding regions of space as well as causes (all of which are construed by Kant as 'conditions'). See *Critique of Pure Reason,* A408–20/B435–48, and the account of 'condition' in the first section of this chapter.

43. Cf. *Critique of Pure Reason,* B150–51. It is there contrasted with the figurative synthesis, which turns out to be the transcendental synthesis of the imagination. The connection between these different kinds of synthesis will be discussed in chapter 7.

44. Cf. *Critique of Pure Reason,* A498/B526. A denial of this principle is equivalent to the denial of a logical connection between premises and conclusions. Kant, to my knowledge, never really considered a skepticism about the laws of logic. In any event, it is not relevant to the question of transcendental realism.

45. I have sketched such an argument, albeit not in this precise form, in "Kant's Refutation of Realism," *Dialectica* 30 (1976): 223–53. As I also suggested in that paper, Kant himself tends to argue in such a manner in the *Prolegomena* and *On the Progress of Metaphysics.*

46. *Prolegomena,* §52, *Ak.* IV, 342.

47. For a significant exception to this, see Norman Kemp Smith, *Commentary,* pp. xlv–xlvii. As he uses the term, it is contrasted with 'subjectivism', which is roughly equivalent to what is here being taken as 'phenomenalism'.

48. A German translation of this work, together with Berkeley's *Three Dialogues* and a critical analysis of both works, was published by Johann Christian Eschenbach. It was entitled, significantly enough, *Samlung der vornehmsten Schriftstellen die die Wirklichkeit ihres eignen Körpers und der ganzen Körperwelt leugnen* (Rostock: Unton Ferdinand Röse, 1756). Lewis Robinson, "Contributions à l'histoire de l'evolution philosophique de Kant," *Revue de Métaphysique et de Morale* 31 (1924): 205–68, and Colin Turbayne, "Kant's Refutation of Dogmatic Idealism," *Philosophical Quarterly* 5 (1955): 225–26, argue convincingly that Kant was in fact familiar with that work. I discuss this issue in "Kant's Critique of Berkeley," *Journal of the History of Philosophy* 11 (1973): 43–63.

49. Arthur Collier, *Clavis Universalis,* in *Metaphysical Tracts by English Philosophers of the Eighteenth Century,* ed. Samuel Parr, pp. 46–50.

50. This is particularly true of the account in the *Prolegomena,* where Kant presents the cosmological Idea as equivalent to "an absolutely existing world of sense," and argues that this concept, like that of a round square, is self-contradictory. This is in turn used to explain

how, as the proofs purportedly show, the contradictory consequences of this conception—that the world is finite and that the world is infinite—can both be false (*Ak.* IV, 341). Collier, *Clavis Universalis,* pp. 46–50, uses virtually the identical argument to prove that "an external world, whose extension is absolute, that is, not relatively depending on any faculty of perception," is self-contradictory. He differs only in that he grounds the self-contradictory nature of this conception (he calls it "repugnancy") on the fact that such a world must be *both* finite and infinite (which Kant could equally well have said). Moreover, while Kant compares the incoherent conception of the world to a round square, Collier compares it to a triangular square.

51. Cf. Robinson, "Contributions," and Arthur O. Lovejoy, "Kant and the English Platonists," in *Essays Philosophical and Psychological,* pp. 284–90.

52. The analysis of transcendental realism in the preceding chapter enables us to understand why Kant should make such a claim. The point is simply that "dogmatic idealism," whether it be Berkeley's or Collier's, is a species of transcendental realism. Since the argument of the Antinomy is intended as a refutation of transcendental realism, if successful, it would also refute this form of idealism. Such a reading is also suggested by Kant's previously cited dictum, "Were we to yield to the illusion of transcendental realism, neither nature nor freedom would be possible" (A543/B571). The question of freedom must be saved for later, but the suggestion that nature would not be possible reflects the likely Kantian interpretation of the idealistic results offered by Collier. Kant's view of Collier would thus seem to parallel closely his view of Berkeley. Finally, an analysis of the first part of *Clavis Universalis* provides further support for this line of interpretation, for it is clear that Collier there construes "mind dependence" or "existence in the mind" in an essentially Cartesian, and thus transcendentally realistic manner.

53. The connection between the Antinomies and the theocentric model of knowledge or, as he terms it, the "theological foundation of truth" is also emphasized by Gottfried Martin, *Kant's Metaphysics and Theory of Science,* pp. 62–64. I can, however, find no evidence for the conclusion which he draws from this; namely, that physical theories are "models produced by men." It seems to me that Kant is here concerned with cosmological questions that go beyond physical theories, and his analysis has no direct implications for the status of such theories. The argument, in other words, does not contain a critique of "scientific realism," if this realism is appropriately characterized as "empirical."

54. Kant's letter to Herz, May 26, 1789 (*Ak.* XI, 55; *Kant's Philosophical Correspondence,* p. 156).

55. Strawson, *Bounds of Sense,* pp. 199–206.

CHAPTER 4

1. Kant's fullest and most suggestive account of the contrast between discursive and intuitive knowledge is to be found in the *Critique of Judgment,* §77, *Ak.* VI, 407–10.

2. Although it is not my intent to argue for it here, I believe that it can also be claimed that the problematic conception of an intuitive intellect also serves to characterize the view of knowledge connected with the theocentric model of transcendental realism. As before, this does not mean that the transcendental realist is saddled with the absurd doctrine that the human mind is intuitive in the sense given by Kant. It is rather that this conception functions more or less implicitly as a normative model to which the transcendental realist appeals in his account of human cognition. For example, when the empiricist regards the immediate apprehension of sensible data, without any conceptualization, as the most fundamental form of knowledge, he can be said to treat human sensible intuition *as if* it were intellectual, that is, of itself sufficient to provide a determinate representation of objects. By contrast, the rationalists frequently appeal to a form of intuitive knowledge that can be characterized as explicitly intellectual. A good example of this is Spinoza's *scientia intuitiva.* From this point of view, then, Kant's insistence that human knowledge is discursive, not

intuitive, can be taken as an integral part of his overall critique of transcendentally realistic epistemologies. Against empiricistic versions it enables him to insist that knowledge requires conceptualization, and against rationalistic versions that it involves sensible, not intellectual, intuition.

3. *Lectures on Logic,* §1, *Ak.* IX, 91.

4. Ibid.

5. Ibid., §6, pp. 94–95.

6. Ibid., §5, p. 94. Cf. Reflexionen 2876, 2878, *Ak.* XVI, 555, 557.

7. *Lectures on Logic,* §1, *Ak.* IX, 91.

8. Ibid.

9. Jaakko Hintikka, "On Kant's Notion of Intuition (*Anschauung*)," *The First Critique,* ed. T. Penelhum and J. MacIntosh, pp. 38–53, and "Kant on the Mathematical Method," *Kant Studies Today,* ed. L. W. Beck, pp. 117–40. Hintikka's denigration of the immediacy criterion has also been criticized, albeit from a quite different perspective, by Charles Parsons, "Kant's Philosophy of Arithmetic," *Philosophy, Science and Method,* ed. S. Morgenbesser, P. Suppes, M. White, pp. 568–94, esp. pp. 578–80, and by Kirk Dalles Wilson, "Kant on Intuition," *Philosophical Quarterly* 25 (1975): 247–65, esp. p. 252. For an overview of the whole dispute, which centers largely on the Beth-Hintikka interpretation of the role of intuition in mathematical proof, see Robert B. Pippin, *Kant's Theory of Form,* pp. 77–84.

10. This was already noted by J. S. Beck in his letters to Kant of Nov. 11, 1791, and May 31, 1792 (*Ak.* XI, 310, esp. pp. 338–40). It has recently been brought up again in connection with Hintikka's interpretation of 'intuition' as the equivalent of a singular term by Manley Thompson, "Singular Terms and Intuitions in Kant's Epistemology," *Review of Metaphysics* 26 (1972): 314–43.

11. H. J. de Vleeschauwer, *La Déduction transcendentale dans l'oeuvre de Kant,* vol. 2, p. 44, points to the difference between Kant and Aristotle on just this issue. For the latter the unity of a representation is attributed to sensibility, and it is derived from the ontological unity of the thing. Consequently, sensibility itself yields a representation of an object. This is just what Kant denies.

12. W. H. Walsh, *Kant's Criticism of Metaphysics,* p. 15.

13. See Kant's marginal comments to Beck's letter of Nov. 11, 1791; *Critique of Pure Reason,* B66; and *Critique of Judgment,* introduction, vii.

14. I am indebted to Lewis White Beck for the distinction between three senses of 'intuition', which he suggested to me in his comments on an earlier draft of this chapter. It should be noted that the distinction between indeterminate and determinate intuition concerns only the first of the three senses of 'intuition' distinguished by Beck; namely, intuitions as representations or mental contents. It should also be noted that this differs from the usual interpretation which distinguishes two senses of 'intuition', the act and the object senses. On this point see Pippin, *Kant's Theory of Form,* pp. 72–73.

15. *Ak.* IX, 101.

16. *Ak.* XXIV, 928.

17. This is specifically claimed by de Vleeschauwer, *La Déduction transcendentale,* vol. 2, pp. 46–47, 131–34.

18. See H. J. Paton, *Kant's Metaphysic of Experience,* vol. 1, p. 251.

19. As Paton points out (ibid., p. 253, n. 3), there is a dispute regarding the question of whether the text reads *Anschauungen* or *Erscheinungen.* Following Paton, Raymond Schmidt, and Kant's own *Handexemplar,* I take *Anschauungen* to be the proper reading. It should be noted, however, that given the distinction between three senses of 'intuition', nothing very much rides on this textual question because 'intuition' here must be taken to mean the intuited and this, for Kant, is always an appearance. The essential point therefore, is not the problematic occurrence of 'intuition' in the passage; it is rather the claim that within

judgment a concept is related to a "given representation" that is itself immediately related to an object. This makes intuition, qua representation, part of the content of judgment.

20. See ibid., pp. 245–48.

21. Ibid., p. 251, n. 3.

22. Reflexion 4634, *Ak.* XVII, 616–17. Similar accounts are contained in numerous other Reflexionen, especially those in the "Lose Blätter aus dem Duisburgischen Nachlass," *Ak.* XVII, 643–73.

23. In his well-known critique of the ontological argument (*Critique of Pure Reason,* A598/B626 ff.), Kant denies that existence is a real predicate or determination because it does not add any content to the description of a thing to say that it exists. He does not, however, deny that it is a logical predicate; consequently, even existential judgments can be said to have two predicates.

24. Kant's standard expression "sich auf etwas beziehen" is generally translated by Kemp Smith as "to relate to." However, as has been pointed out by Richard A. Smyth, *Forms of Intuition,* p. 152, it is more accurately translated as "to refer to." Although I tended to follow Kemp Smith in my own rendition of "On a Discovery," I think that Smyth is correct. Kant is concerned, albeit in his own way, with the problem of reference. In the body of this study I use both expressions, usually depending on the context, but sometimes simply to avoid redundancy.

25. Gerold Prauss, *Erscheinung bei Kant,* pp. 86–87. As textual support he cites A760/B788, where Kant clearly contrasts the two notions. It should also be noted, however, that Kant does on occasion equate them. A case in point is A788/B816. Despite this verbal inconsistency on Kant's part, I believe that Prauss is correct. Kant's analysis of judgment requires that he distinguish between objective validity and truth.

26. This issue is successfully dealt with by Rainer Stuhlmann-Laeisz, *Kants Logik,* pp. 28–53. He draws a distinction between acceptable (*verträglich*) and unacceptable (*unverträglich*) judgments and between transcendental and empirical truth. He notes that Kant himself uses the notion of transcendental truth with respect to concepts at A220/B268, wherein it is equated with objective reality. Building upon Kant's use, he suggests that the transcendental truth of a judgment can be understood as its agreement with the conditions of the possibility of experience, and thus with an object of possible experience. Consequently, an empirical judgment can be acceptable if it has transcendental truth, even if it is false in the empirical sense, that is, does not agree with the actual object to which it makes reference. The judgments of transcendental metaphysics, on this view, are unacceptable, because of this lack of transcendental truth. Nevertheless, precisely because of this lack of transcendental truth they can be regarded as false.

27. *Critique of Pure Reason,* A151/B191.

28. *Prolegomena,* §2, *Ak.* IV, 266–67.

29. See Allison, *Kant-Eberhard Controversy,* pp. 37–38.

30. Lewis White Beck, "Can Kant's Synthetic Judgments be Made Analytic?" in *Kant: Disputed Questions,* ed. Moltke S. Gram, pp. 228–46, esp. pp. 232–35.

31. This is affirmed in criticism of what he takes to be the "Kant-Beck thesis" by Moltke S. Gram, "The Crisis of Syntheticity: The Kant-Eberhard Controversy," *Kant-Studien* 2 (1980): 155–80.

32. Also relevant at this point is the different, but related, objection that was first raised by Eberhard's astute associate J. C. Maass and later developed by C. I. Lewis. According to this line of objection, the distinction between analytic and synthetic judgments is a variable one because any given judgment can be classified as either analytic or synthetic, depending on how one happens to characterize the subject-concept. I have dealt with this objection at some length in the introduction to *The Kant-Eberhard Controversy.*

33. *Lectures on Logic,* §36, *Ak.* IX, 111. I discuss this issue in *Kant-Eberhard Controversy,* pp. 55 ff.

34. This characterization of analytic judgments as involving a "formal extension" of knowledge requires the distinction of such judgments from tautologies. Unfortunately, Kant is inconsistent on this point. For example, in "On the Progress of Metaphysics" (*Ak*. XX, 322), he draws just such a distinction; though in the *Lectures on Logic*, §37 (*Ak*. IX, 111), he treats tautologies as a subset of analytic judgments. For a discussion of this issue see Vleeschauwer, *La Déduction transcendentale*, vol. 3, p. 406.

35. *Lectures on Logic*, §36, *Ak*. IX, 111.

36. As noted by L. W. Beck, in "Can Kant's Synthetic Judgments be Made Analytic?" p. 230, Kant himself makes the point in Reflexion 4674 (*Ak*. XVII, 645) when he remarks that in analytic judgments *Das x fällt weg*.

37. *Ak*. VIII, 239 ff. Allison, *Kant-Eberhard Controversy*, pp. 49–50, 141 ff.

38. L. W. Beck, "Can Kant's Synthetic Judgments be Made Analytic?" p. 231, and "Kant's Theory of Definition," in *Kant: Disputed Questions*, p. 225.

39. Cf. *Critique of Pure Reason*, A728/B756, where Kant asks, "What useful purpose could be served by defining an empirical concept, such, for instance, as that of water? When we speak of water and its properties, we do not stop short at what is thought in the word 'water' but proceed to experiments." As Beck notes in his comments on the passage, "Description suffices; definition which aims at being more than nominal is a useless presumption" ("Kant's Theory of Definition," p. 223). Kant's point seems to be that judgments involving such empirical concepts are normally not analytic; but if one does explicitly endeavor to make an analytic judgment, that is, appeal to meaning, one can appeal only to a purely nominal definition, "what is thought in the word." This makes the judgment arbitrary. One is perhaps tempted to say that such judgments about words, in contrast to the intension of concepts, are empirical claims about linguistic usage. Kant, however, does not seem to have addressed that possibility.

40. *Lectures on Logic*, §36, *Ak*. IX, 111.

41. Ibid.

42. Kant himself limits this claim to theoretical judgments. The point is that he recognizes synthetic judgments of practical reason that do not involve a reference to intuition; for example, "An absolutely good will is one whose maxim can always have as its content itself considered as a universal law." I discuss this issue in *Kant-Eberhard Controversy*, p. 74. For a different view on this point see Gram, "Crisis of Syntheticity," p. 168, n. 24.

43. Kant's letter to Reinhold, Mar. 12, 1789 (*Ak*. XI, 38; Allison, *Kant-Eberhard Controversy*, p. 164).

44. *Ak*. VIII, 228; Allison, *Kant-Eberhard Controversy*, p. 141.

45. In *The Kant-Eberhard Controversy*, pp. 57–59, I argue on the basis of this analysis that the "critical problem" of the synthetic a priori is really equivalent to the problem of the relation between pure concepts of the understanding and objects as Kant presented it in the famous letter to Marcus Herz of February 21, 1772.

46. *Ak*. XX, 266.

47. Cf. Allison, *Kant-Eberhard Controversy*, pp. 60–61.

48. Most notably in the *Critique of Pure Reason*, B3. For a discussion of this see Norman Kemp Smith, *A Commentary to Kant's "Critique of Pure Reason,"* pp. 55–56.

49. I am not here concerned with the question of the cogency of Kant's philosophy of mathematics, but merely with the explication of his claim that synthetic a priori judgments require pure intuitions for their grounding.

CHAPTER 5

1. See P. F. Strawson, *The Bounds of Sense*, p. 70. Strawson's view is typical.

2. H. Vaihinger, *Commentar zu Kants Kritik der reinen Vernunft*, vol. 2, p. 197.

3. Norman Kemp Smith, *A Commentary to Kant's "Critique of Pure Reason,"* pp. 99–105. Paton, *Kant's Metaphysic of Experience*, vol. 1, pp. 110–14.

4. *Critique of Pure Reason,* A22–23 / B37. The concept of presupposition has been much discussed in the recent literature in philosophical logic. In addition, there are long-standing disputes concerning the sense in which Kant takes the notion when, for instance, he speaks of "presuppositions" of geometry and of pure natural science. A helpful discussion of both of these issues is provided by Gordon G. Brittan, Jr., *Kant's Theory of Science,* esp. pp. 32–36. Following Bas van Fraassen ("Presupposition, Implication, and Self-Reference," *Journal of Philosophy* 65 (1968): 136–52), Brittan regards presupposition as a semantic relation which is to be distinguished from implication. According to this view, *A* presupposes *B* if and only if *A* is neither true nor false unless *B* is true. In other words, the truth of *B* (the presupposition) is a necessary condition of the *meaningfulness* (not the truth) of *A.* I think that this does capture the sense of "presupposition" to which Kant appeals when he talks about the Principles as "presuppositions" of experience. It must be kept in mind, however, that this sense of the term applies to the relation between propositions. Here, by contrast, Kant is concerned with the relation between representations or, more accurately, cognitive capacities. Thus the claim is that it is only because I already have the capacity to represent objects as spatial or as in space that I also have the capacity to represent these same objects as distinct from myself (as *ausser mir*) and as numerically distinct from each other.

5. This interpretation is suggested, although not really developed, by Paton, *Kant's Metaphysic of Experience,* vol. 1, p. 111.

6. See *The Leibniz-Clarke Correspondence,* ed. H. G. Alexander, Leibniz's Fifth Paper, §47, pp. 69–72.

7. See H. Allison, *Kant-Eberhard Controversy,* pp. 35–36.

8. See Paton, *Kant's Metaphysic,* vol. 1, p. 112.

9. This point was made by Schulze in his review of the second volume of the *Philosophisches Magazin;* see Allison, *Kant-Eberhard Controversy,* pp. 81, 171.

10. This is especially clear in the temporal portion of the argument in the Inaugural Dissertation, §14, *Ak.* II, 399. Kant there shows that the attempt to explain how the order of time can be derived from experience, that is, from the representaion of things as simultaneous or successive, is inherently question begging.

11. D. P. Dryer, *Kant's Solution for Verification in Metaphysics,* p. 173.

12. Ibid., p. 174. The same point is also made by Rolf P. Horstmann, "Space as Intuition and Geometry," *Ratio* 18 (1976): 17–30.

13. Kemp Smith, *Commentary,* p. 103.

14. See Julius Ebbinghaus, "Kants Lehre von der Anschauung a priori," *Kant: Zur Deutung seiner Theorie von Erkennen und Handeln,* ed. Gerold Prauss, p. 49.

15. Dryer, *Kant's Solution,* p. 175.

16. *Prolegomena,* §10, *Ak.* IV, 283.

17. This is to be contrasted with Ted Humphrey's interpretation of the second argument, "The Historical and Conceptual Relations between Kant's Metaphysics of Space and Philosophy of Geometry," *Journal of the History of Philosophy* 11 (1973): 503–04. Humphrey claims that this argument, which is not present in the Inaugural Dissertation, is intended to establish a stronger form of necessity than the first. This, he contends, reflects the critical turn in Kant's epistemology between 1770 and 1781. Accordingly, Humphrey suggests that in the *Critique,* in contrast to the Inaugural Dissertation, Kant had to show that all awareness is subject to the conditions of sensibility, and that this entails two commitments: "First, that one can be aware of something only if it is spatial and temporal, and second, that one cannot think away space and time." The task of the second argument is thus to secure these results. Although I find myself in basic agreement with the main thrust of this important paper—namely, the claim that Kant's doctrine of the ideality of space is both logically and historically independent of his views on geometry—I cannot accept this reading of the second argument. First, the initial space argument already shows that space is a condition of the awareness of objects as distinct from the self. Second, as already indicated, the claim

that we cannot think away space and time must be interpreted in such a way as to allow for the *thought* of things as they are in themselves. It cannot, therefore, be regarded as an expression of Kant's *Restriktionslehre* in the manner intimated by Humphrey. Finally, Kant had already denied in the Inaugural Dissertation that we can have an "awareness," or intuition, of anything nonsensible. The present argument has no direct bearing on this claim.

18. See Vaihinger, *Commentar*, vol. 2, p. 205.

19. The appeal to possible worlds here will not help, for in the sense that we can speak of other possible worlds, we can also speak of other possible spaces.

20. This is cited by Vaihinger, *Commentar*, vol. 2, p. 233, and referred to by Paton, *Kant's Metaphysic*, vol. 1, p. 122.

21. The following is based largely on the suggestive account of Kant's conception of intuition by Kirk Dalles Wilson, "Kant on Intuition," *Philosophical Quarterly* 25 (1975): 252–56. Much of Wilson's analysis can be accepted independently of his more controversial claim that Kantian intuitions exhibit a mereological structure. The latter is an interesting suggestion, but one that is not really germane to the present considerations.

22. See Jill Buroker, *Space and Congruence*, p. 73.

23. Kant, of course, views this as a regulative principle for the investigation of nature; see *Critique of Pure Reason*, A665–66/B683–84.

24. This line of objection is developed by Vaihinger, *Commentar*, vol. 2, pp. 257 ff.

25. For further elaboration of this matter see Allison, *Kant-Eberhard Controversy*, p. 176.

26. See Vaihinger, *Commentar*, vol. 2, pp. 224 ff.; Kemp Smith, *Commentary*, p. 347; Robert Paul Wolff, *Kant's Theory of Mental Activity*, p. 228.

27. See Reflexion 17, *Ak.* XXIII, 22–23. In this note, which is attached to A26 in his own copy of the *Critique,* Kant remarks that the representation of space and time involve the thought of necessity. He further contends, however, that this is not the necessity of a concept (logical necessity) because there is no contradiction involved in the thought of their nonexistence.

28. J. G. Schulze, *Prüfung der kantischen Critik der reinen Vernunft,* part 2, pp. 41–42.

29. Arthur Melnick, *Kant's Analogies of Experience,* p. 11.

30. Ibid., pp. 17–18.

31. At A20/B34 Kant equates a pure intuition with a pure form of sensibility.

32. Especially significant here is Kant's discussion of the innateness of space in his polemic with Eberhard. See Allison, *Kant-Eberhard Controversy,* pp. 82–83, 135–36.

33. In the recent literature the distinction between a form of intuiting and a form of intuition, together with the attempt to use this distinction to interpret Kant's own distinction between a form of intuition and a formal intuition, has been presented by Gerd Buchdahl, *Metaphysics and the Philosophy of Science,* pp. 579–94, 621; and by Peter Krausser, "The Operational Conception of 'Reine Anschauung' (Pure Intuition) in Kant's Theory of Experience and Science," *Studies in the History and Philosophy of Science* 3 (1972–73): 81–87, and " 'Form of Intuition' and 'Formal Intuition' in Kant's Theory of Experience and Science," *Studies in the History and Philosophy of Science* 4 (1973–74): 279–87. Both, however, tend to conflate the two distinctions with one another. Thus the notion of a form of the intuited, which, I believe, is necessary to capture the claims that Kant makes about space in the Aesthetic, is simply dropped out. I must confess to having made a similar mistake in *The Kant-Eberhard Controversy,* where I tended to equate a form of intuition or indeterminate pure intuition with a disposition or capacity.

34. See Kemp Smith, *Commentary,* pp. 88–92.

35. There is a parallel passage (B137–38) in which Kant likewise claims that the form of intuition *gibt* the manifold of a priori intuition. Interestingly enough, Kemp Smith here translates it as "supplies."

36. The question of whether space as described in the Transcendental Aesthetic should be regarded as a form of intuition (construed as a capacity or disposition to intuit) or as a formal intuition was first raised by Benno Erdmann in his edition of *Reflexionen Kants zur kritischen Philosophie,* pp. 110–11. He claims that the space that is represented as an infinite given magnitude must refer to the mere form of intuition. Vaihinger, *Commentar,* vol. 2, p. 259, argues to the contrary that the merely potential form of intuition is neither finite nor infinite, and thus that it must refer to the determinate formal intuition. According to my analysis, however, neither is right. Clearly, Vaihinger is correct in his rejection of Erdmann's analysis, but he is incorrect in jumping to the conclusion that it must be a formal intuition. The problem with both is that they see only two alternatives, when in fact there are three.

37. This is also clear from *Prolegomena,* §38, *Ak.* IV, 322.

38. Buchdahl, *Metaphysics,* pp. 579–82.

39. I am here largely following the lead of Ted Humphrey, "Historical and Conceptual Relations," pp. 483–512; the same point has also been noted by Rolf P. Horstmann, "Space," pp. 17–30.

40. See *Prolegomena,* §§7–11, *Ak.* IV, 281–84; Allison, *Kant-Eberhard Controversy,* pp. 150–51; *Ak.* VIII, 240; *Reflexionen Kants zur kritischen Philosophie;* ed. Benno Erdmann, Reflexion 1384, pp. 396–97.

41. In the latter work he refers to this argument as providing a "good confirmative ground of proof" (*Ak.* IV, 484).

42. *Ak.* II, 382–83.

43. Ibid., p. 403.

44. Jonathan Bennett, "The Difference between Right and Left," *American Philosophical Quarterly* 7 (1970): 176. A similar sentiment is expressed by Ted Humphrey, "Historical and Conceptual Relations," pp. 488–89, n. 11.

45. This is convincingly demonstrated by Jill Buroker, *Space and Congruence,* pp. 69 ff.

46. Buroker herself seems to acknowledge this (ibid., pp. 79–80), in discussing the criticism of Kant's arguments raised by Bennett and Grunbaum.

47. *Prolegomena,* §13, *Ak.* IV, 286.

48. See Paton, *Kant's Metaphysic,* vol. 1, p. 65.

49. *Prolegomena,* §8, *Ak.* IV, 282.

50. Ibid.

51. Ibid., §9.

52. Ibid.

53. Paton, *Kant's Metaphysic,* vol. 1, pp. 101–02.

54. In his explicit discussion of the concepts of matter and form in the Amphiboly of Concepts of Reflection (A266/B322), Kant defines 'matter' as "the determinable in general" and 'form' as "its determination." These are intended as perfectly general, or "transcendental," definitions, which apply to both judgments and entities. With regard to the latter, however, it should be noted that a thing's determinations make it into the kind of thing that it is. Consequently, the definition is at least compatible with the implicit understanding of 'form' as condition, which we find in both the Transcendental Aesthetic and the Analytic.

55. Paton, *Kant's Metaphysic,* vol. 1, p. 174.

56. *Ak.* XX, 266–68.

57. The same ambivalent attitude toward the Newtonian position seems to underlie Kant's discussion of geometry and its applicability to nature. On the one hand, he claims that, compared with the "metaphysical students of nature" (the Leibnizians), the "mathematical students of nature" (the Newtonians) have the advantage "that they at least keep the field of appearance open for mathematical propositions" (A40/B57). On the other hand, he repeatedly insists that, if space were a thing in itself or pertained to things as they

are in themselves, then geometry, the science of space, would be empirical (something which Kant vehemently denies). A particularly strong formulation of this implication is contained in "On the Progress of Metaphysics" (*Ak.* XX, 268), where Kant remarks that if space were the form of objects as they are in themselves, "our synthetic *a priori* judgments would be empirical and contingent, which is contradictory." Kant's overall view, I take it, is that the Newtonian position is superior to the Leibnizian in that it makes it at least conceivable that geometry applies to nature (since Newtonians regard space as something real, whereas Leibnizians regard it as a "creature of the imagination"), but that neither can explain how mathematics (either pure or applied) can be synthetic and a priori.

58. *Critique of Pure Reason*, B168. Kant is generally taken to be arguing against Crusius on this point.

59. The latter point will prove crucial for the argument of the Analogies of Experience. The whole matter will be discussed in chapters 9 and 10.

60. In the *Metaphysical Foundations of Natural Science* (*Ak.* IV, 559–60), Kant develops a critique of the Newtonian theory of absolute space along these lines. He there concludes against Newton that absolute space is a mere Idea of reason on the grounds that "it cannot be an object of experience, for space without matter is not an object of perception; and yet it is a necessary concept of reason." The Newtonian theory is thus judged guilty of hypostatizing an Idea. This characterization of space as an "Idea of reason" rather than a form of sensibility might seem to contradict the *Critique*. It should be kept in mind, however, that Kant is there talking about Newtonian absolute space, regarded as a presupposed framework with respect to which we distinguish between real and apparent motion, not about the "spatiality" (in Buchdahl's sense) that conditions human experience.

61. The history of the objection is sketched by Vaihinger, who is himself very sympathetic to it; *Commentar*, vol. 2, pp. 134–51. As initially developed by Kant's contemporaries, it took a "strong" and a "weak" form, corresponding to the realistic and the idealistic interpretations of the Leibnizian monadology, respectively. According to the "strong" form, it is deemed possible that space is a form of human apprehension and that things in themselves actually are in space or spatial. According to the "weak" form, it is deemed possible that space is such a subjective form, but that the realm of things in themselves (conceived as Leibnizian monads) contains an analogue of space. The objection was reformulated (without these Leibnizian overtones) in the nineteenth century by Adolf Trendelenburg, who wrote: "Even if we concede the argument that space and time are demonstrated to be subjective conditions which, in us, precede perceptions and experience, there is still no word of proof to show that they cannot at the same time be objective forms" (*Logische Untersuchungen*, p. 184). This led to a lengthy and bitter controversy with Kuno Fischer, who attempted to defend Kant. I have dealt with this issue in "The Non-spatiality of Things in Themselves for Kant," *Journal of the History of Philosophy* 14 (1976): 313–21. My current analysis, however, differs considerably from the one offered there.

62. Kemp Smith, *Commentary*, p. 113.

63. Vaihinger points out (*Commentar*, vol. 2, pp. 300–02) that Fischer and Arnold endeavored to defend Kant in that way. A similar defense is also provided by A. C. Ewing, *A Short Commentary on Kant's "Critique of Pure Reason,"* p. 50.

64. Karl Leonard Reinhold, *Versuch einer neuen Theorie des menschlichen Vorstellungsvermögens*, pp. 244–47.

65. Vaihinger, *Commentar*, vol. 2, p. 313.

66. This is suggested by Jill Buroker, *Space and Congruence*, pp. 95–96, in her critique of my formulation of the argument in "The Non-spatiality of Things in Themselves for Kant."

67. Stephan Körner, *Kant*, p. 17.

CHAPTER 6

1. See *Critique of Pure Reason*, A141/B180.

2. As Lewis White Beck has shown in "Kant's Theory of Definition" and "Can Kant's Synthetic Judgments be Made Analytic?" in *Kant: Disputed Questions*, ed. Moltke S. Gram, real definitions are synthetic judgments. I also discuss this issue in *The Kant-Eberhard Controversy*, pp. 65–66.

3. The conception of pure concepts as second-order rules or rules for the formulation of empirical concepts, which are first-order rules, is developed by Robert Paul Wolff in *Kant's Theory of Mental Activity*, pp. 24–25.

4. I am, of course, ignoring here the complexities raised by the notion of an infinite judgment. In support of this I simply note that Kant himself maintains that, so far as their logical form is concerned, such judgments are really affirmations. See *Critique of Pure Reason*, A72/B97.

5. Ibid., A70–71/B95–96.

6. I say at least one from each set because Kant regards hypothetical and disjunctive judgments as themselves composed of other judgments. The component judgments of any such compound judgment could thus conceivably involve all of the functions.

7. Arthur Melnick, *Kant's Analogies of Experience*, p. 39.

8. It is at this point that my interpretation differs markedly from Melnick's. He argues that the goal of the Metaphysical Deduction is to establish a set of "epistemic concepts," which he characterizes as concepts that "apply to what is given only insofar as what is given is brought under a certain form of judgment." So far we are in agreement. He denies, however, that the argument either establishes or intends to establish the converse; namely, that these epistemic concepts are necessarily used every time that a subject judges under the corresponding form (ibid., p. 41). This latter claim, he contends, is made only in the Transcendental Deduction, where he takes Kant to be arguing that "what is given can be brought under certain forms of judgment only insofar as epistemic concepts apply to what is given" (pp. 46, 55–56). I have two points to make about this interpretation. First, it simply does not depict the structure of the argument of the Transcendental Deduction accurately. We shall see in the next chapter that Kant moves there from the logical functions of judgment to the categories and not vice versa. Second, Melnick contradicts himself. For example, in illustrating the connection between quantification and the concept of quantity, he writes: "Thus, if a subject is going to judge about objects where his judgments have quantificational structure and where it is going to make sense to say that his judgments could be either true or false, he must have some conception of what is to count as an individual or as one object" (p. 40). I believe that Melnick is basically correct here; but it also seems clear that this argument shows that the concept of an individual is necessary for any subject that judges under quantificational forms, and not merely that only a subject that judges under that form can have the concept of an individual. In any event, the former claim much more closely reflects Kant's implicit argument in the Metaphysical Deduction.

9. For the latter thesis see *Critique of Pure Reason*, B146–49, A146–47/B185–87, A239–46/B298–305. The former thesis is especially prevalent in the Second Edition version of the Transcendental Deduction (§§22–23), the Schematism, and the Ground of the Distinction of all Objects in General into Phenomena and Noumena. In these places Kant tends to characterize the pure concepts, apart from their schemata, as empty logical forms and to grant them only a logical significance. I do not believe, however, that there is any contradiction between this and the doctrine that I am currently attributing to him. Any appearance of contradiction can be easily explained in terms of the difference of emphasis. In the Metaphysical Deduction, the concern is to show that there are in fact pure concepts that provide a priori rules for the thought of an object; in the remainder of the Analytic the concern is to show that these rules yield knowledge of objects in synthetic judgments only

when they are applied to the content of sensible intuition. Far from contradicting one another, the "critical" structure of the later part of the Analytic makes sense only in light of the doctrine presently under consideration.

10. H. J. Paton, *Kant's Metaphysic of Experience*, vol. 2, p. 52.

11. See *Critique of Pure Reason*, A240–41 / B300–01. Kant there denies the possibility of a real definition of any of the pure concepts.

12. Ibid., A80 / B106.

13. Ibid., B129, B149, A147 / B186, A242–43 / B300–01.

14. Jonathan Bennett, *Kant's Analytic*, p. 183.

15. This is pointed out by Melnick, in *Kant's Analogies*, p. 39.

16. Melnick (*Kant's Analogies*, p. 51) suggests the appropriateness of the Rylean notion in this context.

17. See *Critique of Pure Reason*, A243 / B301.

18. A confusion on this point underlies one of the most common objections to the argument of the Metaphysical Deduction. This objection consists simply in pointing out that many judgments, particularly categorical and hypothetical judgments, do not presuppose, involve, apply, or in any way embody the corresponding category. In addition to Bennett, the long list of those who criticize Kant on these grounds includes H. A. Prichard (*Kant's Theory of Knowledge*, p. 159); Stephan Körner (*Kant*, p. 55); Graham Bird (*Kant's Theory of Knowledge*, p. 106); and P. F. Strawson (*The Bounds of Sense*, p. 76). Of these, Prichard and Bird suggest that Kant's argument might be said to show that the forms of judgment presuppose the pure concepts. They do not, however, take seriously the possibility that this is precisely what the argument is intended to show.

19. This point is argued vigorously and I think successfully by Paton, both in *Kant's Metaphysic*, vol. 1, pp. 300–02, and in his essay, "The Key to Kant's Deduction of the Categories," in *Kant: Disputed Questions*, pp. 247–68.

20. See Norman Kemp Smith, *A Commentary to Kant's "Critique of Pure Reason,"* pp. 176–86.

21. Following Bird's suggestion in *Kant's Theory*, p. 84, I am here modifying Kemp Smith's translation of the last sentence, or rather, of the clause of the German sentence which Kemp Smith translates as a separate English sentence. He translates this to read "On this account we are entitled to call these representations pure concepts of the understanding . . ." The German, however, says only "weswegen sie reine Verstandsbegriffe hiessen . . ." There is thus no sense of entitlement in the German text, and Kemp Smith's rendering of the passage is seriously misleading.

22. In the main lines of this interpretation, although not in all the details, I am here following Paton, *Kant's Metaphysic*, vol. 1, pp. 281–302, and especially Klaus Reich, *Die Vollständigkeit der kantischen Urteilstafel*, pp. 1–40. The significance of these interpretations consists in the fact that, in contrast to the vast bulk of the secondary literature, they emphasize the identity of the understanding in its logical and transcendental or real employment.

23. This point is particularly emphasized by Robert Paul Wolff, *Kant's Theory of Mental Activity*, pp. 68–77. Wolff's interpretation and criticism of the Metaphysical Deduction closely follows that of Kemp Smith.

24. See Kemp Smith, *Commentary*, pp. 178–80. This whole line of interpretation is succinctly formulated by Paton, in *Kant's Metaphysic*, vol. 1, p. 301.

25. *Ak.* XX, 271–72.

26. See Reich, *Die Vollständigkeit*, pp. 12–13.

27. Ibid., pp. 17–18, and Paton, *Kant's Metaphysic*, vol. 1, p. 288.

28. See Paton, *Kant's Metaphysic*, vol. 1, p. 290.

29. He comes close to doing so at A245 where he writes: "The pure categories are nothing but representations of things in general, so far as the manifold of their intuition must be thought through one of the logical functions of judgment." What is needed here,

but which Kant does not supply, is the converse of this claim. He also claims (A321) that "the form of judgments (converted into a concept of the synthesis of intuitions) yielded categories which direct all employment of understanding in experience." The suggestion that the former can be "converted" (*verwandelt*) into the latter certainly implies that they are distinct.

30. *Prolegomena,* §39, *Ak.* IV, 324.

31. *Ak.* IV, 474.

32. *Ak.* XX, 272.

33. A minor problem is raised by Kant's correlations of the universal judgment with the category of unity and the singular judgment with the category of totality. It seems obvious that these correlations should be reversed.

34. *Critique of Pure Reason,* B111–13.

35. Kant's account does show that the disjunctive function presupposes the category of totality. One cannot argue, however, that to judge disjunctively is just to conceive of the given manifold as constituting a totality. This is a necessary but not a sufficient condition for judging in this mode. It is also necessary to conceive of the elements of the totality as related in such a way as that the affirmation of one entails the negation of the remainder.

36. This claim is virtually a commonplace in the literature. It is suggested by Kant's own arguments for the inclusion of the singular and infinite forms. In addition, it is well established that Kant did not simply take over a commonly accepted list of judgmental forms, but rather selected his list piecemeal from a variety of sources and added some modifications of his own. The standard account of this matter is provided by H. J. de Vleeschauwer, *La Déduction transcendentale dans l'oeuvre de Kant,* vol. 1, pp. 217–48. A similar thesis, based upon a much more thorough consideration of the relevant literature of the seventeenth and eighteenth centuries, is argued for by Giorgio Tonelli, "Die Voraussetzungen zur kantischen Urteilstafel in der Logik des 18. Jahrhunderts," in *Kritik und Metaphysik,* pp. 134–57. Tonelli pays particular attention to the connection between the genesis of the list of the relational forms and the discovery of the relational categories. This conclusion, and indeed the whole claim that the table of logical functions presupposes the categories or that it is based on extralogical considerations, has been challenged by L. Krüger, "Wollte Kant die Vollständigkeit seiner Urteilstafel bewiesen?" *Kant-Studien* 59 (1968): 333–56, esp. pp. 344–53.

37. See *Critique of Pure Reason,* Axiii–xiv, Bxxiii–xxiv.

38. A similar thought is expressed in *Prolegomena,* §36 (*Ak.* IV, 318), and most particularly in Kant's letter to Herz, May 26, 1789 (*Ak.* XI, 51). For a different interpretation of these passages see Malte Hossenfelder, *Kants Konstitutions-theorie und die Transzendentale Deduktion,* pp. 149–50.

39. Reich, *Die Vollständigkeit,* pp. 55–95. In his extremely suggestive but ultimately unpersuasive analysis, Reich endeavors to derive the specific logical functions from the concept of the objective unity of apperception. He further contends that the reason Kant did not in fact do this in the *Critique* is that it is an analytic task that pertains to transcendental philosophy but not to a critique of pure reason. This interpretation of Kant's position and the general claim regarding the possibility of such a derivation of the table of logical function has successfully been criticized by L. Krüger, "Wollte Kant," pp. 333–37.

40. Krüger ("Wollte Kant," pp. 337–43) attempts to give a sense to Kant's completeness claim that is compatible with Kant's claims regarding the ultimate inexplicability of the specific functions of judgment. This attempt constitutes a positive alternative to Reich's attempt to provide a metalogical derivation of these functions from the concept of the objective unity of apperception. Krüger contends that Kant's actual conception of his task is more modest than is usually assumed and is compatible with the recognition of the de facto status of the forms or functions of judgment. He suggests that the completeness argument should be understood in accordance with the Metaphysical Exposition in the Transcendental

Aesthetic. So construed, Kant's concern is not, as Reich suggests, to demonstrate the necessity of a particular set of functions by deriving them from some higher principle; it is rather to show that the given forms, and no others, are the forms of thought (just as space and time and nothing else are the forms of sensibility). Kant accomplishes this, according to Krüger, by providing a criterion for deciding whether putative judgment forms are genuine logical functions of thought: whether they are forms by means of what the understanding is capable of producing unity in its representations (p. 342). Krüger acknowledges that the presence of such a criterion does not of itself guarantee the completion of the table, and he contends that at this point it is necessary to fall back upon Kant's presupposition that the understanding is capable of an exhaustive inventory of its own possessions. I think that Krüger is correct in his interpretation of Kant's intent, and that he is also quite right to distinguish between such an inventory, which is compatible with the de facto status of the items listed, and a logical derivation of these items from some higher principle. The problem, however, is that this does not really make Kant's argument any more plausible. In fact, since it grounds the claim for completeness on the dogmatic assumption of the capacity of the understanding to make such a complete inventory, Krüger's interpretation shows that Kant really begs the whole question. In addition, I think that Krüger's criterion is more appropriately applied to the derivation of the categories than to the logical functions of judgment.

CHAPTER 7

1. *Critique of Pure Reason*, Axvi.

2. See ibid., B138–39, B145. It is only in this sense, I think, that one can accept Strawson's contention (*The Bounds of Sense*, p. 97) that "the thesis of the necessary unity of consciousness can itself be represented as resting on a yet more fundamental premise—on nothing more than the necessity, for any experience at all to be possible, of the original duality of intuition and concept."

3. The problem is raised although not resolved by Rudolf Zocher, "Kants Transzendentale Deduktion der Kategorien," *Zeitschrift für philosophische Forschung* 8 (1954): 163–94, esp. 165.

4. The former interpretation is advocated by Adickes and Paton; the latter by Benno Erdmann and Vleeschauwer. Dieter Henrich, "The Proof-Structure of Kant's Transcendental Deduction," *Review of Metaphysics* 22 (1969): 640–59, provides a good critical analysis of both of these lines of interpretation. See especially pp. 641–45.

5. Henrich, "Proof-Structure," p. 642.

6. Henrich's well-known interpretation turns on a presumed restriction of the conclusion of the first part of the Deduction that is presumably removed in the second. The restriction, expressed in §20, is that "intuitions are subject to the categories *insofar as* they, as intuitions, already possess unity" (B143). Henrich contends that this leaves open the question of "the range *within which* unitary intuitions can be found" (ibid., p. 645). He further contends that the function of the second part is to demonstrate that any intuition which we can have must possess unity and, therefore, be subject to the categories. According to this interpretation, this follows simply from the fact that all our intuitions are in space and time, and these contain unity (p. 646). Rather than engaging in a detailed polemic with Henrich on the interpretive issue, I prefer to let my own alternative interpretation speak for itself. I must say, however, that I find the suggestion that the first part of the Deduction, which speaks of the "manifold of an intuition in general," involves a restriction of the kind affirmed by Henrich to be both artificial and counterintuitive. Moreover, according to this interpretation, the task of the second part becomes largely mechanical. Such a reading, I think, makes it impossible to take seriously Kant's account of the transcendental function of the imagination, which is the central feature in this part of the argument. Finally, despite my disagreement with his results, I readily acknowledge that it was this important essay of

Henrich's that first led me to attempt to rethink the whole problematic of the proof structure of Kant's argument.

7. The importance of this distinction, especially for the understanding of the Deduction, is noted by Heidegger, *Kant und das Problem der Metaphysik,* pp. 183–84. Heidegger also contends, however, that Kant employs the juridical notion of objective validity only in the preliminary formulation of the problem where he raises the *quid juris.* This is simply wrong: references to the objective validity of the categories occur even in the text of the First Edition version of the Deduction, which is, of course, the version which Heidegger believes to contain the authentic Kantian thought. Also, Ralf Meerbote ("Kant's Use of the Notions Objective Reality and Objective Validity," *Kant-Studien* 63 (1972): 51–58) argues for the general importance of this distinction in Kant. His main concern, however, is not with the Deduction or with its relevance to the categories, but rather with Kant's account of the various modes of certainty in the Canon of Pure Reason.

8. The clearest expression of this line of thought is Kant's well-known statement concerning the categories: "If we can prove that by their means alone an object can be thought, this will be a sufficient deduction of them, and will justify their objective validity" (A96–97).

9. See *Critique of Pure Reason,* A109, B148, B150–51, A155/B194.

10. See Klaus Reich, *Die Vollständigkeit der kantischen Urteilstafel,* p. 32.

11. The fullest and most important treatment of the philological issue with which I am familiar is by Bernard Roussett, *La Doctrine kantienne de l'objectivité,* pp. 294–300. Roussett demonstrates the impossibility of making any simple distinction between two senses of 'object', such as phenomenal and noumenal objects or objects of the senses and of the understanding, which would consistently correspond to Kant's use of these terms. He also points out that there are many passages in which they are strict synonyms and in which their juxtaposition seems to be motivated merely by stylistic considerations. Nevertheless, he argues that they have distinct senses, even though they do not refer to distinct entities. Roughly put, *Objekt,* for Roussett, expresses the thought of opposition to the subject, while *Gegenstand* expresses the thought of givenness or presentation to the subject. He regards these as two dimensions of the concept of an object. Unfortunately, Roussett does not deal specifically with the contrast as it is present in the Second Edition of the Deduction; nor, do I believe, does he discuss the purely logical or judgmental sense that is frequently given to "Objekt." Moreover, I am not at all certain that any such general thesis can be consistently carried through. It is, however, interesting that his account of the sense of "Gegenstand" would help to explain why Kant would use this term when he is concerned with establishing the objective reality of the categories.

12. This is especially emphasized by Robert Paul Wolff, *Kant's Theory of Mental Activity,* pp. 109 ff., 280 ff. See also Lewis White Beck, "Did the Sage of Königsberg Have No Dreams?" in *Essays on Kant and Hume,* p. 51.

13. Gerold Prauss, *Erscheinung bei Kant.* This contrast is central to the argument of the entire book. See especially §6, pp. 81–101, wherein Prauss analyzes "der transzendental-objektive Gegenstand," and §16, pp. 292–321, where he deals with "der transzendental-subjektive Gegenstand."

14. I do not wish to suggest by this that Prauss himself intends any such correspondence. He clearly does not. Nevertheless, he does suggest that his two senses of 'object' provide the key to the division of the Deduction. According to his analysis, the first part deals with the connection between the categories and "objective objects" and the second with their connection with "subjective objects." See especially *Erscheinung bei Kant,* pp. 277–78. My disagreement with him on this point shall become apparent during the course of this chapter.

15. Strawson, *Bounds of Sense,* pp. 73–74.

16. See Ross Harrison, "Strawson on Outer Objects," *Philosophical Quarterly* 20 (1970):

pp. 213–21. This is denied, however, by Graham Bird, "Recent Interpretations of Kant's Transcendental Deduction," *Akten des 4. Internationalen Kant-Kongress,* ed. G. Funke and J. Kopper, part 1, p. 372.

17. *Critique of Pure Reason,* B135, B138. The analyticity of the principle has recently been called into question by Paul Guyer, "Kant on Apperception and A Priori Synthesis," *American Philosophical Quarterly* 17 (1980): 205–12. He correctly points out that Kant describes the apperception principle as synthetic in the First Edition (A117), and he argues that, because of its connection with the doctrine of a priori synthesis, he ought to have done likewise in the Second Edition. By contrast, my claim is that this principle is correctly described as analytic in the Second Edition, and that this description is compatible with the account of synthesis.

18. Kant clearly expresses this point in his letter to Marcus Herz, May 26, 1789 (*Ak.* XI, 52).

19. The comparison between James and Kant on this point is noted by Norman Kemp Smith, *A Commentary to Kant's "Critique of Pure Reason,"* p. 459, and by Robert Paul Wolff, *Kant's Theory,* p. 106.

20. There is an interesting contrast here with the First Edition version of the Paralogism, where Kant might be taken to be denying that the principle is analytic. There he denies the possibility of proving "from concepts" the proposition "If a multiplicity of representations are to form a single representation, they must be contained in the absolute unity of the thinking subject" (A352). A consideration of the context, however, clearly indicates that the emphasis must be placed on "absolute," which generally has a metaphysical sense for Kant. Moreover, the only thing which he explicitly denies to be analytic is the quite different and manifestly metaphysical proposition "A thought can only be the effect of the absolute unity of the thinking being" (A353). The original proposition, presumably stripped of its metaphysical sense, is explained as an expression of a necessary condition for apperception. For a different interpretation of this passage see Kemp Smith, *Commentary,* p. 479. According to him this principle is synthetic a priori and is established in the Transcendental Deduction. It seems obvious, however, that it functions as a premise of the Deduction.

21. Dieter Henrich, *Identität und Objektivität,* pp. 54–58.

22. Ibid., pp. 76–79.

23. Ibid., esp. pp. 186–88. This Cartesian aspect of Henrich's interpretation has also been criticized by Malte Hossenfelder (*Kants Konstitutions-theorie und die Transzendentale Deduktion,* p. 132 n.) and by Paul Guyer in his review of Henrich's work (*Journal of Philosophy* 76 (1979): 162).

24. This formulation is used by both Reich (*Die Vollständigkeit,* p. 27) and by H. J. de Vleeschauwer (*La Déduction transcendentale dans l'oeuvre de Kant,* vol. 3, p. 101) to express Kant's apperception principle.

25. The dogmatic nature of Kant's claim is emphasized by Kemp Smith, *Commentary,* p. 284, and by A. C. Ewing, *A Short Commentary on Kant's "Critique of Pure Reason,"* p. 115, who makes specific reference to the Second Edition. The latter point is affirmed by Henrich, *Identität und Objektivität,* pp. 7, 21.

26. Kant asserts this in the First Edition (A94), when he suggests that there is a "synopsis" of the manifold attributable to sense, while still insisting upon the necessity of a synthesis.

27. Kant's letter to Beck, July 1, 1797 (*Ak.* XI, 514).

28. See *Critique of Pure Reason,* B132.

29. Ibid., A117 n.

30. This interpretation is suggested by the analyses of Reich, *Die Vollständigkeit,* pp. 34–36, and of Rainer Stuhlmann-Laeisz, *Kants Logik,* pp. 81–83.

31. Although he expresses it differently, I believe that this is basically equivalent to the objection of Hossenfelder, *Kants Konstitutions-theorie,* pp. 128–30.

32. Reflexion 6350, *Ak.* XVIII, 676. Other Reflexionen which refer to this same conception of an object include 4372, 4674, 5726, and 5923.

33. Henrich, *Identität und Objektivität,* pp. 44–46.

34. See Kemp Smith, *Commentary,* p. 385; Vleeschauwer, *La Déduction transcendentale,* vol. 3, pp. 123–24; Paton, *Kant's Metaphysic,* vol. 1, pp. 517–18.

35. *Prolegomena,* §18, *Ak.* IV, 298–99.

36. *Prolegomena,* §20, *Ak.* IV, 300.

37. Ibid., §22, *Ak.* IV, 304.

38. Ibid., §19, *Ak.* IV, 299 n.

39. Ibid., §20, *Ak.* IV, 301.

40. Ibid., §19, *Ak.* IV, 298.

41. See Ralf Meerbote, "Kant's Use of the Notions Objective Reality and Objective Validity," p. 55. In his discussion of the contrast between objective reality and objective validity as it occurs in the Canon of Pure Reason, Meerbote notes that the latter conception is explicated in terms of intersubjective agreement.

42. This is the basic characterization of these judgments that Prauss provides in *Erscheinung bei Kant,* esp. pp. 199–252.

43. Prauss contends (ibid., pp. 234 ff. and elsewhere) that judgments of perception are incorrigible. This, however, is irrelevant to the present context, where we are concerned merely with the question of their objective validity.

44. See Lewis White Beck, "Did the Sage of Königsberg Have No Dreams?" p. 51.

45. Ibid., pp. 52–53.

46. *Prolegomena,* §18, *Ak.* IV, 298.

47. I take this to be basically the view of Prauss (*Erscheinung bei Kant,* pp. 150–51); later, however (pp. 155 ff.), he does seem to interpret these as judgments of inner sense. Moreover, it should also be noted that Prauss explicitly asserts that such judgments involve the categories. His contention is that they involve them in a different way than do judgments of experience or "objective judgments." The latter involve the application, these merely the use, of the categories (pp. 272–92). This is connected with his interpretation of experience as the *Deutung* of appearances, an issue with which we are not presently concerned.

48. L. W. Beck, "Did the Sage of Königsberg Have No Dreams?" p. 54. Beck, however, does not seem to be concerned about this difference, although his analysis suggests that both must involve the categories.

49. I have no wish to dwell here on particular difficulties that may be associated with the notion of dreaming, in contrast to Kant's own examples of judgments of perception. It should be noted, however, that one cannot escape from this conclusion by arguing with Malcolm that we cannot be meaningfully said to judge in dreams. Even if that is the case, we then at least dream that we judge, and this must presuppose the categories.

50. L. W. Beck, "Did the Sage of Königsberg Have No Dreams?" p. 54.

51. *Ak.* XI, 52; *Kant's Philosophical Correspondence 1759–99,* ed. and trans. A. Zweig, pp. 153–54.

52. Reflexion 6315, *Ak.* XVIII, 621; L. W. Beck, "Did the Sage of Königsberg Have No Dreams?" p. 45.

53. L. W. Beck, "Did the Sage of Königsberg Have No Dreams?" p. 45, suggests that this involves an inspectional, not a functional sense of intuition. This means simply that intuitions are themselves represented as objects rather than being used to represent objects.

54. For an account of the contrast between the "I" as subject and the "me" as object of thought, see Pierre Lachièze-Rey, *L'Idealisme kantien,* esp. pp. 149–207.

55. See also *Critique of Pure Reason,* B139. In the sentence immediately following the one just discussed Kant writes: "Therefore the empirical unity of consciousness, through association of representations, itself concerns an appearance, and is wholly contingent." Presumably, 'empirical unity' is equivalent to 'subjective unity'.

56. Cf. Paton, *Kant's Metaphysic*, vol. 1, p. 520. I shall deal with the question of the nature of empirical apperception in chapter 12.

57. I believe that this is basically the interpretation suggested by Prauss, *Erscheinung bei Kant*, pp. 284–85. Prauss does not acknowledge any problem here because he sees empirical apperception as the mode of consciousness through which we apprehend a subjective object. This is quite true as far as it goes, but it should also be noted that the judgment through which even a subjective object is represented is objectively valid.

58. This is the interpretation affirmed by Paton. He fails to see, however, the incompatibility of this with the conception of empirical apperception as a mode of consciousness through which subjective states are represented.

59. A somewhat similar interpretation and criticism of Kant on this point is affirmed by Arthur Melnick, *Kant's Analogies of Experience*, pp. 31–37. He shows that Kant tends to conflate the judgment-nonjudgment distinction with the distinction between subjective and objective judgment. My difference with Melnick here concerns merely his interpretation of subjective unity as a unity of concepts rather than of intuitions or images.

60. See *Critique of Pure Reason*, B163–65.

61. Ibid., A247/B304.

62. Ibid., B151–52.

63. Heidegger, *Kant und das Problem*, p. 146.

64. Heidegger notes (ibid., p. 148) that in *Nachträge* XII Kant changed "soul" to "understanding."

65. See *Critique of Pure Reason*, B147.

66. I have modified somewhat Kemp Smith's translation. He construes *derselben* to refer to empirical intuition *simpliciter,* rather than to the manifold thereof.

67. See Paton, *Kant's Metaphysic*, vol. 1, p. 528 n.

68. A similar point is made in the note attached to B137.

69. *Critique of Pure Reason*, A100.

70. Cf. ibid., A120, B168, A320/B376.

71. Cf. ibid., A110, B218.

72. Kant sometimes seems to slide from the former claim to the latter. A typical passage is B164–65.

73. A markedly different but, I believe, unconvincing interpretation of this passage is given by Paton, in *Kant's Metaphysic*, vol. 1, pp. 444–45.

74. These difficulties largely concern the problematic doctrine of transcendental affinity, which I discuss in "Transcendental Affinity—Kant's Answer to Hume?" in *Kant's Theory of Knowledge*, ed. Lewis White Beck, pp. 119–27. In brief, the problem with the doctrine of affinity is that it involves a slide from claims about "appearances" construed as the contents of empirical consciousness to claims about "appearances" construed in the transcendental sense as things that are known as they appear. This parallels roughly the slide from perception to experience in the Second Edition.

75. Prauss, *Erscheinung bei Kant*, p. 277.

76. *Ak.* IV, 474.

77. An interesting discussion of the difference between the anti-Cartesian and anti-Humean lines of argument in Kant, as well as a critique of interpreters such as Strawson who fail to notice this difference, is provided by Margaret Wilson, "Kant and the Refutation of Subjectivism," in *Kant's Theory of Knowledge*, pp. 208–17.

78. Jonathan Bennett, *Kant's Analytic*, p. 100.

CHAPTER 8

1. Kant's letter to Reinhold, May 12, 1789 (*Ak.* XI, 30).

2. H. J. Paton, *Kant's Metaphysic of Experience*, vol. 1, p. 72.

3. Martin Heidegger, *Kant und das Problem der Metaphysik*, p. 105.

4. H. A. Prichard, *Kant's Theory of Knowledge,* pp. 246–47.

5. G. J. Warnock, "Concepts and Schematism," *Analysis* 8 (1949): pp. 77–82.

6. See Eva Schaper, "Kant's Schematism Reconsidered," *Review of Metaphysics* 18 (1964): 267–92; Moltke S. Gram, *Kant, Ontology,* and *the A Priori;* and Lauchlan Chipman, "Kant's Categories and Their Schematism," *Kant-Studien* 63 (1972): 36–49.

7. Cf. Paton, *Kant's Metaphysic,* vol. 2, p. 67.

8. A similar point is made by Gram in his discussion of Warnock's objection, albeit without specific mention of a "logical use"; *Kant, Ontology,* and *the A Priori,* pp. 89–91.

9. Reflexion 5133, *Ak.* XVIII, p. 392.

10. This is pointed out by Ernst Robert Curtius, "Das Schematismuskapitel in der Kritik der reinen Vernunft," *Kant-Studien* 19 (1916): pp. 338–66, esp. p. 348; and by Norman Kemp Smith, *A Commentary to Kant's "Critique of Pure Reason,"* p. 336.

11. *Critique of Pure Reason,* A137/B176. I am here following the original version of the text rather than Vaihinger's emendation, which was adopted by Kemp Smith in his translation. For a discussion of this point see Paton, *Kant's Metaphysic,* vol. 2, p. 26, n. 1.

12. Kemp Smith, *Commentary,* pp. 335–36. He is essentially following Curtius. The line of objection which I have tried to sketch is intended to capture the main thrust of the criticisms of both Curtius and Kemp Smith.

13. Paton, *Kant's Metaphysic,* vol. 2, p. 26, n. 1.

14. Cf. Gerold Prauss, *Erscheinung bei Kant,* p. 103.

15. Both Curtius ("Das Schematismuskapitel," pp. 348 ff.) and Kemp Smith, (*Commentary,* p. 336) acknowledge the suitability of this model for the presentation of the problematics of the schematism, but then proceed to criticize Kant for not adhering to it.

16. See Allison, *Kant-Eberhard Controversy,* esp. p. 60.

17. *Ak.* V, 68.

18. *Ak.* VI, 251.

19. Gram, *Kant, Ontology,* esp. pp. 128–29.

20. Ibid., pp. 91–94.

21. See Allison, *Kant-Eberhard Controversy,* pp. 86–88.

22. The distinction is also implicit in the response to Eberhard, wherein Kant denies the innateness of the actual representations of space and time (Allison, *Kant-Eberhard Controversy,* p. 136; *Ak.* VIII, 222–37). Perhaps even more germane, in a Reflexion that deals specifically with the Schematism, Kant distinguishes between *Zeitanschauung* and *Zeitbestimmung,* the intuition and the determination of time (Reflexion 6359, *Ak.* XVIII, 686).

23. In this regard, it is worthy of note that in his polemic with Eberhard Kant explicitly characterizes mathematical construction as "schematic" rather than "mechanical"; Allison, *Kant-Eberhard Controversy,* p. 111; *Ak.* VIII, 192. The point is that what is constructed is the schema of the concept.

24. See *Critique of Pure Reason,* B153–56, where Kant talks specifically about the determination of inner sense and his letter to Beck, July 3, 1792 (*Ak.* XI, 348).

25. So construed, a "transcendental determination of time" is also equivalent to "the synthesized in general" (*das Zusammengesetzten überhaupt*) to which Kant refers in his correspondence with Beck and Tieftrunk. See especially Kant's letter to Tieftrunk, Dec. 11, 1797, *Ak.* XII, 222–25.

26. Paton, *Kant's Metaphysic,* vol. 2, pp. 28–30.

27. A plausible explanation of this is provided by Paton, *Kant's Metaphysic,* vol. 2, pp. 63–64.

28. Lewis White Beck, "Can Kant's Synthetic Judgments be Made Analytic?" *Kant: Disputed Questions,* ed. Moltke S. Gram, p. 241.

29. See Robert E. Butts, "Kant's Schemata as Semantical Rules," *Kant Studies Today,* ed. Lewis White Beck, pp. 290–300.

30. See *Critique of Pure Reason,* A242, A248/B305.

31. L. W. Beck, "Can Kant's Synthetic Judgments be Made Analytic?" p. 241, maintains that "schematizing a category is very different from defining it." This is certainly true if one is talking about a nominal definition. In any event, providing a schema and giving a real definition serve the same purpose: they establish the objective reality of the concept in question. Kant himself is somewhat ambiguous on the point. As we have already seen in chapter 6, he remarks that "we cannot define any of them [the categories] in a real [added in B] fashion, . . . without at once descending to the conditions of sensibility" (A240/B300). Since to descend to the conditions of sensibility is to schematize, Kant might be taken to be implying that the various schemata are real definitions of the categories.

32. Ibid., pp. 241–42.

33. Ibid., p. 242.

34. Paton, *Kant's Metaphysic*, vol. 2, pp. 52–53.

35. According to Paton, the schema is simply the product of the synthesis according to the schematized category; ibid., p. 53, and more generally pp. 42–43.

36. This distinction is almost a commonplace in the literature, and they are frequently treated as if they were two distinct sets of concepts. This is certainly true of Paton's account and even more so of Gram's. For the latter, see especially *Kant, Ontology*, pp. 126–27. I do not believe, however, that this has any warrant in the text. If one wishes to distinguish between pure and schematized categories, then the distinction should not be construed as between two sets of concepts, but between two functions (judgmental and perceptual or experiential) that are exercised by the pure concepts. So construed the distinction corresponds to the division between the two parts of the Transcendental Deduction in the Second Edition.

37. Jonathan Bennett, *Kant's Analytic*, p. 151, suggests that "the schema of any category, then, is just the category itself with the condition of temporality added." But then our question becomes, How, in each case, do we determine the specific condition of temporality?

38. In emphasizing the conception of transcendental schema as product of the transcendental synthesis, I am following Paton, *Kant's Metaphysic*, vol. 2, pp. 43 ff.

39. The "rule theory" is presented by Curtius. In the recent literature its most rigorous advocate is Robert Paul Wolff, *Kant's Theory of Mental Activity*, pp. 206–23.

40. Gram provides a convincing critique of the "rule theory" along similar lines; *Kant, Ontology*, pp. 95–100.

41. *Critique of Pure Reason*, A220–21/B267–68.

42. This is argued for by Gregg E. Franzwa, "Space and the Schematism," *Kant-Studien* 69 (1978): 149–59.

43. *Ak.* IX, 51. Additional references to *logische Wirklichkeit* are to be found in Kant's letter to Reinhold, May 19, 1789 (*Ak.* XI, 47; *Critique of Pure Reason*, A75/B101; and *Reflexion* 2181, *Ak.* XVI, 261). The notion is also discussed by Paton, *Kant's Metaphysic*, vol. 2, p. 58; Klaus Reich, *Die Vollständigkeit der kantischen Urteilstafel*, pp. 44, 56–60; and Rainer Stuhlmann-Laeisz, *Kants Logik*, p. 63.

44. Paton, *Kant's Metaphysic*, vol. 1, p. 60.

45. Kant (*Critique of Pure Reason*, A242/B300) does use the locution *ein Dasein zu aller Zeit* in his characterization of permanence (*Beharrlichkeit*).

46. It is interesting that this is precisely what Strawson takes to be the main thrust of the argument of the Transcendental Deduction. See *Bounds of Sense*, pp. 100–12. The possibility of finding such an argument in Kant and its limitations is also discussed by Henrich, *Identität und Objektivität*, esp. pp. 34, 43.

47. Kant states that the Postulates contain only "explanations of the concepts of possibility, actuality and necessity in their empirical employment" (A219/B266), and he denies that they are "objectively synthetic" (A233/B286). That is why these principles are best characterized as schema judgments.

48. See Paton, *Kant's Metaphysic*, vol. 2, pp. 180–81.

49. Ibid., pp. 180–83.

50. *Critique of Pure Reason*, A179–80/B222.

51. I discuss Kant's critique of this conception of the principle of sufficient reason in *Kant-Eberhard Controversy*.

52. For a discussion of this issue with specific reference to the Kant criticism of C. I. Lewis, see L. W. Beck, "Can Kant's Synthetic Judgments be made Analytic?" pp. 235–38; the same issue is treated more fully in Beck's "Lewis' Kantianism," in *Studies in the Philosophy of Kant*, pp. 108–24.

CHAPTER 9

1. Kant initially refers to "modes of time" at A177, where he characterizes them as permanence or duration (*Beharrlichkeit*), succession, and coexistence. Each of the Analogies is there correlated with one of the modes as the rule for its determination. These passages raise two exegetical issues: one concerns the meaning of the expression 'mode of time'; the other concerns the compatibility of the claim that permanence or duration, as well as succession and coexistence, are such modes with what Kant says elsewhere in the Analogies. For example, we find Kant claiming (A183/B226) that change (or succession) does not affect time itself, but only appearances in time. He further claims in the same context that simultaneity is not a mode of "time itself" because the parts of time are not simultaneous but successive. I believe that Paton indicates the correct way out of the interpretive morass when he points out that these modes are not to be construed as properties or characteristics of time itself, but rather as relational properties of things in time (*Kant's Metaphysic of Experience*, vol. 2, pp. 165 ff.).

2. The contrary thesis is the basis of Melnick's interpretation of the First Analogy; *Kant's Analogies of Experience*, pp. 58–71.

3. This line of argument is developed by W. H. Walsh in "Kant on the Perception of Time," *The First Critique*, eds. T. Penelhum and J. MacIntosh, pp. 70–88, and in *Kant's Criticism of Metaphysics*, pp. 129–35.

4. *Critique of Pure Reason*, A183.

5. See Paton, *Kant's Metaphysic*, vol. 2, p. 196.

6. *Critique of Pure Reason*, A184/B227.

7. I have here modified Kemp Smith's translation to render the second clause as a separate sentence. His version reads: "For it is that in which, and as determinations of which succession or coexistence can alone be represented." I believe that this misleadingly suggests that Kant is making two distinct claims here: that succession and coexistence can be represented only in *time;* and that they can be represented only as *determinations* of time. The German, however, says only "Die Zeit also in der aller Wechsel der Erscheinungen gedacht werden soll, bleibt und wechselt nicht; weil sie dasjenige ist, in welchem das Nacheinander oder Zugleichsein nur als Bestimmungs derselben vorgestelt werden können."

8. This reconstruction of the argument can be compared with Paton's six-step reconstruction, in *Kant's Metaphysic*, vol. 2, pp. 120–21. The basic difference is that he lumps together my steps 5 and 6. His version is justified by a literal reading of the text (since 5 and 6 are combined in a single sentence). Nevertheless, I believe that they involve quite distinct claims and must be treated as such.

9. This citation is taken from Norman Kemp Smith, *A Commentary to Kant's "Critique of Pure Reason,"* p. 359 n.

10. Robert Paul Wolff, *Kant's Theory of Mental Activity*, p. 251.

11. This is suggested by Kemp Smith, *Commentary*, p. 359.

12. Gerd Buchdahl, *Metaphysics and the Philosophy of Science*, p. 647, suggests that this rejected assumption represents the Newtonian view.

13. Paton, *Kant's Metaphysic*, vol. 2, p. 191.

14. Jonathan Bennett, *Kant's Analytic*, p. 182.

15. James Van Cleve, "Substance, Matter, and Kant's First Analogy," *Kant-Studien* 70, (1979): 153.

16. Kemp Smith's translation of *Wechsel* is also criticized by D. P. Dryer, in *Kant's Solution for Verification in Metaphysics*, pp. 351–52. Basing his analysis on B233, where Kant seems to equate *Wechsel* with *Sukzession*, he suggests that *Wechsel* be rendered 'succession'; thus, the principle on his formulation reads: "All succession is change." This is also misleading, however, for in spite of B233, Kant does not simply equate *Wechsel* with *Sukzession*. He rather equates it with 'succession of appearances' or 'appearances of succession' (*Erscheinungen der Zeitfolge*) (B232). Presumably, this refers to the kind of succession in which something is replaced or succeeded by something else, which is, in effect, "replacement change."

17. Bennett, *Kant's Analytic*, pp. 187–88.

18. Dryer, *Kant's Solution*, pp. 353–59.

19. This argument should be contrasted with the argument attributed to Kant by Van Cleve, in "Substance, Matter, and Kant's First Analogy," pp. 155–57. The argument, as he constructs it, involves a non sequitur in the move from the premise that some antecedent object must have existed at t_1 (if one is to experience a replacement change at t_2), to the conclusion that the new state of affairs that comes into existence at t_2 must be merely a determination or state of the object existing at t_1. The argument sketched here, however, links the state of affaris that comes into existence at t_2 with a prior and contrary state of affairs (symbolized by 'non-x' and 'x'), not with an antecedently existing object. It contends that if the coming into existence of the later state of affairs (the replacement change) is to be experienced, it must be contrasted with the earlier state of affairs (otherwise there would be no change), and this requires that *both* states of affairs (non-y and x) be experienced as successively existing states or determinations of an enduring object (y). Thus, while I agree with Van Cleve that the argument which he cites does involve a non sequitur, I see no reason to accept his reconstruction of the argument.

20. Among those who maintain this in one form or another are Jonathan Bennett, *Kant's Analytic*, p. 199; D. P. Dryer, *Kant's Solution*, pp. 367–68; Arthur Melnick, *Kant's Analogies*, p. 67; P. F. Strawson, *Bounds of Sense*, pp. 128–30.

21. This is the argument that has been developed by W. H. Walsh; see note 3, above.

22. It has frequently been noted that Kant's claim here is very close to that of the Second Analogy. If one were to characterize Kant's position in Aristotelian terms, it could be said that the First Analogy is concerned with the demonstration of the necessity of a material cause for every event and the Second Analogy with the demonstration of the necessity of an efficient cause.

23. Critics who attack Kant on this point include C. D. Broad, "Kant's First and Second Analogies of Experience," *Proceedings of the Aristotelian Society* 25 (1926): 189–210; Jonathan Bennett, *Kant's Analytic*, p. 200; and Robert Paul Wolff, *Kant's Theory*, p. 251. The whole matter is discussed by James Van Cleve, "Substance, Matter, and Kant's First Analogy," pp. 158–61.

24. A somewhat similar argument, which turns on an appeal to the Axioms of Intuition, is suggested by Carl Friedrich Weizsäcker, "Kant's 'First Analogy of Experience' and Conservation Principle of Physics," *Synthese* 23 (1971): 84. Support for this interpretation is also provided by Reflexion 81, *Ak.* XXIII, 30–31, where Kant remarks:

If substance persists while the accidents change [*wechseln*] but, at the same time, substance apart from all of its accidents is the empty substantial [*das leer substantiale ist*], what is it that persists? The only thing in experience that can be distinguished from the changing determinations is quantity [*Quantität*], and this can only be measured through the magnitude [*Grösse*] of the merely relative effect with respect to equivalent outer relations. *It therefore applies only to bodies.*

25. *Metaphysical Foundations of Natural Science, Ak.* IV, 541.

26. For a discussion of the empirical nature of Kant's concept of matter see Robert Walker, "The Status of Kant's Theory of Matter," in *Kant's Theory of Knowledge,* ed. Lewis White Beck, pp. 151–56.

27. *Metaphysical Foundations of Natural Sciences, Ak.* IV, 503.

28. Ibid.

29. Ibid.

30. For a discussion of this point see Paton, *Kant's Metaphysic,* vol. 2, pp. 211–12.

31. *Metaphysical Foundations of Natural Science, Ak.* IV, 541–42.

32. James Van Cleve, "Substance, Matter, and Kant's First Analogy," pp. 160–61.

33. The latter position is affirmed vigorously by Gerd Buchdahl (*Metaphysics,* pp. 672–81).

34. Wolff, *Kant's Theory,* p. 249.

35. Gordon G. Brittan, Jr., *Kant's Theory of Science,* pp. 143–44.

36. Perhaps the best-known expression of the aspect of Descartes's theory of substance is contained in his analysis of the perception of the piece of wax in the Second Meditation.

37. See *Critique of Pure Reason,* A205/B251–52. For a discussion of this point, see Paton, *Kant's Metaphysic,* vol. 2, pp. 215–17.

38. For a discussion of this aspect of Kant's thought, including an analysis of the relevant passages in the *Lectures on Metaphysics,* see Allison, "Kant's Critique of Spinoza," in *The Philosophy of Baruch Spinoza,* ed. Richard Kennington, pp. 205–07.

CHAPTER 10

1. David Hume, *A Treatise of Human Nature,* ed. L. A. Selby-Bigge, book 1, part 3, section 4, p. 78.

2. Lewis White Beck, "A Prussian Hume and a Scottish Kant," in *Essays on Kant and Hume,* pp. 111–29.

3. A helpful account of this is provided by L. W. Beck in "A Reading of the Third Paragraph in B," *Essays on Kant and Hume,* pp. 141–46.

4. Kant seems to have recognized this in the Second Edition, for in the account of the general principle of the Analogies (B219) he provides a more concise version of the same line of argument.

5. This point is noted by numerous commentators including H. J. Paton, *Kant's Metaphysic of Experience,* vol. 2, p. 231; Arthur Melnick, *Kant's Analogies of Experience,* p. 85; L. W. Beck, "A Reading," p. 144; and James Van Cleve, "Four Recent Interpretations of Kant's Second Analogy," *Kant-Studien* 64 (1973): 69–87, esp. p. 75.

6. This is indicated by Gerd Buchdahl, *Metaphysics and the Philosophy of Science,* esp. pp. 641–46. In fact, although my own formulation certainly differs in some respects from his, I am greatly indebted to him for his criticisms of an earlier version of this and the preceding chapter.

7. We shall see in chapter 12 that when in the judgment of inner sense this so-called "subjective order" is made into an object it is experienced as part of the objective temporal order of the phenomenal world. Strictly speaking, there is only one temporal order because there is only one time.

8. This premise is included in the parallel passage at B219.

9. The Newtonian position is obviously the test case here. My interpretation is largely based on H. G. Alexander's analysis of Newton's characterization of absolute or real time in the famous scholium to Definition 8 of the *Principia* as time as it is measured by the period of revolution of Jupiter's moons and by pendulums. *The Leibniz-Clarke Correspondence,* ed. and trans. H. G. Alexander, pp. xxxv–xxxvi. The point, then, is that not even Newtonian absolute or real time is held to be itself perceived.

10. See Paton, *Kant's Metaphysic*, vol. 2, pp. 224–25. He follows the tradition of Adickes and Kemp Smith.

11. See Norman Kemp Smith, *A Commentary to Kant's "Critique of Pure Reason,"* pp. 375–76, who is closely followed by Robert Paul Wolff, *Kant's Theory of Mental Activity*, p. 373; for a more developed critique, see A. C. Ewing, *Kant's Treatment of Causality*, pp. 73–75. A helpful restatement of these criticisms is provided by W. A. Suchting, "Kant's Second Analogy of Experience," *Kant-Studien* 58 (1967): 355–69. An interesting attempt at a defense of Kant against these objections is offered by Paton, *Kant's Metaphysic*, vol. 2, pp. 254–56.

12. See Suchting, "Kant's Second Analogy," p. 357, and Van Cleve, "Four Recent Interpretations," p. 73.

13. *Critique of Pure Reason*, B4–5.

14. This interpretation is supported by Kant's language in the Second Analogy. See, for instance, A193/B239, A200/B246, A201/B247.

15. See Suchting, "Kant's Second Analogy," p. 356, and Van Cleve, "Four Recent Interpretations," pp. 73–74.

16. Suchting, "Kant's Second Analogy," p. 356, n. 7, correctly remarks that, if we assume that the motion of the ship is rectilinear and uniform, its motion cannot be described as a change of state. He thus suggests that the various German terms translated as 'alteration', 'event', 'happening', and 'occurrence' be taken to signify "the coming to be or passing away of some 'determination' of a substance." This, however, is a subtlety which has little bearing on the argument. For the most part I intend to follow Kant's customary usage and take 'state' in this context as equivalent to 'determination'. The point is simply that states or determinations of substances are the sorts of things that come into being or pass away, and that such "happenings" are events.

17. See Graham Bird, *Kant's Theory of Knowledge*, p. 155, and Melnick, *Kant's Analogies*, pp. 79–80. This is in response to an objection raised at this point by Jonathan Bennett, *Kant's Analytic*, p. 222.

18. Typical of this are the interpretations of Wolff, *Kant's Theory*, p. 267; and Melnick, *Kant's Analogies*, pp. 80–82.

19. Wolff, *Kant's Theory*, p. 268.

20. The same assumption is criticized from a different point of view by Melnick, *Kant's Analogies*, pp. 81–83.

21. In spite of the criticism cited above, this is recognized by Wolff, who writes: "The real point of the argument, as Kant makes clear later in the Analogy, is not that we must *perceive* B after A, but that we must represent or *think* B after A. Objectivity is a characteristic of cognition not of apprehension" (*Kant's Theory*, p. 268). I believe this point to be perfectly correct, and I differ from Wolff only in regarding it as a statement of Kant's consistent position throughout the Analogy.

22. A211/B258.

23. See Van Cleve, "Four Recent Interpretations," pp. 75–76, for his discussion of Ewing's interpretation; and Melnick, *Kant's Analogies*, pp. 81–82, for his critique of Paton in this point.

24. Lewis White Beck, "Once More into the Breach," in *Essays on Kant and Hume*, p. 131.

25. Ibid., pp. 132–35.

26. This formulation is taken from Gordon G. Brittan, Jr., *Kant's Theory of Science*, p. 189. In fairness, however, it should be noted that this does not reflect his own interpretation of the argument, although he does endeavor to connect the Second Analogy with the problem of induction.

27. This is basically the line of interpretation advocated by Melnick, *Kant's Analogies*, pp. 85–94.

28. The essential point is clearly stated by Bird (*Kant's Theory,* p. 162, n. 1), when he writes: "The fact that we employ our empirical knowledge of particular causal laws in order to check the time order of phenomena is important for Kant's argument in the Postulates, but not especially for that of the Second Analogy. It could be used in this latter context to stress the usefulness, even indispensability, of the concept in its empirical or scientific employment, but this is in any case assumed in the argument, and not at issue between Kant and Hume." Although this was written many years before the publication of Melnick's book, it indicates, to my mind at least, precisely the error in Melnick's interpretation of the Second Analogy.

29. Melnick, *Kant's Analogies,* pp. 110 ff., introduces this conception and contrasts "initiating" with "standing conditions."

30. Arthur Schopenhauer, *Ueber die vierfache Wurzel des Satzes vom zureichenden Grunde,* vol. 1, *Sämtliche Werke,* ed. J. Frauenstadt, §23, pp. 85–92.

31. Although he does not have the precise problem with which we are presently concerned in mind, a characterization of such a situation is suggested by Melnick with his analysis of a "closed system" (*Kant's Analogies,* p. 117). According to Melnick, "a closed system is one whose description at a certain time is governable by laws whose conditions of application constitute a description of the system at some other time." The movement of the planets is an example of such a system because "the position of the planets at any time is a function of their mass and position at other times." This can perhaps be taken as the description of a situation in which the earlier state of a "substance" is the cause or condition of its later state.

32. Buchdahl, *Metaphysics,* p. 650.

33. Arthur Lovejoy, "On Kant's Reply to Hume," *Kant: Disputed Questions,* ed. Moltke S. Gram, p. 303.

34. Ibid., pp. 300–01.

35. P. F. Strawson, *The Bounds of Sense,* p. 137.

36. Ibid., p. 138.

37. Ibid.

38. Lewis White Beck, "A *Non-Sequitur* of Numbing Grossness," in *Essays on Kant and Hume,* pp. 151–52.

39. These alternatives are suggested by Van Cleve, "Four Recent Interpretations," p. 75.

40. The point is clearly shown by Buchdahl, *Metaphysics,* pp. 670–71.

CHAPTER 11

1. I discuss this aspect of Kant's analysis in "Things in Themselves, Noumena, and the Transcendental Object," *Dialectica* 32 (1978): 42–76. The argument of this chapter follows closely the account that I gave in that paper.

2. The most interesting and informed discussion of the two senses in which Kant construes the "thing in itself" is provided by Bernard Rousset, *La Doctrine kantienne de l'objectivité,* pp. 167 ff.

3. A firm adherent of this view is Prichard, who assumes that when Kant construes the distinction between appearances and things in themselves to refer to two entities, he requires things in themselves in order to "produce" appearances (*Kant's Theory of Knowledge,* pp. 73–76). It also seems to have been held by Norman Kemp Smith, *A Commentary to Kant's "Critique of Pure Reason,"* esp. pp. 216–18. In more recent literature, it can be found in Nicholas Rescher, "Noumenal Causality," in *Kant's Theory of Knowledge,* ed. L. W. Beck, pp. 175–83; and Moltke S. Gram, "How to Dispense with Things in Themselves (I)," *Ratio* 18 (1976): 1–15.

4. This interpretation is adhered to by Erick Adickes, *Kant und das Ding an sich,* p. 5; and by Paton, *Kant's Metaphysic of Experience,* esp. vol. 2, pp. 445–46. In the more recent

literature its proponents include Horst Seidl, "Bemerkungen zu Ding an sich und Transzendentalen Gegenstand in Kants *Kritik der reinen Vernunft,*" *Kant-Studien* 63 (1972): 305–14; and W. H. Walsh, *Kant's Criticism of Metaphysics,* pp. 162–67.

5. An interesting treatment of the problem along these lines is provided by Gerold Prauss, *Kant und das Problem der Dinge an sich,* esp. pp. 32–43. See also Ralf Meerbote, "The Unknowability of Things in Themselves," in *Kant's Theory of Knowledge,* ed. L. W. Beck, pp. 166–74.

6. The point is made by Prauss, *Kant und das Problem,* pp. 42–43.

7. See *De Mundi Sensibilis atque Intelligibilis Forma et Principiis,* §4, *Ak.* II, 392.

8. The emphasis on the methodological basis of the conceptions of the noumenon, the thing as it is in itself, and the transcendental object separates the interpretation provided here from the "as if" interpretations of Vaihinger and more recently of Eva Shaper, "The Kantian Thing-in-itself as a Philosophical Fiction," *Philosophical Quarterly* 16 (1966): 233–43.

9. I have attempted this in my paper "Kant's Concept of the Transcendental Object," *Kant-Studien* 59 (1968): 165–86. I must admit, however, that the views expressed in this present work differ substantially from those expressed there.

10. Cf. A253; A358; Reflexion 5554, *Ak.* XVIII, 250.

11. It should be noted that in the Note to the Amphiboly of Concepts of Reflection, which remains unchanged in the Second Edition, we find a different version of the distinction between a positive and a negative sense of the noumenon or "intelligible object" (A286–88/B342–44). This distinction is between the idea of a thing "thought through pure categories, without any schema of sensibility" (positive sense), which is said to be impossible, and the "objects of a non-sensible intuition" (negative sense). This negative sense is identical to what later becomes the positive sense.

12. Erik Stenius ("On Kant's Distinction between Phenomena and Noumena," *Philosophical Essays Dedicated to Gunnar Aspelin on the Occasion of his 65th Birthday,* pp. 231–45) has argued (p. 241) that "the so-called 'noumena in the negative sense' ought not to be called 'noumena' at all—but rather the transcendental object, which is completely indeterminate." In this he is perfectly correct. However, as part of his critique of the Second Edition version he proceeds to claim that this leads Kant into a contradiction in terms: "For this means that the idea of a 'thing as it is in itself' will be identified with the idea of a thing that is in no way at all. But then the argument of the Transcendental Analytic as well as that of the Transcendental Aesthetic loses its point." What Stenius misses, and what has been stressed here throughout, is the epistemic thrust of Kant's analysis. The idea of a thing as it is in itself is not identified with the idea of a thing that "is in no way at all," but with that of a thing that *for us* can be nothing more than a mere something $= x$.

13. Interestingly enough, Kant returned to his earlier locutions in the *Opus Postumum,* especially Convolut VII (*Ak.* XXII, 3–131), where the methodological interpretation sketched here seems to find ample support. The following is typical of many passages from this section: "Jede Vorstellung als Erscheinung wird als von dem was der Gegenstand an sich ist unterschieden gedacht (das Sensibile einem Intelligibelen) das letztere aber = x ist nicht ein besonderes ausser meiner Vorstellung existierendes Objekt sondern lediglich die Idee der Abstraktion vom Sinnlichen welche als notwendig anerkannt wird. Es ist nicht einmal ein *cognoscibile* als Intelligibele sondern x weil es ausser der Form der Erscheinung ist aber doch ein *cogitabile* (und zwar als notwendig denkbar) was nicht gegeben werden kann, aber doch gedacht werden muss, weil es in gewissen anderen Vehältnissen die nicht sinnlich sind, vorkommen kann" (p. 23).

14. Henri Lauener, *Hume und Kant,* p. 129.

15. According to Adickes, *Kant und das Ding an sich,* the affection by things in themselves is unambiguously asserted in the following places in the *Critique:* A44/B61, B72, A190/B235, A358, A380, A393, and A494/B522. Of these the last five refer specifically to

the transcendental object. Other passages from the *Critique*, such as A288/B344 and A613–14/B641–42, could be added to this list, as could many from other works.

16. F. H. Jacobi, *David Hume über den Glauben, oder Idealismus und Realismus*, Beilage, *Ueber den transzendentalen Idealismus, Werke*, ed. F. Roth and F. Köppen, vol. 2, pp. 291–310.

17. The most forceful proponent of this view is Fichte, especially in his *Zweite Einleitung in die Wissenschaftslehre*, in *Erste und zweite Einleitung in die Wissenschaftslehre*, ed. Fritz Medicus, pp. 68–75.

18. H. Vaihinger, *Commentar zu Kants Kritik der reinen Vernunft*, vol. 2, p. 53.

19. Erick Adickes, *Kants Lehre von der doppelten Affektion unseres Ich als Schlüssel zu seiner Erkenntnistheorie*.

20. See Kemp Smith, *Commentary*, pp. 612 ff., Robert Paul Wolff, *Kant's Theory of Mental Activity*, pp. 169 ff., 222 ff.

21. Cf. Pierre Lachièze-Rey, *L'Idéalisme kantien*, pp. 450–63; Graham Bird, *Kant's Theory of Knowledge*, pp. 18–35, Bernard Rousset, *La Doctrine*, pp. 190–97; Gerold Prauss, *Kant und das Problem*, pp. 192 ff.; and Moltke S. Gram, "The Myth of Double Affection," *Reflections on Kant's Philosophy*, ed. W. H. Werkmeister, pp. 29–69.

22. Prauss, *Kant und das Problem*, pp. 192–207.

23. Ibid., pp. 205 ff.

24. Adickes is typical in this regard. He certainly recognizes that Kant formulates the distinction in this way (*Kants Lehre*, p. 3), but his whole analysis is in total variance with this fact.

25. For a discussion of empirical affection passages see Adickes, *Kants Lehre*, pp. 5–15.

26. I think that some such line of thought is at work, at least implicitly, in Prauss's analysis.

27. The importance of the reference to the transcendental object in the discussions of affection has been noted by others. See Herbert Herring, *Das Problem der Affektion bei Kant, Kant-Studien*, Ergänzungshefte 67 (1953): 65–69. The first part of this important study provides a valuable survey of the literature on the problem of affection. In the second part, Herring develops an interpretation of affection by means of the transcendental object (distinguished from the thing in itself) which differs from the one offered here in its ontological focus. More recently, Henri Lauener (*Hume und Kant*, p. 130) has emphasized both the importance of distinguishing between the thing in itself and the transcendental object and of viewing the latter as "der rechtmässige Grund (*Frage quid iuris*) der transzendentalen Affektion, die die Norwendigkeit der empirischen verbürgt."

28. Among the passages wherein the appeal to the transcendental object serves, as it were, to cut off debate, the most noteworthy are A277–78/B333–34, A479/B507 n. and A613–14/B641–42.

29. Bird, *Kant's Theory*, p. 69.

30. *Ak.* VIII, 215; H. Allison, *Kant-Eberhard Controversy*, p. 130.

31. Precisely the opposite is claimed by Prauss (*Kant und das Problem*, p. 103, n. 22) who asserts that the present passage contains one of the most extreme examples of the *transzendent-metaphysischen Entgleisungen* to be found in the Kantian corpus.

32. *Ak.* VIII, 219; Allison, *Kant-Eberhard Controversy*, p. 133.

33. Kant refers to "the transcendental matter of all objects as things in themselves" (A143/B182) and to "matter in the transcendental sense," which is defined as the "determinable in general" (A266/B322) and equated with the "things themselves which appear" (A268/B324). A precritical version of this conception is found in the Inaugural Dissertation (*Ak.* II, 389).

34. Eberhard conflated these grounds with the simple parts of which space and time are allegedly composed. In the present context Kant is concerned with underlining the distinction between ground (which is transcendental) and matter or part (which is empirical). He

also, however, attacks Eberhard's conception of space and time as composed of simples. See Allison, *Kant-Eberhard Controversy*, pp. 117–23.

CHAPTER 12

1. H. J. Paton, *The Categorical Imperative*, p. 233.

2. Inaugural Dissertation, §15, *Ak.* II, 405.

3. See H. J. Paton, *Kant's Metaphysic of Experience*, vol. 1, pp. 148–49.

4. This discussion is suggested by the treatment of the topic by Dennis C. Holt, "Timelessness and the Metaphysics of Temporal Existence," *American Philosophical Quarterly* 18 (1981): 149–56. Holt, however, does not deal with Kant.

5. See *Critique of Pure Reason*, B154–55.

6. Ibid., A178–79 / B220–22.

7. See ibid., A34 / B50–51, A342 / B400; *Prolegomena*, §49, *Ak.* IV, 336; *Anthropologie*, §24, *Ak.* VII, 161.

8. *Anthropologie*, §24, *Ak.* VII, 161.

9. Ibid.

10. For a discussion of this point see the note by Mary J. Gregor to her translation of *Anthropology from a Pragmatic Point of View*, pp. 198–99.

11. *Ak.* V., 206. See also *Ak.* V, 219–20, and *Ak.* VII, 153.

12. T. D. Weldon, *Kant's Critique of Pure Reason*, pp. 256–70.

13. Robert Paul Wolff, *Kant's Theory of Mental Activity*, pp. 198–200.

14. See Johann Nicholas Tetens, *Philosophische Versuche über die menschliche Natur und ihre Entwicklung*, vol. 1, pp. 46–48.

15. *Anthropologie*, §24, *Ak.* VII, 161.

16. *Critique of Pure Reason*, B151; *Anthropologie*, §15, *Ak.* VII, 153.

17. See *Critique of Pure Reason*, B66; Reflexionen 5456 and 6319, *Ak.* XVIII, 187, 633.

18. This point is also noted by Wilfred Sellars, ". . . This I or he or it (the thing) which thinks . . . ," *Proceedings and Addresses of the American Philosophical Association* 44 (September 1971): 8.

19. Reflexion 5453, *Ak.* XVIII, 186; cf. Reflexion 6354, *Ak.* XVIII, 680.

20. For a criticism of this argument see Malte Hossenfelder, *Kants Konstitutions-theorie und die Transzendentale Deduktion*, pp. 31, 61–63.

21. See *Critique of Pure Reason*, B68.

22. Paton, *Kant's Metaphysic*, vol. 2, pp. 238–40.

23. The reader is referred back to chapter 7 for a discussion of the connection between these two kinds of synthesis.

24. Michael Washburn, "The Problem of Self-Knowledge and the Evolution of the Critical Epistemology, 1781 and 1787," esp. pp. 194–215. Much of the following analysis was suggested to me by Washburn's interesting discussion.

25. For an interesting discussion of this issue formulated with reference to Strawson see Graham Bird, *Kant's Theory of Knowledge*, pp. 181–88.

26. Reflexion 5655, *Ak.* XVIII, 314.

27. *Critique of Pure Reason*, B291–92.

28. *Ak.* IV, 474–76.

29. Perhaps the best discussion of this topic is that of A. C. Ewing, *Kant's Treatment of Causality*, pp. 124–68.

CHAPTER 13

1. Kant affirms this explicitly in the *Anthropologie*, §7, *Ak.* VII, 142; and *Die Fortschritte*, *Ak.* XX, 270.

2. *Prolegomena*, §46, *Ak.* IV, 334n.

3. See chapter 7.

4. See Heinz Heimsoeth, "Personlichkeitsbewusstsein und Ding an sich in der kant-ischen Philosophie," *Studien zur Philosophie Immanuel Kants, Metaphysiche Ursprüng und Ontologische Grundlagen*, pp. 229–55; and Gottfried Martin, *Kant's Metaphysics and Theory of Science*, trans. P. G. Lucas, esp. pp. 176–81.

5. See H. J. Paton, *Kant's Metaphysic of Experience*, vol. 1, p. 400.

6. *Anthropologie*, §7, *Ak*. VII, 141.

7. Ibid., *Ak*. VII, 142.

8. *Critique of Pure Reason*, A115.

9. This distinction is suggested by the account of Ingeborg Heidemann, *Spontaneität und Zeitlichkeit*, pp. 226–27.

10. See *Critique of Judgment*, introduction, sections 4 and 5, *Ak*. V, 179–86.

11. Reflexion 5661, *Ak*. XVIII, 318–19.

12. This is noted by A. C. Ewing in his discussion of the Reflexion (*Kant's Treatment of Causality*, p. 137).

13. *Ak*. XVIII, 319. Although I have made some changes, I have basically followed Ewing's English rendering of the passage (ibid., pp. 136–37).

14. Kant makes a similar claim with respect to number in a letter to Johann Schulze written at about the same time as the Reflexion. Kant's letter to Schulze, Nov. 25, 1788, Ak. XI, 554–57.

15. *Ak*. XVIII, 319.

16. Bernard Williams, "The Certainty of the Cogito," in *Descartes: A Collection of Critical Essays*, ed. Willis Doney, p. 95. Spinoza's statement is from *Principles of Cartesian Philosophy*, I, Prolegomena.

17. G. W. Leibniz, *New Essays on Human Understanding*, trans. P. Remnant and J. Bennett, book 4, chap. 7, §7 (p. 411).

18. Ibid.

19. For a very different account of this topic see Norman Kemp Smith, *A Commentary to Kant's "Critique of Pure Reason,"* p. 330 n. Kemp Smith claims that Kant's denial that 'existence' here functions as a category is incompatible with the doctrine of the postulates. 'Existence' on his view differs from the categories of relation in that "it would seem to be impossible to distinguish between a determinate and an indeterminate use of it. Either we assert existence or we do not." This, however, is simply not the case. As we have seen in our account of the Schematism (chapter 8), the schema of actuality (*Wirklichkeit*) is "exis-tence in some determinate time" and the pure concept (logical actuality) is just the concept of assertion. In light of this, we can see that what Kant is doing in this note is denying that the schema of actuality is applied to the subject of apperception in the present case. Nevertheless, there is still an assertion and with it a "logical use" of the category, or, equivalently, a use of the "pure category." Whatever general difficulties such a doctrine may involve, they are no greater in the case of the modal than in the cases of any of the other categories.

20. In support of this rejection it is customary to cite Descartes's claim, "He who says '*I think, hence I am* or exist,' does not deduce existence from thought by a syllogism but, by a simple act of mental vision recognizes it as if it were a thing that is known *per se*" (Response to the Second Set of Objections, in *Philosophical Works of Descartes*, trans. E. S. Haldene and G. R. T. Ross, vol. 2, p. 38). The interpretive issue, however, is not nearly as clear cut as this and similar passages might suggest. For example, according to Anthony Kenny (*Descartes: A Study of His Philosophy*, p. 51), "the premise '*cogito*' in conjunction with the presupposition that it is impossible for that which is thinking to be non-existent yield the conclusion '*sum*.' " Kenny also points out that the only thing that is required to interpret this inference as a simple syllogism is the acceptance of the thesis that 'existence' is a predicate. Since Kant criticizes Descartes's version of the ontological argument precisely on

the grounds that it treats 'existence' as a (real) predicate, it is certainly reasonable for him to construe the cogito inference in the same way. Moreover, given this reading he is perfectly correct in his contention that it implies that everything that thinks exists necessarily, "for in that case the property of thought would render all beings who possess it into necessary beings." The issue is discussed by Bernard Williams, "The Certainty of the Cogito," p. 94.

21. Williams, "The Certainty of the Cogito," p. 106.

22. Jonathan Bennett (*Kant's Dialectic*, pp. 66–69) talks about the "Cartesian basis" of the Paralogism, by which he means "the intellectual situation in which one attends to nothing but one's mind and its states" (p. 66). Given the importance of the apperception–inner sense contrast for Kant, this is a bit misleading and does not quite capture Kant's point that the 'I think' is "the sole text of rational psychology." Moreover, as Bennett himself seems to acknowledge (p. 83, n. 4), the actual arguments under review in this section of the *Critique* cannot all be attributed to Descartes. For an account of the Leibnizian roots of the Second Paralogism, see Margaret Wilson, "Leibniz and Materialism," *Canadian Journal of Philosophy* 3 (1974): 495–513, esp. pp. 509–13.

23. This identification is easily subject to misunderstanding. It should, therefore, be noted that Kant distinguishes between a moral and a psychological sense of personality (*Die Metaphysik der Sitten, Ak.* VI, 223). The former is construed as the "freedom of a rational being under moral law," and the latter as "the capacity to be conscious of the identity of oneself in the various conditions of one's existence." Clearly, the latter conception is the one at work in the Paralogisms. The same conception is to be found in *Anthropologie,* §1, *Ak.* VII, 127.

24. Descartes, Sixth Meditation, in *Philosophical Works of Descartes,* vol. 1, p. 190.

25. On this point see Wilfred Sellars, ". . . this I or he or it (the thing) which thinks. . . ," *Proceedings and Addresses of the American Philosophical Association* 44 (September 1971): esp. p. 9.

26. Much of the general thrust of the argument of this section, although not all the details, was suggested by the discussion of Pierre Lachièze-Rey, *L'Idéalisme kantien,* pp. 149–207.

27. Reflexion 6001, *Ak.* XVIII, 420–21.

28. See *Critique of Pure Reason,* A361, A358–59; *Critique of Judgment,* introduction, *Ak.* V, 175. Such a position is attributed to Kant by Kemp Smith, *Commentary,* pp. 322–26, as well as by Heimsoeth and Martin (see note 4, above).

29. See *Anthropologie,* §4, *Ak.* VII, 134 n.; *Die Fortschritte, Ak.* XX, 270.

30. The original critics of this aspect of Kant's doctrine were Lambert and Mendelssohn. He deals with their criticism in his famous letter to Marcus Herz of February 21, 1772. Similar criticisms were later voiced by Pistorius against the doctrine of inner sense as it appears in the *Critique.* For an account of these criticisms see Benno Erdmann, *Kants Kriticismus in der ersten und in der zweiten Auflage der Kritik der reinen Vernunft,* pp. 106–07.

31. Strawson, *The Bounds of Sense,* p. 248.

32. Ibid.

33. Ibid., p. 249. It is worthy of note that Lachièze-Rey anticipates the gist of Strawson's criticism when he remarks "Ainsi l'unité des deux moi ne peut être justifée par on théorie qui ferait du moi empirique le phénomène de moi déterminant" (*L'Idéalisme kantien,* p. 156).

34. Ludwig Wittgenstein, *Tractatus Logico-Philosophicus,* trans. D. F. Pears and B. F. McGuinness, 5.631, p. 117.

35. Ibid., 5.632, p. 117.

36. Ibid., 6.000, p. 119.

37. Lachièze-Rey (*L'Idéalisme kantien,* pp. 188–89) points out in this connection that the real problem is that we are lacking a concept, not simply an intuition of the I as subject.

38. See ibid., p. 158.

39. Wittgenstein, *Tractatus*, 5.633, 5.6331, p. 117.

40. Essentially the same point is argued forcefully by Ingeborg Heidemann, *Spontaneität und Zeitlichkeit*, pp. 211–12.

CHAPTER 14

1. A typical example of this line of interpretation is to be found in the well-known paper of Barry Stroud, "Transcendental Arguments," first published in the *Journal of Philosophy* (1968): 241–56, and reprinted in *The First Critique*, ed. T. Penelhum and J. MacIntosh.

2. I discuss this issue in "Kant's Critique of Berkeley," *Journal of the History of Philosophy* 11 (1973): 43–63.

3. See Reflexionen 5653–54 and 6311–16, *Ak.* XVIII, 305–16, 607–23.

4. The major treatments of this topic are by Pierre Lachièze-Rey, *L'Idéalisme kantien*, pp. 60–148, and Bernard Rousset, *La Doctrine kantienne de l'objectivité*, pp. 139–61.

5. See also Reflexionen 5653, 5655, *Ak.* XVIII, 309, 314.

6. See Rousset, *La Doctrine kantienne*, pp. 148–51; Myron Gochnauer, "Kant's Refutation of Idealism," *Journal of the History of Philosophy* 12 (1974): 195–206, esp. p. 198; and Richard E. Aquila, "Personal Identity and Kant's Refutation of Idealism," *Kant-Studien* 70 (1979): 259–78, esp. pp. 260–61.

7. See note 3, above.

8. See Reflexionen, 5653, 6315, *Ak.* XVIII, 308, 618–20. The issue is discussed by Rousset, *La Doctrine kantienne*, p. 155.

9. Such an objection was raised by G. E. Schulze, *Aenesidemus oder über die Fundamente der von dem Herrn Prof. Reinhold in Jena gelieferten Elementar-Philosophie;* reprinted in *Aetas Kantiana*, pp. 105–08.

10. See Reflexion 5461, *Ak.* XVIII, 189.

11. This problem is raised, although not resolved, by Myron Gochnauer, "Kant's Refutation of Idealism," pp. 205–06.

12. This is how Kant himself expresses the matter at Bxli n., where he remarks: "I am just as certainly conscious that there are things outside me, which are in relation to my sense, as I am conscious that I myself exist as determined in time."

13. See Bennett, *Kant's Analytic*, pp. 203 ff.

14. G. E. Moore, "Four Forms of Scepticism," *Philosophical Papers*, pp. 200–01.

15. Ibid., p. 211.

16. See *Critique of Pure Reason*, A113.

17. Bennett, *Kant's Analytic*, pp. 218–19.

18. Sidney Shoemaker, *Self-Knowledge and Self-Identity*, p. 135.

19. *Critique of Pure Reason*, A363 n.

20. See Bennett, *Kant's Dialectic*, p. 109.

CHAPTER 15

1. *Critique of Practical Reason*, *Ak.* V, 4–5.

2. For a recent discussion of this historical issue see Bernard Carnois, *La Cohérence de la doctrine kantienne de la liberté*, pp. 79–132. He goes so far as to characterize the discovery of the principle of autonomy as a second Copernican revolution (p. 79).

3. For Kant's characterization of mechanism see *Critique of Practical Reason*, *Ak.* V, 97, and Reflexion 5978, *Ak.* XVIII, 413.

4. Kant indicates as much in the observation on the thesis, where he refers explicitly to the concept of a prime mover (A451/B480). The argument is also interpreted in this way by Lewis White Beck, *A Commentary on Kant's "Critique of Practical Reason,"* p. 184.

5. This step is clearly the locus of the difficulty in the argument, and the problem begins with the question of what exactly is being claimed. The text reads:

> If, therefore, everything takes place solely in accordance with laws of nature, there will always be only a relative [*subalternen*] and never a first beginning, and consequently no completeness of the series on the side of the causes that arise the one from the other. But the law of nature is just this, that nothing takes place without a cause *sufficiently* determined *a priori*. The proposition that no causality is possible save in accordance with laws of nature, when taken in unlimited universality, is therefore self-contradictory; and this cannot, therefore, be regarded as the sole kind of causality. [A446/B474]

The exegetical question centers around the meaning of the phrase "a cause sufficiently determined *a priori*" and the connection between the 'laws of nature' and the 'law of nature' that is allegedly being contradicted by the antithesis. According to the standard interpretation, by the former is meant merely a cause sufficient to determine its effect, or a sufficient cause. Schopenhauer, however, had already pointed out that, on this interpretation, the argument never really gets off the ground. The point is simply that the question of whether *A* itself is caused is irrelevant to the question of whether *A* (being given) is sufficient to produce *B*. This objection is repeated by Norman Kemp Smith (*A Commentary to Kant's "Critique of Pure Reason,"* p. 493), who, following Schopenhauer, reads the text in this way. More recently the Schopenhauer-Kemp Smith reading has been rejected by Jonathan Bennett on the grounds that it fails to make any sense of the argument (*Kant's Dialectic*, pp. 185–86). Bennett, however, does not provide any alternative. Following Al-Azm's reconstruction of the arguments of the Antinomies in light of the Leibniz-Clarke dispute, I am here taking "a cause sufficiently determined *a priori*" to be equivalent to a sufficient reason in the Leibnizian sense. See Sadik Al-Azm, *The Origins of Kant's Arguments in the Antinomies*, pp. 92–93. Correlatively, by 'law of nature' (*Gesetz der Natur*) I understand the principle of sufficient reason. The 'laws of nature', on the other hand, are just the laws of mechanistic causality. The argument thus asserts the incompatibility of the universality of mechanistic causality with the adherence to the principle of sufficient reason. As Al-Azm suggests, this can be taken as a reductio of the Leibnizian position, at least as it is presented in the debate with Clarke.

6. See *Critique of Pure Reason*, A529–32/B557–60, and *Prolegomena*, §53, *Ak*. IV, 443–47.

7. *Critique of Pure Reason*, A558/B586.

8. See *Prolegomena*, §53, *Ak*. IV, 343–48.

9. The way in which Kant formulates his indirect proof (A506–07/B534–35) seems to reflect his awareness of this fact.

10. *Critique of Practical Reason*, *Ak*. V, 42–50.

11. *Groundwork of the Metaphysics of Morals*, *Ak*. IV, 446.

12. Ibid.

13. Kant, in effect, anticipates this distinction at A548/B576, where he contrasts two possible objects of the will: the pleasant and the good. The former is connected with sensibility and the latter with reason.

14. Admittedly, there are some passages in the Dialectic that seem to point in a different direction. We shall deal with these later. For the present, however, it suffices to note A557/B585, where Kant writes of the will: "We can know that it is free, that is, that it is determined independently of sensibility, and that in this way it may be the sensibly unconditioned condition of appearances."

15. I take Kant's position here to be significantly different from his position in the *Critique of Practical Reason*, where, in somewhat similar fashion, he treats God and immortality as postulates of practical reason (*Ak*. V, 122–34). The essential difference is that in the First Critique God and immortality seem to be necessary props for the moral law itself,

while in the Second Critique these postulates presuppose the validity of the moral law and are necessary only for the realization of the highest good (the combination of virtue and happiness). For an interesting discussion of this whole issue in terms of Kant's *absurdum practicum* argument, see Allen W. Wood, *Kant's Moral Religion.*

16. On this point at least I find myself in disagreement with the important analysis of Karl Ameriks, "Kant's Deduction of Freedom and Morality," *Journal of the History of Philosophy* 19 (1981): 53–79, and *Kant's Theory of Mind*, pp. 189–233. Making extensive use of passages from the *Reflexionen* and the lectures, Ameriks argues that although Kant does state repeatedly that practical freedom is sufficient for morality (the acceptance of the categorical imperative), he cannot mean this literally. He also offers an ingenious (but I think unconvincing) explanation of why Kant should be read in this way. Contrary to Ameriks, I maintain that such passages are, indeed, to be taken literally. I believe that the key point here is the distinction between the recognition of the categorical imperative as the principle or criterion of moral action, which Kant certainly did affirm well before 1781, and the affirmation of the principle of autonomy, which demands that one act out of respect for the law. Transcendental freedom, I contend, is required for the latter, but not for the former.

17. Chief among these are Albert Schweitzer, *Die Religionsphilosophie Kants von der Kritik der reinen Vernunft bis zur Religion innerhalb der Grenzen der blossen Vernunft;* Victor Delbos, *La Philosophie pratique de Kant,* esp. pp. 157–200; Martial Gueroult, "Canon de la raison pure et critique de la raison pratique," *Revue Internationale de Philosophie* 8 (1954): 331–57; and Bernard Carnois, *La Cohérence de la doctrine kantienne de la liberté,* pp. 92 ff.

18. *Critique of Practical Reason, Ak.* V, 97–98.

19. Kant introduces the notion of a "transcendental location" in the Amphiboly of Concepts of Reflection (A268/B324) in order to characterize the "place" to which we assign concepts in transcendental reflection; namely, to either sensibility or understanding. Although Kant does not use the expression here, it would seem that the same idea is at work in the present context.

20. *Critique of Pure Reason,* A535–37/B563–65. Although there is no need to dwell on it here, it is at least worth noting that the difference between the two problems is reflected in the difference in the ways in which Kant uses the transcendental distinction in dealing with each of them. Moreover, the latter difference itself reflects the difference between the two categories of noumena that Kant recognizes. It will be recalled that by a 'noumenon' (in the positive sense) is meant the object of a nonsensible cognition. Such an object, however, could be either one that cannot be represented sensibly at all, such as God, or an object that is identical with a sensible object (phenomenon) but is known in a nonsensible manner (as it is in itself). In the resolution of the Third Antinomy the transcendental distinction is used to allow for the conceivability of a noumenon of the former kind, while in the case of the problem of freedom it is a noumenon of the latter kind that is required. Kant's failure to spell all of this out is one of the main reasons for the obscurity of the discussion.

21. The fullest discussions of the topic in the recent literature are in Carnois, *La Cohérence,* pp. 113 ff.; Ingeborg Heidemann, *Spontaneität und Zeitlichkeit,* pp. 226 ff.; and, most important, Heinz Heimsoeth, *Transzendentale Dialektik,* pp. 349–61, 397–406.

22. For Kant's definition of character from a specifically anthropological point of view, see *Anthropologie,* §89, *Ak.* VII, 285.

23. Kant uses this expression in Reflexion 6286, *Ak.* XVIII, 557, to characterize this very process of arriving at the intelligible by stripping away everything pertaining to sensibility. Although he is there explicitly concerned with the thought of God, the same principle applies in the present context.

24. This line of criticism is emphasized by Lewis White Beck, *A Commentary on Kant's "Critique of Practical Reason,"* p. 188.

25. I have here altered considerably the translation of Kemp Smith, who renders this

sentence as: "That our reason has causality, or that we at least represent it to ourselves as having causality, is evident from the *imperatives* which in all matters of conduct we impose upon our active powers." My changes serve both to provide a more literal reading and to show the connection between this account of practical reason and the previous discussion of theoretical reason.

26. One of the most striking of such passages is Reflexion 4904 (*Ak*. XVIII, 24), where Kant remarks that transcendental freedom "is the necessary hypothesis of all rules, and consequently of any employment of the understanding" and that it is "the property of beings in whom consciousness of a rule is the ground of their actions." This Reflexion is cited and discussed by Stephan Körner, "Kant's Conception of Freedom," *Proceedings of the British Academy* 53 (1967): 203. Other Reflexionen making a similar claim include 4220, 4336, 4723, 7440, and 7441 (all of which are noted by Ameriks, *Kant's Theory of Mind*, p. 196). The same doctrine is also prominent in the *Lectures on Metaphysics;* see especially *Metaphysik L, Ak.* XXVIII, 267–69.

27. On this point see Heidemann, *Spontaneität und Zeitlichkeit,* pp. 240–41.

28. Wilfred Sellars, ". . . This I or he or it (the thing) which thinks . . . ," *Proceedings and Addresses of the American Philosophical Association* 44 (September 1971): 24–25.

29. A similar thought is expressed at A548–49 / B576–77.

30. David Hume, *A Treatise of Human Nature,* ed. L. A. Selby-Bigge, book 2, §3, p. 415.

31. Two such places are *Metaphysik L* (*Ak*. XXVIII, 267–68) and the *Opus Postumum* (*Ak*. XXI, 470). Also, in the *Vorarbeiten zu die Metaphysik der Sitten* (*Ak*. XXIII, 383), he distinguishes between reason as *causa instrumentalis* and *causa originaria*.

32. Sellars, ". . . This I or he or it," p. 26.

33. A parallel account of the compatibility of the predictability and freedom of the same action is contained in the *Critique of Practical Reason* (*Ak*. V, 99).

34. Lewis White Beck is typical of the sympathetic critics. See *Commentary,* pp. 191–94.

35. *Critique of Judgment,* §§69–71, *Ak*. VI, pp. 385–92. Interestingly enough, interpreters who are broadly sympathetic to Kant's overall conception of freedom, but who cannot accept his compatibility thesis, have called attention to this later account and have argued that the doctrine of the *Critique of Pure Reason* must be revised in light of it. On this point see Beck, *Commentary,* pp. 191–95; Stephan Körner, "Kant's Conception of Freedom," pp. 193–217; and John Silber, "The Ethical Significance of Kant's Religion," in the introduction to the English translation of Kant's *Religion within the Limits of Reason Alone,* trans. T. M. Greene and H. H. Hudson, pp. xcviii–ciii. The claim made here however is that the "regulative reading" is in accord with the actual position of the *Critique of Pure Reason.* Thus, rather than a revision of Kant's doctrine in light of his later insights, all that is needed here is a closer attention to the actual doctrine of the First Critique.

36. Kant's sharpest statement of this view is in *Religion within the Limits of Reason Alone* (*Ak*. VI, 24). This formulation, of course, reflects his later theory of freedom, where, in virtue of the moral law, the will is claimed to be free in the transcendental sense. The same general point, however, is found in Kant's earlier discussions of freedom, where there is no such assumption. For example, in the *Lectures on Ethics* he remarks: "However much, for instance, we may try by torture to force a man to action we cannot compel him to do it if he does not will it; if he so will it he can withstand every torment and not yield. In a relative sense he can be compelled, but not in an absolute sense. In spite of every instigation of the senses, a man can still leave an action undone. This is the characteristic of *liberum arbitrium*" (*Eine Vorlesung Kants über Ethik,* ed. Paul Menzer, p. 34).

37. It should be clear from the above that Kant's analysis really cuts across the reason-cause distinction that is central to contemporary action theory. On the one hand, Kant, like Davidson, regards reasons (incentives) as causes of actions, while on the other hand his insistence on the "act of incorporation" differentiates his position decisively from that of

Davidson and others who appeal to an essentially Humean model for their understanding of agency.

38. See *Critique of Pure Reason,* bxxvii–xxix, B430–32.

39. For a list of some of these texts see note 26, above. Also significant in this regard are Kant's review of Schultz's *Sittenlehre* (*Ak.* VIII, 10–14) and the discussion of freedom in the third part of the *Groundwork of the Metaphysics of Morals,* (*Ak.* IV, 448–49). For a discussion of these latter two texts and their connection with the doctrine of the *Critique of Practical Reason* see Karl Ameriks, "Kant's Deduction of Freedom and Morality," esp. pp. 58–73.

CONCLUSION

1. An interesting and informed neo-Hegelian critique of Kant, which focuses on difficulties raised by Kant's "formalistic methodology," has recently been published by my colleague Robert Pippin (*Kant's Theory of Form: An Essay on the Critique of Pure Reason*). Pippin's analysis calls for a serious and sustained reply, but for now I can only record my conviction that many of the difficulties that he, and others before him, find in Kant's "formalism" can be dealt with adequately in terms of the conception of an epistemic condition.

2. For recent discussions of this issue see Lewis White Beck, "Toward a Meta-Critique of Pure Reason," in *Essays on Kant and Hume,* pp. 20–37, and W. H. Walsh, *Kant's Criticism of Metaphysics,* pp. 249–55.

3. I have dealt previously with Husserl's criticisms of Kant in "The *Critique of Pure Reason* as Transcendental Phenomenology," in *Dialogues in Phenomenology,* ed. Dan Ihde and Richard M. Zaner, pp. 136–55. The issues raised by Hegel's Kant criticism are extremely complex, but it should be noted that many of these criticisms reflect the standard picture. Thus Hegel typically presents Kant as a subjective idealist and skeptic, who separates knowledge or, rather, a subjectivistic surrogate for knowledge, from "Truth." A good example of this is his discussion of Kant at the beginning of the *Encyclopedia,* esp. §§40–43. I think that my remarks about the standard picture and its inadequacies apply equally well to this aspect of Hegel's Kant criticism. Finally, I also think that the account of apperception in chapter 13 helps to explain how Kant can justify his fundamental claim about the discursive nature of human cognition, which is a major part of the problem of a "metacritique." The essential point is simply that apperception, insofar as it is "something real," is a consciousness of the spontaneity of thinking. Thus the conceptualizing activity of the mind is a datum of ordinary reflection, and this provides the basis for a transcendental or specifically philosophical reflection on the "forms" and "conditions" of this activity. This, of course, makes Kant's philosophy a "philosophy of reflection" in the Hegelian sense; the issue, which cannot be dealt with here, therefore becomes the cogency of Hegel's overall critique of this philosophical "standpoint" and of his own alternative to it.

Bibliography

WORKS BY KANT

Anthropology from a Pragmatic Point of View, ed. and trans. Mary J. Gregor. The Hague: Martinus Nijhoff, 1974.

Critique of Practical Reason, trans. L. W. Beck. Indianapolis: Bobbs-Merrill, 1956.

Critique of Pure Reason, trans. N. Kemp Smith. New York: St. Martin's Press, 1929.

Gesammelte Schriften, ed. Königlich Preussischen Akademie der Wissenschaften. Berlin and Leipzig: de Gruyter, 1922.

Kant's Critique of Judgement, trans. J. C. Meredith. Oxford: Clarendon Press, 1952.

Kant's Philosophical Correspondence 1759–99, ed. and trans. A. Zweig. Chicago: University of Chicago Press, 1970.

Kritik der reinen Vernunft, ed. R. Schmidt. Hamburg: Felix Meiner, 1954.

Metaphysical Foundations of Natural Science, trans. J. Ellington. Indianapolis: Bobbs-Merrill, 1970.

"On a Discovery According to Which Any New Critique of Pure Reason Has Been Made Superfluous by an Earlier One," in *The Kant-Eberhard Controversy,* ed. and trans. H. E. Allison. Baltimore: Johns Hopkins University Press, 1973.

Die Philosophischen Hauptvorlesungen Immanuel Kants, ed. Arnold Kowalewski. Hildescheim: George Olms, 1965.

"A New Exposition of the First Principles of Metaphysical Knowledge," trans. F. E. England, in *Kant's Conception of God: A Critical Exposition of its Metaphysical Development Together with a Translation of the "Nova Dilucidatio."* London: Allen & Unwin, 1929.

Prolegomena to Any Future Metaphysics, trans. L. W. Beck. Indianapolis: Bobbs-Merrill, 1950.

Reflexionen Kants zur kritischen Philosophie, ed. Benno Erdmann. Leipzig: Feuss Verlag, 1882.

Religion within the Limits of Reason Alone, trans. T. M. Greene and H. H. Hudson. New York: Harper & Row, 1960.

Selected Pre-Critical Writings and Correspondence with Beck, trans. G. B. Kerferd and D. E. Walford. Manchester: Manchester University Press, 1968.

Eine Vorlesung Kants über Ethik, ed. Paul Menzer. Berlin: Pan Verlag Rolf Geise, 1924.

OTHER WORKS

Adickes, Erich. *Kants Lehre von der doppelten Affektion unseres Ich als Schlüssel zu seiner Erkenntnistheorie.* Tübingen: J. C. Mohr, 1929.

———. *Kant und das Ding an sich.* Berlin: Pan, 1924.

Al-Azm, Sadik J. *The Origins of Kant's Argument in the Antinomies.* Oxford: Oxford University Press, 1972.

Allison, Henry E. *Benedict de Spinoza.* Boston: Twayne, 1975.

———. "The *Critique of Pure Reason* as Transcendental Phenomenology," in *Dialogues in Phenomenology,* ed. Don Ihde and Richard N. Zaner, 136–55. The Hague: Martinus Nijhoff, 1975.

———. (ed. and trans.) *The Kant-Eberhard Controversy.* Baltimore: Johns Hopkins University Press, 1973.

———. "Kant's Concept of the Transcendental Object," *Kant-Studien* 59 (1968): 165–86.

———. "Kant's Critique of Berkeley," *Journal of the History of Philosophy* 11 (1973): 43–63.

———. "Kant's Critique of Spinoza," *Studies in Philosophy and the History of Philosophy,* vol. 7, *The Philosophy of Baruch Spinoza,* ed. Richard Kennington, 199–227. Washington, D.C.: The Catholic University Press of America, 1980.

———. "Kant's Non-Sequitur," *Kant-Studien* 62 (1971): 367–77.

———. "Kant's Refutation of Realism," *Dialectica* 30 (1976): 223–53.

———. "Kant's Transcendental Humanism," *The Monist* 55 (1971): 182–207.

———. "The Non-Spatiality of Things in Themselves for Kant," *Journal of the History of Philosophy* 14 (1976): 313–21.

———. "Things in Themselves, Noumena, and the Transcendental Object," *Dialectica* 32 (1978): 41–76.

———. "Transcendental Affinity—Kant's Answer to Hume?" in *Kant's Theory of Knowledge,* ed. L. W. Beck (see below), 119–27.

———. "Transcendental Idealism and Descriptive Metaphysics," *Kant-Studien* 60 (1969): 216–23.

———. "Transcendental Schematism and the Problem of the Synthetic A Priori," *Dialectica* 35 (1981): 57–83.

Ameriks, Karl. "Kant's Deduction of Freedom and Morality," *Journal of the History of Philosophy* 19 (1981): 53–79.

———. *Kant's Theory of Mind.* Oxford: Clarendon Press, 1982.

———. "Recent Work on Kant's Theoretical Philosophy," *American Philosophical Quarterly* 19 (1982): 1–24.

Aquila, Richard E. "Personal Identity and Kant's Refutation of Idealism," *Kant-Studien* 70 (1979): 257–78.

Barker, Stephen. "Appearing and Appearances," reprinted in *Kant Studies Today*, ed. L. W. Beck (see below), 278–89.

Bayle, Pierre. *Historical and Critical Dictionary*, selections ed. and trans. Richard H. Popkin. Indianapolis: Bobbs-Merrill, 1965.

Beck, Jacob Sigismund. *Einzig möglicher Standpunct aus welchem die critische Philosophie beurtheilt werden muss.* Riga: Johann Friedrich Hartnoch, 1796. Reprinted in *Aetas Kantiana.* Brussels: Culture et Civilisation, 1969.

Beck, Lewis White. *The Actor and the Spectator.* New Haven: Yale University Press, 1975.

———. "Analytic and Synthetic Judgments before Kant," in *Essays on Kant and Hume* (see below), 80–100.

———. "Can Kant's Synthetic Judgments be Made Analytic?" reprinted in *Kant: Disputed Questions,* ed. Moltke S. Gram (see below), 228–46.

———. *A Commentary on Kant's "Critique of Practical Reason."* Chicago: University of Chicago Press, 1960.

———. "Did the Sage of Königsberg Have No Dreams?" in *Essays on Kant and Hume* (see below), 38–60.

———. *Essays on Kant and Hume.* New Haven: Yale University Press, 1978.

———. (ed.) *Kant Studies Today.* La Salle, Ill.: Open Court, 1969.

———. "Kant's Theory of Definition," reprinted in *Kant: Disputed Questions,* ed. Moltke S. Gram (see below), 215–27.

———. (ed.) *Kant's Theory of Knowledge.* Dordrecht: Reidel, 1974.

———. "Lovejoy as a Critic of Kant," in *Essays on Kant and Hume* (see above), 61–79.

———. "A *Non-Sequitur* of Numbing Grossness?" in *Essays on Kant and Hume* (see above), 147–53.

———. "Once More into the Breach: Kant's Answer to Hume, Again," in *Essays on Kant and Hume* (see above), 130–35.

———. "A Prussian Hume and a Scottish Kant," in *Essays on Kant and Hume* (see above), 111–29.

———. "A Reading of the Third Paragraph in B," in *Essays on Kant and Hume* (see above), 11, 141–46.

———. *Studies in the Philosophy of Kant.* Indianapolis: Bobbs-Merrill, 1965.

Bennett, Jonathan. *Kant's Analytic.* Cambridge: Cambridge University Press, 1966.

———. "The Difference between Right and Left," *American Philosophical Quarterly* 7 (1970): 175–91.

———. *Kant's Dialectic.* Cambridge: Cambridge University Press, 1974.

———. *Locke, Berkeley, Hume.* Oxford: Oxford University Press, 1971.

Berkeley, George. *The Works of George Berkeley, Bishop of Cloyne,* ed. A. A. Luce and T. E. Jessop. London: Thomas Nelson and Sons, 1948.

Bird, Graham. *Kant's Theory of Knowledge.* London: Routledge and Kegan Paul, 1962.

———. "Recent Interpretations of Kant's Transcendental Deduction," in *Akten des 4. Internationalen Kant-Kongress,* ed. G. Funke and J. Kopper, part 1, 1–15. Berlin: de Gruyter, 1974.

Brittan, Gordon G., Jr. *Kant's Theory of Science.* Princeton: Princeton University Press, 1978.

Broad, C. D. "Kant's First and Second Analogies of Experience," *Proceedings of the Aristotelian Society* 25 (1926): 189–210.

Buchdahl, Gerd. "The Conception of Lawlikeness in Kant's Philosophy of Science," in *Kant's Theory of Knowledge,* ed. L. W. Beck (see above), 128–50.

———. *Metaphysics and the Philosophy of Science.* Cambridge, Mass.: M.I.T. Press, 1969.

———. "The Kantian 'Dynamic of Reason' with Special Reference to the Place of Causality in Kant's System," in *Kant Studies Today,* ed. L. W. Beck (see above), 187–208.

Buroker, Jill. *Space and Congruence, The Origins of Kant's Idealism.* Dordrecht: Reidel, 1981.

Butts, Robert E. "Kant's Schemata as Semantical Rules," in *Kant Studies Today,* ed. L. W. Beck (see above), 290–300.

Caird, Edward. *The Critical Philosophy of Kant.* Glasgow: J. Maclehose, 1909.

Carnois, Bernard. *La Cohérence de la doctrine kantienne de la liberté.* Paris: Editions du Seuil, 1973.

Cassirer, Ernst. *Das Erkenntnisproblem in der Philosophie und Wissenschaft der neueren Zeit,* vols. 1 and 2. Berlin: Bruno Cassirer, 1911.

———. *Kants Leben and Lehre.* Berlin: Bruno Cassirer, 1918.

Chipman, Lauchlan. "Kant's Categories and Their Schematism," *Kant-Studien* 63 (1972): 36–49.

Cohen, Hermann. *Kants Theorie der Erfahrung.* Berlin: Dümmler, 1871; 2nd ed., 1885.

———. *Kommentar zu Immanuel Kants Kritik der reinen Vernunft.* 4th ed. Leipzig: Felix Meiner, 1925.

Cohn, Jonas. *Geschichte des Unendlichkeitsproblems in abendländischen Denken bis Kant.* Reprint. ed. Hildesheim: Georg Olms, 1960.

Collier, Arthur. *Clavis Universalis,* in *Metaphysical Tracts by English Philosophers of the Eighteenth Century,* ed. Samuel Parr, 1–100. London: Edward Lumley, 1837.

Curtius, Ernst Robert. "Das Schematismuskapitel in der Kritik der reinen Vernunft," *Kant-Studien* 19 (1916): 338–66.

Daval, Roger. *La Metaphysique de Kant.* Paris: Presses Universitaires de France, 1951.

Delbos, Victor. *La Philosophie pratique de Kant.* 3rd ed. Paris: Presses Universitaires de France, 1969.

Descartes, René. *Philosophical Works of Descartes,* trans. E. S. Haldene and G. R. T. Ross. 2 vols. New York: Dover, 1955.

Donnellan, Keith S. "Reference and Definite Descriptions," *Philosophical Review* 75 (1968): 281–304.

Dryer, D. P. *Kant's Solution for Verification in Metaphysics.* Toronto: University of Toronto Press, 1966.

Ebbinghaus, Julius. "Kants Lehre von der Anschauung a priori," in *Kant, Zur Deutung seiner Theorie von Erkennen und Handeln,* ed. G. Prauss (see below), 44–61.

Eberhard, J. A. (ed.) *Philosophisches Archiv.* 2 vols. Berlin: C. Massdorf, 1792–93. Reprinted in *Aetas Kantiana.* Brussels: Culture et Civilisation, 1968.

———. *Philosophisches Magazin.* 4 vols. Halle: J. J. Gebouer, 1789–92. Reprinted in *Aetas Kantiana.* Brussels: Culture et Civilisation, 1968.

Engel, Morris S. "Kant's Copernican Analogy: A Re-examination," *Kant-Studien* 54 (1963): 243–51.

Erdmann, Benno. *Kants Kriticismus in der ersten und in der zweiten Auflage der Kritik der reinen Vernunft.* Leipzig: Leopold Voss, 1878.

Eschenbach, Johann Christian. *Samlung der vornehmsten Schriftstellen die die Wirklichkeit ihres eignen Körpers und der ganzen Körperwelt leugnen.* Rostock: Unton Ferdinand Röse, 1756.

Ewing, A. C. *Kant's Treatment of Causality.* London: Kegan Paul, Trench, Trubner & Co., 1924.

———. *A Short Commentary on Kant's "Critique of Pure Reason."* 2nd ed. London: Methuen, 1950.

Fichte, J. G. *Zweite Einleitung in die Wissenschaftslehre,* in *Erste and zweite Einleitung in die Wissenschaftslehre,* ed. Fritz Medicus. Hamburg: Felix Meiner, 1961.

Franzwa, Gregg E. "Space and the Schematism," *Kant-Studien* 69 (1978): 149–59.

Gibson, James. *Locke's Theory of Knowledge and its Historical Relations.* Cambridge: Cambridge University Press, 1917.

Gochnauer, Myron. "Kant's Refutation of Idealism," *Journal of the History of Philosophy* 12 (1974): 195–206.

Gram, Moltke S. "The Crisis of Syntheticity: The Kant-Eberhard Controversy," *Kant-Studien* 7 (1980): 155–80.

———. "How to Dispense with Things in Themselves (I)," *Ratio* 18 (1976): 1–15.

———. (ed.) *Kant: Disputed Questions.* Chicago: Quadrangle Books, 1967.

———. "Kant's First Antinomy," *The Monist* 51 (1967): 499–518.

———. *Kant, Ontology,* and *the A Priori.* Evanston, Ill.: Northwestern University Press, 1968.

———. "The Myth of the Double Affection," in *Reflections on Kant's Philosophy,* ed. W. H. Werkmeister (see below), 29–69.

Gueroult, Martial. "Canon de la raison pure et critique de la raison pratique," *Revue Internationale de Philosophie* 8 (1954): 331–57.

Gurwitsch, Aron. *Leibniz, philosophie des panlogismus.* Berlin: de Gruyter, 1974.

Guyer, Paul. "Identität und Objectivität" (review), *Journal of Philosophy* 76 (1976): 151–67.

———. "Kant on Apperception and A Priori Synthesis," *American Philosophical Quarterly* 17 (1980): 205–12.

Hanson, Norwood Russell. "Copernicus' Role in Kant's Revolution," *Journal of the History of Ideas* 20 (1959): 274–81.

Harrison, Ross. "Strawson on Outer Objects," *Philosophical Quarterly* 20 (1970): 213–21.

Heidegger, Martin. *Kant und das Problem der Metaphysik.* 3rd ed. Frankfurt am Main: Vittorio Klostermann, 1965.

Heidemann, Ingeborg. *Spontaneität und Zeitlichkeit.* Cologne: Kölner Universitäts-Verlag, 1958.

Heimsoeth, Heinz. "Personlichkeitsbewusstsein und Ding an sich in der kantischen Philosophie," in *Studien zur Philosophie Immanual Kants, Metaphysiche Ursprüng und Ontologische Grundlagen.* Cologne: Kölner Universitäts-Verlag, 1956.

———. *Transzendentale Dialektik.* 4 vols. Berlin: de Gruyter, 1969.

Henrich, Dieter. *Identität und Objectivität, Eine Untersuchung über Kants transzendental Deduktion.* Heidelberg: Carl Winter Universitäts-Verlag, 1976.

———. "The Proof-Structure of Kant's Transcendental Deduction," *Review of Metaphysics* 22 (1969): 640–59.

Herring, Herbert. *Das Problem der Affektion bei Kant, Kant-Studien,* Ergänzungshefte 67 (1953).

Hinske, Norbert. *Kants Weg zur Transzendental-philosophie: Der driessigjährige Kant.* Stuttgart: W. Kohlhammer, 1970.

Hintikka, Jaakko. "Kant on the Mathematical Method," *Kant Studies Today,* ed. L. W. Beck (see above), 117–40.

————. "On Kant's Notion of Intuition (Anschauung)," in *The First Critique,* ed. T. Penelhum and J. MacIntosh (see below), 38–53.

Holt, Dennis C. "Timelessness and the Metaphysics of Temporal Existence," *American Philosophical Quarterly* 18 (1981): 149–56.

Horstmann, Rolf P. "Space as Intuition and Geometry," *Ratio* 18 (1976): 17–30.

Hossenfelder, Malte. *Kants Konstitutions-theorie und die Transzendentale Deduktion.* Berlin: de Gruyter, 1978.

Hume, David. *A Treatise of Human Nature,* ed. L. A. Selby-Bigge. Oxford: Clarendon Press, 1888.

Humphrey, Ted. "The Historical and Conceptual Relations between Kant's Metaphysics of Space and Philosophy of Geometry," *Journal of the History of Philosophy* 11 (1973): 483–512.

Ishiguro, Hide. *Leibniz' Philosophy of Logic and Language.* Ithaca: Cornell University Press, 1972.

Jacobi, F. H. *David Hume über den Glauben, oder Idealismus und Realismus,* in *Ueber den transzendentalen Idealismus, Werke,* ed. F. Roth and F. Köppen, vol. 2, 291–310. Darmstadt: Wissenschaftliche Buchgesellschaft, 1968.

Jammer, Max. *Concepts of Space: The History of Theories of Space in Physics.* Cambridge, Mass.: Harvard University Press, 1954.

Kemp Smith, Norman. *A Commentary to Kant's "Critique of Pure Reason."* 2nd ed., revised and enlarged. New York: Humanities Press, 1962.

Kenny, Anthony. *Descartes: A Study of His Philosophy.* New York: Random House, 1968.

Körner, Stephan. *Kant.* London: Penguin Books, 1955.

————. "Kant's Conception of Freedom," *Proceedings of the British Academy* 3 (1967): 199–217.

Krausser, Peter. " 'Form of Intuition' and 'Formal Intuition' in Kant's Theory of Experience and Science," *Studies in the History and Philosophy of Science* 4 (1973–74): 279–87.

————. "The Operational Conception of 'Reine Anschauung' in Kant's Theory of Experience and Science," *Studies in the History and Philosophy of Science* 3 (1972–73): 81–87.

Krüger, L. "Wollte Kant die Vollständigkeit seiner Urteilstafel bewiesen?" *Kant-Studien* 59 (1968): 333–55.

Lachièze-Rey, Pierre. *L'Idéalisme kantien.* Paris: Librairie Philosophique J. Vrin, 1950.

Lauener, Henri. *Hume und Kant.* Bern: Francke Verlag, 1969.

Leibniz, G. W. *Discourse on Metaphysics,* trans. G. R. Montgomery. La Salle, Ill.: Open Court, 1962.

———. *The Leibniz-Clarke Correspondence,* ed. and trans. H. G. Alexander. Manchester: Manchester University Press, 1956.

———. *New Essays on Human Understanding,* trans. P. Remnant and J. Bennett. Cambridge: Cambridge University Press, 1981.

Locke, John. *An Essay Concerning Human Understanding,* ed. A. C. Fraser. 2 vols. New York: Dover, 1959.

Lovejoy, Arthur O. "Kant and the English Platonists," in *Essays Philosophical and Psychological, in Honor of William James,* 265–302. New York: Longmans Green and Co., 1908.

———. "On Kant's Reply to Hume," in *Kant: Disputed Questions,* ed. Moltke S. Gram (see above), 284–308.

Martin, Gottfried. *Kant's Metaphysics and Theory of Science,* trans. P. G. Lucas. Manchester: Manchester University Press, 1955.

Matthews, H. E. "Strawson on Transcendental Idealism," *Philosophical Quarterly* 19 (1969): 204–20.

Meerbote, Ralf. "Kant's Use of the Notions Objective Reality and Objective Validity," *Kant-Studien* 63 (1972): 51–58.

———. "The Unknowability of Things in Themselves," in *Kant's Theory of Knowledge,* ed. L. W. Beck (see above), 166–74.

Melnick, Arthur. *Kant's Analogies of Experience.* Chicago: University of Chicago Press, 1973.

Moore, G. E. "Four Forms of Scepticism," in *Philosophical Papers.* London: George Allen and Unwin, 1959.

———. *Some Main Problems of Philosophy.* London: George Allen and Unwin, 1953.

Parsons, Charles. "Kant's Philosophy of Arithmetic," in *Philosophy, Science, and Method,* ed. S. Morgenbesser, P. Suppes, and M. White, 568–94. New York: St. Martins Press, 1969.

Paton, H. J. *The Categorical Imperative.* London: Hutchinson Co., 1958.

———. *Kant's Metaphysic of Experience.* 2 vols. New York: Macmillan, 1936.

———. "The Key to Kant's Deduction of the Categories," in *Kant: Disputed Questions,* ed. Moltke S. Gram (see above), 246–68.

Penelhum, T., and MacIntosh, J. (eds.) *The First Critique: Reflections on Kant's Critique of Pure Reason.* Belmont, Calif.: Wadsworth, 1969.

Pippin, Robert B. *Kant's Theory of Form.* New Haven and London: Yale University Press, 1982.

Prauss, Gerold. *Erscheinung bei Kant.* Berlin: de Gruyter, 1971.

―――. *Kant und das Problem der Dinge an sich.* Bonn: Bouvier, 1974.

―――. (ed.) *Kant: Zur Deutung seiner Theorie von Erkennen und Handeln.* Cologne: Kiepenhauer and Witsch, 1973.

Prichard, H. A. *Kant's Theory of Knowledge.* Oxford: Clarendon Press, 1909.

Reich, Klaus. *Die Vollständigkeit der kantischen Urteilstafel.* Berlin: Diss. Rostock, 1932.

Reinhold, Karl Leonard. *Versuch einer neuen Theorie des menschlichen Vorstellungsvermögens.* Prague and Jena: C. Widtmann and I. M. Marke, 1789.

Rescher, Nicholas. "Noumenal Causality," in *Kant's Theory of Knowledge,* ed. L. W. Beck (see above), 175–83.

Robinson, Lewis. "Contributions à l'histoire de l'evolution philosophique de Kant," *Revue de Mêtaphysique et de Morale* 3 (1924): 205–68.

Roussett, Bernard. *La Doctrine kantienne de l'objectivité.* Paris: Librairie Philosophique J. Vrin, 1967.

Russell, Bertrand. *Our Knowledge of the External World.* London: George Allen and Unwin, 1914.

Schaper, Eva. "Kant's Schematism Reconsidered," *Review of Metaphysics,* 18 (1964): 267–92.

―――. "The Kantian Thing-in-itself as a Philosophical Fiction," *Philosophical Quarterly* 16 (1966): 233–43.

Schopenhauer, Arthur. *Ueber die vierfache Wurzel des Satzes vom zureichenden Grunde,* vol. 1, *Sämtliche Werke,* ed. J. Frauenstadt. Leipzig: F. U. Brochaus, 1919.

Schulze, G. E. *Aenesidemus oder über die Fundamente der von dem Hernn Prof. Reinhold in Jena gelieferten Elementar-Philosophie,* 1792. Reprinted in *Aetas Kantiana.* Brussels: Culture et Civilisation, 1969.

Schulze (or Schultz), J. G. *Erläuterungen über des Herrn Professor Kant Critik der reinen Vernunft.* Königsberg: Hartung, 1791. Reprinted in *Aetas Kantiana.* Brussels: Culture et Civilisation, 1968.

―――. *Prüfung der kantischen Critik der reinen Vernunft.* Königsberg: Hartung, 1789. Reprinted in *Aetas Kantiana.* Brussels: Culture et Civilisation, 1968.

Schweitzer, Albert. *Die Religionsphilosophie Kants von der Kritik der reinen Vernunft bis zur Religion innerhalb der Grenzen der blossen Vernunft.* Freiburg: J. C. D. Mohr, 1899.

Scott-Taggart, M. J. "Recent Works on the Philosophy of Kant," *American Philosophical Quarterly* 3 (1966): 171–209.

Seidl, Horst. "Bemerkungen zu Ding an sich und Transzendentalen Gegenstand in Kant's *Kritik der reinen Vernunft*," *Kant-Studien* 63 (1972): 305–14.

Sellars, Wilfred. ". . . This I or he or it (the thing) which thinks . . . ," *Proceedings and Addresses of the American Philosophical Association* 44 (September 1971): 5–31.

Shoemaker, Sydney. *Self-Knowledge and Self-Identity.* Ithaca: Cornell University Press, 1963.

Silber, John. "The Ethical Significance of Kant's Religion," in the introduction to *Religion within the Limits of Reason Alone* (see above), lxxix–cxxxvii.

Smyth, Richard A. *Forms of Intuition: An Historical Introduction to the Transcendental Aesthetic.* The Hague: Martinus Nijhoff, 1978.

Spinoza, Benedict de. *The Chief Works of Spinoza,* trans. R. H. M. Elwes. 2 vols. New York: Dover, 1951.

———. *The Principles of Descartes' Philosophy,* trans. H. H. Briton. La Salle, Ill.: Open Court, 1961.

Stenius, Erik. "On Kant's Distinction between Phenomena and Noumena," in *Philosophical Essays Dedicated to Gunnar Aspelin on the Occasion of his 65th Birthday,* 231–45. Lund: C. W. R. Gleerup, 1965.

Strawson, P. F. *The Bounds of Sense, an Essay on Kant's Critique of Pure Reason.* London: Methuen, 1966.

Stroud, Barry. "Transcendental Arguments," *Journal of Philosophy* (1968). Reprinted in *The First Critique,* ed. T. Penelhum and J. MacIntosh (see above), 54–70.

Stuhlmann-Laeisz, Rainer. *Kants Logik.* Berlin: de Gruyter, 1976.

Suchting, W. A. "Kant's Second Analogy of Experience," *Kant-Studien* 58 (1967): 355–69.

Swinburne, Richard. *Time and Space.* London: MacMillan, 1968.

Tetens, Johann Nicholas. *Philosophische Versuche über die menschliche Natur und ihre Entwicklung.* 2 vols. Leipzig: M. G. Weidmanns Erben und Reich, 1777.

Thompson, Manley. "Singular Terms and Intuitions in Kant's Epistemology," *The Review of Metaphysics* 26 (1972): 314–43.

Tonelli, Giorgio. "Die Voraussetzungen zur Kantischen Urteilstafel in der Logik des 18. Jahrhunderts," in *Kritik und Metaphysik, Festschrift für H. Heimsoeth.* Berlin: de Gruyter, 1966.

Trendelenburg, Adolf. *Logische Untersuchungen.* Leipzig: Hinzel, 1862.

Turbayne, Colin. "Kant's Refutation of Dogmatic Idealism," *Philosophical Quarterly* 5 (1955): 225–44.

Vaihinger, H. *Commentar zu Kants Kritik der reinen Vernunft.* 2 vols. Stuttgart: W. Spemann, 1881–92.

Van Cleve, James. "Four Recent Interpretations of Kant's Second Analogy," *Kant-Studien* 64 (1973): 69–87.

———. "Substance, Matter, and Kant's First Analogy," *Kant-Studien* 70 (1979): 149–61.

van Fraassen, Bas. "Presupposition, Implication, and Self-Reference," *Journal of Philosophy* 65 (1968): 136–52.

Vleeschauwer, H. J. de. *La Déduction transcendentale dans l'oeuvre de Kant.* 3 vols. Paris: Leroux, 1934–37.

Walker, Ralph. *Kant. The Arguments of the Philosophers.* London: Routledge and Kegan Paul, 1978.

———. "The Status of Kant's Theory of Matter," in *Kant's Theory of Knowledge,* ed. L. W. Beck (see above), 151–56.

Walsh, W. H. *Kant's Criticism of Metaphysics.* Edinburgh: Edinburgh University Press, 1975.

———. "Kant on the Perception of Time," in *The First Critique,* ed. T. Penelhum and J. MacIntosh (see above), 70–88.

Warnock, G. J. "Concepts and Schematism," *Analysis* 8 (1949): 77–82.

Washburn, Michael. "The Problem of Self-Knowledge and the Evolution of the Critical Epistemology, 1781 and 1787." Ph.D. diss.: University of California, San Diego, 1970.

Weizsäcker, Carl Friedrick. "Kant's 'First Analogy of Experience' and Conservation Principle of Physics," *Synthese* 23 (1971): 75–95.

Weldon, T. D. *Kant's Critique of Pure Reason.* Oxford: Clarendon Press, 1958.

Werkmeister, William. (ed.) *Reflections on Kant's Philosophy.* Gainesville: University Presses of Florida, 1975.

Williams, Bernard. "The Certainty of the Cogito," in *Descartes: A Collection of Critical Essays,* ed. Willis Doney, 88–107. New York: Doubleday, 1967.

Wilson, Kirk Dalles. "Kant on Intuition," *Philosophical Quarterly* 25 (1975): 247–65.

Wilson, Margaret. "Kant and the Refutations of Subjectivism," in *Kant's Theory of Knowledge,* ed. L. W. Beck (see above), 208–17.

———. "Leibniz and Materialism," *Canadian Journal of Philosophy* 3 (1974): 495–513.

Wittgenstein, Ludwig. *Tractatus Logico-Philosophicus,* trans. D. F. Pears and B. F. McGuinness. London: Routledge and Kegan Paul, 1961.

Wolff, Robert Paul. *Kant's Theory of Mental Activity.* Cambridge, Mass.: Harvard University Press, 1963.

Wood, Allen W. *Kant's Moral Religion.* Ithaca: Cornell University Press, 1970.

Zocher, Rudolf. "Kants Transzendentale Deduktion der Kategorien," *Zeitschrift für philosophische Forschung* 8 (1954): 161–94.

Index